Operational Risk Capital Models

May 12, 2015

Hi John,

Great data leads to better analytics and decisions. Thanks for the inspiration.

Best,
Brenda Boultwood

Operational Risk Capital Models

**Edited By Rafael Cavestany, Brenda Boultwood
and Laureano F. Escudero**

Published by Risk Books, a Division of Incisive Media Investments Ltd

Incisive Media
32–34 Broadwick Street
London W1A 2HG
Tel: +44(0) 20 7316 9000
E-mail: books@incisivemedia.com
Sites: www.riskbooks.com
www.incisivemedia.com

© 2015 Incisive Risk Information Limited

ISBN 978 1 78272 201 4

British Library Cataloguing in Publication Data
A catalogue record for this book is available from the British Library

Publisher: Nick Carver
Commissioning Editor: Sarah Hastings
Managing Editor: Lewis O'Sullivan
Designer: Lisa Ling
Copyeditor: MFE Editorial

Typeset by Mark Heslington Ltd, Scarborough, North Yorkshire
Printed and bound in the UK by PrintonDemand-Worldwide

Contents

Acknowledgements

The authors wish to thank Professor David Rios Insua for his contributions to the sections on scenario analysis modelling, stressed correlations and adversarial risk analysis, and for his thorough editing and reviewing of the book content.

The authors also wish to thank SKITES for the editing and reviewing performed by SKITES's partner Professor Javier Martínez Moguerza.

Foreword

These are interesting times for operational risk. Since the beginning of this century when it became a more established risk discipline blessed by the Basel II accord, operational risk has had a lesser status than market and credit risk. These financial risks would be more visible to the board and executive management; and, if business units want any change in the risk profile, such as a value-at-risk limit increase, these business requests would have to be vetted by market and credit risk managers.

Operational risk managers would not have the same interaction, mostly because the models used by risk managers were not designed with sensitive analysis tools that would allow analysts to understand the impact of new deals or transactions in the overall capital requirement. Most recently, financial institutions have been subject to very large losses that originated from bad conduct during the financial crisis or even after that period. These large losses are obviously made to the bank's operational loss databases and create a significant challenge for modellers.

Considering that operational risk severity distributions are already heavy-tailed, the inclusion of these extremely large settlements caused a spike and also brought volatility to the regulatory capital for these firms. These losses were so important that they impacted on the results of these large financial institutions, turning operational profits into losses on their quarter and annual earnings results. These settlements helped to call the attention of the board of directors and executive management to the importance of having a robust operational risk management within their organisations.

Currently, operational risk is seen as a key risk in financial institutions and operational risk managers are beginning to get invited to opine in key decisions and large strategic deals. However, the modelling challenge persists, and this is where *Operational Risk Capital Modelling: Compliance and Integration into Management* comes with a significant contribution to close this gap.

The book covers in detail all the building blocks of operational risk modelling with a very pragmatic, step-by-step view from industry practitioners, so the reader can see how the operational risk capital is actually calculated and stress-tested. The authors move from the technicalities of capital calculation to the integration of this capital into the strategic and tactical decisions of the financial institution. In my view, this book is a strong contribution to operational risk management in this new era.

Marcelo Cruz
Professor, New York University
Editor-in-Chief, *Journal of Operational Risk*

List of Abbreviations

(see also Glossary for explanations of many of the terms below)

A–D	Anderson–Darling GoF (*q.v.*) test
BCSG-AMA	the document issued by Basel Committee on Banking Supervision named "Operational Risk – Supervisory Guidelines for Advanced Measurement Approaches", June 2011
BEICFs	business environment and internal control factors
CDF	cumulative distribution function
CIP	critical infrastructure protection.
ED	external data
EDA	exploratory data analysis
ERM	enterprise risk management
EVT	extreme value theory
GEV	generalised extreme value distribution used for the implementation of extreme value theory
GoF	goodness-of-fit
GRC	governance, risk and compliance
ICDF	inverse CDF
ILD	internal loss data
KRI	key risk indicators
K-S	Kolmogorov–Smirnov
LDA	loss distribution approach
LS	least squares
MLE	maximum-likelihood estimator
NPV	net present value
ORA	operational risk appetite
ORMS	operational risk measurement system
ORC	operational risk category or unit of measure
pdf	probability density function
RAROC	risk-adjusted return on capital
RCSA	risk and control self-assessment

RLS	robust least square
SA	scenario analysis
SBA	scenario-based approach
SBC	Schwarz Bayesian criterion
SLA	single loss approximation
SSA	structured scenario analysis
UoM	unit of measure or ORC (*q.v.*)
VR	violation ratio
WLS	probability-weighted least squares

Glossary

(This list of terms has been created mainly from *Wikipedia* and has been validated by the authors and editors)

Advanced Operational Risk Capital Model: Methods for the estimation of capital requirements using statistical approaches, such as LDA and SBA. These models use inputs such as ILD, ED, SA and BEICFs to determine the loss distribution of different ORCs and determine the aggregated loss distribution from which capital requirements are derived. These methods are used to comply with the regulatory requirements for AMA models in Basel II/III and Solvency II internal models for operational risk.

Aggregated (operational) loss distribution: This is the result of the aggregation of the loss distributions of a group of ORCs.

Basel II: The second of the Basel Accords, (now extended and effectively superseded by Basel III), which are recommendations on banking laws and regulations issued by the Basel Committee on Banking Supervision.

Basel Committee on Banking Supervision: This is a committee of banking supervisory authorities that was established by the central bank governors of the Group of Ten countries in 1974. It provides a forum for regular cooperation on banking supervisory matters. Its objective is to enhance the understanding of key supervisory issues and improve the quality of banking supervision worldwide. The committee also frames guidelines and standards in different areas – some of the better known among them are the International Standards on Capital Adequacy, the Core Principles for Effective Banking Supervision and the Concordat on Cross-border Banking Supervision.

Basic indicator approach: This is an operational risk measurement technique proposed under Basel II. It is based on the original Basel Accord, and banks using it must hold capital for operational risk equal to the average over the previous three years of a fixed percentage of positive annual gross income. Figures for any year in which annual gross income is negative or zero should be excluded from both the numerator and denominator when calculating the average. The fixed percentage "alpha" is typically 15% of annual gross income.

BCSG-AMA: This is the document issued by Basel Committee on Banking Supervision named "Operational Risk – Supervisory Guidelines for Advanced Measurement Approaches". It was published in June 2011.

Bespoke models: These are models created in-house with limited use of graphical user interfaces and data sources interphases, suboptimal integrated data flows, limited reporting capabilities and scarce model governance such inexistence of audit trail or user control.

Body losses: Those most likely to be observed and of smaller relative magnitude, generally, close to the mode of the distribution. Tail losses are relatively of much higher severity, are less likely and are of increasing magnitude, some of them representing a high multiple of the distribution mode and mean.

Bootstrapping: A resampling method with replacement from the set data points used for the estimation of the sampling distribution of almost any statistic using only very simple methods.

Capital charge: The amount of capital required to guarantee a target solvency standard assigned to an ORC (or operational risk category, *q.v.*). It is determined based on a regulatory or economic calculation framework.

Convolution: The mathematical process used to derive a total loss distribution from the loss frequency and loss severity distributions. The process consists of first sampling a random number from a frequency distribution determining the number, λ, of operational events of the period. Then, λ random numbers are sampled from the severity distribution, which determine the actual loss value of each of the λ operational events. Finally, the addition of the loss values of the λ events represents the total operational loss value of the period. In a Monte Carlo simulation, this process is iterated multiple times to create the total operational loss distribution until an adequate stability of results is achieved in the high percentiles of the total operational loss distribution.

Copula: In probability theory and statistics, a copula is a multivariate probability distribution for which the marginal probability distribution of each variable is uniform. Copulas are used to describe the dependence between random variables. Sklar's theorem states that any multivariate joint distribution can be written in terms of univariate marginal distribution functions and a copula that describes the dependence structure between the variables.

Correlation: A measure of the relationship between two mathematical variables or measured data values.

Credit risk: This is defined by Basel as the possibility of losses associated with diminution in the credit quality of borrowers or counterparties.

Cumulative distribution function: This is the function that describes the probability that a random variable will have a value less than or equal to it.

Data elements: The four data elements mentioned in BCSG-AMA, which are ILD, ED, SA and BEICFs.

Dependence: Any statistical relationship between two random variables or two sets of data.

Distribution threshold: *See* Threshold.

Earnings-at-risk (EaR): This measures the quantity by which net income might change in the event of an adverse change in interest rates. It is a risk measurement that is closely linked with value-at-risk (VaR) calculations. The difference is that, while VaR looks at the change in the entire value over the forecast horizon, EaR looks at potential changes in cashflows or earnings.

Empirical distribution function: This is when the pdf, CDF and ICDF are derived directly from the observed data sample, rather than from a mathematical function. It consists of a double vector that relates the observed loss values with their cumulative probabilities. When the desired value is not among the observed sample, it can be interpolated from those observed. In this work, we also use the term "empirical distribution" to refer to the actual empirical loss data used to feed the fitting process to determine the parametric distribution. We also use the term "observed distribution" to refer to the empirical distribution.

Empirical loss data: This is the collection of loss events that have occurred in the past. They may have been observed internally by the institution (as ILD) or by other institutions (as ED). We also refer to empirical loss data as empirical distribution.

Exceedances: This refers to the number of loss observations used to fit a distribution as those of a smaller severity are taken out of the fitting sample. Analysing the impact on distribution characteristics by the number of exceedances in the sample is a standard analytical technique in extreme value theory (*q.v.*).

Expected loss: Is the probability-weighted average of all possible operational loss values of an ORC or group of ORCs. It can be calculated from the Monte Carlo simulation as the mean value of the loss replications.

Expected value: In probability theory, the expected value (or expectation, mathematical expectation, EV, mean, or first moment) refers, intuitively, to the value of a random variable we would "expect" to find if we could repeat the random variable process an infinite number of times and take the average of the values obtained. More formally, the expected value is the average of all possible values weighted to their probability.

Exploratory data analysis: In statistics, this is an approach to analysing datasets to summarise their main characteristics, often with visual methods.

External loss data: loss events that have occurred outside of your particular organisation. They can be acquired from an external source such as vendors or data consortia.

Extreme value theory: This is a branch of statistics dealing with extreme deviations from the median of probability distributions. It seeks to assess, from a given ordered sample of a given random variable, the probability of events that are more extreme than any previously observed.

Fit differences: The differences between the distribution fitting input loss data and the prediction of the fitted distribution function. Also called fit discrepancies, fit errors.

Fitted distribution: The distribution that results from the fitting process.

Fitting process: This is the statistical process used to find a distribution function and its parameters that best replicate the input data (historical loss data, scenario analysis, etc).

Frequency: The frequency (or absolute frequency) of an event i is the number n_i of times the event occurred during the observation period used for operational risk modelling.

Goodness-of-fit (GoF): This encompasses all different tests, analyses and plots that can be implemented to evaluate how well a parametric distribution replicates the input data (historical loss data, scenario analysis, etc). In the case of operational risk modelling, the input data may include the four data elements: ILD, ED, SA and BEICFs.

Governance, risk and compliance (GRC): This typically encompasses activities such as corporate governance, enterprise risk management (ERM) and corporate compliance with applicable laws and regulations. Software supporting GRC includes operational risk management solutions to capture and manage all inputs to a capital model, which include internal loss data, external loss data, scenario analysis, and business environment and internal control factors. Leading GRC vendors also provide specific solutions also for Sarbanes–Oxley, quality management, vendor management, IT risk, internal audit, etc.

Hybrid model (HM): In the hybrid model, both the scenario analysis and the historical loss data are used to determine the loss distributions. This can be done by complementing loss data frequency and severity distributions with scenario analysis, by merging the loss distributions independently generated from historical losses or scenarios.

Input data: This refers to the dataset used in the modelling. It can be ILD, ED or SA.

Internal loss data: The loss data from loss events that have occurred in the institution and have been internally collected.

Inverse CDF: This function is the inverse of the CDF.

Jackknife: A resampling method for estimating the precision of sample statistics (medians, variances, percentiles) by using subsets of available data without replacement from a set of data points.

Joint distribution: *See* total loss distribution.

Key risk indicators (KRIs): Measures of risk that are meant to act as an early warning of changes in the risk profile of an institution, department, process, activity, etc. Examples of KRIs are level of rotation of key personnel (as a high rotation of key personnel increases the probability of internal process errors) and external fraud rates (as they will increase the likelihood of suffering fraudulent attacks). An institution may develop a dash board of KRIs to cover for the monitoring diversity of operational risks.

Kurtosis: This is any measure of the "peakedness" of the probability distribution of a real-valued random variable. There are various interpretations of kurtosis, and of how particular measures should be interpreted. These are primarily peakedness (width of peak), tail weight and lack of shoulders (distribution of primarily peak and tails, not in between).

Least squares: The method of least squares is a standard approach to the approximate solution of overdetermined systems, ie, sets of equations in which there are more equations than unknowns. "Least squares" means that the overall solution minimises the sum of the squares of the errors made in the results of every single equation.

Loss distribution approach (LDA): To implement LDA, an institution first segments operational losses into homogeneous segments, called units of measure (UoMs) or operational risk categories (ORCs). For each ORC, the institution then constructs a loss distribution representing its expectation of total losses that can materialise in a one-year horizon. The loss distribution is constructed by developing a frequency distribution that describes the number of loss events in a given year, and a severity distribution that describes the loss amount of a single loss event. The frequency and severity distributions are assumed to be independent. The convolution of these two distributions then gives rise to the (annual) loss distribution.

Market risk: According to the Basel Committee, this is the risk that the value of an investment will decrease due to moves in market factors.

Mathematical optimisation: This consists of maximising or minimising a real function by systematically choosing input values from within an allowed set and computing the value of the function. More generally, optimisation includes finding "best available" values of some objective function given a defined domain, including a variety of different types of objective functions and different types of domains.

Mean of the distribution: This is the expected value and refers to one measure of the central tendency either of a probability distribution or of the random variable characterised by that distribution.

Median: The median is the numerical value separating the higher half of a data sample, or a probability distribution, from the lower half.

Mode of the distribution: The mode is the value that appears most often in a set of data. The mode of a discrete probability distribution is the value x at which its probability mass function takes its maximum value.

Modelling sample: The set of operational losses used to create the distribution model, by fitting a parametric distribution or other means.

Modelling threshold: This refers to the minimum size below which loss observations are not used to fit the distribution modelling, and only those losses larger than the threshold are used for the distribution modelling. This can also be called the truncation point.

Modified LDA: This refers to the use of a modified LDA model for stress-testing purposes. Under this approach, baseline model parameters are stressed, such as frequencies, tail parameters, mean severity, etc. Via Monte Carlo simulation, the modified LDA distribution is derived and percentiles of such a distribution lower than the 99.9th are used to determine the losses under stress and severely adverse scenarios, for instance, 70% for the former and 98% for the later.

Observed data: This is also referred to as observed losses, and it is the operational risk losses that have been observed, internally or externally. They may be used as a modelling sample in a fitting process.

Observed distribution: *See* empirical distribution function.

Operational risk: Basel II defines this as "the risk of loss resulting from inadequate or failed internal processes, people and systems or from external events".

Operational risk appetite: This can be defined as the total acceptable level of operational risk that the top management is willing to take. *See also* risk appetite.

Operational risk category (ORC): This is the level (for example, organisational unit, operational loss event type, risk category) at which the bank's quantification model generates a separate distribution for estimating potential operational losses. This term identifies a category of operational risk that is homogeneous in terms of the risks covered and the data available to analyse those risks.

Operational risk measurement system: This consists of the systems and data used to measure operational risk in order to estimate the operational risk capital charge.

Operational risk profile: The amount and characteristics of the operational risk being faced by the institution at a point in time. The term is also used to refer to the metrics that describe such a risk profile, which are derived from the operational risk total aggregated loss distribution, including total and allocated capital at different confidence intervals and expected losses. The risk profile metrics may also incorporate other qualitative measurements from the ORMS, such as KRIs and RCSA.

ORX: This refers to the Operational Riskdata eXchange Association, which is a leading operational risk data consortium.

Parametric distributions: This refers to the distribution functions that have been obtained from a fitting process.

Percentile: This is a measure indicating the value below which a given percentage of observations in a group of observations fall. For example, the 20th percentile is the value (or score) below which 20% of the observations may be found.

Positive semi-definitive matrix: A positive semi-definite matrix is a Hermitian matrix all of whose eigenvalues are non-negative. It is a requirement for a matrix to be used a correlation matrix.

Primary cause: The risk type of the operational risk event.

Probability density function: This is the function that provides the relative likelihood for the random variable on a given value.

Probability-weighted least squares: *See* probability weighted-least squares fit (WLS) page 134.

Projected distribution: The distribution function used to project capital requirements.

P-value: The probability of obtaining a test statistic at least as extreme as the one that was actually observed, assuming that the null hypothesis is true.

Quantiles: These are points taken at regular intervals from the cumulative distribution function (*q.v.*) of a random variable. Dividing ordered data into q essentially equal-sized data subsets is the motivation for q-quantiles; the quantiles are the data values marking the boundaries between consecutive subsets.

Replications versus simulation and scenarios: We refer to replication as the number of times a Monte Carlo simulation repeats a random calculation process to create a distribution. Sometimes, the term "replication" also refers to scenarios, as each of the replications of a Monte Carlo simulation represents a possible risk scenario. However, in this work, we restrict the use of term "scenario" to scenario analysis, for clarity purposes. By simulation, we refer to the act of launching one Monte Carlo process, which will generate multiple replications until the desired distribution is created.

Resampling: This is a method used in statistics for estimating the precision of sample statistics (medians, variances, percentiles) by using subsets of available data (jackknifing) or drawing randomly with replacement from a set of data points (bootstrapping).

Risk and control self-assessment: This is a business practice that helps an institution's top management to identify and appraise significant risks inherent in the company's activities. An RCSA programme also instructs departmental managers and segment-level employees on how to ensure that internal controls, policies and procedures are functional and adequate.

Risk appetite: A high-level determination of how much risk a firm is willing to accept taking into account the risk–return attributes; it is often taken as a forward-looking view of risk acceptance. "Risk toler-ance" is a more specific determination of the level of variation a bank is willing to accept around business objectives, and is often consid-ered to be the amount of risk a bank is prepared to accept. In this document the terms are used synonymously.

Risk tolerance: *See* risk appetite.

Risk type: The standards for operational risk classification defined by the regulatory frameworks such Basel and Solvency II. Risk Type I risks in Basel II/III are internal fraud; external fraud; employment practices and workplace safety; clients, products and business prac-tice; damage to physical assets; business disruption and systems failures; and execution, delivery and process management. A detailed description of operational risk class can be found in the various documents of "Operational Risk Data Collection Exercise" published by the Basel Committee for Banking Supervision.

Risk Type II: This refers to the standards for operational risk classifi-cation defined by the regulatory frameworks such Basel and Solvency II. This classification is divided in Levels, I, II, III, etc. A detailed description of the operational risk classification can be found in the various documents of "Operational Risk Data Collection Exercise" published by the Basel Committee for Banking Supervision.

Robust least square: *See* robust least-squares (RLS) fit, page 137.

Return on Equity (ROE): This is used as a measure of the return obtained on the capital invested.

Scaled external data: External data that has been transformed in order to reflect the magnitude of losses of the institution risk profile.

Scenario analysis: *See* robust scenario analysis framework, as described in Chapter 3.

Scenario-based approach: This differs from the loss distribution approach (*q.v.*) in that the institution uses scenario analysis to determine the severity and/or the frequency distributions. When scenario analysis is not used to determine the frequency distribution, internal loss data analysis might be used instead.

Simulation: *See* Replications versus simulation and scenarios.

Single loss approximation: *See* Single Loss Approximation: Analytical Derivation of the Loss Distribution.

Skewness: This is a measure of the asymmetry of the probability distribution of a real-valued random variable about its mean.

Solvency II: An EU directive that codifies and harmonises the EU insurance regulation. Primarily, this concerns the amount of capital that EU insurance companies must hold to reduce the risk of insolvency.

Standard approach: In the context of operational risk, the standard or standardised approach is a set of operational risk measurement techniques proposed under Basel II capital adequacy rules for banking institutions. Basel II requires all banking institutions to set aside capital for operational risk. The standardised approach falls between the basic indicator approach and the advanced measurement approach in terms of the degree of complexity.

Tail losses: *See* Body losses.

Theoretical distribution: This refers to the parametric distribution that results from the fitting process.

Threshold, or distribution threshold: A boundary defined to restrict the range of a parametric distribution. Threshold can also refer to the data collection threshold above which operational risk events are not reported for capital modelling purposes. We also refer to this concept with the term "truncation point".

Total aggregated (operational risk) distribution: This refers to the operational loss distribution that aggregates the losses from a group of ORCs.

Total loss distribution: The joint distribution or the distribution resulting from the convolution of the frequency and severity distributions and which represents the total losses of an ORC.

Trimmed mean: The trimmed mean is a family of measures of central tendency. The trimmed mean of the values is computed by sorting all the values, discarding an x percentage of the smallest and an x percentage of the largest values, and computing the remaining values.

Truncation point: See Threshold.

Units of measure (UoM): These are the basic modelling units in an operational risk capital (ORC) model. They are generally made of a frequency and a severity distribution. An ORC represents the possible loss values from a risk scenario, a risk type of a business unit, or other criteria the capital model is structured on.

Use test: This is the means by which an institution introduces the capital calculations into the its day-to-day risk management.

Violation ratio: *See* Other Selection Methods: Schwarz Bayesian Criterion (SBC), Likelihood Ratio, Violation Ratio

About the Editors

Brenda Boultwood is the senior vice president of Industry Solutions at MetricStream. Previously, she served as senior vice president and chief risk officer at Constellation Energy, before which she served as global head of strategy for alternative investment services at JP Morgan Chase. At Bank One Corporation, she served as head of corporate market risk management and counterparty credit and head of corporate operational risk management, before advancing to head, global risk management for the company's Global Treasury Services group.

Boultwood has also worked with PricewaterhouseCoopers (PwC) and Chemical Bank Corporation. In addition, she has spent time teaching at the University of Maryland's MBA programme. She was a member of the CFTC Technology Advisory Committee, and has also served on the Board of the Global Association of Risk Professionals (GARP). She currently serves on the board of the Committee of Chief Risk Officers (CCRO).

Boultwood graduated with honours from the University of South Carolina with a bachelor's degree in international relations. She also earned a PhD in economics from the City University of New York.

Rafael Cavestany has over 15 years of experience in the financial services industry covering the banking and insurance sectors. He currently works as a director in True North Partners Group and SKITES. Before, Cavestany worked at Everis as executive director of the risk management practice and at PwC as senior manager.

He has worked on projects for a number of leading financial institutions in the USA, Canada, the UK, Spain, Italy, Latin America and South Africa, and his experience is focused on consulting projects for the development of risk management analytics software solutions and the corresponding methodologies, workflows and data requirements with special emphasis on economic capital and operational risk modelling. Regarding operational risk modelling, he has undertaken projects in the insurance, banking, energy, oil and gas, and food industries and led the development of the software solution used in the examples of this book, OpCapital Analytics.

Cavestany received the MBA from the University of Michigan in 1997 and a degree in economics from Universidad Autonoma de Madrid. He is currently completing his PhD thesis in statistics.

Laureano F. Escudero received a PhD in economics from the Universidad de Deusto, Bilbao, in 1974 and a degree in computer science from Universidad Politécnica de Madrid in 1972. He was professor of statistics and operations research at the Universidad Rey Juan Carlos, Spain from 2007 to 2013.

In the period 2003–4, he was president of EURO (Association of European Operational Research Societies). He worked at IBM Research scientific and development centres in Madrid (Spain), Palo Alto (California), Sindelfingen (Germany) and Yorktown Heights (NY) from 1972 to 1991. He taught mathematical programming at the Mathematical Sciences School, Universidad Complutense de Madrid, from 1992 to 2000 and stochastic programming at the Universidad Miguel Hernandez, Spain from 2000 to 2007. Escudero is the author of five books, has co-edited five others, has published more than 135 scientific papers in leading journals and written more than 30 chapters in edited books.

Escudero has worked in different mathematical programming fields (linear, integer, nonlinear, stochastic) and their risk management applications to finance, energy, supply chain management and air traffic, among other sectors.

About the Authors

Lutz Baumgarten is a partner and the chairman of True North Partners. He has more than 15 years' experience in consulting in the financial services industry, two of which he spent as a partner at KPMG's global risk management practice and two further years as managing director at KDB. Previously, he was with Oliver Wyman in London and Frankfurt for nine years

He has worked with senior management of leading financial institutions and regulators around the world, including the UK, Germany, Austria, Benelux, Spain, Portugal, South Africa, Turkey, the Gulf region, Singapore, Korea, the US and Mexico. His project experience focuses on themes in finance, risk and strategy, including topics at the interface of those three disciplines such as planning and budgeting, capital and risk profile management, group-wide economic value management and others.

Baumgarten holds an M.Eng in engineering science and an M.Phil and D.Phil in economics, all from Oxford University.

Javier M. Moguerza received his PhD in mathematical engineering from University Carlos III in 2000. He has been associate professor and researcher at Rey Juan Carlos University since 2000.

Between 2004 and 2008, he was the academic director for international relations and, during 2009, vice-dean for research at the Computer Science School at Rey Juan Carlos University. He is currently a member of the Global Young Academy. Moguerza has taken part in research projects with private and public funding, and he collaborates on projects of consultancy.

Moguerza's professional expertise is focused on computational and applied mathematics, optimisation, Six Sigma quality, data mining, pattern recognition methods and energy risk management. He has publications in highly ranked scientific journals.

Daniel Rodríguez has over 10 years' experience in the financial services industry, covering the banking and insurance sectors. His experience is focused on consulting projects for the development of risk management tools and the corresponding methodologies. He has worked on projects for a number of leading financial institutions in the UK, Spain, Italy, Latin America and South Africa. He has a degree in physics from the Universidade de Santiago de Compostela and he received his PhD by Universidad Politécnica de Madrid, in 2015.

Furthermore, Rodríguez is the author of numerous scientific papers in leading journals and he has contributed several statistics packages to CRAN, the software package repository of the R Project for Statistical Computing.

Fabrizio Ruggeri works for the Italian National Research Council, and his major research interests are Bayesian and industrial statistics (especially in reliability and risk). He holds a BSc in mathematics (Milano), an MSc in statistics (Carnegie Mellon) and a PhD in statistics (Duke). Ruggeri is a former President of the International Society for Bayesian Analysis and of the European Network for Business and Industrial Statistics.

1

Introduction

Rafael Cavestany

We write this book (2015) while the world economy is still recovering from the largest economic crisis since the Great Depression. Many of the current crisis causes can be traced to consecutive operational failures (Robertson 2011), including mortgage fraud, model errors, negligent underwriting standards and failed due diligence combined with loosely implemented innovation trends in finance. Mortgage originators, mortgage bundlers, credit-rating agencies, asset managers, investors and, ultimately, regulatory agencies were responsible for many of these operational failures.

The consequences have included severe depletion of capital and undermined confidence in the financial system, causing the downfall of many large, well-established financial institutions, and forcing a deep restructuring of the financial sector in many of the most advanced economies.

The Basel II Committee defines operational risk as "the risk of loss resulting from inadequate or failed internal processes, people and systems or from external events". Internal processes, people, and systems or external events directly impact on the institution's business and strategy execution, endangering the institution's survival, if operational risk is not managed adequately. In fact, even individual operational risk events have caused the collapse of historical institutions (instance Baring PLC in 1995) or produced great damage into their capital base (Société Générale in 2008 and UBS in 2011) in addition to undermining the confidence in these institutions' capacity for managing risks.

These past events remind us how vulnerable our organisations are to new threats and that institutions should thoroughly identify emerging menaces. For instance, innovation trends in banking, such as smartphones, tablets and self-service technologies, are energetically exploding, while the sophistication of cyber-attackers seems to increase, too frequently, faster than the institutions' capacity to respond effectively. On top of this, the upsurge of social networks dramatically increases the reputational impact and the development speed of some operational risk events.

Hence, operational risk should be pervasively analysed, quantified and managed for an adequate understanding of its potential economic and operative consequences, identification of causes and introduction of effective remedies. For this purpose, a granular operational risk capital modelling is a critical tool that allows institutions a deep understanding of the operational risk profile and permits enterprise-wide operational risk management.

In spite of the highly disruptive impact and unexpected nature of operational risk events, operational risk capital modelling is far too often considered less critical than the modelling of credit and market risk capital. Many institutions have successfully integrated credit and market risk quantification into management, in critical processes such as asset approvals, pricing, risk appetite, risk limits and performance measurement. On the other hand, operational risk quantification remains all too frequently dedicated principally to the calculation of a regulatory capital figure and has little integration into the daily mitigation of operational risk.

This is due, in part, to the more evident link of credit and market risk capital with specific assets in the balance sheet and their risk characteristics (probability of default, price volatility and others), enabling a risk management differentiated by asset. On the contrary, in operational risk, capital is calculated at organisational-entity level (business unit (BU), business area, department or other), sometimes being more challenging in its calculation down to a very granular level. Additional reasons include the absence, until now, of sufficiently robust models to determine an accurate operational risk profile, together with the impact of mitigation actions in such a risk profile; and the underimplemented methods and procedures for the integration of the operational risk capital results into the day-to-day risk management of the institution and strategic and business planning.

However, the implementation of a robust operational risk capital model[1] framework, in a financial institution, including its solid integration into the institution management, can provide the organisation with great benefits, far beyond the regulatory compliance with Basel II/III or Solvency II, or the capital cost savings with respect to the standardised or basic indicator approaches.

The inputs used in capital modelling – internal loss data (ILD), external data (ED), scenario analysis (SA) and business environment and internal control factors (BEICFs) – deliver us an insightful view of the operational risk profile faced by the institution: the collection and modelling of ILD allows an understanding of the likely losses segmented by risk type and organisational entity, and their projection to unlikely but possible events. SA offers information on rare but highly disruptive events for the financial institution that are not captured in the internal-loss-data set. Scenarios can be complemented with ED, which provides the experience of other institutions into the analysis, complementing the view of the potential risks being faced by the institution. BEICFs provide us with an updated operational risk profile and its future possible evolution, thanks to the use of key risk indicators (KRIs), risk and control self-assessment (RCSA) and internal audit scores. These inputs to the capital model can be used to identify areas requiring mitigation action plans and can be embedded into other risk management processes.

Also, the studies required in determining SA, risk dependencies, stress testing and distribution tails provide a unique opportunity for different risk owners to meet in order to analyse and discuss the risks faced in their departments, increasing risk awareness and identifying the most effective mitigation. The construction of predictive analytics on BEICFs can help in identifying loss drivers and create early warnings about changes in risk profile and so on, while being used for creating a more foreseeing estimation of capital.

Finally, the capital figures estimated by the model can be embedded in the strategic and operational business planning process for more accurate financial planning, resource allocation, performance measurement and management of the risk profile. The capital model outputs can be used in the institution's risk appetite framework, helping to enforce the risk management mandate by the board of directors of the institution and a more efficient control of the financial resources of the organisation. All this will facilitate a better implementation of the institution strategy. Then, the capital model helps to determine the economic business case for the implementation of mitigation plans, providing a risk–reward perspective on risk mitigation.

All in all, an advanced operational risk capital model allows for a more reliable operational environment and significant cost savings from fewer loss events, prevention of high-severity events, capital costs and precision in financial planning. This represents an important win for the institution, given the disruptive and unexpected nature of operational risk events.

Indeed, it is hard to imagine that means other than an advanced operational risk capital model would be able to provide such benefits. It is worth noting that an advanced operational risk capital model probably provides risk mitigation information at least as useful as those more commonly implemented capital models of credit and market risks, such as Moody's KMV and RiskMetrics.

In this context, methodologies for operational risk quantification are less consolidated than those of market and credit risks, and calculation standards are yet to be widely accepted.

Some of the reasons for the absence of widely accepted calculation standards are the significant challenges involved in performing robust operational risk modelling and its integration into the daily management of the institution. The robust calculation of operational risk depends on a strong modelling methodology and a thorough collection of institution-specific high-quality operational risk data from multiple processes and organisational units. Also, the integration of capital calculation into the institution's daily management depends on the development of information and analytical processes, allowing the link between operational risk calculations and risk mitigation measures such as action plans, insurance, and process improvements. Finally, all of the above is highly dependent on the support of automated processes and the provision of an adequate governance over those processes.

More specifically, the modelling challenges in operational risk quantification include: data quality; difficulty of modelling extreme events; need for a forward-looking capital estimates; the qualitative nature of SA; the need for stable operational risk capital estimates; the selection of modelling assumptions; the diversity of nature and origin of operational losses; the integration of different data elements; the availability of a technology that adequately supports all analytical processes, data integrity and governance functions; and the requirement of a regulatory validation.

Overcoming these challenges requires a deep analysis and the collection of valuable operational risk information on exposures, dependences and potential events. The modelling of operational risk capital in fact requires a deep understanding of these. Moreover, if these are linked to risk mitigation, the institution obtains one of the greatest benefits, if not the greatest benefit, of the advanced operational risk capital modelling approach.

This book contains the experience of its authors during the successful implementation in organisations of operational risk capital models, best practices and industry standards, and the integration of the capital results into day-to-day risk management. We use the challenges described above to define the required elements in the operational risk capital modelling framework. Figure 1.1 shows all the interconnected elements involved in the process of achieving a robust estimation of operational risk capital that correspond to the chapters in the book.

Figure 1.1 High-level workflow for robust operational risk capital modelling framework

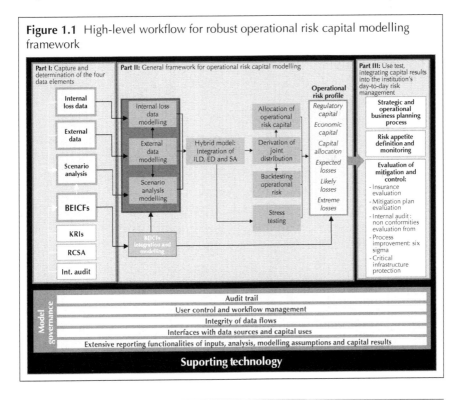

This framework is structured in three parts which correspond to the chapters and parts of this book.

Part I, "Capture and Determination of the Four Data Elements", defines the foundation of an operational risk modelling framework, since the capital model outputs' quality cannot exceed that of its inputs. Within Part I, we present two chapters:

❑ "Collection of Operational Loss Data: ILD and ED". This chapter presents a common understanding of what is operational risk loss and what are the key considerations when collecting operational risk internal losses and using external data.
❑ "Scenario Analysis Framework and BEICFs Integration". Here, we present the key elements for scenario analysis collection, including all supporting information (including BEICFs), actions for bias mitigation, scenario rating and scenario validation methods.

Part II, "General Framework for Operational Risk Capital Modelling", includes a thorough description of the end-to-end process to quantify the operational risk profile of the institution, including the modelling of each of the data elements, creating a hybrid model, estimating operational risk correlations, generating the join distribution, allocating capital, and more. This part has the following chapters:

❑ "Loss Data Modelling: ILD and ED". This chapter presents the process for modelling loss data, starting with exploratory data analysis (EDA), defining the appropriate modelling granularity, defining an optimal threshold, determining the tail weight, fitting distributions and goodness of fit (GoF) analysis under different methods, analysing stability of capital estimates, evaluating the realism of the models created and external data scaling.
❑ The chapter titled "Scenario Analysis Modelling" describes how to translate the results of scenario analysis into distributions in a scenario-based approach (SBA). It provides methods for controlling the tail shape during the fit and splitting scenarios into lower organisational entities.
❑ "BEICFs Modelling and Integration into the Capital Model"

presents methods of integrating BEICFs into a capital model, including a score-card method, its modelling or its use to estimate operational risk correlations based on expert judgement.

❑ The chapter titled "Hybrid Model Construction: Integration of ILD, ED and SA" introduces different methods for creating a hybrid model using different data elements, including implementation of credibility theory for determining the weight that each data element should have in the hybrid model.

❑ "Derivation of the Joint Distribution and Capital Allocation" introduces the methods for creating a joint distribution from which to derive the operational risk profile for the use test. This includes the Monte Carlo simulation, operational risk correlations, copulas for the aggregation of the different operational risk categories (ORCs), capitalisation of operational risk and allocation of the operational risk capital.

❑ Next, "Backtesting, Stress Testing and Sensitivity Analysis introduces different methods to backtest and stress test the operational risk model.

❑ "Evolving from a Plain Vanilla to a State-of-the-Art Model" concludes Part II. Here we present the typical path describing the evolution from a plain vanilla model to a highly developed model fully integrated in the day-to-day management of the institution.

In Part III, "Use Test, Integrating Capital Results into the Institution's Day-To-Day Risk Management", management and information processes are implemented to integrate the operational risk profile into the daily risk management of the institution. Part III is divided into two chapters:

❑ "Strategic and Operational Business Planning and Monitoring" presents the key consideration when integrating the risk profile from the capital model into the business planning process, and its monitoring of the implementation of the plan using an operational risk appetite framework.

❑ In "Risk–Reward Evaluation of the Mitigation and Control Effectiveness" we introduce several detailed examples of how to embed the operational risk capital results into daily risk management together with the risk/reward evaluation of the impact of mitigation actions, into the risk profile, and the determination of an optimal mitigation portfolio using Adversarial Risk Analysis.

All the above informational and analytical processes should have a governance framework that includes audit trail, user control, extensive reporting, workflow management for the validation of modelling assumptions, etc. Finally, the technology around this framework limits modelling error possibilities and facilitates a solid and timely execution of all the modelling, documentation and governance.

The purpose of this book is to present to the practitioner the methods and processes required to address all the above challenges and to help in making the practical decisions for determining the most adequate model for projecting the institution operational risk capital needs. In the different sections, ample references are provided to support the different methodologies proposed.

Additionally, since in practical terms, the main challenge is the fact that operational risk capital models in financial institutions need a regulatory approval, we refer these methods to the guidelines issued by the Basel Committee on Banking Supervision named "Operational Risk – Supervisory Guidelines for Advanced Measurement Approaches" (BCSG-AMA). We use this reference because it is the most comprehensive international document for operational risk capital supervisory purposes. The other major regulatory initiative, Solvency II, is initially a European Union legislative measure, although it is likely to be adopted by many other jurisdictions once it is finally approved and implemented in the European Union. Nevertheless, the methods proposed are valid for any regulation. After all, regulators and supervisors share concerns when seeking to guide institutions in their implementation of solidly supported capital models, which can be externally validated for their use in guaranteeing solvency.

Therefore, the methodologies described in the book can be directly applied to Solvency II operational risk capital internal models also. In fact, we have developed some of these methods working for companies that seek to be Solvency II-approved.

We provide now a more extensive explanation of each of the modelling challenges and, later, Parts I, II and III present the mathematical and methodological processes that may be used to deal with these modelling challenges.

Although this work is focused on providing answers to the regulatory guidelines of Basel II/III and Solvency II, the methods proposed are perfectly applicable to operational risk modelling in any financial and nonfinancial organisation. In fact, the regulatory guidelines are meant to provide robustness, transparency and governance over a quantitative model, and thus can be used for the same purpose by companies in any industry. The implementation of this type of model in a nonfinancial industry may provide the organisation with even greater benefits than those that would be enjoyed by a financial institution, because operational risk is frequently more significant than other risks.

CHALLENGES OF OPERATIONAL RISK ADVANCED CAPITAL MODELS

The data quality of the capital inputs

Data quality represents the foundation of an operational risk capital model, as the quality of the model output cannot exceed that of its inputs. Data quality affects all the four data elements of the capital model (ILD, ED, SA and BEICFs).

ILD must be collected with completeness (BUs, size, risk types and other considerations), ensuring its consistency with accounting, and each event should contain specific data fields appropriately populated. Additionally, the collection should follow a particular definition and methodologies, permitting the correct modelling of operational risk loss distributions (an example of these definitions and methodologies can be found in the "Operational Risk Reporting Standards" of the Operational Riskdata eXchange Association (ORX)). To guarantee the adherence to these, it is necessary to implement a workflow with the corresponding approvals where the data quality is validated before being ratified for quantification. Finally, the ILD collection ideally should guarantee a trail and have adequate data certificates (see Chapter 2).

To obtain an SA with the adequate quality, several issues should be addressed, such as avoiding biases, participant training, validation processes and consistency analysis with other metrics from the Operational Risk Measurement System (ORMS), see Chapter 3.

BEICFs' incorporation into the capital model is probably the most challenging and will require that elements such as RCSA and KRIs to have sufficient frequency and completeness for their embeddedness into the capital model (see Chapters 3 and 6).

Perhaps ED is the least problematic of the four data elements regarding data quality. ED is delivered, in most cases, by an external provider who has adequate data quality controls. Frequently, the ED provider is a data consortium where data from several institutions is shared. This permits us to enjoy the data quality of more experienced member institutions, as the consortium requests strong quality standards to all participants. Nevertheless, receiving loss data from consortia most frequently implies sharing the institution's own ILD, which, in turn, should have the appropriate quality and be compliant with consortium standards. Therefore, access to consortium data is eventually subject to the institution's ILD quality. Finally, external data entails other issues such as its representativeness of the institution's risk profile, which are later addressed in Chapters 2 and 4.

Modelling operational risk extreme events

In any risk type (market, credit, operational and so forth), capital charge is driven by extreme and exceptional events. In fact, under regulatory frameworks (Basel II/III and Solvency II), capital should be sufficient to absorb losses occurring with a higher probability than 0.001 in a year (corresponding to a confidence interval of 99.9%). The use of such a low probability of losses to determine capital implies that exceptional loss events have not necessarily been observed by the institution. This requires the creation of a statistical model to project out from observed loss data.

Determining operational risk capital under Solvency II or Basel II/III's solvency standards is even more challenging, as operational risk distributions generally have strong fat-tail behaviour. Fat-tail behaviour implies that those extreme exceptional events represent a large multiple of what is usually observed. Because traditional modelling is mostly based on observed data, calculating operational risk extreme events requires a challenging projection beyond the observed data.

For the sake of clarity, consider the example in Figure 1.2, which represents the histogram of internal loss data with fat-tail behaviour in a linear scale.[2] The required capital, computed under a 99.9% solvency standard by fitting a generalised Pareto distribution to the loss sample with fat-tail behaviour and using the single-loss-

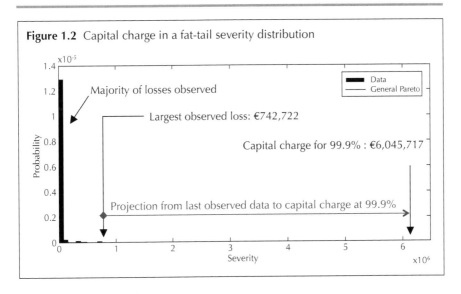

Figure 1.2 Capital charge in a fat-tail severity distribution

approximation method, demonstrates this point. It can be seen that the capital charge is approximately nine times larger than the higher observed loss. Also, the capital charge is a very large multiple of the average observed loss.

Modelling extreme events can be addressed with extreme value theory (EVT) and fat-tail distributions (see Chapter 4). Nevertheless, fat-tail distributions are highly sensitive to changes in the underlying modelling sample and may deliver unstable capital charges.

The scarcity of observed extreme losses can be tackled by the use of external data and expert judgement as an input to the modelling. In fact, the use of expert judgement in operational risk modelling is required by the supervisory guidelines and it is named SA (see Chapter 3).

Performing a forward-looking capital estimation
Any capital requirement calculation is addressed to absorbing losses occurring in the years ahead. Most commonly, capital requirements are calculated for a time horizon of one to three years. Therefore, these requirements should be calculated with a forward-looking spirit. Forward-looking operational risk capital calculation is challenging, as the institution's control environment continuously evolves, business progresses and the external environment changes.

These evolving circumstances imply that historical operational risk data is less representative when it originates from several years prior to the modelling date. As time passes, internal controls may have been improved, processes automated, new products or services launched or part of existing offerings may have increased their weight in total activity. Also, the external business environment may affect activity levels, the nature of fraudulent actions or attacks, new technologies implemented by the institution and clients, alternative distribution channels used, and so on. All of this changes the size and frequency of the operational losses of the institution decreasing the historical data relevancy.

Additional issues can be found when institutions initially implement their formal operational risk management programmes. The loss data collection process may take a couple of years to be perfected and achieve a complete coverage within the institution. The implementation of a solid internal loss data collection process from the very start of the operational risk management programme will help to mitigate this issue. Moreover, a formal and systematic operational risk management programme is expected to reduce the size and frequency of operational losses diminishing the relevance of data collected before the implementation of the programme. Thus, the older the loss data, the less relevant it is for determining future capital requirements.

The problem of old data representativeness is present in any science using historical data to predict future events, such as actuarial, engineering, manufacturing, etc. This problem is addressed using several methods including the following: assigning a lower weight to older data during the distribution fit or simulation of total losses see Chapter 4); introduction of additional data elements such as expert judgement in the form of scenario analysis (see Chapter 7); implementation of credibility theory (see Chapter 7) to determine the weight of the different data elements; analysing frequency trends and distribution characteristics' evolution and projecting them accordingly (see Chapter 4).

In fact, the BCSG-AMA requires financial institutions to use BEICFs as one of the four main elements for the modelling (ILD, ED and SA are the other three elements) to reflect the forward-looking character of the operational risk capital. Embedding BEICFs into capital estimation is a challenge given the difficulty in establishing a direct link, through the use of statistical analysis, into the capital modelling (see Chapter 6). Nevertheless, predictive models relating KRIs, internal audit scores or even RCSA scores can be created for adjusting the expected frequencies of the capital model and other capital metrics (see Chapter 6). This type of analysis is facilitated by the existence of an appropriate database of BEICFs and event data, generally supported by a governance, risk and compliance (GRC) solution.

The qualitative nature of scenario analysis

Scenario analysis is one of the data elements that should be part of an advanced capital model for operational risk. It is a critical component used to complement the modelling of potential extreme losses, which have not been observed by the institution but are possible.

Scenario analysis is based on expert judgement and, therefore, is subject to well-reported human cognitive biases, which pose a significant threat to the quality of the answers obtained. Also, given the qualitative nature of the answers to the scenario analysis, a validation process should be established. Therefore, to maximise the quality of a scenario analysis, the institution should establish a solid process to inform the experts on all available information, provide training for helping experts in structuring their analysis, establish strategies for the mitigation of cognitive biases, articulate adequately scenario questions and, finally, establish a strong process for the validation of expert answers.

The need for stable capital estimates

Stability of results in operational risk modelling is required because the capital budgeting process needs stable capital estimations in order to programme resource allocation, capital-raising actions, dividend payments, etc. Additionally, the robustness of the operational risk model may be in doubt if capital requirements change significantly every time newly collected loss data is added to the modelling sample.

Unstable capital estimates may have several origins, which include the selection of the model type and the insufficiency of historical data for modelling.

The selection of an inadequate model, for instance, looking simply at the goodness of fit, can have a major impact on capital stability, when the model is very sensitive to changes in the fitting sample. Figure 1.3 illustrates the impact on capital stability estimates by

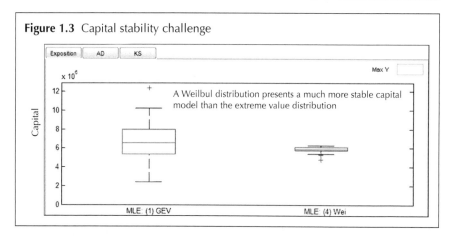

Figure 1.3 Capital stability challenge

selecting different modelling options. The capital stability calculations have been performed following the resampling method described in Chapter 4. The box plot graph represents the potential capital dispersion given new losses coming from the same loss-generation process. It can be seen how modelling with one distribution provides more stable capital estimates.

Figure 1.4 illustrates the stability of capital estimates due to insufficiency of historical data for modelling. It represents capital stability as the number of exceedances used in the fitting process (see Chapter 4). It can be seen that capital is more stable the higher the number of exceedances used, and becomes more volatile the fewer the number of exceedances. The reason is that, as the size of the sample decreases, there is more uncertainty on the real loss distribution explaining the behaviour. As an example, in Figure 1.4, the divergence in capital estimates increases as the size of the sample decreases, by increasing the modelling threshold.

Therefore, in operational risk capital modelling, the modeller should implement processes to evaluate the stability of modelling results. Some methods of performing this analysis are described in Chapter 4.

Selection of modelling assumptions

While, for market risks and credit, the distribution modelling standards are restricted to some distribution families (normal, lognormal, binomial and so on), operational risk modelling does not have any restrictions on the distribution family, provided it delivers

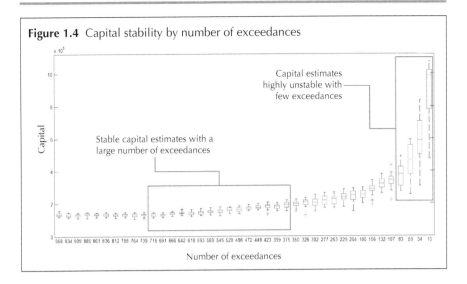

Figure 1.4 Capital stability by number of exceedances

an adequate fit. Therefore, a wide variety of distributions are used for modelling operational risk as described in Appendix I.

If p-values from tests are solely considered, the modeller may face multiple distribution assumptions to select from and no solid argument to prioritise one over the rest. The modelling process should incorporate extensive analysis to allow a solid modelling assumption selection (see Part II for methods of selecting distributional assumptions, including graphical and numerical goodness-of-tests analysis, stability of capital estimates, goodness-of-fit measures adjusted to the degrees of freedom of the distribution, evaluation method of the realism of the distribution estimates, tail control measures, and others).

Wide variety of sources and risk types of operational losses

Operational losses originate in any process or organisational unit in the institution and may be of very different natures. The source and nature of losses determine the loss frequency and severity distribution, making operational risk losses a highly heterogeneous sample of losses with different frequencies and distributional characteristics.

Figure 1.5 provides examples of operational risks in a financial institution spread over all activities, departments, BUs, etc. A similar representation can be done for insurance, asset management and so forth, or even for nonfinancial sectors such as energy and utilities.

Ideally, these circumstances would be resolved by creating a specific model for every process and loss type. In practice, this implies segmenting an already limited data sample, thus preventing a robust modelling of highly specific operational risks.

The creation of a larger modelling sample, can be addressed by aggregating losses by risk type Level 1 (after Basel Committee classification and Solvency II guidelines) and BUs. Although sample aggregation creates larger datasets, allowing its modelling, the aggregated data sample becomes a highly heterogeneous amalgamation of losses, resulting in other modelling challenges.

This heterogeneity can be addressed by segmenting the data sample by severity segments, as size is a clear differentiation factor for loss nature (see Chapter 4). Small losses may come from noncritical processes, while large losses may stem from processes impacting on serious aspects of the bank's activity, involving large monetary amounts and stronger controls. Loss severity distribution can be modelled according to multiple segments, to differentiate high-severity tail events from medium-sized and small-sized losses. Lower losses are generally most frequent and can be integrated into the simulation by directly resampling over the historical distribution. Tail losses are generally modelled using fat-tail distributions and body losses using a light-tail distribution.

Figure 1.5 High-level description of the activities in a financial institution

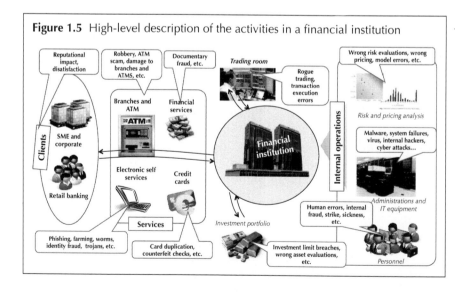

The integration of multiple data elements

Each of the four data elements (ILD, ED, SA and BEICFs) provides an important piece of information for the correct modelling of the complete operational risk distribution, from likely losses to highly unlikely but possible losses. Also, the weight and influence of each of the data elements should be determined using an unbiased method.

This represents a challenge for modelling, as it requires the use of nonstandard statistical and simulation methods to consolidate the different sources of information into a single joint risk distribution and determine the weight that each data element should have in the joint distribution.

Modelling operational risk dependencies

As the ORMS matures with improved data quality and a well-trained modelling team, the institution may decide to implement a more precise modelling of operational risk dependencies. This allows it to acquire a better understanding of common drivers of operational risk events, more precise capital allocation and, potentially, capital savings.

Nevertheless, the calculation of operational risk dependencies presents several challenges, which include the definition of a correlation framework with a dimension consistent with the amount of data available; data series arrangement and mitigating the data non-linearity; seasonality; and limited data availability (see Chapters 6 and 7). Also, the determination and replication of a dependency between severity and frequency dependency require the use of nonstandard correlation calculation and simulation methods (see Chapter 8).

Technology supporting the modelling process

As a result of the challenges presented above, operational risk modellers need to establish multiple analytical documentation and control processes to determine and justify operational capital results and guarantee their governance. Given the absence of widely accepted modelling standards, models are too frequently based on bespoke tools,[3] which frequently lack adequate data integrity, audit trail, automatic assumption documentation and interfaces with data sources and uses, as well as displaying other weaknesses.

The use of these types of limited bespoke tools induces more time-consuming modelling, maintenance and documentation, increases model error and makes the knowledge transfer of model functioning and methodology more difficult. Also, it becomes very hard to implement any change in model parameters or rerun the model under different assumptions. As a result, the institution develops strong dependence on the group of specialists who have developed the model and, in addition, may not have the adequate governance over the capital modelling process.

The technology supporting the modelling represents, last but not least, the very significant challenge of operational risk capital modelling. It is worthy of note that the use of the appropriate technology facilitates the implementation of all the methods and analytics described in this work into a highly doable task requiring a reasonable number of resources, thanks to the elimination of non-value-added manual tasks.

REGULATORY COMPLIANCE AND SUPERVISION OF THE OPERATIONAL RISK CAPITAL MODEL

The challenges of extreme event modelling with little historical and relevant data, forward-looking estimates and so on are shared with many areas of science, such as actuarial pricing, electronics and nuclear energy. However, when these challenges are involved in financial institutions' solvency reporting, a potential conflict of interest emerges: while capital is scarce and expensive for financial institutions, lenders and investors need these financial institutions to have sufficient capital for solid solvency. In fact, the solvency level of the institution will have a direct impact on the institution's financing costs and financial results.

To guarantee that this conflict of interest does not influence capital determination in any institution, an independent review and approval of the model is performed by supervisors. Here, the supervisory role is to ensure that capital calculation is not only acceptable for internal use, but also satisfactory as a solvency measure for external parties.

It follows that the modelling should incorporate governance processes, as a means of reassuring supervisors and external parties with the capital results and calculation processes. For the reassurance and model approval, supervisors across countries and industries share expectations such as the following:

❏ Robust processes to capture and determine capital modelling inputs: The quality of capital estimations is fully dependent on the inputs to the model. Therefore, supervisors expect institutions to have implemented solid collection and determination processes for internal loss data, external data and scenario analysis, and business environment and internal control factors (see Chapter 2).

❏ Audit trail of data sources and their transformations: To validate capital model results, all data sources and their transformations, additions and so on need to be thoroughly documented, so as to permit the replication of the modelling sample used and the capital results. Figure 1.6 shows an example of how to trail and document modelling assumptions.

❏ Solid justification and documentation of modelling assumptions: The selection of distribution type, fitting method, modelling threshold, data elements aggregation method, correlations and so on should be solidly justified and documented (see Part II, "General Framework for Operational Risk Capital Modelling"). Extensive documents and illustrations describing the analysis performed and modelling decisions taken need to be created in order to adequately justify modelling decisions to supervisors.

❏ Consistency of modelling criteria: The practitioner should apply the same criteria in modelling all risk types and BUs without directing the modelling to obtain a specific result. Modelling consistency can be documented by detailed workflows describing the analysis step by step and the decisions taken at each step.

Figure 1.6 Audit trail of operational risk modelling

	User	Operation type	Time	Date	Application module	Data Origin	Operation Data	Operation Details
1	Rafa	Create Audit Trail	18.20	19/12/2013	Scenario modeling			
2	Rafa	Read data	18.20	19/12/2013	Scenario modeling	GRC Scen	Read data info	
3	Rafa	Select data	18.20	19/12/2013	Scenario modeling	APPLICATI	Risk of costs of	
4	Rafa	Data Modify	18.20	19/12/2013	Fit Quant	Application	FIT	
5	Rafa	Data Modify	18.21	19/12/2013	Fit Quant	Database	SET	Set Skewness (5.100000e+000)and Kurtosis (33) from data
6	Rafa	Data Modify	18.21	19/12/2013	Fit Quant	Application	FIT	
7	Rafa	Data Modify	18.21	19/12/2013	Fit Quant	User	SET	Stress frequency to NaN
8	Rafa	Data Modify	18.21	19/12/2013	Fit Quant	User	SET	Stress severity to 30
9	Rafa	Data Modify	18.21	19/12/2013	Fit Quant	Application	FIT STRESS SEV	
10	Rafa	Data Modify	18.22	19/12/2013	Fit Quant	User	SET	Mean to 700
11	Rafa	Data Modify	18.22	19/12/2013	Fit Quant	Application	FIT STRESS SEV	

❏ Analysis of capital estimates stability: The modelling quality and forward-looking nature of the capital estimations receive a solid evaluation by the analysis of the capital results stability (see Chapter 4).

❏ Capital results validation process: Results of capital estimations acquire additional support when they are validated against losses occurring after the modelling date with techniques such as backtesting to verify the adequateness of distribution assumptions etc.

❏ Full understanding of the modelling process and methodology: The institution needs to fully understand the complexities of the modelling process. It follows that the complexity of the analytical processes has to be in accordance with the institution resources, knowledge and experience. In fact, institutions generally start modelling with simpler approaches – for instance, only internal-loss-data-based – and, as experience is gained, they incorporate additional inputs such as external data and scenario analysis. When technology is assisting the modelling, black boxes should be avoided and the institution should have access to and fully understand the modelling code.

❏ User control and approvals: When multiple BUs, departments or modellers participate in the input collection and model building, control and audit over contributors helps in governing the model. Also, validations and approvals over different steps of the modelling constitute a solid control the modelling process.

Many of these supervisory expectations add significant efforts and challenges to the internal operational risk modelling process.

An additional element of governance by supervisors is the use test. This means that capital estimations should be embedded within decision-making practices and on an ongoing business-as-usual basis. Supervisors expect financial institutions to accept and trust the capital estimations so that they can be used in their daily decisions. If a capital determination process is related only to regulatory compliance, the institution may be tempted to underestimate capital charges.

In fact, BCSG-AMA explicitly says, "The purpose and use of an AMA should not be solely for regulatory compliance purposes." Also, the regulatory approval of a capital model implies that the institution has developed a risk-based management, which provides additional trust in the institution's capacity to mitigate risks. It follows that operational risk modelling results should be embedded in the risk mitigation investment evaluation, performance measurement, financial budgeting, resource allocation, strategic plan definition, etc.

The advanced approach for capital calculation, together with the use test, creates a strong virtuous circle for operational risk management. The required data elements for its implementation provide an understanding of the risk profile, permitting a thorough risk mitigation. The fact that the inputs to the capital model are also used for mitigation incentivises a much deeper analysis, thus improving, in turn, the quality of the inputs to the capital model. This virtuous circle is probably the largest benefit an institution may get from an advanced approach for operational risk capital calculation. Indeed, it is uncommon to see such systematic and thorough operational risk mitigation in financial institutions calculating operational risk capital under standard or basic indicator approaches. This suggests that the advanced approach represents a very strong stimulus for solid operational risk mitigation.

Embedding capital results into the day-to-day risk management requires the development of strong analytical and management processes, see Part III.

The evaluation of risk mitigation investment requires the implementation of financial analysis incorporating operational risk capital. The evaluation of insurance requires the modelling of all insurance features, limitations and so forth into the operational loss simulation. Embedding the capital calculations into the performance management, financial budgeting and so on requires the integration of operational risk capital into the rest of the economic capital programme.

Finally, from the technology perspective, supervisors expect that it should minimise model error and facilitate timely modelling and assumption documentation and an effective enforcement of model governance. Model error is minimised through an optimal integrity of data flows and the automation of analytical and documentation processes. Model governance is facilitated with audit trail and user control functionalities embedded in operational risk management and modelling technology.

All these requirements are, either explicitly or implicitly, included in the previously mentioned Basel Committee on Banking Supervision's "Operational Risk – Supervisory Guidelines for Advanced Measurement Approaches" (BCSG-AMA). The focus of this work is to address aspects more closely related to the modelling (and data collection, preparation and statistical processes) of capital. Table 1.1 summarises the different requirements of the Basel Committee document and how the chapters of this work can help to address them. Needless to say, however, the final regulatory approval of an operational risk capital model will eventually depend on the views, evaluations, negotiations and final discretion of the relevant national supervisor.

Table 1.1 Supervisory requirements and sections of this work

Supervisory quotation	Part or chapter of this Book
Model Inputs	
"An AMA for calculating the operational risk capital charge of a bank requires the use of four data elements which are: (1) internal loss data (ILD); (2) external data (ED); (3) scenario analysis (SBA) and (4) business environment and internal control factors (BEICFs)."	Part I, "Capture and Determination of the Four Data Elements" Part II, "General Framework for Operational Risk Capital Modelling"
"The purpose of the standards is to provide insight into supervisors' minimum expectations regarding data integrity and comprehensiveness, both of which are critical to the effective implementation of an AMA."	Part I, "Capture and Determination of the Four Data Elements"
"To maintain consistency, a bank should develop data policies and procedures that include, for example, guidelines around perimeter of application, minimum observation period, reference date, de minimis modelling thresholds, and data treatment."	Part I, "Capture and Determination of the Four Data Elements"
Modelling assumptions	
"Supervisors expect ILD to be used in the operational risk measurement system (ORMS) to assist in the estimation of loss frequencies; to inform the severity distribution(s) to the extent possible."	Chapter 2, "Collection of Operational Loss Data" Chapter 4, "Loss Data Modelling"
"In accordance with paragraph 669(c) of the Basel II Framework, an AMA bank's risk measurement system 'must be sufficiently granular to capture the major drivers of operational risk affecting the shape of the tail of the loss estimates'."	Chapter 4, "Loss Data Modelling"
"The bank should put in place methodologies to reduce estimate variability and provide measures of the error around these estimates (eg confidence intervals, p-values)."	Chapter 4, "Loss Data Modelling"
"It generates a loss distribution with a realistic capital requirements estimate, without the need to implement 'corrective adjustments' such as caps."	Chapter 4, "Loss Data Modelling"

Supervisory quotation	Part or chapter of this Book
"Supervisors expect ED to be used in the estimation of loss severity as ED contains valuable information to inform the tail of the loss distribution(s)."	Chapter 2, "Collection of Operational Loss Data: ILD and ED" Chapter 4, "Loss Data Modelling: ILD and ED"
"A data scaling process involves the adjustment of loss amounts reported in external data to fit a bank's business activities and risk profile. Any scaling process should be systematic, statistically supported, and should provide output that is consistent with the bank's risk profile."	Chapter 4, "Loss Data Modelling: ILD and ED"
"A robust scenario analysis framework is an important element of the ORMF. This scenario process will necessarily be informed by relevant ILD, ED and suitable measures of BEICFs."	Chapter 3, "Scenario Analysis Framework and BEICFs Integration" Chapter 5, "Scenario Analysis Modelling"
"A bank should thus ensure that the loss distribution(s) chosen to model scenario analysis estimates adequately represent(s) its risk profile."	Chapter 5, "Scenario Analysis Modelling"
"A robust governance framework surrounding the scenario process is essential to ensure the integrity and consistency of the estimates produced."	Chapter 3, "Scenario Analysis Framework and BEICFs Integration"
"BEICFs are operational risk management indicators that provide forward-looking assessments of business risk factors as well as a bank's internal control environment."	Chapter 3, "Scenario Analysis Framework and BEICFs Integration" Chapter 6, "BEICFs Modelling and Integration into Capital Model"
"The bank should follow a well specified, documented and traceable process for the selection, update and review of probability distributions and the estimate of its parameters."	Chapter 4, "Loss Data Modelling: ILD and ED"
"A bank should carefully consider how the data elements are combined and used to ensure that the bank's operational risk capital charge is commensurate with its level of risk exposure."	Chapter 7, "Hybrid Model Construction: Integration of ILD, ED and SA"
"The combination of data elements should be based on a sound statistical methodology."	Chapter 7, "Hybrid Model Construction: Integration of ILD, ED and SA"
"The techniques to determine the aggregated loss distributions should ensure adequate levels of precision and stability of the risk measures."	Chapter 7, "Hybrid Model Construction: Integration of ILD, ED and SA"
"A bank should pay particular attention to the positive skewness and, above all, leptokurtosis of the data when selecting a severity distribution."	Chapter 4, "The Scale and Shape Scaling Method" Chapter 5, "Scenario Analysis Modelling"
"When separate distributions for the body and the tail are used, a bank should carefully consider the choice of the body-tail modelling threshold that distinguishes the two regions."	Chapter 4, "Loss Data Modelling: ILD and ED"
"As such, simulation, numerical or approximation methods are necessary to derive aggregated curves (e.g. Monte Carlo simulations, Fourier Transform-related methods, Panjer algorithm and Single Loss Approximations)."	Chapter 8, "Derivation of the Joint Distribution and Capitalisation of Operational Risk"

Supervisory quotation	Part or chapter of this Book
"Robust estimation methods (such as alternatives to classical methods as the Maximum Likelihood and the Probability Weighted Moments), proposed recently in operational risk literature, are reasonably efficient under small deviations from the assumed model."	Chapter 4, "Loss Data Modelling: ILD and ED"
"A bank should assess the quality of fit between the data and the selected distribution. The tools typically adopted for this purpose are graphical methods (which visualise the difference between the empirical and theoretical functions) and quantitative methods, based on goodness-of-fit tests. In selecting these tools, a bank should give preference to graphical methods and goodness-of-fit tests that are more sensitive to the tail than to the body of the data (e.g. the Anderson Darling upper tail test)."	Chapter 4, "Loss Data Modelling: ILD and ED"
"Moreover, the results of the goodness-of-fit tests are usually sensitive to the sample size and the number of parameters estimated. In such cases, a bank should consider selection methods that use the relative performance of the distributions at different confidence levels. Examples of selection methods may include the Likelihood Ratio, the Schwarz Bayesian Criterion and the Violation Ratio."	Chapter 4, "Loss Data Modelling: ILD and ED"
"The bank may be permitted to use internally determined correlations in operational risk losses across individual operational risk estimates, provided it can demonstrate to the satisfaction of the national supervisor that its systems for determining correlations are sound, implemented with integrity and take into account the uncertainty surrounding any such correlation estimates (particularly in periods of stress). The bank must validate its correlation assumptions using appropriate quantitative."	Chapter 8, "Derivation of the Joint Distribution and Capitalisation of Operational Risk"
"A bank should also gather information on the expected loss. Due to its high sensitivity to extreme losses, the arithmetic mean can cause an inaccurate picture for the expected losses. In light of this, the use of statistics that are less influenced by extreme losses (e.g. median, trimmed mean) is recommended, especially in the case of medium/heavy tailed datasets."	Chapter 8, "Derivation of the Joint Distribution and Capitalisation of Operational Risk"
"Whatever approach is used, a bank must demonstrate that its operational risk measure meets a soundness standard comparable to that of the internal ratings-based approach for credit risk (ie comparable to a one year holding period and a 99.9th percentile confidence interval)."	Chapter 8, "Derivation of the Joint Distribution and Capitalisation of Operational Risk"
"However, a bank must be able to demonstrate that its approach captures potentially severe 'tail' loss events."	Chapter 4, "Loss Data Modelling: ILD and ED" Appendix I, "Distributions for Modelling Operational Risk Capital"
"Exploratory Data Analysis (EDA) for each ORC to better understand the statistical profile of the data and select the most appropriate distribution ...	Chapter 4, "Loss Data Modelling: ILD and ED"
"Appropriate techniques for the estimation of the distributional parameters; ..."	Chapter 4, "Loss Data Modelling: ILD and ED"
"Appropriate diagnostic tools for evaluating the quality of the fit of the distributions to the data, giving preference to those most sensitive to the tail."	Chapter 4, "Loss Data Modelling: ILD and ED"

Supervisory quotation	Part or chapter of this Book
"Capital allocation to internal business lines should be a factor when choosing ORCs, as these ORCs may be used as part of the capital allocation process."	Chapter 8, "Derivation of the Joint Distribution and Capitalisation of Operational Risk" Chapter 1, "BEICFs Modelling and Integration into Capital Model"
"Moreover, a bank should perform sensitivity analyses and stress testing (e.g. different parameter values, different correlation models) on the effect of alternative dependence assumptions on its operational risk capital charge estimate.	Chapter 2, "Backtesting, Stress Testing and Sensitivity Analysis"
Verification and validation	
"Verification of the ORMF includes testing whether all material aspects of the ORMF have been implemented effectively …: … a comparison of scenario results with internal loss data and external data."	Chapter 3, "Scenario Analysis Framework and BEICFs Integration"
"Validation ensures that the ORMS used by the bank is sufficiently robust and provides assurance of the integrity of inputs, assumptions, processes and outputs."	This work focuses in the modelling. However, in the introduction we mention these topics in:
"Verification activities test the effectiveness of the overall ORMF, consistent with policies approved by the board of directors, and also test ORMS validation processes to ensure they are independent and implemented in a manner consistent with established bank policies."	This chapter, "Regulatory compliance and supervision of the operational risk capital model"
"Results from verification and validation work should be documented and distributed to appropriate business line management, internal audit, the corporate operational risk management function and appropriate risk committees. Bank staff ultimately responsible for the validated units should have access to, and an understanding of, these results".	Chapter 4, "Backtesting, Stress Testing and Sensitivity Analysis"
"The validation process of the ORMS should provide enhanced assurance that the measurement methodology results in an operational risk capital charge that credibly reflects the operational risk profile of the bank."	Chapter 5, "Backtesting, Stress Testing and Sensitivity Analysis"
Use test	
"The bank should have adequate processes in place to monitor identified controls, ensuring that they are appropriate to mitigate the identified risks to the desired residual level and operating effectively."	Chapter 6, "Risk–Reward Evaluation of the Mitigation and Control Effectiveness"
"A bank´s board of directors should approve and review a clear statement of operational risk appetite and tolerance."	Chapter 7, "Strategic and Operational Business Planning and Monitoring"
"A bank´s strategic and business planning process should consider its operational risk profile, including outputs from the ORMS."	Chapter 8, "Strategic and Operational Business Planning and Monitoring"

1　We refer to operational risk capital bottom-up models such as LDA, SBA and hybrid models. In financial industry regulation, this type of model is called AMA (advanced measurement approach) in Basel II/III and internal models in Solvency II.
2　In this book, all graphs and calculations referring to capital modelling have been performed using OpCapital Analytics, a software solution based on MatLab specifically designed for the calculation of operational risk capital requirements under advanced approaches.

3 Bespoke models refer to those created in-house with limited use of GUIs and data sources' interphases, suboptimal integrated flows, limited reporting capabilities and scarce model governance such as nonexistence of audit trail or user control.

REFERENCES

Robertson, Douglas, 2011, "So That's Operational Risk!", OCC Economics Working Paper 2011-1, March.

Part I

Capture and Determination of the Four Data Elements

The results of an operational risk capital model are primarily dependent on the inputs provided to the modelling. This dependence is even higher than in other risk models, because, in the case of operational risk capital, inputs include significant portions of expert opinions and very diverse sources, and many inputs are internally generated by the institution.

According to the BCSG-AMA (the abbreviation used in this book for referring to the document issued by Basel Committee on Banking Supervision named "Operational Risk – Supervisory Guidelines for Advanced Measurement Approaches"),[1] "an AMA for calculating the operational risk capital charge of a bank requires the use of four data elements, which are: (1) internal loss data (ILD); (2) external data (ED); (3) scenario analysis (SA) and (4) business environment and internal control factors (BEICFs)".

Each of the data elements provides very distinctive and necessary information about the capital model. ILD informs us about the specific risk profile of the institution based on its historical high-frequency loss events. ED provides insights on the high-severity events experienced by peer institutions that might not be reflected in the ILD. SA captures information on low frequency risk scenarios very specific to the institution provided by manager expert judgment. Finally, BEICFs (business environment and internal control factors) point to operational weaknesses that may anticipate potential failures in delivering forward-looking information into the estimation of capital requirements.

Part I presents methods for capturing and determining the four data elements with the required quality for capital calculation purposes. Chapter 2 examines loss data (ILD and ED) and Chapter 3 looks at SA and BEICFs as input into SA.

We will refer to Governance Risk and Compliance (GRC) platforms, as they provide a robust technology for capturing quality inputs required for a robust estimation of operational risk capital.

---

1 This work bases its regulatory references on various Basel Committee documents. Nevertheless, we believe these references are perfectly applicable to other regulated industries, such as the insurance sector. In fact, regulatory frameworks across industries and jurisdictions share basic principles. We also believe that the operational risk principles defined in this work are usable for the modelling of operational risk even in nonfinancial industries such as energy and utilities. Indeed, most of the principles defined in the financial sector regulation can be used for the internal governance of modelling activity in nonregulated industries.

2

Collection of Operational Loss Data: ILD and ED

Brenda Boultwood

In this chapter, we will examine the key considerations around operational loss data, both internal loss data (ILD) and external data (ED), the first two data elements of an operational risk capital model. The chapter starts with the understanding of operational loss and its key considerations and the need for completeness of data collection and consistency with accounting. Finally, we will define an understanding of ED, discuss the available ED sources and introduce the ED uses.

TOWARDS A COMMON UNDERSTANDING OF OPERATIONAL LOSS

What are operational losses?

Defining operational risk is an important first step in developing a common understanding of operational loss. Conceptually speaking, operational risk has evolved steadily over time. Recognising the growing impact of operational risk on the long-term health of organisations, the Basel II accords moved away from a classification of operational risk as simply all "other risk" not subsumed under the categories of market or credit risk and towards a specific definition – "The risk of direct or indirect loss resulting from inadequate or failed internal processes, people and systems or from external events" (BIS 2001, Section II, subsection 6).

To be sure, the Basel II definition is just one of many definitions of operational risk currently in circulation. A number of firms and industries have used the Basel II framework to guide the

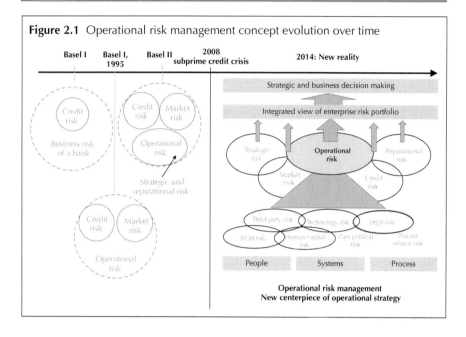

Figure 2.1 Operational risk management concept evolution over time

development of their own definitions.[1] However, given the breadth of the Basel II guidelines, as well as their foundational role in providing a basis for subsequent definitions, the Basel II definition provides us with a useful point of departure for discussing operational losses.

While the Basel II definition of operational risk is broad, it does make clear that operational losses are linked to particular causal factors. Specifically, operational losses are losses that can be attributed to human error, flawed processes, failed systems and external events that disrupt day-to-day business operations. To put these into a more concrete perspective, examples of operational losses can include everything from the banal (minor accounting errors) to the extreme (rogue trading, data breaches, noncompliance with regulatory standards and even natural disasters that impact on business continuity).

On further inspection, the broad nature of operational loss raises a number of questions:

❑ What constitutes a loss?
❑ What differentiates direct from indirect losses?

- ❏ What distinguishes operational losses from market and credit losses?
- ❏ How do we adequately capture, collect and assess operational loss data?
- ❏ Why is the collection of loss data crucial to an organisation's risk management posture?

Guided by these core questions, in this chapter, we explore the significance of operational loss and provide a framework for internal data collection as well as loss analysis and predictive modelling.

Why capture operational losses?

According to the Basel Committee on Banking Supervision (BCBS), "The tracking of internal loss event data is an essential prerequisite to the development and functioning of a credible operational risk measurement and management system" (Wilson 2008; BIS 2001) – and with good reason. There is little doubt that unmitigated operational risks will result in operational losses, but not every operational risk is worth mitigating simply because it may lead to a loss. On what basis can organisations make the determination as to which risks are worth mitigating and which are not? How can organisations allocate resources and capital in order that the risks being targeted are truly those risks that will cause the most significant financial losses?

Answering these questions requires organisations to conduct internal investment calculations that determine whether or not the investment required to mitigate a specific risk significantly outweighs the cost of the risk itself. These types of calculations play a central role in helping an organisation develop its risk appetite by making clear distinctions between risks that require constant mitigation and those that fall within an acceptable risk threshold.

Internal investment calculations, however, are largely qualitative in nature. Given the ubiquitous nature of operational risk, as well as its relationship to business operations, operational risk can escape hard quantitative analysis. As a result, short- and long-term risk impacts and losses are often assessed through probabilistic calculations that can be difficult to quantify.

It is precisely at this juncture that capturing operational losses becomes essential. The collection of operational loss data provides a historical record that allows for a more comprehensive and acute understanding of past risk incidents and operational losses. This offers two important benefits. First, operational loss data can be fed back into risk assessments and risk mitigation efforts to inform more accurate internal investment calculations. Second, as operational loss data is captured over time, it can be used for more sophisticated qualitative and quantitative risk modelling and analysis in order to gauge the frequency of specific types of risk incidents or the likelihood of particular losses.

In short, the historical perspective offered by operational loss data can play an indispensable role in guiding future risk decisions, and it allows organisations to adjust their risk posture based on the experience of actual losses.

How do operational losses differ from credit and market losses?

The *raison d'être* of Basel II was to develop an accord that was more risk-sensitive than earlier versions, which, as was previously mentioned, was tied to "the realisation that risks other than credit and market can be substantial" (BIS 2001). As such, understanding the differences between operational losses, credit losses and market losses requires an appreciation of how operational risk differs from credit and market risk.

Market and credit segments of an organisation involve areas of risk that possess the potential for gains as well as losses. Given the potential upside, when it comes to an organisation's market and credit functions, a complete avoidance of risk is not only impossible, it's also undesirable. Accordingly, an optimal level of exposure to market and credit risk can actually help maximise returns, facilitate business growth and foster innovation.

As opposed to credit and market risk, however, operational risk involves little to no upside. As a result, operational losses are not simply a normal part of an organisation's larger risk landscape, necessary to absorb because of the potential gains they offer. This means that organisations should work to mitigate all possible operational risks in order to prevent the negative impact – both financial and reputational – of operational losses. Though a certain measure of risk is unavoidable in the realm of credit and market functions, when confronted with operational losses, the best strategy is to mitigate and avoid risk at all costs.

In comparison with credit and market losses, operational losses, by their very nature, are also harder to detect and track. Market and credit risks can be linked to distinct areas of an organisation staffed with dedicated teams and personnel equipped with an acute understanding of the risk landscape. This type of organisational transparency increases accountability and responsiveness to risk. In addition, because market and credit risks are confined to particular business units, the collection and reporting of loss data presents less of an organisational challenge.

Operational risks, however, are dispersed throughout the entirety of an organisation. Losses can emerge from just about anywhere – from the initial point of customer contact all the way to the IT architecture in the back of the house. This also means that tracking and reporting operational losses presents a unique challenge. Collecting and aggregating operational loss requires a far more integrated and holistic approach to enterprise-wide risk management in order to be effective.

THE IMPORTANCE OF BUILDING A COMMON UNDERSTANDING OF OPERATIONAL LOSSES

What constitutes a loss? On its face, the question seems simple enough. However, being able to arrive at a common understanding of operational losses is fundamental to the success of an organisation's operational risk management efforts. According to the Bank of International Settlements (BIS 2001),

> In order to use a bank's internal loss data in regulatory capital calculation, harmonisation of what constitutes an operational risk loss event is a prerequisite for a consistent approach. Developing workable supervisory definitions, in consultation with the industry, of what constitutes an operational loss event for different business lines and loss types will be critical to the robustness of the Internal Measurement Approach.

The issue of common understanding becomes even more important in light of the core differences between operational losses and market and credit losses discussed in the previous section. Credit and market risks are isolated to specific segments of an organisation. From loan instruments to trading processes, those intimately involved with credit and market transactions on a daily basis possess a common language and shared taxonomy for assessing these particular types of risk.

Operational risk, however, permeates the entirety of an organisation. From the administrative desk to the IT department, an operational loss can occur at almost any point in a business process across the organisation. This makes the development of a common set of definitions and practices essential. Developing and maintaining a robust approach to operational loss collection depends on a shared lexicon for assessing, categorising, recording and reporting loss data. Common understanding will allow for a much easier, more effective and efficient harmonisation of risk processes and aggregation of data from across the organisation.

KEY CONSIDERATIONS ON OPERATIONAL LOSSES
Indirect versus direct losses

At the outset, it is worth noting that a measure of ambiguity exists when it comes to drawing clear distinctions between direct and indirect losses. This is perhaps best demonstrated by way in which the Basel II definition of operational risk has evolved over time. In its initial definition of operational risk, the Basel II accords made explicit reference to "direct and indirect" losses. However, the absence of a clear understanding as to the constitutive differences between them engendered significant industry criticism. In response, the BIS offered a "refined definition of operational risk" that excluded explicit reference to direct and indirect losses (Chernobai, Rachev and Fabozzi 2007, p. 17).[2]

Despite this ambiguity, however, delineating between direct and indirect losses remains vital to developing a common understanding of operational loss. It is also instrumental in creating a more nuanced understanding of operational risk and guarding against the errors that can arise from double counting. Typically, direct losses are easier to characterise because they can be linked to specific operational control failures. Take, for example, the case of losses arising from an act of rogue trading in which a particular trader is able to circumvent the system in place that restricts daily trading limits. In this instance, systemic failure leads directly to organisational losses. As in the case of the rogue trader, direct losses that can be linked to control failures are easily recognisable and thus easily quantifiable.

The costs associated with indirect losses, however, are not as readily apparent. While risk incidents generate certain impacts that organisations feel immediately, there are others that may unfold slowly over a longer period. For example, while businesses are able to attach specific dollar amounts to lawsuit settlements, the longer-lasting reputational impacts will prove difficult to quantify. In addition, certain losses may be latent, unrealised as losses in the immediate, or contingent on a host of variables and circumstances that may or may not occur. All of which produces a level of uncertainty when it comes to calculating indirect losses.

Difficulties also arise in relation to those cases in which direct and indirect losses overlap with one another. In these instances, maintaining a rigid boundary between the two becomes not only difficult but also impractical. Overlap may present significant challenges for organisations in terms of data collection and calculation. Furthermore, because every organisation establishes different risk appetite parameters, the question of where to draw the boundary can certainly vary. These challenges clarify the need for every organisation to make determinations regarding the assessment of direct and indirect losses. This will ensure that the reporting and collection of operational loss data aligns with larger business goals and objectives.

Holding period of losses

In addition to distinguishing between direct and indirect losses, designing a robust loss data collection programme requires determining the appropriate holding period of losses. Limiting the variation of losses entails a lower sensitivity of operational risk estimates to the chosen time horizon or holding period, which implies a higher probability of extreme losses. As a result, establishing the proper holding period for operational losses is essential.

To this end, there are a number of suggested guidelines for defining the optimal holding period of losses. According to standards set forth in the Basel II framework, organisations are required to collect losses for at least three years in order to meet the data requirements for historical analysis. While the Australian Prudential Regulation Authority (APRA) Advanced Measurement Approach (AMA) notes that organisations can determine their required capital based on whatever method or model deemed appropriate, they suggest that the operational risk regulatory capital requirement must be comparable to a 99.9% confidence level over a one year holding period.

However, beyond these benchmarks, each organisation needs to decide how long it will hold loss data. Best practices involve ascertaining how long specific organisational losses remain valid and at what point they cease to provide relevant insight for organisational risk management practices.

Observation period of historical losses

As we saw earlier, one of the core benefits of collecting internal loss data is the historical perspective it provides, which can inform an organisation's risk posture as well as improve its strategic decision-making capabilities. Therefore, when designing a risk methodology and framework for analysis, one of the most important questions involves establishing a timeline for the observation of historical losses.

Generally, a bank's operational risk data and assessment system includes a minimum historical observation period of five years' worth of operational losses. However, with the approval of a primary federal supervisor, a bank could implement a shorter historical observation period in order to address transitional situations such as integrating a new business line.

Determining the observational scope of loss assessment is important because it establishes a field of risk intelligibility – rendering certain events visible while masking others. Selecting a timeline for observation will help tell a particular story about operational losses. Changing the observational timeline, however, will impact on the analysis, conveying a different history of operational loss and risk.

When setting parameters for observation, organisations need to be careful about including crisis moments, catastrophic incidents and other exceptional events known as "black swans". Because of their rarity, the inclusion of these types of events in a historical sample of operational losses will result in a skewed dataset, which in turn will hamper an organisation's ability to create workable probabilities that provide actionable insights for risk assessment. In these instances, it is best to omit outlying events and subject them to risk scenario analysis instead – a subject to be covered at length in later chapters.

The role of judgement in data collection and consolidation

At this point, there should be little doubt that effective operational loss analysis is dependent on a set of shared practices that allow organisations not only to collect and aggregate data but to ensure its integrity and quality as well. However, with so much emphasis on data, calculation and quantification, it might lead to the assumption that internal loss collection is as much about removing the human element entirely as it is about laying the groundwork for a historical analysis that enables organisations to optimally shape their risk management programmes.

The key to successful data collection is to make the process as objective and systematic as possible. But, in truth, judgement and decision making play a substantial role in developing and designing the best possible approach to data collection. From drawing boundaries between direct and indirect losses to making determinations regarding the holding period and observational timeline for historical losses, key decision makers have a role to play in ensuring that collection and consolidation efforts ultimately align with larger business goals, generate the right questions and provide the right answers that ensure that an organisation's risk posture, armed with the insights of the past, is able to successfully and effectively mitigate future losses.

In addition, there is also a behavioural aspect to loss collection that can have a significant impact on an organisation's ability to gain an accurate perspective of its operational losses. For example, the negative connotation surrounding the idea of loss often leads managers and business owners to mask losses out of fear that it will reflect poorly on their own abilities and performance. This can lead to delays and inconsistencies in the reporting process as well as the complete absence of loss reporting in some instances. Consequently, a focus on enterprise-wide risk training and awareness can play a crucial role in addressing the subjective aspects of judgement and decision making around operational risk. Building a culture of transparency is important for developing an internal loss-collection programme that doesn't just work, but works well.

COMPLETENESS OF DATA COLLECTION
Loss event capture lifecycle
The lifecycle of a loss event capture contains a number of specific organisational processes and components used to identify, record and remediate operational losses. We begin this section with a broad overview of the complete workflow involved in the loss event

lifecycle and examine the key considerations that comprise loss event data collection. Following this general introduction, we move on to a detailed exploration of the components associated with data collection – from identification to calculation.

The first step in a loss event workflow is all about definition. It begins with an individual or group identifying a loss event based on the common threshold and risk appetite criteria established by the organisation. Once an event is identified as a loss event, it is then formally recorded. The recording process involves entering all inputs and parameters associated with the event into requisite loss data fields, which will be discussed at greater length in subsequent sections of this chapter. Following the recording process, the loss event then moves through an approval cycle, where it is vetted and assessed in order to determine the appropriate response and remedial action.

Once a loss event has been identified, initiated, recorded and properly vetted through the approval cycle, there are two basic types of action that can occur in response. The first involves subjecting the loss event to a causal analysis in which the primary objective is to uncover what specifically caused the loss to occur. The purpose of causal analysis is to define the field of possibilities for specific remedial action. Applying this process, however, requires a significant number of organisational resources. Given the costs associated with remediation, subjecting every loss event to this process would prove inefficient and also unnecessary. As a result, this type of action is typically reserved for particularly large loss events responsible for significant financial losses.

The second course of action, which is a more common approach to assessing and incorporating internal losses into an organisation's operational risk framework, relates back to the sophisticated risk perspective that having a historical record offers. Creating this historical record involves integrating the captured loss event data into your organisation's larger database of historical losses. Specific loss event data can then be included in larger capital models of historical risk analysis in order to arrive at a more accurate value-at-risk (VaR) number. This approach enables efficient and systematic handling of internal loss event data with benefits for long-term operational risk management and assessment.

In addition to the general loss event workflow described above, there are a number of other important points to consider in order to ensure the quality and integrity of the data being collected. These core considerations will be explored below.

Establishing the minimum materiality threshold

From a resource perspective, capturing every loss presents a significant burden for an organisation. As we mentioned in our discussion of the loss event life cycle, data collection begins first and foremost with the identification of a loss event that is significant enough to warrant data capture. This, of course, prompts the following question: on what basis can an organisation identify loss data worth capturing?

The process of identifying losses significant enough for data collection requires establishing a minimum materiality threshold for every operational risk class. "Thresholds need to be defined for data capturing and loss reporting so that management has the ability to evaluate and react to operational risk events" (State Bank of Pakistan 2013). This establishes a baseline for determining which losses should be considered loss events for the purposes of data collection. Defining the minimum materiality threshold is a business-specific process that will change depending on the size and needs of an organisation, which makes it a crucial part of developing a common organisational understanding of loss. In addition, loss-collection thresholds are not static but rather dynamic numbers that need to be evaluated on a periodic basis as the organisation scales to ensure that the "choice of threshold includes all material operational risk losses for risk management purposes" (State Bank of Pakistan 2014).

Determining frequency and severity of loss events

Once the minimum materiality threshold is established and guidelines are in place for the identification and recording of loss event data, an organisation can begin to determine the frequency and severity of loss events. However, if each loss event is viewed as unique, and every loss has its own category or classification, being able to understand a more holistic and comprehensive picture of the frequency and severity of losses is all but impossible. Ultimately, in order for internal loss collection to be effective, data has to be properly categorised. Optimal risk assessment and statistical analysis requires aggregating data according to specific classifications that can in turn provide the organisation with a clear picture of operational losses.

Classification systems enable organisations to identify those loss events that occur more frequently than others as well as those loss events that may produce greater and more severe organisational impacts in need of remediation and correction. Consequently, the appropriate classification of loss data may provide valuable insights that necessitate a shift in resources and risk posture, or even a re-evaluation of the procedures being used to capture losses themselves.

Mapping losses to supervisory event types and business lines

Similar to the way in which gauging the frequency and severity of loss events requires a particular scheme for data classification, the appropriate mapping of losses to organisational business lines also plays a critical role in effective data analysis. Once again, given that every organisation possesses a unique internal structure, the mapping process is indeed business-specific. For instance, while some banks may have wealth management and retail banking combined in a single business unit, others may have defined boundaries between the retail banking and wealth management sides of their organisation.

Thus, it is crucial that organisations establish a common set of practices to ensure that loss data is categorised along shared business lines. In fact, the ability to correlate enterprise-wide loss data that will yield information useful to organisational risk decision making depends on it. To aid in this process, the Basel Accords outline specific business lines common to most banks. These guidelines, which will be discussed in greater detail below, provide a starting point for organisations to begin mapping their internally unique structures to these more general business line categories.

Identifying and leveraging existing historical loss databases

Beginning the process of internal loss collection may seem like a daunting task, especially for organisations that are initiating loss collection for the first time. However, while locating a point of departure might seem difficult, there are certainly places already embedded within an organisational structure that can provide a useful foundation. In short, organisations do not have to start building loss databases from scratch.

There are sources of loss data that, while not officially classified as loss databases, hold a wellspring of information that can be used to begin building a historical loss database. In banking and financial institutions, existing fraud databases are centralised repositories of valuable information that can be mined for relevant loss event data. In addition, corporate security, insurance and legal departments also hold vital information that can be leveraged to begin building a foundation for historical loss databases.

Establishing an automated process of collection, validation, attribution and reporting that aligns with incentives

The efficacy of any loss-capture programme depends on making it an enterprise-wide process. The more people engaged in identifying and reporting losses, the greater the amount of data available for risk assessment and analysis. A broader dataset provides a more comprehensive picture of organisational losses and has the potential to impact on strategic decision making. The incorporation of large datasets, however, comes with its own set of challenges. How can an organisation ensure the effective management of large volumes of operational loss data? In addition, how can it ensure the integrity and quality of that data?

The effective collection of loss data requires a system in place for data management. But this cannot be accomplished manually. The implementation of a set of automated processes for the management, validation and approval of all recorded loss data will ensure that organisations are well equipped to work with large historical loss databases as well as ensure a set of core processes for data capture workflow.

Setting the boundary between operational risk and "other" risk types

The definition of operational risk outlined in the Basel II accords makes explicit distinctions between different types of risk. For example, it begins by recognising "risks other than credit and market can be substantial" and goes on to state that "strategic and reputational risk is not included in this definition [of operational risk] for the purpose of a minimum regulatory operational risk capital charge" (BIS 2001). Earlier in this chapter, we discussed the differences between operational losses and market and credit losses on the basis of their differences as types of risk categories. In this section, we explore how, given the exclusion of reputational risk from the Basel II definition, organisations distinguish between operational and reputational risk.

This is a question of significant importance given that there are a number of areas in which the boundary between operational and reputational risk remains porous. Furthermore, though Basel II excludes reputational risk from the definition of operational risk, it does recognise that the measurement and modelling of operational risk continues to develop and progress, which opens the door to the possibility of integrating reputational risk into an operational risk framework.[3]

In the absence of a common standard that explicitly establishes where the boundary should be set between operational risk and other types of risk, such as strategic and reputational risk, organisations need to develop a set of internal standards and best practices to guide their assessment of risks and losses. However, similar to establishing the minimum materiality threshold, organisations should approach these boundaries as dynamic and flexible, subject to change over time depending on organisational needs and changing industry standards.

Recognising losses

In the previous sections, we broke down the anatomy of a loss data workflow. In this next section we turn to an exploration of the primary elements to consider while capturing loss data for the purpose of aggregation and analysis. Specifically, internal loss capture involves the following core attributes:

- ❏ Cause – an investigation as to the cause of the loss event. What was the actual source of the loss? Was the loss caused by internal factors, such as control failure or negligent personnel, or was it caused by an external event?
- ❏ Classification – a classification of the loss according to the three levels outlined in the Basel II framework.
- ❏ Consequence – the specific consequences of the loss. Involves a description of the particular type of loss and how it will impact on the organisation.
- ❏ Discovery – an account of how the loss event was detected, including how and when the loss was discovered.

❏ Cost – a determination of the particular type of monetary loss as well as the actual loss value.
❏ Disclosure – the timeline for disclosing losses can vary depending on the type of loss. For example, while some losses have to be disclosed in real-time, others can be reported monthly or quarterly.

Structure of loss data fields

The Basel II operational risk framework requires classifying losses by event type and mapping those losses to specific business lines. However, when developing inputs for loss event data, there are a variety of additional fields that are essential for creating a robust database of historical losses. While these may vary slightly from organisation to organisation, there are a number of fairly standard fields that will help organisations keep track of the most vital operational loss information. Each data point can then be aggregated for analysis in larger calculations and incorporated into an organisation's overall risk assessment profile.

Standard loss data fields for database modelling may include the following:[4]

General information:
❏ loss ID;
❏ reporting unit;
❏ geographic location; and
❏ reporting person.

Incident information:
❏ description of loss incident;
❏ individual involved;
❏ incident cause;
❏ mitigation and remedial actions;
❏ status;
❏ discovery;
❏ business line as defined by Basel (Level 1, 2 or 3);
❏ event type – (Category 1, 2 or 3);
❏ incident date;
❏ detection date;
❏ accounting date;

❏ follow-up action;
❏ gross loss;
❏ currency;
❏ recovered amount;
❏ recovery date; and
❏ loss categorisation according to Basel II.

The Basel II accords provide a framework for loss categorisation to aid in the development of historical loss databases. The framework offers the following three-tiered system for classifying loss events:

❏ Level 1: event-type category;
❏ Level 2: loss category; and
❏ Level 3: activity example.

Each level of loss categorisation provides a different layer of information, from broader and more general classifications of event types to highly detailed and granular data regarding the specific activities that caused the loss in question. Combined, these three levels of classification help aggregate and align the appropriate data related to specific operational loss events.
    Level 1 event types include (BIS 2002):

❏ internal fraud – unauthorised transactions resulting in losses, embezzlement;
❏ external fraud – cybersecurity breaches and hacking incidents, physical robbery;
❏ employment practices and workplace safety – harassment and discrimination, health and safety violations;
❏ clients, products and business practices – money laundering, lender liability;
❏ damage to physical assets – natural disasters, terrorism;
❏ business disruption and system failures – power and utility outages, server failure; and
❏ execution, delivery and process management – data entry errors, missing or incomplete legal documents.

Following Level 1, the Basel II framework further subdivides these loss events in Level 2, which comprises 20 specific loss categories, each corresponding to specific Level 1 event-types.

Level 2 categories include (BIS 2002):

- ❏ unauthorised activity;
- ❏ theft and fraud;
- ❏ systems security;
- ❏ employee relations;
- ❏ safe environment;
- ❏ diversity and discrimination;
- ❏ suitability, disclosure and fiduciary;
- ❏ improper business or market practice;
- ❏ product flaws;
- ❏ selection, sponsorship and exposure;
- ❏ advisory activities;
- ❏ disasters and other events;
- ❏ systems;
- ❏ transaction capture, execution and maintenance;
- ❏ monitoring and reporting;
- ❏ customer intake and documentation;
- ❏ customer/client account management;
- ❏ trade counterparties; and
- ❏ vendors and suppliers.

The final level of loss event classification, Level 3, provides the most detailed and specific data of the Basel II categories. Level 3 information focuses on specific loss-related activities that correspond to the event type and event categories provided by Levels 1 and 2. Level 3 activities include, but are not limited to, unreported and unauthorised transactions, forgery, smuggling, tax evasion and non-compliance, fiduciary breaches, insider trading, product defects, natural disaster losses, utility outages, data entry error, outsourcing and vendor disputes (BIS 2002).

In addition to the three-tiered system for loss event classification, Basel II also offers a specific structure for business line mapping, which, as we mentioned earlier in this chapter, provides a framework for individual institutions to align their internal business lines with the categories established by the Basel II framework.

The Basel Committee's framework for business line mapping includes the following eight categories (BIS 2002):

❏ corporate finance;
❏ trading and sales;
❏ retail banking;
❏ commercial banking;
❏ payment and settlement;
❏ agency services;
❏ asset management; and
❏ retail brokerage.

Though these eight standard business lines may not correspond directly to the pre-existing structure of every bank and financial institution, organisations have the latitude to map their own corporate structures to the Basel framework in order to properly align their loss data collection process.

Defining the loss amount

Defining the loss amount is one of the most critical aspects of loss event data collection. It can be used to guide future decisions regarding appropriate response and remediation measures as well as to inform changing risk appetites. Determining the correct loss amount also provides an important data point that can be factored into larger models of operational risk assessment and analysis.

When defining the loss amount, organisations need to begin by distinguishing between loss and gross loss. Specifically, gross loss represents the negative impact on profit and loss statements before "recoveries of any type".[5] While gross loss calculations include "costs incurred as a consequence of the event", as well as the "external expenses with a direct link to the operational risk event",[6] they exclude any costs associated with general property or equipment maintenance along with investments to enhance the business and strengthen its risk posture following an event. Gross loss also excludes the cost of specific insurance premiums (State Bank of Pakistan 2013).

While organisations may begin by calculating the gross loss number, ultimately, in order to develop a more accurate loss amount, the gross loss number must be entered into a larger calculation that takes into account a number of additional variables. For example, a calculation for defining the actual loss amount may include the following:

Cost of the loss-event – the amount recovered + the cost of recovery – the cost of the insurance claim and insurance premium + the cost of the internal investigation and resolution = total loss amount [7]

This equation makes clear that, though there are a number of ways to define the loss amount, an accurate depiction of losses incurred as the result of an operational risk event requires a variety of numerical inputs. Given the number of variables, and the potential for fairly large and complex calculations, an automated rather than manual process can play an essential role in standardising this type of data analysis.

Reporting rules

Along with establishing a common understanding of what constitutes an operational loss, as well as developing working parameters for classifying loss data and calculating loss amounts, organisations need levels of governance that dictate exactly how losses should be reported, evaluated and approved.

Reporting rules are meant to provide guidance on everything from definitional questions regarding types of losses to the specific structure for loss reporting. Certainly, organisations need to institute reporting criteria that "fulfill centrally defined data requirements based on Basel guidelines and operational risk management standards" (Moffitt and van de Lagemaat 2003). However, beyond those specific requirements, organisations need to develop governance standards for loss reporting that align with larger business management needs and organisational goals.

CONSISTENCY WITH ACCOUNTING
Governance to ensure accuracy of data

When recording operational losses, one of the central challenges involves validating operational loss data against an organisation's accounting procedures and larger financial records. A sound governance framework can play an important role in ensuring the accuracy of operational loss data by defining a set of policies and procedures designed to authenticate and correlate loss data with financial records. Importantly, this is another area in which the need to move away from manual processes and towards automation can help successfully validate similar amounts and eliminate the potential for discrepancies between loss reporting and financial accounting.

EXTERNAL DATA
Towards an understanding of external loss data

ED contains information on loss events that have occurred outside of your particular organisation. According to the Bank of International Settlements (BIS 2011), "ED provides information on large actual losses that have not been experienced by the bank, and is thus a natural complement to ILD [Internal Loss Data] in modelling loss severity." The value of external loss data lies in its ability to provide a broader historical framework for assessing operational losses. Organisations can make use of external loss data in tandem with internal datasets to increase the accuracy of their risk calculations and make more informed decisions regarding wider risk management efforts. The use of external loss event data in capital modelling can be direct and indirect. External loss events can be normalised and added to a company's historical loss event database to broaden the set of loss events used in the loss distribution analysis approach to capital modelling. External losses can also be used to assist a company develop scenarios of internal losses, and can contribute to a scenario-based approach to capital modelling when the organisation has an insufficient number of internal loss events in a business or for a Basel category.

Being able to identify risk event patterns and areas of unexpected losses is vital to enhancing the risk posture of an organisation. External loss data can help organisations develop a greater understanding of the control failures and breakdowns that commonly occur across a range of similar institutions. Armed with a larger dataset consisting of critical information on industry-wide losses, external loss data can enhance risk scenario analysis as well as internal risk assessments for new business lines and initiatives.[8]

In the following sections, we examine external loss data in greater detail and provide an overview of how it can be leveraged to inform better risk decision making by complementing, and at times even enhancing, internal loss databases.

Available sources of external loss data

Though external loss data can provide substantial industry-wide benefits, it is understandable that most, if not all, institutions are reticent to share their own loss data publicly. Fears regarding potential reputational damage and concerns related to competitive advantage have created the need for publicly available databases and third-party consortium data on operational losses. To be sure, there are certainly differences between publicly available databases and their nonpublic, membership-only counterparts. While publicly available databases such as OpData offer accurate loss information, as well as an analysis of control breakdowns and emerging risk patterns, nonpublic consortia such as ABA and ORX provide a wider range of loss severities and more complete institutional loss profiles (Baruh 2010). The differences notwithstanding, both types of organisations maintain robust and anonymous databases replete with qualitative and quantitative external loss data for statistical use and integration.

While some third-party loss databases are regionally specific, others are international. A brief list of regional third-party databases includes:

❏ ABA (US);
❏ Dakor (Germany);
❏ DSGV Datapool (Germany);
❏ Diplo (Italy);
❏ Gold (UK); and
❏ Hunor (Hungary).

A brief list of international external loss data consortia includes:

❏ ORX;
❏ ORIC;
❏ Algorithmics Algo First; and
❏ OpRisk Global Data.

The most important point of differentiation between these organisations is with regard to their membership bodies. Similar to building a robust internal loss event database, when it comes to external loss data consortia, a greater number of participants will yield a greater amount of information for the purposes of research and analysis.

Expelling concerns and myths about public data
External loss data is a space in which collective action can be leveraged for individual gains. Specifically, the pooling of operational losses from a large number of organisations can be used to enhance

internal risk decision making. Undoubtedly, however, a pervasive fear exists among organisations when it comes to sharing loss data beyond their own borders. As a result, it is imperative to dispel the myths circulating around public loss data in order to encourage greater levels of support and participation.

When it comes to consortium data, there is a misperception that the public has unfettered access to this information. However, accessing external loss data provided by third-party consortia is contingent on active membership and participation. Consortium membership requires shared engagement. Organisations must be willing to share their internal loss data in order to access this vital information.

In terms of the data itself, there is also the commonly held perception that information on external losses lacks relevance because of the significant variances that may exist between control environments from organisation to organisation. However, despite potential differences, external data can offer a more comprehensive understanding of the context in which losses occur. Organisations can thus make use of external loss data to assess the health of their internal risk taking based on an analysis of the control failures that caused the external losses. These types of control breakdowns can be used as benchmarks for gauging an organisation's own levels of risk preparedness (Baruh 2010).

Similarly, loss data from different types of institutions or from different geographic regions does not negate the value of that data for your own organisation. Heterogeneous data still provides useful insights that can be leveraged internally. For example, regardless of geographic differences and distinct regulatory climates, all organisations are exposed to similar types of risk and compliance issues. Being able to analyse where breakdowns and failures occurred in other contexts can empower firms to make more informed decisions about their own risk posture as well as optimise their approach issues of governance and compliance (Baruh 2012).

Uses of external loss data

The previous sections clarify the power of external loss data to inform organisationally specific risk management programmes. Being able to identify loss event triggers, control failures, key control indicator threshold breaches and other factors that contribute to external losses serves to deepen an organisation's internal risk assessments. By understanding risk events in a broader industry-wide context, organisations can ensure that their risk profile and risk appetite accurately reflect the business environment in which they are operating (Baruh 2010). Indeed, linking external loss data to controls in their organisational risk assessments allows companies to generate the right set of questions regarding their own risk profiles to enhance the effectiveness of their risk management efforts.

Road map for using external loss data

There is, however, an inherent challenge that exists when working with external data. As the BIS guidelines (BIS 2011) acknowledge,

> ... while ED can be a useful input into the capital model, external losses may not fit a particular bank's risk profile due to reporting bias. Reporting bias is inherent in publicly sourced ED and therefore focuses on larger, more remarkable losses. A bank should address these biases in their methodology to incorporate ED into the capital model.

The information in external loss databases is not only vast but also nonspecific to your organisation. Thus, in order for external loss data to be effective, it has to be scaled appropriately before it can be successfully incorporated into an organisational framework for identifying and assessing losses.

Doing so requires that organisations apply specific data quality controls to make external loss data germane to their specific business needs and risk programmes. Typically, this involves a two-step process of filtering and scaling the data accordingly. When filtering external loss data, subject-matter experts within an organisation need to identify appropriate and relevant data from external databases that meet their specific threshold criteria for loss collection. The BIS does offer guidance on this process, stating (BIS 2011) that,

> ... a data filtering process involves the selection of relevant ED based on specific criteria and is necessary to ensure that the ED being used is relevant and consistent with the risk profile of the bank. To avoid bias in parameter estimates, the filtering process should result in consistent selection of data regardless of loss amount.

This process typically involves bringing consistent expertise to the decisions about the correct loss events to apply to a business unit within the entity. This workflow should also include an approval step where rationale is provided for including the particular loss event.

Once relevant losses are identified and mapped to the appropriate entity, organisations can then move to apply revaluation and currency conversion where appropriate in order to assess actual loss amounts and financial impact (Butler 2010) Finally, organisations can then scale loss events to correspond to their own organisational structure in terms of size, resources and business objectives.

According to the BIS guidelines, the "data scaling process involves the adjustment of loss amounts reported in external data to fit a bank's business activities and risk profile. Any scaling process should be systematic, statistically supported, and should provide output that is consistent with the bank's risk profile" (BIS 2011) Like the filtering process, the scaling step should require workflow to incorporate reviews and approvals from appropriate subject-matter experts and ultimate business owners of the operational loss capital model result.

It is important to note that in the absence of a singular method for effectively incorporating external loss data, the process of filtering and scaling data is subjective and can differ from institution to institution. Similar to the necessity of establishing internal guidelines to distinguish between direct and indirect losses or operational and reputational risks, there is also the need to establish filtering and scaling criteria that conform to the organisational logic of your particular institution – processes that will no doubt vary from bank to bank. However, each organisation should be prepared to demonstrate the workflow approval steps and audit trail for the decision to include each external loss data point into its operational risk capital model.

How to use external loss data

Once external loss data has been properly filtered and scaled to meet the specific capital requirements of an organisation, it can play an integral role in enterprise-wide risk assessments and be used to support larger risk management practices and risk scenario analysis (Butler 2010).

In terms of a direct role, external data can be used to "complement the paucity of internal data" (Baruh 2010). Though internal data is certainly beneficial for providing a historical perspective on operational losses, the data itself may be incomplete or actually provide limited information on specific types of losses that could prove critical for determining an organisation's capital requirements. For example, a number of commentators point to the fact that "regularly encountered losses", which comprise the lion's share of the internal loss database, "may provide limited information on the size and frequency of large, rarely occurring losses that are the major factor in determining capital requirements" (Guillen *et al* 2007). In these instances, external data can fill in the gaps around unexpected losses and be used as a point of reference for statistical comparisons dealing with large-scale loss events. In short, combining scaled and relevant information on external losses with pre-existing internal loss data provides the most comprehensive picture of the risk environment organisations find themselves operating in (Baruh 2010).

Beyond its ability to complement internal data in capital modelling, external data can play an even larger indirect role in shaping risk management efforts. First, by comparing internal loss data against external losses from peer organisations, external data can be used as a benchmark to validate internal loss models and help organisations make determinations regarding strategic changes to their processes for collecting and evaluating internal losses.

Second, external data can provide an additional layer of contextual depth for generating potential risk scenarios. An examination of large-scale loss events that have taken place at similar institutions can help validate practices for operational risk analysis as well as provide the basis for more robust risk assessments regarding potential and unexpected losses.

Finally, external data can be used to inform risk control assessments. Information on external losses from peer organisations can be "linked" to an organisation's internal controls and serve to highlight potential exposures and help identify areas where similar failures in control could occur. As such, companies can use external loss data to evaluate their own internal control mechanisms to ensure that sufficient processes are in place to effectively mitigate expected and unexpected operational risks (Baruh 2010). These risk assessment results could motivate important discussions about the costs and benefits of additional investments in business controls.

How to optimise the use of external loss data

In addition to external data's value as a quantitative input, it also has a number of important qualitative benefits. Information on external losses can provide significant lessons for organisations on emerging risk patterns and establish a foundation for critical discussions on risk preparedness with upper management (IBM 2003). By offering insight into unexpected, large-scale losses in similar organisations, external data can be used to prompt discussions regarding the necessity of developing, maintaining and strengthening internal risk management efforts and investments in additional controls or control enhancements. Cultivating an awareness that, "if it happened there, it can happen here" can provide the impetus for assessing the relative strengths and weaknesses of an organisation's operational risk and control infrastructure (IBM 2003).

In this regard, external loss data can also play a role in establishing a stronger and more risk-aware corporate culture. Being able to observe significant unexpected losses at similar companies may make an organisation more attuned to its internal risk profile. In addition to providing a basis for strengthening basic risk functions, insights from external data may even facilitate a re-evaluation of an organisation's internal loss-collection process. For instance, identifying significant gaps in the tail or body of your loss data matrix can necessitate a shift in an organisation's loss event workflow and result in revamping the process of reporting and evaluating losses internally.

In order to ensure that external data points remain organisationally relevant, data should be refreshed on a periodic basis. The optimal refresh rate, however, is not static. It varies from organisation to organisation based on need, and can fluctuate within an organisation as goals and risk programmes change over time. For companies using external data to assess larger regulatory shifts and ongoing compliance changes, a monthly refresh of external loss data may be in order. However, for enterprises engaged in using external data for their yearly scenario analysis, an annual to biannual rate may be sufficient (IBM 2003).

CONCLUSION

This chapter has presented a common framework for operational losses, which will enable a complete and consistent collection of loss data containing the necessary information for a robust capital modelling, in addition to governance over the data collection to reflect the real economic losses captured in the accounting system. ILD is a critical data element in the capital modelling, providing the unique characteristics of the operational risk profile of the institution. Finally, we introduced an understanding of the value of external data to establish the standards for its use in capital modelling. ED will greatly enrich the capital model by contributing with the loss experience of peer institutions which cannot be found in ILD.

1   For example, Deutsche Bank defines operational risk as "potential for incurring losses in relation to employees, contractual specifications and documentation, technology, infrastructure failure and disasters, external influences and customer relationships", while the US Securities and Exchange Commission (SEC) defines it as "the risk of loss due to the breakdown of controls within the firm including, but not limited to, unidentified limit excesses unauthorised trading, fraud in trading or in back office functions, inexperienced personnel, and unstable and easily accessed computer systems". For more examples, see Chernobai, Rachev and Fabozzi (2007).

2   It is, however, important to note that the BIS consultative document on operational risk issued in accordance with the initial Basel II framework explicitly recognised that this was ambiguous terrain. For instance, in Section II, Subsection 8, they acknowledge that, "In practice, such distinctions [between direct and indirect losses] are difficult as there is often a high degree of ambiguity inherent in the process of categorizing losses and costs, which may result in omission or double counting problems. The Committee is cognizant of the difficulties in determining the scope of the charge and is seeking comment on how to better specify the loss types for inclusion in a more refined definition of operational risk." See Bank for International Settlements (BIS) (2001)

3   The BIS document states, "This definition focuses on the causes of operational risk and the Committee believes that this is appropriate for both risk management, and ultimately, measurement. However, in reviewing the progress of the industry in the measurement of operational risk, the committee is aware that causal measurement and modelling of operational risk remains at its earliest stages" (BIS 2001).

4   For examples, see State Bank of Pakistan (2013).

5   For examples, see State Bank of Pakistan (2013).

6   According to the State Bank of Pakistan's guidelines (State Bank of Pakistan 2013), these include legal expenses directly related to the event and fees paid to attorneys and costs of repair or replacement to restore the position that was prevailing before the operational risk event.

7   "Internal Loss Data Collection in a Global Banking Organisation," Kevin Moffitt and Gerrit Jan van de Lagemaat, ABN-AMRO: http://www.newyorkfed.org/newsevents/events/banking/2003/con0529h.pdf

8   For example, though the BIS document (2011) highlights the fact that "supervisors expect ED to be used in the estimation of loss severity as ED contains valuable information to inform the tail of the loss distribution(s)", it goes on to note that "ED is also an essential input into scenario analysis as it provides information on the size of losses experienced in the industry. Note that ED may have additional uses beyond providing information on large losses for modelling purposes. For example, ED may be useful in assessing the riskiness of new business lines, in benchmarking analysis on recovery performance and in estimating competitors' loss experience."

REFERENCES

Baruh, Nedim, 2010, "Incorporating External Loss Data within the ORM Framework", available at: www.febraban.org.br/7Rof7SWg6qmyvwJcFwF7I0aSDf9jyV/site-febraban/Nedim%20Baruh.pdf

BIS, 2001, "Consultative Document. Operational Risk. Supporting Document to the New Basel Capital Accord", Basel Committee on Banking Supervision.

BIS, 2002, "Operational Risk Data Collection Exercise", Basel Committee on Banking Supervision), June, available at: www.bis.org/bcbs/qis/oprdata.pdf

BIS, 2011, "Operational Risk – Supervisory Guidelines for the Advanced Measurement Approaches", Basel Committee on Banking Supervision, June, available at: www.bis.org/publ/bcbs196.pdf.

Butler, Daniel, 2010, "OpRisk Modelling & External Databases: Solvency II", AON Global, March, available at: http://theirm.org/events/documents/OpRisk_modelling_and_external_databases.pdf

Chernobai, Anna S., Svetlozar T. Rachev and Frank J. Fabozzi, 2007, *Operational Risk: A Guide to Basel II Capital Requirements, Models and Analysis* (ed. Fabozzi) (New York: John Wiley & Sons).

Guillen, Montserrat, *et al,* 2007, "Using External Data in Operational Risk" *The Geneva Papers* 32, 178–189. doi:10.1057/palgrave.gpp.2510129

IBM, 2013, "Improving Operational Risk Management with External Loss Data", "Operational Risk & Regulation", IBM webinar.

Moffitt, Kevin, and Gerrit Jan van de Lagemaat, 2003, "Internal Loss Data Collection in a Global Banking Organization", Kevin Moffitt and Gerrit Jan van de Lagemaat, ABN-AMRO, available at: www.newyorkfed.org/newsevents/events/banking/2003/con0529h.pdf

State Bank of Pakistan, 2013, "Guidelines on Operational Risk Data Collection and Implementation", June, available at: www.sbp.org.pk/bsrvd/pdf/DCGuidelines/Draft%20Guidelines%20-%20Operational%20Risk%20Data%20Collection%20&%20Implementation.pdf

State Bank of Pakistan, 2014, "Implementation of Operational Risk Management Framework", May, available at: www.sbp.org.pk/bprd/2014/C4-Annexure-1.pdf

Wilson, Shane, 2008, "The Utilization of Internal Loss Data in the Measurement and Management of Operational Risk in Australian AMA Banks", Australian Prudential Regulation Authority.

Scenario Analysis Framework and BEICFs Integration

Rafael Cavestany, Brenda Boultwood, Daniel Rodriguez

Having defined the collection process and sourcing of loss data in Chapter 2, in this chapter we present a scenario analysis (SA) framework that will permit the ability to collect scenarios in an adequate format and quality for its use in the capital model. The SA framework includes the incorporation of business environment and internal control factors (BEICFs), the fourth and last of the data elements of capital, as an input to SA.

SA allows the introduction of expert judgement within operational risk management and quantification. Expert judgement is used in many areas of science, business and policy making for forecasting future events when little relevant data is available. It is also used by credit and market risk management via stress testing and sensitivity analysis, which are based on expert defined scenarios. Expert judgement is used even when a model is created with wide historical data, since it provides circumstances not sufficiently represented in such historical data. In fact, it is those circumstances with little or no historical data that organisations generally worry most about, while those with abundant historical data are commonly better understood and generally have controls providing sufficient comfort.

Expert judgement via SA is particularly valuable in operational risk management and quantification. Exceptional and extreme operational risk events that determine capital have a severity distinctly larger than commonly observed events, making these events very difficult to model based only on historical experience. Also, the historical loss data loses relevancy because of the continuous evolution of the institution's control factors, business environment, activity, etc. Finally, SA creates a clearer link between operational risk quantification and its mitigation, because the quantification can be performed at a much more granular level than ILD modelling. This allows the analysis of very specific risk events and requires a deep analysis of causes, consequences and so forth, benefiting the mitigation strategy and increasing risk awareness.

The Basel Committee recognises the need for SA in its Supervisory Guidelines, saying, "A robust scenario analysis framework is an important element of the ORMF." and, "A robust governance framework surrounding the scenario process is essential to ensure the integrity and consistency of the estimates produced."

Although the granularity of the SA varies depending on the institution, it is generally structured to evaluate risks by business unit. For risk measurement purposes, scenarios are most frequently defined, within a business unit, by risk type Level II (BIS, 2002) This may result in a significant number of scenarios.

Scenarios can be modelled individually or grouped into risk categories to create higher-level models. Each specific modelling unit is called a unit of measure (UoM) or an operational risk category (ORC).

The SA is most commonly assessed in workshops, where various subject-matter experts from the evaluated activities or business units take part in the identification and evaluation of potential risks. Once the risk scenarios have been identified, each scenario can be analysed following the steps below (which are presented in detail in subsequent sections):

❑ Support data and preparation phase: All scenario-supporting data available is collected and prepared to be used during the risk scenario evaluation. Additionally, training on statistical concepts is given to participating experts and strategies in order to mitigate cognitive biases, so that the quality of their answers is maximised and the risk analysis is facilitated in the workshops.
❑ Scenario-rating phase: Risk scenarios are evaluated implementing robust elicitation methods. Elicitation methods consist of questions posed to the expert referring to potential losses resulting from the risk materialisation. These questions are

designed to be directly translated into distributional characteristics for the scenario modelling (see Chapter 5).

❏ Scenario-validation phase: As SA is expert-opinion-based, validation processes add major value to mitigating biases and subjectivity. Different options can be implemented to provide solid scenario governance, including the advanced expert elicitation methods such as Structured Scenario Analysis, benchmark with ED and ILD and others.

❏ BEICFs as an input into SA: In this section, we introduce BEICFs, the fourth of the data elements, and their use as an input to SA.

Governance over the scenario modelling and input determination is of particular supervisory concern, given the qualitative and subjective nature of the exercise. It is recommended that the support and validation phases of SA be given special emphasis. Also, the use test will be given special attention, as supervisors expect capital calculations to be trustworthy and therefore used within the daily management of the institution. The method through which to embed operational risk quantification into the daily management is described in Part III.

The following sections present an approach for implementing the robust SA process mentioned in the above phases.

SCENARIO SUPPORT DATA AND PREPARATION

Scenario analysis is a purely qualitative assessment by expert judgement of potential risks. Human judgement has very positive properties when only limited information is available and probability theory is insufficient. Its benefits include intuitive decisioning or smart heuristics (read *Gut Feelings: The Intelligence of the Unconscious* by Gerd Gigerenzer).

Nevertheless, our judgement is also influenced by the subjectivity of the participating experts and subject to cognitive biases (Tversky and Kahneman 1973). The support and preparation phase is directed to mitigate the limitations and subjectivity of our qualitative judgement by providing supporting information, implementing strategies to mitigate cognitive biases and training experts on the required analytics. By mitigating these limitations, human intuitive judgement is educated and structured, thus enhancing the expert predictions on potential risk scenarios.

Supporting information

Modelling inputs and assumptions should be justified and documented for the regulatory and internal approval of an SA-based capital. The collection and documentation of information on the scenario development, causes and consequences representing critical pieces of the model justification may include: detailed scenario description; causes and common drivers; risk control situation; opportunities for mitigation; and historical data such as internal and external losses, key risk indicators (KRIs), evolution of risk and control self-assessment (RCSA) and results from internal audits. The consideration of this supporting information during the scenario evaluation will also help to mitigate cognitive biases, as explained in "Bias mitigation strategies" below, and facilitate a high-quality analysis of the potential consequences of the scenario.

Regarding the SA supporting information, the BCSG-AMA also states, "A robust scenario analysis framework is an important element of the ORMF. This scenario process will necessarily be informed by relevant ILD, ED and suitable measures of BEICFs."

The enunciation and documentation of a detailed scenario description should drive the in-depth analysis of risk causes and consequences, allowing for a more accurate risk evaluation. This may include common causes with other risk scenarios for the determination of correlations across ORCs (see Chapter 6). The scenario description should focus on the storyline of the scenario development, the causal pathway – including different steps or required elements for the loss materialisation – and the analysis of the drivers and causes of the scenario development. Finally, nonfinancial consequences, including the reputational and operational impacts – such as processes interrupted and clients affected – should be part of the scenario description and feed the risk mitigation of the scenario (financial consequences are later captured in the rating phase for capital calculation).

The risk control situation focuses on documenting and analysing how the assessed risk is currently mitigated and the identification of potential gaps in the existing risk controls and mitigations. The identification and analysis of past control failures also help to evaluate the potential for similar situations and provide the means to identify opportunities for mitigation. Results and diagnosis of internal audit – including nonconformities and so forth – should add additional insight and views about the control situation of the risk.

The analysis and documentation of scenario risk mitigation opportunities is the main instrument for proving the use test and making the scenario-based capital trustworthy. Probably, one of the greatest benefits of SA is that it triggers discussions within the business units regarding the potential risks and mitigation opportunities. Mitigation discussions are an incentive for expert involvement into the SA exercise by emphasising the risk–reward nature of the relationship between risk and mitigation. It also incentivises a more comprehensive analysis of the scenario consequences that should be mitigated. Hence, SA documentation should include potential risk mitigation action plans and the analysis of the business case for the corresponding necessary investment/cost, risk-versus-mitigation benefits, etc. Part III includes the examination of the use of SA modelling results in risk mitigation.

As mentioned by BCSG-AMA, SA should be informed by the relevant loss data. Loss data provides objective and abundant reference to the experts during the risk evaluation of the scenario potential consequences. When available, loss data should include the internal losses suffered by the institutions in similar scenarios. Also, external losses from similar events suffered by peer institutions are a valuable reference, after being adequately scaled. Detailed descriptions of the circumstances that led to the materialization of the loss data events will help experts to orient their analysis during the evaluation of the scenario potential losses.

Finally, SA documentation includes BEICFs, as described below in "BEICFs as an input into scenario analysis" below, sources of information such as KRIs and their link to risk frequency and severity help the expert in estimating future impacts, by analysing the evolution and projection of the indicators. To conclude, the results and information collected during the RCSA of the underlying processes involved in the scenario development may provide additional valuable information detailed at process level for the evaluation of the severity and frequency of the scenario risk.

Bias mitigation strategies[1]
It is said that a properly phrased question may provide us with half of the pursued answer. This definitively applies to the design of SA exercises. The design of the questionnaires, their delivery method, the development of the workshop and even the filling method can

influence, consciously or unconsciously, the results of risk evalua-tions. The reason for this is that SA is subject to human judgement and cognitive biases (read *Judgement Under Uncertainty: Heuristics and Biases* by D. Kahneman, P. Slovic and A. Tversky), which may pose a significant threat to the quality of the SA for determination of opera-tional risk capital.

In fact, cognitive biases may have played their role in historical financial decisions, such as influencing the perception on the riski-ness of products such as "junk bonds", renamed "high-yield" or "AAA-rated structured products", denominated instruments that had subprime mortgages as backing assets. Therefore, the SA exer-cise should give special attentions to strategies for cognitive bias mitigation.

Next, we present the most relevant biases for SA (mainly herding, self-herding, anchoring, denial and recency) as well as strategies for their mitigation (additional references can be found in *Wikipedia*'s "List of Cognitive Biases" chapter). Note that SA-supporting infor-mation plays a major role in the strategy to mitigate cognitive biases.

Anchoring bias

The anchoring bias is very influential in SA, and in human judge-ment in general. This bias refers to the situation in which experts use a specific reference to assess the answers to questions. Anchoring may have many sources such as examples contained in the scenario questionnaire, known answers from somewhat similar personal experiences, the answers given in previous questions, etc. This may result in approximate, similar or correlated values in their responses.

An example in which the anchoring bias manifests with strength is in the relative values provided by the expert in different consecutive questions of the SA questionnaire. During the SA exercise, in which the expert indicates the severity or frequency of multiple events, the first event can become a reference for the next. If the events have been ordered by increasing potential impact, it may be that the answers will show an increasing growth, as the second must be greater than the first, the third greater than the second and so on, thus accumulating estimation errors. If the events had been ordered decreasingly, the opposite effect would hold.

The way to address this issue is by giving a random order to the events, thus avoiding an order resulting in an increasing or decreasing impact pattern. Also, after the questions for all the events have been obtained, the different events can be ranked by impact and/or frequency to ensure that they keep both a rational relative order and a rational absolute amount.

Another way through which the anchoring bias may have a subtle influence is due to the figures provided as examples in the SA forms. There have been experiments where participants were asked about the price they would be willing to pay on different goods. In the experiment, the participants had been previously asked for the last two digits of their social security number. The result showed a significant positive correlation between the social security number and the price provided in the answers, when the social security number is strictly random and should present no correlation (Ariely, Loewenstein and Prelec 2006). The main conclusion is that even a random number (the social security number, employee number, number of query or page) may, in some cases, introduce some sort of interference in the assessment when the amounts to be assessed are not known *a priori*.

Anchoring may be mitigated by reinforcing the analytical exercise. A thorough and structured analysis of the scenario causal pathway and development steps helps the expert deriving answers from the analysis, rather than using the original reference. Also, anchoring can be mitigated by providing experts with internal and external data events of a similar nature and analysing the causal pathway of each of the historical events. This exercise trains experts in deriving risk impacts analytically rather than using references.

It can also be useful for avoiding the presence of previous values in the questionnaires, when possible, such as "Enter value in thousands of euros (eg, 100 for €100,000)".

Herding bias

The herding bias, or group-thinking bias, refers to the tendency to do (or believe) things because many other people do (or believe) the same. It is common in SA when participating staff are new or untrained in the exercise, and it is stronger in organisations with a hierarchical culture. The herding bias is usually reinforced when staff with higher rank take dominating attitudes during the risk evaluations. It can also be caused by natural leaders without a formal position. This bias is the easiest to address with the design of the workshops. You can start by selecting attendees to avoid, as much as possible, the presence of formal leaders who can determine the opinions of subordinates.

Later in the voting process, there are different methods to reduce the conditioning by the experts. These methodologies are based primarily on obtaining the evaluation privately, and subsequently discussing the results in the workshop. This allows the experts to develop independent views and evaluations, rather than leveraging on group opinions.

If higher-rank employees participate in the workshop and the later discussions, they should be particularly sensitive about the time and way they express their opinions. With methods such as structured scenario analysis, where experts provide answers individually, analysis can also be used to address this bias (see "Structured scenario analysis: validating SA through the analysis of expert performance" below).

Self-herding bias

Self-herding is the psychological tendency of people to justify their past decisions and maintain them over time regardless of the reasoning behind their initial decision. This situation is not motivated by social interactions, but by the need to maintain a consistent opinion with previous decisions. Also, to some extent, it is motivated by a desire to avoid reassessing these previously made decisions.

Self-herding can be addressed by alternating risk the topic of questions, to prevent experts from maintaining their previously given opinions. In SA reviews, experts should not be given access to previous assessments on the same risks, in order to avoid their "reuse" in the new assessment. It is also important the experts do not have access to the opinions, current or past, of other experts, again in order to avoid herding or anchoring.

Denial bias

The denial bias refers to the situation in which interviewees might not feel comfortable or be willing to answer questions such as their own error rate, internal fraud, institutional employment practices, weaknesses in the process they manage, etc. In fact, experts might feel responsible for the situation, and bias their answers. This type of situation should be identified in advance and addressed during the workshops. Generally, it can be mitigated by using the appropriate positive language when phrasing the questions by avoiding negative sentences such as "How many errors may you make in a year?" Instead, questions should be phrased suggesting the expert's lack of personal responsibility: "Given the current control and automation level, how many errors may process 'A' produce in a year?"

Another effective way to manage the denial bias is shifting the risk analysis from the traditional single-sided threat and potential losses view into a risk–reward evaluation. Under this approach, the threats and potential losses are analysed together with their possible mitigation and the corresponding mitigation cost (see Chapter 12). This approach results in an increased expert involvement and a more comprehensive identification of impacts in need of mitigation. Additionally, it provides important mitigation insights, thanks to the expert collaborative efforts and idea sharing during the SA workshops.

Recency bias
Recency is a cognitive bias that results from disproportionate salience attributed to recent stimuli or observations – the tendency to weight recent events more than earlier events.

Similar to the anchor bias, recency may be mitigated by providing the expert with multiple data and information from similar events for their analysis during the SA. The availability of multiple additional observations decreases the influence of the more recent occurrences.

Insensitivity to sample size
Finally, an insensitivity to the size of the sample may also introduce a bias. Generally, the expert, through their own experience, has observed only a limited number of events. This creates a tendency to exaggerate the variance of the sample. This bias can be augmented by an overconfidence effect that overweights the expert's own experience. Again, the principal means by which to address this bias are to provide statistical training to the expert to facilitate a robust analytical effort and inform them of other, similar, cases from ED or other sources. The information provided on other events will permit the expert to a make better estimation of the range of possible outcomes on the risk evaluated.

Other influencing circumstances

SA might be influenced by other circumstances in which the intervie-wees show little interest and pay limited attention to the questionnaire in their rush to finish. It can also be influenced by the fear of looking unknowledgeable in front of peers and/or superiors. Attention and involvement of interviewees may be obtained by communicating the importance and management benefits of the SA exercise. Linking SA results with potential mitigation plans affecting participants' work should increase the perception of the potential benefits of the exercise. Also, the use of multi-answer validation tech-niques such as structured scenario analysis (see "Structured scenario analysis: validating SA through the analysis of expert performance" below) improves the involvement of participants. Multi-answer vali-dation techniques rank SA participants by the quality of their answers. This peer comparison and expert ranking provides a strong stimulus for good performance. Also, since the scenario answers are given individually rather than in a group exercise, there is no reason to remain quiet to avoid looking unsmart.

Needless to say, these mitigation methods are not magic and cannot completely avoid cognitive biases. However, the experts' awareness of difficulties, their training on analytics, as well as the above suggestions, permit their mitigation to a certain extent. In *Experts Under Uncertainty*, Roger M. Cooke provides additional guide-lines for addressing cognitive biases.

Training on analytics to complement judgemental heuristics

Given cognitive biases, major attention should be paid to the statis-tical training of the participants as a way of maximising the quality of expert answers. Understanding the heuristics used by human judge-ment and complementing them with appropriate analytics represents a robust means of mitigating cognitive biases (we point the reader to *Decision Behaviour, Analysis and Support* written by S. French, J. Maule and N. Papamichail).

During the rating phase, the SA questionnaire will typically include questions requiring the understanding of statistical concepts. For instance, it may include questions that inquire about the worst loss in 5, 25 or 40 years or values of the mean, mode, etc. These answers will vary strongly, depending on whether they refer to light- or fat-tail progression phenomena. Expert adequate understanding of such questions may be ensured by first training them in practice.

The training questions should have the same format as those used in the actual questionnaire/workshop, but the content of these practice questions will be much more general, referring to events that may occur in normal everyday life, as in the following examples:

❏ Ask participants for the largest goal score in 1, 20 or 50 years in a major soccer competition. This might correspond to a light-tail phenomenon. The answer may be something like 6 goals in one year, 9 in 20 years and 12 in 50 years. This progression clearly demonstrates a light tail, as the low and high values are relatively close.
❏ Ask participants for the worst number of casualties from tsunami or earthquakes in 1, 20 or 50 years. This might correspond to fat-tail behaviour. The answer would be similar to 200 casualties in one year, 10,000 in 20 years and 500,000 in 50 years. This progression has a strong fat-tail behaviour, as the exceptional severity represents a large multiple of what usually happens in any year.
❏ Provide training on basic statistical concepts such as mean, median, mode, percentiles. The first three coincide in a normal distribution, but would be very different in typical operational risk distributions. Non-experts on statistics will probably ignore the difference, making their answers highly inaccurate.

Following this training, a similar exercise can then be carried out for operational risk events. External or internal loss data can be used to show the different progression and tail behaviours of different risk types and business units, so get the expert acquainted with this analysis for the actual operational risks workshops.

Also, providing a structured analysis to determine risk frequencies and severities adds a lot of value; popular frameworks for structuring the analysis of risk assessment are the BowTie (Nordgård 2008 and Swiss Cheese (Reason 1990)) models. Frequency is the more challenging variable and its structured analysis is critical. The expert may be asked to determine how many different independent circumstances are required to trigger the risk materialisation. The more independent circumstances required, the lower the likelihood of the scenario. Also, the number of points in an organisation where it can happen should be taken into consideration. The larger the number of points, the higher the likelihood of the scenario. Finally, the analysis of the number of existing controls and their effectiveness will permit an evaluation of the final probability of the risk materialisation.

Severity can be assessed first in the different phases of the risk materialisation. After the risk has materialised, the institution may react and take mitigation actions to reduce the impact. The effectiveness of these potential measures should be analysed to determine the final severity of the scenario.

Assume we have the following risk scenario example to evaluate: an employee's laptop drive is stolen in a hotel, containing sensitive product pricing information and the details of potential clients in the pipeline. This information is sold to a competitor who clones the product and markets it before we do, thereby capturing some of our potential clients.

This scenario evaluation may start by analysing the number of independent events required for such risk to materialise. There are at least four independent events: (1) a laptop containing sensitive information is stolen; (2) the thief has the capability to find the sensitive information and contact the appropriate competitor; (3) the competitor is willing to clone the product and launch it; (4) cloning the product actually makes economic sense and fits within the competitor's strategy and skills. Therefore, it sounds highly unlikely that the event will materialise into a loss beyond the computer cost, from the random theft of a laptop in a hotel room. However, if the events are not independent, the scenario sounds more like industrial spying, a situation in which a specific computer containing valuable information has been targeted, and the likelihood of occurrence is much higher. Then, the scenario should be redefined as "industrial spying", and would be like many other types of industrial espionage, increasing again the likelihood of a significant loss materialising.

SCENARIO RATING

Once the information supporting the SA has been collected and, bias mitigation strategies put in place, the scenario's financial impacts can be determined. The collection of SA financial impacts is carried out using elicitation methods, which are questions designed to be translated into distributional characteristics (see Chapter 5). Such features permit us to model SA through distributions and eventually to incorporate scenario analysis into capital calculations. Only financial impacts should be taken into consideration for capital determination, excluding reputational impacts.

The goal of the elicitation method is to request information in an intuitive and tangible format. For instance, rather than ask the expert for the 95th percentile of the severity distribution, the elicitation method phrases the question through, "What would be your worst loss if the risk materialises 20 times?" Using more intuitive formats is of particular value in financial institutions' scenario analysis, as participating experts may not have the quantitative background that would enable them to respond directly on distributional characteristics. It is also crucial that the elicitation methods include questions on infrequent but extreme events. Far too often experts only focus their analysis on the most likely or expected outcome, giving little consideration to unexpected extreme events which provide the information on the tail shape.

There are several elicitation methods used by the financial industry to model capital under the SBA (scenario-based approach). We will examine some of them here.

Frequency-by-severity segment
The expert is asked to estimate frequencies according specific severity segments. This method is very effective when consolidating scenarios from more granular risk types into a higher level and in facilitating the modelling of aggregated units of measure. For instance, it can be used to aggregate frequencies by the risk type Level II severity segment, such as employee relations, safe environment, and diversity and discrimination, into risk type Level I, employment practices and workplace safety. Examples of how to phrase the scenario questions according to this method would be:

❏ What is the annual frequency for events costing between US$0 and US$10.000?
❏ What is the annual frequency for events costing between US$10,000 and US$100,000?
❏ What is the annual frequency for events costing between US$100,000 and US$1,000,000?
❏ What is the annual frequency for events costing between US$1,000,000 and US$10,000,000?
❏ How many events are there costing more than US$10,000,000?

This format is appropriate for evaluating high-frequency events, when the annual frequencies are not much lower than 1. This approach is commonly used when internal and external data feed into the scenario analysis and low-severity segments are directly informed from these sources of information. When the scenarios being evaluated have very low frequencies (1/100 or 1/500), the method is more subject to potential estimation errors, if experts are not adequately trained.

Worst losses by time horizon

The expert is asked to estimate the worst losses over a period of time. It is implicitly assumed that the risk levels will remain constant for the time horizon, rather than evolve, as happens in reality. The annual frequency must also be requested in the questionnaire. An implicit assumption is that the risk environment should constant over the time horizon rather than evolve. Examples of this scenario phrasing would be:

❏ What would be the worst loss within 5 years?
❏ What would be the worst loss within 25 years?
❏ What would be the worst loss within 100 years?
❏ What would be the worst loss within 250 years?
❏ What is the annual frequency of the scenario?

This format is more appropriate for evaluating extreme low-frequency events. The expert finds it easier to determine high severities for unlikely events, than to estimate very low frequencies for very high-severity segments.

Worst losses by number of events

This has the advantage of facilitating the analysis detached from a time horizon. Examples of how to phrase the scenario questions are:

❏ What is your worst loss per 10 events materialised?
❏ What is your worst loss per 100 events materialised?
❏ What is your worst loss per 1,000 events materialised?
❏ What is the annual expected frequency of the scenario?

This format is more appropriate for evaluating events of high frequency, as the expert can better imagine several events according to their own experience. The percentile of the distribution can be easily derived from the questions.

Expected and worst loss estimations
A simpler approach would be to ask the expert for two points in the severity distribution, the expected[2] and worst losses. The worst loss is linked with a high percentile of the severity distribution, such as 99%. This method provides two points for the distribution fitting, the mean and a percentile, permitting to fit two parameter distributions.

Single figure
This format is appropriate for risk scenarios with only one potential outcome or an outcome very close to a specific figure. For instance, a fire in the headquarters destroys the building, or there are other natural disasters such as earthquakes and floods. In this case, the expert is asked to provide a single figure or a range of figures for the scenario and its probability of occurrence.

Combined method
All these elicitation methods can be easily translated into distribution characteristics such as percentiles, distribution mean, expected frequencies, or even skewness and leptokurtosis. The different methods can be made equivalent via the implicit distribution percentiles, and questions can be adapted to obtain the same answer in any of the formats. Using this property, several methods can be combined to better extract the information from the body and tail of the severity distribution or as a consistency check procedure (see "Cross consistency validation of expert answers" below). Examples of this combined approach would be:

❏ What is the annual frequency for events costing between US$0 and US$6,000?
❏ What is the annual frequency for events costing between US$6,000 and US$60,000?
❏ What is the annual frequency for events costing between US$60,000 and US$300,000?
❏ What is the annual frequency for events costing more than US$300,000?
❏ What would be the worst loss in 10 years' time?
❏ What would be the worst loss in 25 years' time?
❏ What would be the worst loss in 100 years' time?

Figure 3.1 Elicitation method combining body and tail questions

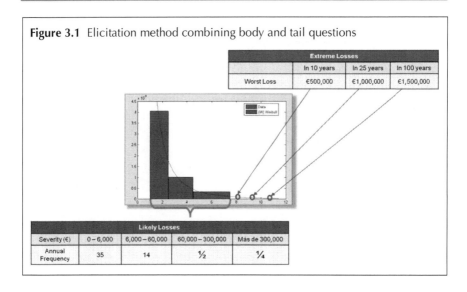

Extreme Losses			
	In 10 years	In 25 years	In 100 years
Worst Loss	€500,000	€1,000,000	€1,500,000

Likely Losses				
Severity (€)	0 – 6,000	6,000 – 60,000	60,000 – 300,000	Más de 300,000
Annual Frequency	35	14	½	¼

In the illustrative example depicted in Figure 3.1, the first four questions are directed to capture most usual high-frequency events and the last three focus on tail events. When combined, the time horizon on the tail questions (worst loss in …) needs to be coordinated with the frequencies provided in the body questions (annual frequency for events …). Otherwise, there will be an overlap between the body and tail questions and it will be more difficult to link percentiles and quantiles from the SA answers. A criticism of this method is that it requires a deeper involvement by the experts, in an already effort intensive exercise, and its use may be justified only in the evaluation of the most disruptive events.

Once the experts have provided their estimations for the risk scenarios, these can be translated into distribution characteristics and fed into the distribution modelling process, as presented in Chapter 5.

Nevertheless, the quality of the scenario answers is significantly enhanced when they are run through a validation process. The means of validating the scenario analysis are now described.

SCENARIO VALIDATION

Given the subjective nature of scenario analysis, supervisors have special concerns with respect to all governance elements in the scenario determination. The governance should include a process for the validation of the experts' answers.

In fact, BCSG-AMA explicitly mentions the verification needs of scenario analysis when it states, "Verification of the ORMF includes testing whether all material aspects of the ORMF have been implemented effectively … a comparison of scenario results with internal loss data and external data." It also says, "A robust governance framework surrounding the scenario process is essential to ensure the integrity and consistency of the estimates produced."

Below are some alternatives to validate the scenario analysis results.

Validation against internal and external losses

Answers to scenario analysis questions should be compared with available historical internal and external data in order to evaluate the reasonability of the estimates implicit in the scenario answers. Generally, there will be little available data, and discrepancies can be expected, which need to be clearly justified.

When significant data is available, quantiles obtained during the scenario analysis should be compared with those from historical data. P-P and Q-Q plots can be created. If data is insufficient, various SA and answers can be aggregated by similarity, and mean accuracy may be estimated.

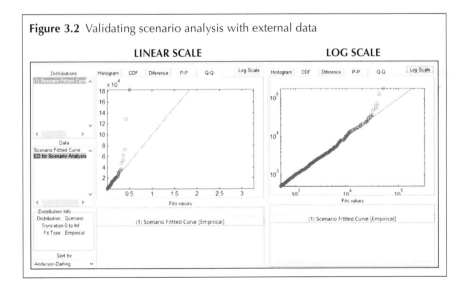

Figure 3.2 Validating scenario analysis with external data

Figure 3.2 shows the results of comparing external loss data with the SA-fitted distribution, in linear (left) and log (right) scales. It shows that, while for the low-severity data there is a clear matching, the results are not replicating very high-severity events in the external loss data. It should then be analysed whether such extreme external events are actually possible in the incumbent institution. After all, external data events may have been generated by institutions under a different jurisdiction, with different business profile or activity volumes and thus may not be used as a perfect reference.

Structured scenario analysis: validating SA through the analysis of expert performance

The SA too frequently presents significant issues such as discussions and answers dominated by the most influential people, lack of involvement of participants, difficulty in selecting workshop participants, and cognitive biases (anchoring, overconfidence, group thinking, fear of looking unknowledgeable and others). These deserve careful attention and efforts for guaranteeing the quality of the risk evaluations.

On the other hand, SBA is effort intensive requiring the evaluation of numerous risk scenarios by business unit which, in addition, should be re-evaluated twice a year. This implies that the scenario analysis exercise needs to be relatively direct and practical in terms of time and resources. Otherwise, it will quickly become a burdensome exercise, decreasing the involvement of participants and most likely damaging its quality.

In this context, the institution's operational risk profile ends up being dominated by a limited number of particularly threatening risk scenarios (such as cybercrime, rogue trading, internally infiltrated hackers, data thefts, model errors and epidemic diseases). Noticeably, these deserve a differentiated approach for a more accurate determination of their potential impact and corresponding capital requirements.

Structured scenario analysis[3] (SSA) is a statistics-driven[4] method – derived from the technology and engineering sectors – that can significantly improve the quality of expert judgement based risk assessments. It permits a robust and transparent validation of expert assessments on uncertain events when little data is available and leverages on the collective knowledge of the expert group to enhance the final risk evaluation. It also reduces the discusion time thus making SA workshops more efficient.

In SSA, the limited available data is used to determine the answers to "seed" questions which are included in the scenario analysis questionnaire to evaluate the expert prediction skills of uncertain events. Two to eight seed questions[5] are sufficient for the expert performance evaluation.

Questions may be phrased according to any of the elicitation methods presented earlier ("What would be the worst loss within 5 years?", for instance, and so on) and answers are provided in a range format (between X and Y). Experts answer the SA questionnaire individually rather than collectively and usually after a group discussion, training and knowledge-sharing session. The answers to seed questions are used to derive each expert calibration (the answer range proximity to the seed value) and informative level (the width of the range provided by the expert). An expert can have a high calibration, because the seed answers fall within the provided range, but may add low informative value, because the range is too wide.

Figure 3.3 represents the answers by four different experts to the same seed question analysed under SSA. Expert 1 has provided a wide range that includes the real value of the seed question. The answer is calibrated but provides little informative value. Expert 2's answer is highly informative, since the expert provides a narrow

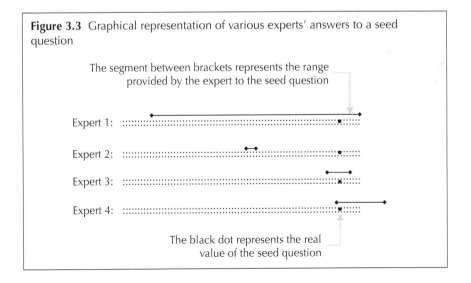

Figure 3.3 Graphical representation of various experts' answers to a seed question

The segment between brackets represents the range provided by the expert to the seed question

Expert 1:

Expert 2:

Expert 3:

Expert 4:

The black dot represents the real value of the seed question range, but completely misses the real value and hence has no calibration. Expert 3 is highly informative because the expert has provided a narrow range, and it is also well calibrated, showing high expert performance. Finally, Expert 4 is also well calibrated but is less informative then Expert 3 because it has provided a wider range. This example shows how SSA provides a transparent means to evaluate expert performance during SA.

This analysis can also be used to identify overconfidence and anchoring cognitive biases in the answers. The former is identified through very narrow ranges in expert answers missing the correct value of the seed questions (Expert 2 in Figure 3.3 probably shows overconfidence). The latter may be identified because answers have similar values. The expert could be using a central reference value as an anchor and adjust other answers to this reference.

Then, experts are ranked according to the quality of their answers and given relative weights, typically according to Cooke's classical model (1991). The weights are used to build the final distribution with the aggregation of the answers from all the experts. Logically, experts with higher ranking are given more weight and become more influential in the final estimation. To finish, the values of the aggregated answers are fed into the distribution fitting process (see Chapter 5), as part of the operational risk capital model.

Experience (Wisse, Bedford and Quigley 2006) shows that the collective answers aggregated using performance-based weights have more predictive power than even the best-performing individual expert. Moreover, the best-performing individual expert would be identified only if the above-described expert performance evaluation procedure is implemented. Note that, in the traditional method for SA (one answer from an expert group workshop), the SA answer is typically dominated by the most influential participants but not necessarily by the best performers.

In fact, SSA surfaces and mitigates weaknesses of the individual expert answers. In Figure 3.4, individual answers are represented, graphically illustrating how different expert performance can be. The vertical axis represents the informativeness (the higher in the axis, the wider range provided by the) and the horizontal the calibration (represented in statistical significance, being 5% of the red threshold). It can be seen that only a fraction of the individual experts

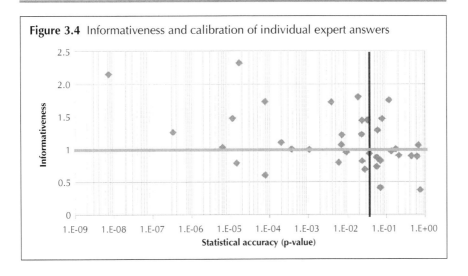

Figure 3.4 Informativeness and calibration of individual expert answers

are in the low right quadrant of acceptable quality answer (food for thought).

However, when these same individual answers are aggregated following SSA, the aggregated answer significantly gains in both informativeness and calibration, being the great majority in the low right quadrant, as illustrated in Figure 3.5. This represents a dramatic improvement for the quality of the SA results. In fact, Figures 3.3, 3.4

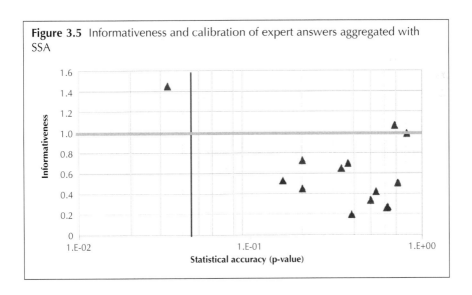

Figure 3.5 Informativeness and calibration of expert answers aggregated with SSA

Figure 3.6 Structured scenario analysis workflow

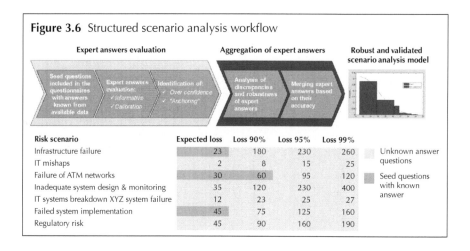

Risk scenario	Expected loss	Loss 90%	Loss 95%	Loss 99%	
Infrastructure failure	23	180	230	260	Unknown answer questions
IT mishaps	2	8	15	25	
Failure of ATM networks	30	60	95	120	Seed questions with known answer
Inadequate system design & monitoring	35	120	230	400	
IT systems breakdown XYZ system failure	12	23	25	27	
Failed system implementation	45	75	125	160	
Regulatory risk	45	90	160	190	

and 3.5 can be used to analyse and track the progress in the quality of the SA exercise, as the process matures within the institution.

Figure 3.6 shows the workflow of SSA. The questionnaire has its seed questions, from which the expert calibration and informativeness are derived. Seed questions values are generally derived from the medium and high percentiles of the most data-populated ORCs or mean and low percentiles of lowly populated ORCs. Then, the answer aggregation is constructed, based on weights calculated from each expert performance on the seed questions, to arrive at the weighted ORC distribution. The right-hand side of the figure represents how the weighted distribution is modelled and integrated into the capital calculations as presented in Chapter 5.

The quality of the overall results is assessed based on discrepancy and a robustness analysis. The discrepancy analysis evaluates the disparity of expert answers. Ideally, expert answers should be as consistent as possible. The robustness analysis assesses how expert performance weights change by removing any of the seed questions from the sample. Ideally, expert weights should remain stable regardless of which specific seed question is removed from the analysis.

SSA requires the determination of seed answers and other analytics. However, its use in highly critical risks provides the required validation and reduces cognitive biases, increasing the precision of the estimation of harmful impacts. Also, it incentivises the involvement of experts, thanks to the embedded peer comparison (the expert ranking by answer quality), thus improving the quality of the overall results. SSA also increases efficiency by reducing the workshop complexity and discussion time, since answers are provided individually, rather than in a group effort directed to reach a collective agreement. It also permits the incorporation of more experts into the scenario evaluation, including those of lower rank actually managing the processes and probably having the required deep understanding of how a risk scenario may develop.

In addition, the aggregation of individual answers based on the expert performances should typically provide results superior to the common procedure of providing a single answer from a group workshop. In fact, experience (Wisse, Bedford and Quigley 2006) shows that the most influential workshop participants (charismatic, communication-savvy or higher-rank) too frequently perform poorer than other, less outspoken, participants (lower-rank or timid).

Summarising, SSA leverages from the collective knowledge by identifying most qualified individual assessments and enriching these with other expert views, following a scientific model. It also provides traceable and transparent means for a solid justification and validation of the qualitative evaluations of risk scenarios.

In conclusion, SA can be scientifically validated and, hence, it should be validated – at least those most threatening risk scenarios – to significantly increase the quality of the assessments. Some SSA researchers say that using expert judgement with a unique answer (as in the standard SA elicitation process) is like playing Russian roulette with only one bullet missing in the cylinder

The SSA method can also be used to improve the quality of other risk evaluations driven by expert judgement, such as the determination of stress scenarios of market, credit and business risks, stressed dependencies (market and credit) and others.

Goodness-of-fit validation and reasonability of results

Validation of the scenario analysis can also be performed by evaluating the reasonability of the corresponding distribution modelling results. This includes the analysis of the reasonability of the goodness of fit (GoF, see Chapter 4), the parameters of the fit and the analysis of the distribution quantiles and resulting capital.

When there is sufficient historical data available, there is almost

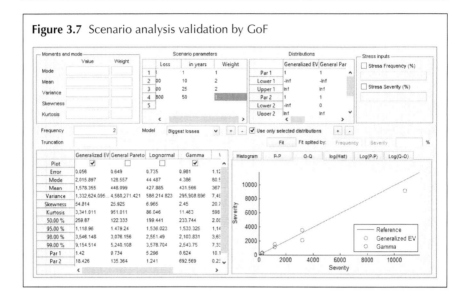

Figure 3.7 Scenario analysis validation by GoF

always a parametric distribution that provides a reasonable fit. It follows that the SA modelling GoF insights into its quality. The implicit assumption is that, if sufficient loss data for the risk scenario was available to fit a parametric distribution, then it would be possible to obtain a good fit using a parametric distribution.

For this validation method, see the screen grab in Figure 3.7, where the distribution is fitted to the scenario data, as explained in Chapter 5. The scenario inputs are: annual frequency, 2; worst loss in 1 year, 256; worst loss in 10 years, 1,200; worst loss in 25 years, 3,200; and worst loss in 50 years, 10,800. The worst losses are translated into the percentiles 50, 95, 98 and 99 (see Chapter 5). The graphic in the bottom right corner is a Q-Q plot (see Chapter 4), where it can be perceived that the generated extreme value (GEV) distribution (see Appendix 1) closely replicates the inputs provided, suggesting that the scenario answers follow the pattern of operational losses.

The analysis of different fit parameters may also provide an insight into its quality. For instance, analysing the σ and μ from the lognormal distribution fit provides a mean to evaluate tail behaviour (see Chapter 4). σ values higher than 3 and a negative μ suggest fat-tail behaviour, which should be consistent with the perception of risk.

Sometimes, rougher estimates are given to questions for losses

Figure 3.8 SA sensitivity analysis

mu	-5.30
sigma	7.23
Frequency	1
Percentile	99.9
SLA	25,301,635
Mode	66,412
Mean	209,812
Variance	92,944,746,284,919
Skewness	63.61
Kurtosis	4,254

under very long time horizons (for instance, worst loss in 500 years), given the difficulties of estimating the impact of such low probabilities. The results may lead to an extremely high σ, variance and kurtosis in the fit, resulting in unrealistic capital estimates. Figure 3.8 illustrates the parameters of a fitted lognormal with very high σ (7.23) and very negative μ (−5.296) and the 99.9th percentile of the severity distribution is over 25 million. It should be confirmed that such strong fat-tail behaviour is not due to estimation errors and that it corresponds with the real risk profile.

Finally, an evaluation of how realistic the losses produced by the severity distribution and capital charges are may also be evaluated for consistency. Figure 3.9 shows capital charges produced under the single loss approximation for multiple percentiles, allowing for an evaluation against the perception of potential risk impacts.

An additional means of validating the reasonability of scenario ratings is to compare the scenario severities/frequencies by ranking them. Following this method, you will create a rank of scenarios based on their severity/frequency. This provides multiple benchmarks per scenario for validating that the scenario severity/frequency makes sense in relative terms to other scenarios. The exercise can be done in various percentiles or time horizons and will

Figure 3.9 Scenario analysis validation by the realism of losses generated

	Lognormal (MLE)
Percentile 99.98	26,470,666
Percentile 99.95	16,459,554
Percentile 99.93	13,782,674
Percentile 99.90	11,397,688
Percentile 99.00	3,179,663

easily reveal scenarios that are over- or underrated, facilitating the verification of the quality of the risk assessment.

Cross-consistency validation of expert answers

The quality of expert answers can also be validated by checking whether the expert would provide equivalent answers if given the same question in different formats. As described in Chapter 5, all elicitation methods can be tuned to ask for the same percentile of the distribution. If experts provide consistent answers given the same question in different formats, it suggests that they are analysing the problem in a sound way and that they understand the implicit analytics. The understanding of implicit analytics helps to mitigate cognitive biases.

This test can be performed by checking the consistency between the answers provided in the likely-losses-format questionnaires (frequency by severity buckets) and the extreme-losses format (losses given time horizon). The validation can be performed in several steps:

❑ Step 1: Provide the expert with questions on frequency by severity segments.
❑ Step 2: Questions for the extreme scenarios are generated consistently with the frequencies answered in Step 1. The initial and/or second questions of the extreme scenarios can be used to check consistency between the two formats (see Figure 3.10).
❑ Step 3: Finally, the additional questions can be generated automatically and consistently with the first step to obtain information on the tail, which is not captured by the likely scenario format.

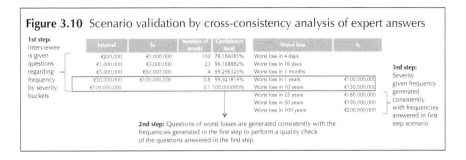

Figure 3.10 Scenario validation by cross-consistency analysis of expert answers

BEICFS AS AN INPUT INTO SCENARIO ANALYSIS

Following from the previous sections of this chapter, where we have presented a process for a robust scenario analysis, we now look to the last of the four data elements, business environment and internal control factors (BEICFs), and their use as an input into SA. In Chapter 6 we will examine the use of BEICFs as a direct input into the capital model.

BEICFs are tools used in the measurement and management of operational risk. Examples of BEICFs are RCSA, KRIs, internal audit scores, mitigation plans and statistics on regulatory exam issues. Together with internal loss data (ILD), external data (ED) and scenario analysis (SA), they are one of the four data elements that should be considered in an AMA operational risk capital estimation.

The benefits of BEICFs are recognised by BCSG-AMA when it says, "BEICFs are operational risk management indicators that provide forward-looking assessments of business risk factors as well as a bank's internal control environment."

The BEICFs may include the following elements:[6] business environment; internal controls; factors. Let us now look at each in turn.

Business environment

This refers to the internal and external circumstances that may materially affect the operational risk profile of the institution:

❏ the quality and ability of the institution's employees, vendors and other resources;
❏ the complexity and riskiness of the business, products and processes they use to deliver them;
❏ the degree of automation of the product processes and capacity of the institution for automation;

❏ the legal and regulatory environment of the business; and

❏ the evolution of the institution's markets, including the diversity and sophistication of its customers and counterparties, the liquidity of the capital markets it trades in and the reliability of the infrastructure that supports those markets.

Internal controls

These are the detective and preventive processes the firm has in place to reduce or eliminate the severity and frequency of operational risk events. They can be specific, such as a confirmation after a trade or the due diligence on a hire. They can also be general, as is the RCSA. They can also have different degrees of automation, from purely manual to fully automatic.

A useful list of internal control attributes to be considered during the risk evaluation of scenario analysis:

❏ control test date;

❏ control tested by XXX;

❏ preventative or detective;

❏ manual or automated;

❏ imbedded control;

❏ shared control with business;

❏ shared control with corporate;

❏ external third party reliance;

❏ external third party name;

❏ model used;

❏ historical events over the last twelve months;

❏ QA testing monitoring;

❏ supporting documentation;

❏ procedure documentation;

❏ documented procedures meet standards;

❏ training;

❏ no controls in place;

❏ partial coverage gap;

❏ design coverage gap;

❏ performance coverage gap; and

❏ control effectiveness rating.

Factors

These are leading measures or indicators of change in the environment or in control effectiveness:

❏ measures of business expansion, such as numbers of new products and increase in gross and net revenues;
❏ the number of customer complaints;
❏ the number of audit points and other measures tracking regulatory and policy compliance and progress in closing any gaps in existing practice;
❏ outputs from risk and control self-assessments, including indicators reflecting the emergence of new risks, the effectiveness of existing controls, control gaps and progress in closing them; and
❏ other risk indicators, including general indicators such as staff turnover and specific ones such as peak capacity utilisation in a trading system.

In general, it is assumed that it is hard to establish a significant statistical relationship between BEICFs and future losses. Therefore, the inclusion of BEICFs into the capital estimations can be implemented in a qualitative fashion, which includes their use as an input into the scenario analysis evaluation and correlation calculations; as a driver for the capital attribution; and/or as an *ex post* adjustment to the capital model results. Nevertheless, we propose in Chapter 6 some basic statistical modelling of BEICFs that can be used for making capital estimations more forward-looking.

When embedding BEICFs into the capital estimations, it is important to ensure that the double accounting of BEICFs is avoided. For instance, if they are used as an input into scenario analysis, they probably should not be used as an *ex post* adjustment to capital calculations. However, it is compatible to use any of these two applications together with the capital attribution and calculation of operational risk correlations.

In the following sections, we provide an overview of BEICFs and explore their relationship to SA. Our discussion will begin with an explanation of BEICFs and SA as core components of an operational risk framework. We then consider how BEICFs can be factored into SA and the ways in which BEICFs impact on an organisation's capital requirement calculations.

Understanding BEICFs[7]

There are four elements that can comprise an operational risk capital model:

❑ internal loss data;
❑ external loss data;
❑ BEICFs; and
❑ scenario analysis.

While internal and external loss data offers a quantitative, historical perspective, scenario analysis and BEICFs are meant to provide organisations with a more qualitative, forward-looking assessment of operational risks (BIS 2011).

According to the Bank for International Settlements (BIS), "BEICFs are indicators of a bank's operational risk profile that reflect underlying business risk factors and an assessment of the effectiveness of the internal control environment" (BIS 2006). BEICFs allow organisations to gain a greater understanding of key risk exposures and identify potential areas of vulnerability. Developing an acute understanding of inherent day-to-day risks – as well as the control factors used to mitigate those risks – is critical to shaping an organisation's operational risk profile.

Information on BEICFs can be gathered through risk and control self-assessments (RCSAs). RCSAs are used to define internal and external risks, assess potential quantitative and qualitative factors, or inherent risks, and assess the controls in place to mitigate and prevent risks before they have a chance to result in significant operational losses, to arrive at a residual risk rating. In the RCSA process, risks for a business, process, legal entity or other asset are assessed. If residual risk levels are higher than the risk appetite of the organisation, a plan for remediation can be developed. Often, this plan will include actions to evaluate the design and effectiveness of internal controls. This allows organisations to determine their operational risk profiles by determining appropriate levels of residual risk under which they operate on a daily basis (Watchorn and Levy 2008). Through this process, organisations can track the level of investment in controls required to get to the desired level of residual risk.

Metrics tied to operational risk are called key risk indicators (KRIs). KRIs allow the level of risk to be monitored and can also be used to measure the level of residual risk. Consistent capture and monitoring of KRIs allows an organisation to observe the ways in which a risk level changes over time. KRIs provide a quantitative basis to assess the quality of internal controls for risk mitigation and remediation (Watchorn and Levy 2008). Similar to RCSAs, the measurement and analysis of KRIs is an ongoing process used to shape an organisation's operational risk profile. By helping to identify potential sources of vulnerability, KRIs can focus organisational attention and direct resources towards specific risks and engender larger conversations regarding their relationship to daily business operations. Similar to KRIs, organisations can link metrics to controls to allow monitoring of the performance and effectiveness of the control. These metrics are called key control indicators (KCIs). KCIs are often the result of control testing results (see Table 3.1).

BEICFs provide a picture of an organisation's operational risk profile in the present. This raises the question of how BEICFs relate to scenario analysis. This is especially the case given the fact that "scenario analysis typically considers the extreme, low-frequency/high-impact (LFHI) operational events, while BEICFs measures are usually associated with the day-to-day, high-frequency/low-impact (HFLI) events" (Watchorn and Levy 2008). Despite this designation, however, BEICFs can inform future risk scenarios by identifying early-warning signs of risks that have the potential to cause substantial future losses (Watchorn and Levy 2008). To this end, we now turn to a discussion of the ways in which BEICFs can play an integral role in SA.

Table 3.1 Examples of KRIs and KCIs

Risk	KRI
Employee fraud	Number of fraud incidents
Failure of an application	System downtime
Control	**KCI**
Restricted physical access	Number of unauthorised people
Management sign-off	Number of cases where management sign-off did not occur

What is scenario analysis?

At its core, SA is future-oriented assessment typically focused on understanding maximum losses and gains. The analysis typically focuses on low-probability events or events that have yet to occur. More specifically, scenario analysis is used by organisations to "systematically assess extreme but plausible events" (KPMG 2011) that can result in significant and catastrophic losses. Due to their exceptional nature, these types of loss incidents have the potential to skew capital model calculations. Scenario analysis provides a method for examining these hypothetical situations in order to effectively integrate potential losses into an organisation's capital calculations for operational risk. This is helpful for capital modelling purposes in cases where there is a lack of internal or external loss event data.

Conducting a scenario analysis involves three distinct phases. First, an assessment of internal and external loss data, along with BEICFs, is used to establish a set of scenario definitions and parameters. Following the initial identification phase, business line experts subject the range of potential scenarios to a quantification and review process. This often involves a group or workshop review of the risk factor and expert opinion applied to assess maximum losses if controls failed. Finally, a committee comprising senior management is brought in to review and approve the full set of scenarios and finalise operational risk scenario figures (Palmer 2005). These steps are critical to ensure business buy-in for the scenarios, given that they can have a large impact on operational risk capital calculations, particularly in the case where there is a paucity of internal loss events.

While SA helps financial institutions prepare for potential crises before they occur, challenges remain. SA in operational risk management is a largely qualitative process. Workshops that combine input from internal and external loss data, as well as a broad range of subject matter and normative experts, are used to define a range of potential scenarios for further discussion with key stakeholders and executive management. Given the significant investment of time and resources that SA requires, the question of how to define the finite number of plausible future events worth analysing is of paramount importance.

Though internal and external loss data can play an important role in helping define scenario parameters, their utility for SA is limited. Indeed, the strength of internal and external loss data is dependent on the accurate disclosure and reporting of loss events (Palmer 2005). As a result, loss data often provides information regarding those events that are most frequently reported. For example, while large loss events that occur as a result of rogue trading tend to garner a substantial amount of publicity, technology-related losses often receive less attention and may even go unreported (Palmer 2005). What's more, because the collection of operational loss data is a fairly recent development, organisations cannot rely on a deep historical record from which to cull significant data points to guide scenario analysis.

The use of BEICFs in scenario analysis

BEICFs can play an important role in not only mitigating potential biases but also helping to identify potential events for SA. By providing a robust picture of an organisation's current business environment and internal control factors, "consideration of BEICFs can assist the scenario assessors in making estimates that are relevant to the current and future residual risk profile of the bank" (Watchorn and Levy 2008). The factors that organisations use to define their BEICFs, including RCSAs and KRIs, provide a point of focus for determining potential scenarios in need of further analysis.

RCSAs and KRIs offer insight into daily exposures and vulnerabilities, which can be used to identify areas in which the potential for substantial losses is possible. For example, consider the case of system downtime. As a KRI, system downtime indicates a level of risk inherent in an organisation's core banking system. While data that indicates regular instances of downtime creates questions as to its root causes, it can also provide the basis for identifying a larger risk and potential loss for SA. Consideration of small-scale system outages on a daily basis can inspire the larger what-if question. This includes an SA of what would happen if the bank's entire server were brought down by a malicious cyber attack or natural disaster. What losses would the bank incur as a result? What safeguards can be instituted to prevent this type of catastrophic loss from occurring in the future? In this regard, BEICFs can direct organisational attention towards loss events that, while infrequent, have the potential to cause substantial losses.

How do BEICFs affect the capital model?

Without BEICFs the capital model remains primarily historical in nature, comprising internal and external loss data. The emphasis on past events, however, may fail to reveal hidden biases that can ultimately affect statistical analysis. In response, BEICFs provide an important post-analysis correction to various anomalies that occur as a result of the overwhelmingly historical nature of the capital model in two important ways.

First, BEICFs help mitigate hidden biases in the capital model by providing a host of qualitative information, including KRIs, RCSAs and audit findings that come directly from the practitioners operating actual business lines and organisational units. Unlike internal and external loss data, these assessments are informed by daily interactions with risks and controls. While the model provides important statistical risk mapping on the basis of events that have already taken place, it can never fully replace or account for the qualitative assessments and experiential knowledge of practitioners on the ground. In this regard, BEICFs allow your organisation to integrate vital information into the model that would otherwise remain absent from your overall capital calculations.

Second, BEICFs are meant to provide the most up-to-date assessments of an organisation's risk profile. By highlighting present risk realities, BEICFs, such as KRIs and RCSAs, provide a mechanism for incorporating current perspectives into an otherwise historically oriented capital model. In short, BEICFs not only correct statistical anomalies but also present a more comprehensive picture of an organisation's overall risk reality, which ultimately helps create a more robust capital model.

To be sure, integrating qualitative information into a quantitative model represents a significant challenge. There is no single blueprint or general framework governing the use of BEICFs in capital calculations. Doing so effectively requires developing processes that are organisationally specific and in line with an institution's business units, operations and risk framework. Once established, these processes can facilitate the successful integration of BEICFs from throughout the organisation into the capital model.

The inherent challenge of incorporating BEICFs into the capital model does, however, underscore the importance of developing a shared risk taxonomy. Ensuring that key stakeholders from across the organisation have a common language through which they can communicate about and understand disparate risk-related data is critical. Developing a shared taxonomy will serve to create a level of commonality among the diverse group of data inputs and allow for their aggregation, analysis and integration into the capital model.

In conclusion, this chapter presents us an end-to-end scenario analysis process that allows for its solid preparation, rating and validation. The process ensures that experts receive the appropriate information for the risk evaluation; it increases the expert involvement; it mitigates cognitive biases; and, finally, it establishes a strong scenario validation. In fact, in spite of the subjective nature of scenario analysis, there exist robust methods for their validation that make SA a high-quality information source.

The implementation of this process will greatly complement the capital model with expert judgement information regarding the incertitudes faced by the institution and incrementing the forward-looking character of the capital estimates.

We have reached the end of Part I, which presents the foundation of an operational risk capital model: the definition and collection process of its four data elements. In fact, the quality of these elements determines the quality of the overall capital estimates and therefore maximum attention and care should be given. Additionally, a solid foundation on the four data elements is also the basis an effective operational risk management, beyond obtaining more precise capital estimates, as we will examine in Part III.

1   This section has been contributed by Daniel Rodriguez.
2   Alternative to the expected loss, the loss mode can potentially be asked as one of the two points of the distribution. The mode is attractive from an information-collection point of view. Experts frequently find it simpler to assess the mode – the most typical value of a loss – than the mean loss. For a correct mean loss evaluation, the expert should consider extreme values weighted by their probability of occurrence, which most likely have not been witnessed by them. On the other hand, the mode represents the expert's most common experience and hence is more directly estimated. However, the mode is linked with the skewness of the distribution and may determine the full distribution shape in a two-para-meter distribution, making it hard to obtain robust results. Therefore, it is more practical to use the mean as an input to the loss distribution determination, than the mode.
3   Structured scenario analysis is frequently called "structure expert judgement" or "performance-based expert judgement".
4   SSA has a solid academic background and it is sponsored by intergovernmental initiatives such as COST, Europe's longest-running intergovernmental framework for cooperation in science and technology, by its programme COST Action IS1304, European Expert Judgment Network.

5   IS1304 COST Expert Judgement.
6   BEICFs survey performed by Advanced Measurement Approach Group (AMAG).
7   This and the next three sections have been contributed by Brenda Boultwood.

REFERENCES

Ariely, Dan, George Loewenstein, Drazen Prelec, 2006, "Tom Sawyer and the construction of value", *Journal of Economic Behaviour & Organisation* 60.

BIS, 2002, "Operational Risk Data Collection Exercise", Basel Committee for Banking Supervision.

BIS, 2006, "Observed Range of Practice in Key Elements of Advanced Measurement Approaches (AMA)", Basel Committee on Banking Supervision, October.

BIS, 2011, "Operational Risk Supervisory Guidelines for the Advanced Measurement Approaches", Basel Committee on Banking Supervision, June.

Cooke, Roger M. 1991. *Experts in Uncertainty: Opinion and Subjective Probability in Science.* Oxford: Oxford University Press.

French, S., Maule, J. and Papamichail, K. N. *Decision Behaviour, Analysis and Support.* Cambridge: Cambridge University Press, 2009.

Gigerenzer, Gerd. 2007. *Gut Feelings: The Intelligence of the Unconscious.* New York: Viking.

Kahneman, Daniel., Paul Slovic and Amos Tversky. 1982. *Judgment under Uncertainty: Heuristics and Biases*, New York, Cambridge University Press.

KPMG, 2011, "Preparing for the Unexpected: Leading Practice for Operational Risk Scenarios, Headline Findings", March.

Nordgård, Dag Eirik, 2008, "Quantitative Risk Assessment using Bow-Tie Modelling", Norwegian University of Science and Technology, Trondheim.

Palmer, David, 2005, "Using Scenario Analysis to Estimate Operational Risk Capital", presentation to OpRisk Europe Conference, March.

Reason, James, 1990, "Human error: models and management", Department of Psychology, University of Manchester.

Tversky, Amos and Daniel Kahneman, "Judgment under Uncertainty: Heuristics and Biases", *Science* 27 Vol. 185, no. 4157 pp. 1124–1131, September 1974.

Watchorn, Emily, and André Levy, 2008, "Developing Business Environment and Internal Control Factors for Operational Risk Measurement and Management", APRA, April.

Wisse, Bram, Tim Bedford and John Quigley, 2006, "Expert judgment combination using using moment methods. Reliability Engineering and System Safety", 93(5):675—686, 2008.

Part II

General Framework for Operational Risk Capital Modelling

Operational risk modelling requires a robust determination of its inputs as presented in Part I. This includes the definition of criteria for the collection of, and quality control for, internal losses; sourcing of external data; a robust process for the capture of scenario analysis and the incorporation of BEICFs into the capital model.

Once quality inputs are available, they can be used in the appropriate modelling processes to obtain adequate capital estimations. Part II describes the modelling processes that permit a quality capital estimation and describes the circumstances in which these processes should be applied.

Most institutions calculate their operational risk capital requirements based on either a loss distribution approach (LDA) – mainly based on loss data – or a scenario-based approach (SBA). A more advanced approach is the hybrid model (HM), where loss data and scenario analysis are combined into a single model to compute capital using, in effect, the four data elements requested in the BCSG-AMA.

The choice of LDA, SBA or HM depends on the financial sector and the maturity of the operational risk capital modelling programme. Banking institutions generally start with an LDA and later migrate to an HM, as they generally have sufficient data to start capital modelling using ILD. On the other hand, insurers most commonly start with an SBA, as, in their case, ILD is less abundant.

Part II describes the modelling processes required to construct a fully developed operational risk capital model, which includes the modelling processes for a LDA, SBA and HM methods. The part examines the modelling topics that correspond to the following chapters:

❏ "Loss Data Modelling";
❏ "Scenario Analysis Modelling";
❏ "BEICFs Modelling and Integration into the Capital Model";
❏ "Hybrid Model Construction: Integration of ILD, ED and SA";
❏ "Derivation of the Joint Distribution and Capitalisation of Operational Risk";
❏ "Backtesting, Stress Testing and Sensitivity Analysis"; and
❏ "Evolving from a Plain Vanilla to a State-of-the-Art Model".

4

Loss Data Modelling: ILD and ED

Rafael Cavestany and Daniel Rodriguez

In this chapter, we examine the modelling of operational loss data, which can be applied in the modelling of internal loss data (ILD) and external data (ED). The use of ILD in the capital model permits us to incorporate relevant information on the specific characteristics of the risk profile of an institution, as reflected in its loss experience dominated by high frequency events. The use of ED permits us to complement the modelling with the experience of peer institutions, which is not reflected in the ILD, accompanying ILD with low frequency/high severity events.

Loss data is generally modelled by determining the frequency and severity distributions of the loss data of each operational risk category (ORC). The importance of using ILD in capital modelling is recognised by the Basel Committee on Banking Supervision in a 2011 document titled, "Operational Risk – Supervisory Guidelines for Advanced Measurement Approaches" (BCSG-AMA): "Supervisors expect ILD to be used in the operational risk measurement system (ORMS) to assist in the estimation of loss frequencies; to inform the severity distribution(s) to the extent possible." In addition, the BCSG-AMA states, "Supervisors expect ED to be used in the estimation of loss severity as ED contains valuable information to inform the tail of the loss distribution(s)."

Loss data severity modelling is performed by evaluating several important aspects including, but not restricted to, the determination of the distribution shape; adequate tail modelling for correct estimation of potential extreme losses determining capital; goodness of fit (GoF) of the selected distribution to the data used for the modelling; stability of capital estimations given changes in the modelling sample; and evaluation of the realism of the losses generated by the distribution function used for the modelling.

Loss data frequency distribution modelling is simpler because it is focused more on determining the frequency mean and less on the distribution shape. Aspects of goodness of fit, evaluation of the time evolution of loss frequencies and consistency with the severity fit are all critical for a sound frequency distribution fit.

In this chapter, we present the loss data detailed modelling divided in the following sections (which address the issues mentioned above):

❏ "Exploratory analysis and selection of a homogeneous data sample": This presents several analyses for the evaluation of the loss data available for the modelling and presents an initial understanding for selecting the modelling venue.
❏ "Optimum modelling granularity": This section looks at the methods for defining the appropriate modelling granularity that permits us to properly capture the tail shape of the ORC and a robust modelling.
❏ "Tail shape and threshold determination through extreme value theory": In this section, we present several methods for the determination of the distribution tail type choice and modelling threshold. These methods permit us to adequately model the tail shape and a stable capital modelling.
❏ "Severity distributions fitting": This section presents several methods to determine loss distributions for better capturing the tail behaviour and reflecting a current risk profile. These methods include time-weighted least squares (to address the issue of combining old and new data), probability weighted least squares (to increase the weight of extreme losses during the fit) and robust least squares (for samples with outliers and other issues).
❏ "Frequency distribution fitting": In this section, we look at the key considerations when determining frequency distributions.
❏ "Goodness-of-fit evaluation": This presents different methods for the evaluation of the correct fit of the distribution function and the loss data used in the modelling, including numerical tests such as p-value and other, graphical, analysis.
❏ "Stability analysis of capital estimates, distribution parameters,

and GoF": In this section, we look at methods for determining models that produce stable capital estimates, given the new losses that the institution will experience in the future. The methods include the re-sampling and what-if? methods.

❏ "Evaluating whether the capital estimates are realistic": This section presents methods for evaluating the losses that the distribution models produce and verifying that they are commensurate with the risk profile of the institution.

❏ "External data scaling": This section examines the necessary previous transformation of ED, before it is modelled and integrated with the rest of the data elements in the institution's capital model.

❏ "Definition of a loss data modelling process": In this section, we look at the need to define a modelling process that permits us to apply consistent criteria in the selection of the modelling assumptions.

Figure 4.1 illustrates the workflow in loss data modelling that is later developed in the sections of this chapter.

Nevertheless, the methods presented in this chapter are equally applicable in the modelling of external data.

EXPLORATORY ANALYSIS AND SELECTION OF A HOMOGENEOUS DATA SAMPLE[1]

The modelling of internal loss data starts with the analysis and selection of the actual data sample. The final data sample will constitute

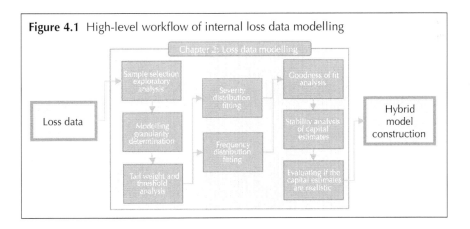

Figure 4.1 High-level workflow of internal loss data modelling

the basis of the ORC's ILD modelling. The goal is to define a data sample selection criterion that is sufficiently homogeneous and provides a minimum-size sample to permit a solid modelling.

A homogeneous sample is achieved by segmenting the data mainly by organisation unit and risk category. When segmenting the analysis by organisational unit, business line is an appropriate criterion to follow. In fact, Basel II proposes standard business units (retail banking, commercial banking, sales and trading, and so on) for the modelling, although these can be adapted to the specific organisation of the institution. The rationale of this segmentation is to group losses with consistent risk profile to permit solid modelling.

Once the homogeneous sample has been defined, some initial analysis can be performed in order to understand the characteristics of the data, including the following:

❑ Moments of the distribution: Mean, variance, skewness and leptokurtosis – when high leptokurtosis and skewness are identified, this suggests that the distribution has strong tail behaviour.
❑ Percentiles of the distribution: Low and high percentiles should be analysed and then the multiples of low to high percentiles should be assessed.
❑ Log analysis: The mean and the standard deviation of the logarithm of the losses (μ and σ of the corresponding lognormal distribution respectively) is analysed so as to determine tail behaviour. When σ is higher than three and μ is very low or even negative, it suggests a fat behaviour. More on the log analysis can be found under "Tail shape and threshold determination through extreme value theory".
❑ Other values of the sample: These, too, can be analysed, such as the number of events; the number of unique values (value repetitions indicates data quality issues or specific loss patterns); the difference between the minimum and the maximum; the frequency by bin; and histogram shape under linear and lognormal scales.

BCSG-AMA states that, for selecting the probability distribution, "a bank should generally adhere to the following: Exploratory Data

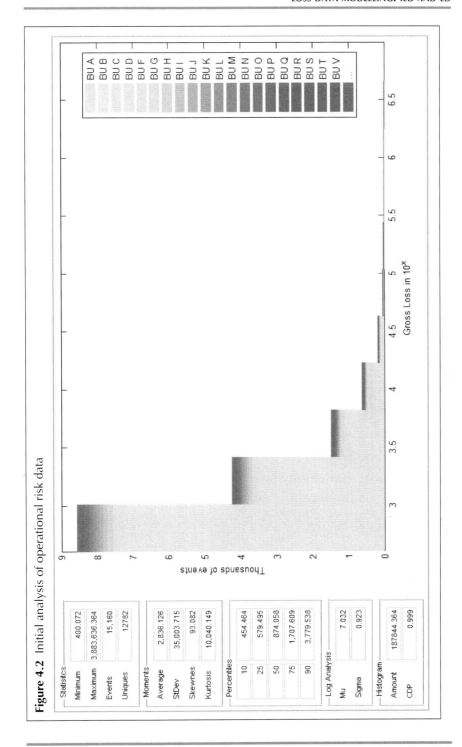

Figure 4.2 Initial analysis of operational risk data

Analysis (EDA) for each ORC to better understand the statistical profile of the data and select the most appropriate distribution ..."

Figure 4.2 shows the analysis of these characteristics of an operational risk sample[2] of 15,160 events. Among these, there are 12,782 unique values, which suggest multiple values repeated, which might be due to data quality or real loss values repeated (credit-card limits, damaged assets with identical value and so forth). Note that all graphs and calculations referring to capital modelling in this book have been performed using OpCapital Analytics, a software solution based on MatLab specifically designed for the calculation of operational risk capital requirements under advanced approaches.

The histogram shows the gross losses broken into 30 bins. The log analysis shows a strong μ, 7.032, and a low σ, 0.923. The analysis of moments suggests a strong leptokurtosis, 10,040, and skewness, 93, in the sample. Percentiles 10%, 50%, 90%, 95%, 99% and 99.9% are analysed and percentile 99.9% is about 214 times the size of the median, 66 times the mean and 5 times the standard deviation. This last can be compared to the normal distribution assumption, typical of market risk, where the 99.9th percentile is approximately 3.1, suggesting strong tail behaviour of the analysed sample. Also, the frequencies by business unit and loss size are analysed in lineal and log scales.

The data sample frequencies should be analysed also. Figure 4.3 shows the representation of the frequency distribution under different time bucketing. The distribution on the left refers to the frequency by week. We can observe that there are many weeks with no losses observed. The value of 0 weekly losses is the most common in the data sample. The frequency on the right is monthly, and it can be observed this time that the shape resembles a standard Poisson distribution assumption.

Regarding frequencies, the time evolution of the frequencies may also be analysed. Figure 4.4 shows the frequency time evolution of the same sample. It can be observed how there is a growth on the loss frequency. It should be determined whether this is due to improvements in the data collection processes or due to the operational risk profile becoming more dangerous or out of control.

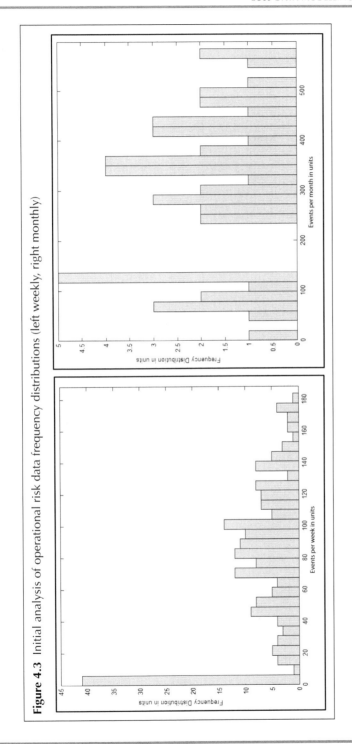

Figure 4.3 Initial analysis of operational risk data frequency distributions (left weekly, right monthly)

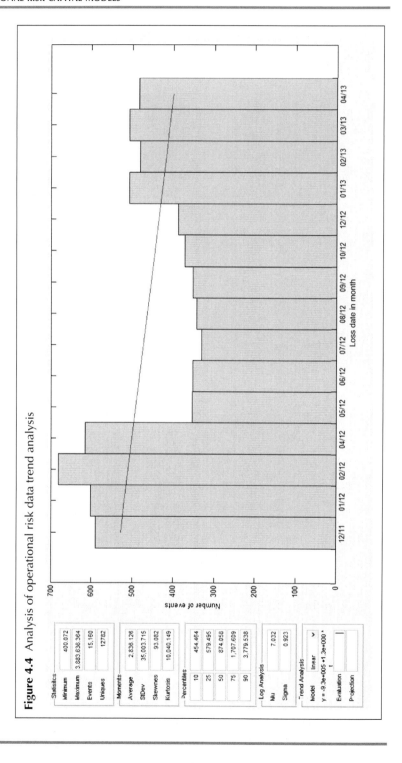

Figure 4.4 Analysis of operational risk data trend analysis

OPTIMUM MODELLING GRANULARITY

Modelling granularity is an important matter on operational risk quantification. The implementation of a more detailed granularity than the standard (7 risk categories x 8 business lines[3]) provides significant benefits. Detailed modelling permits a better capture of the ORC tail shape and of the institution's idiosyncrasies – that is, the organisational structure and business complexities. Additionally, it allows a more specific capital allocation and hence a more insightful understanding of the operational risk profile. In turn, the detailed capital allocation can help in a more precise evaluation of the impact into such risk profiles of potential new mitigation plans and controls (see Chapter 12 and Figure 12.6), as mitigation and controls most frequently refer to particular processes or organisational entities, rather than to the complete high-level business line.

On the other hand, the ORC split should have a sufficient number of observations for a robust distribution fitting. Finally, correlations should also be adapted to avoid the exaggeration of the diversification benefits (see Chapters 6 and 8). Similar concerns are also mentioned in BCSG-AMA in its "Granularity" section, paragraphs 160–9.

When the available ILD sample is broken one level down in the organisational structure or operational risk classification, the loss observations will typically not be evenly split across the new segments. Most frequently, only one or two of the new segments will contain a sufficient number of observations for robust individual modelling. Many of the rest will need to be aggregated to sum up sufficient observations for their solid modelling.

Similar circumstances exits when modelling the 56 ORC of the standard busine lines and risk types. There are multiple lowly populated individual ORC that can be aggregated for their modelling.

Here, the challenge is grouping the lowly populated segments into adequately homogeneous data samples to permit their sound distribution fitting. The goal is to aggregate those segments with the most similar distribution characteristics as reflected in their sample moments, percentiles or lognormal fit parameters. Grouping samples with homogeneous distributional characteristics allows for significant distribution fits and more stable capital estimates.

This can be achieved by a combination of qualitative and quantitative methods. A qualitative method will look at the risk drivers of each of the segmented ILD samples to determine ILD segment groups. The qualitative method can be complemented or informed by a clustering algorithm over the ILD samples' distribution attributes (moments, percentiles or lognormal fit parameters) to identify those having sufficient similarity for their grouping. The advantage in the use of quantitative methods is that they provide an objective and transparent measure of the samples' similarities and grouping criteria, and facilitate the implementation of consistent grouping criteria across ORCs and modelling dates. Modelling consistency is a requirement from supervisors.

Table 4.1 presents an example of clustering 12 corporate and investment banking business areas, based on their ILD distribution moments, percentiles and mu and sigma of the lognormal fit. The clustering algorithm we used is Pham (Pham, Dimov and Nguyen 2004). It differs from a standard k-means in that it does not require a number of desired clusters because Pham provides its optimal number given a minimum degree of similarity. This is particularly convenient, since it permits us to create clusters with a consistent degree of similarity across different ORCs. The standard k-means clustering method, where a number of clusters is a required input, creates the provided number of clusters but with inconsistent degrees of similarity.

The algorithm has clustered the 12 business areas into 6 modelling ORCs with the most similar distributional characteristics. The clustering is in fact dominated by tail shape attributes such as highest percentiles and sigma parameter of the lognormal fit. This can also be observed in Table 4.2, where the cluster centres of the highest percentiles and sigma are clearly distinctive. In fact, the tail shape should be a major concern when defining granularity, as mentioned by BCSG-AMA: "... an AMA bank's risk measurement system must be sufficiently granular to capture the major drivers of operational risk affecting the shape of the tail of the loss estimates".

TAIL SHAPE AND THRESHOLD DETERMINATION THROUGH EXTREME VALUE THEORY

After an adequately granular and homogeneous sample has been defined and its major characteristics identified, the analysis turns into modelling the severity distribution. Most frequently, the severity distribution is modelled separating the tail from the body, in

Table 4.1 Business areas assigned to clusters based on distributional characteristics

	Banking and custody operations	Banking services	Corporate and investment banking operations	Fund administration	Global markets	Investment banking	Operations and support	Personal and business banking	Priority banking	Risk management	Transactional products and services	Trust
# of Events	34	12	560	29	444	39	88	73	43	118	1198	7
Average	8,540	1,775	35,673,180	85,179	315,732	827,296,445	445,355	3,207	1,453	34,321	178,910	1,301
StandDev	27,093	3,648	8.432E+08	225,463	2.975E+06	5.165E+09	2.725E+06	9,529	2,308	201,333	2.109E+06	1,487
Skewness	4,602.0	2.6	23.0	2.8	16.0	6.0	8.5	4.9	3.6	7.1	16.7	1.4
Kurtosis	24.0	8.6	558.0	9.5	301.0	37.0	77.0	29.9	18.4	55.9	305.7	3.7
percentil 25	$209	$62	$206	$901	$1,004	$4,215	$1,938	$269	$162	$215	$49	$219
percentil 50	$997	$309	$568	$4,461	$4,399	$19,719	$8,620	$400	$921	$734	$343	$1,182
percentil 75	$3,078	$1,677	$2,314	$45,933	$24,110	$100,924	$25,785	$1,098	$1,693	$2,749	$2,864	$1,563
percentil 90	$18,949	$6,421	$9,098	$334,597	$192,675	$611,912	$385,511	$7,903	$3,447	$12,385	$30,822	$3,927
percentil 95	$48,032	$12,313	$46,079	$7,468,502	$763,608	$2,072,165	$751,782	$14,208	$5,162	$44,640	$126,633	$4,511
Mu	6.8	5.6	6.7	8.3	8.6	10	8.9	6.4	6.34	6.8	6.1	6.4
Sigma	2.1	2.2	2.2	3	2.6	3.3	2.9	1.5	1.561	2.1	2.9	1.5
Number of assigned cluster	2	2	4	3	6	1	5	2	2	2	5	2

105

Table 4.2 Centres of the clusters

	Centers of Cluster 1	Centers of Cluster 2	Centers of Cluster 3	Centers of Cluster 4	Centers of Cluster 5	Centers of Cluster 6
Average	8.27E+08	8.43E+03	8.52E+04	3.57E+07	3.13E+05	3.16E+05
Standard deviation	5.17E+09	4.09E+04	2.25E+05	8.43E+08	2.60E+06	2.97E+06
Skewness	6.00	770.26	2.80	23.00	13.73	16.00
Kurtosis	37.00	23.42	9.50	558.00	227.90	301.00
percentil 25	4,215	189	901	206	997	1,004
percentil 50	19,719	757	4,461	568	4,454	4,399
percentil 75	100,924	1,976	45,933	2,314	17,586	24,110
percentil 90	611,912	8,839	334,597	9,098	203,003	192,675
percentil 95	2,072,165	21,478	7,468,502	46,079	547,341	763,608
Mu	10.00	6.39	8.30	6.70	7.87	8.60
Sigma	3.30	1.83	3.00	2.20	2.80	2.60
Events per cluster	39	287	29	560	1,286	444
Business areas	Investment banking	Banking and custody operations, banking services, personal and business banking, priority banking, risk management and trust	Fund administration	Corporate and investment Banking operations	Operations and support, transactional products and services	Global markets

order to ensure tail extreme losses are correctly modelled. This requires the definition of an optimal threshold (severity separation of body and tail, also known as truncation point) and the analysis of the tail behaviour.

The BCSG-AMA says, "A bank is responsible for defining and justifying appropriate thresholds for each operational risk class, both for data collection and modelling." The same document later says, "When separate distributions for the body and the tail are used, a bank should carefully consider the choice of the body-tail modelling threshold that distinguishes the two regions."

This section proposes several methods to determine the modelling threshold and to analyse the tail behaviour for loss severity distributions, in the context of loss data (ILD and ED), with the corresponding references on the methods. They represent an *ex ante* analysis directed to orient the modelling and justify the distribution assumption selections.

The proposed methods follow extreme value theory (EVT) (Beirlant *et al* 2005; Coles 2001). BCSG-AMA mentions the need to analyse and capture extreme events: "However, a bank must be able to demonstrate that its approach captures potentially severe 'tail' loss events", or, in other words, extreme values of the operational losses that can be addressed with EVT.

EVT suggests that tail data above a specific threshold follows a fat-tail distribution, is independent of the distribution body and, therefore, can be modelled independently of the body. A common assumption for the tail modelling is a Pareto distribution.

In operational risk modelling, using separate distributions for tail and body is particularly useful, as ORCs are the result of grouping losses of a very diverse nature stemming from multiple processes of different natures. Therefore, determining a threshold for tail losses permits the creation of a much more homogeneous loss data sample for the modelling. The correct modelling of the distribution tail is critical for the determination of operational risk capital, as capital is determined by extreme, highly infrequent events or tail events. Although there are no fixed rules for selecting the truncation point, the purpose is to concentrate the weight of the fit on the extreme observations while preserving sufficient data for a robust fit.

The EVT methods proposed in Figure 4.5 analyse tail behaviour by creating multiple subsamples, which we call tail subsamples.

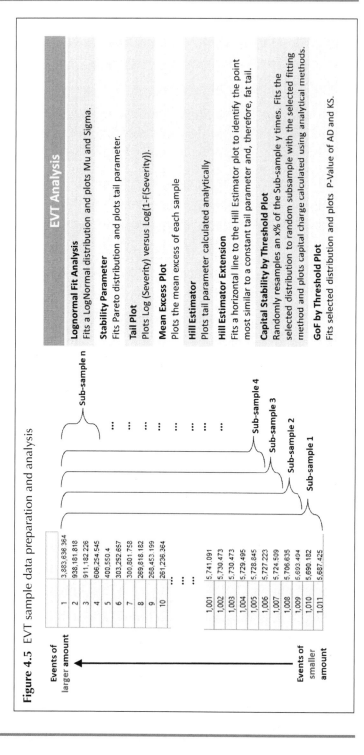

Figure 4.5 EVT sample data preparation and analysis

They are created by excluding additional portions of smaller-severity events. Consecutive subsamples include fewer data points, called exceedances, and only those with the largest severity, as in the numbers in the left-hand-side table shown in Figure 4.5. Then, the analytics summarised in the table that is part of Figure 4.5 are performed over the subsamples.

The effectiveness of these tests depends on the nature of the empirical data analysed, meaning that conclusions will sometimes be obvious and, at other times, the results may be less conclusive.

Lognormal fit analysis by exceedances

This test is based on the analysis of the lognormal fit in the exceedance subsamples (Dekkers, Einmahl and de Haan 1989). The aim is to help establish an optimal truncation point by adjusting (via maximum-likelihood estimator, or MLE) the excesses with a lognormal distribution and observing at which truncation point the estimated values of parameters μ and σ become stable or converge to a specific value.

The test is performed by fitting a lognormal to each of the subsamples, as shown in Figure 4.6. Then, the resulting μ and σ parameters of the lognormal distribution are plotted versus the number of exceedances or severity used in the fit, as illustrated. The representation of the confidence intervals of the μ and σ parameters, dotted external lines around the solid one, provides additional robustness to the analysis.

The criterion is based on the graph ending. When σ is higher than 3 and μ is negative, it suggests fat-tail behaviour and, alternatively, light-tail behaviour. This criterion, applied to Figure 4.6, suggests light-tail behaviour as the σ, the blue line of the top graphic is always below 3, and the μ, the centre line of the bottom graphic, is positive. The external lines above and below the centre line represent the 95% confidence intervals around the σ and μ estimations. On the other hand, Figure 4.7 shows the opposite case: fat-tail distribution as μ is negative and σ higher than 3.

Stability parameter

The aim of the stability parameter test is to evaluate the adequateness of modelling the tail distribution with a generalised Pareto distribution (GPD) type of fat-tail distribution, via the tail stability plot (see

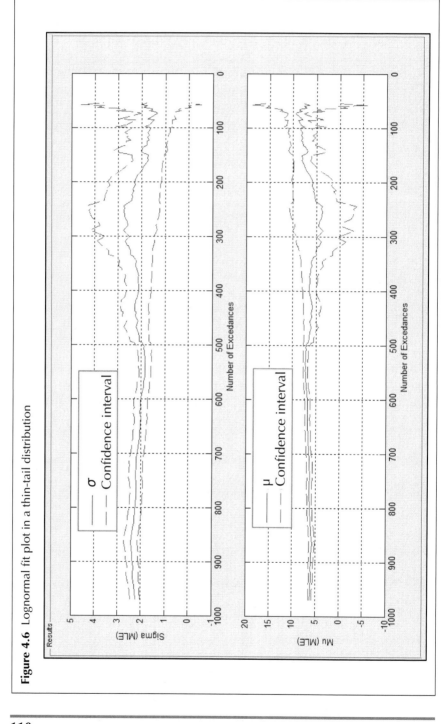

Figure 4.6 Lognormal fit plot in a thin-tail distribution

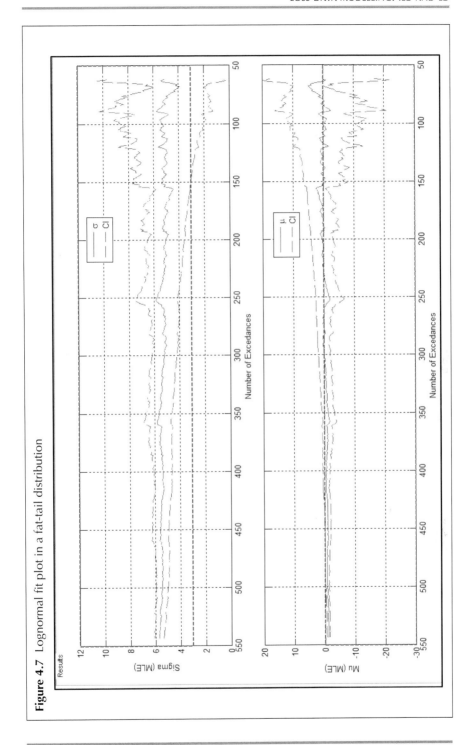

Figure 4.7 Lognormal fit plot in a fat-tail distribution

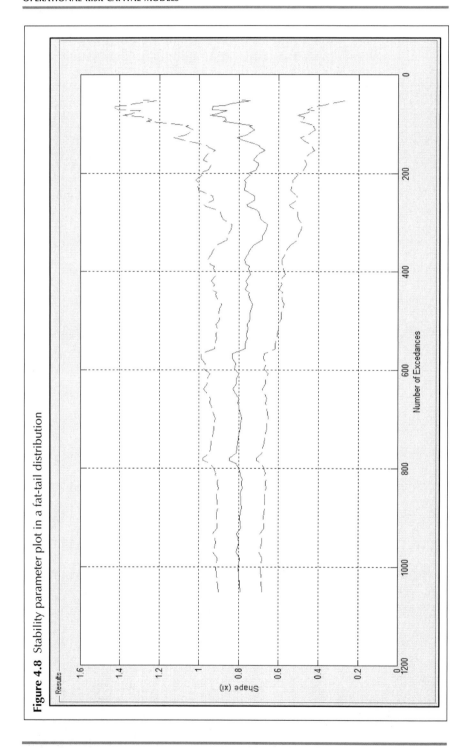

Figure 4.8 Stability parameter plot in a fat-tail distribution

Figures 4.8 and 4.9). Different tail behaviours can be identified based on the tail stability plot, which helps to determine an optimal truncation point. Additionally, the tail stability plot indicates the minimum number of exceedances required to obtain a reliable fit using fat tail distributions.

EVT states that, for a GPD-type tail distribution, after a given threshold, the estimated tail index parameter (ξ) is independent of the threshold, remaining stable, provided the threshold point leaves a sufficient number of exceedances to obtain a reliable empirical estimate of tail parameter (ξ). In other words, if the threshold is progressively increased, the tail parameter (ξ) resulting from the fit will remain stable, in the case that the distribution excesses or tail samples show fat-tail behaviour. On the other hand, thin-tail behaviour will be identified if the estimated ξ values tend to zero. While tail parameter is supposed to remain stable to pass the test, the scaling factor of the distribution may vary as the threshold is increased.

The calculation process consists of fitting a GPD to each of the subsamples, as explained above and in Figure 4.8. The tail index from the GPD fit is plotted against the number of subsample exceedances, as shown.

Figure 4.8 shows clear, stable, fat-tail behaviour for the distribution. The tail index parameter (ξ) remains stable at 0.8, after around 400 exceedances, indicating also that a minimum of approximately 400 exceedances is required for a reliable tail modelling.

The graph in Figure 4.9, shows the opposite example, in which the tail index parameter (ξ) tends to zero, suggesting a light tail.

Tail plot

The purpose of the tail plot (de Fontnouvelle, Rosengren and Jordan 2007) is to identify fat- or thin-tail behaviour in the empirical data, by analysing the log of the cumulative probability function versus the log of the severities.

Assuming a series of observations {x} have a cumulative empirical distribution F*(x), the tail plot is obtained by drawing log (1–F*(x)) in the vertical axis Y of a graph, in relation to log(x) in the horizontal axis X. When the graph is linear with a stable positive slope, it suggests a fat tail. When the slope of the line increases progressively with a convex curve, it suggests a light tail. At the same time, the

Figure 4.9 Stability parameter plot in a thin-tail distribution

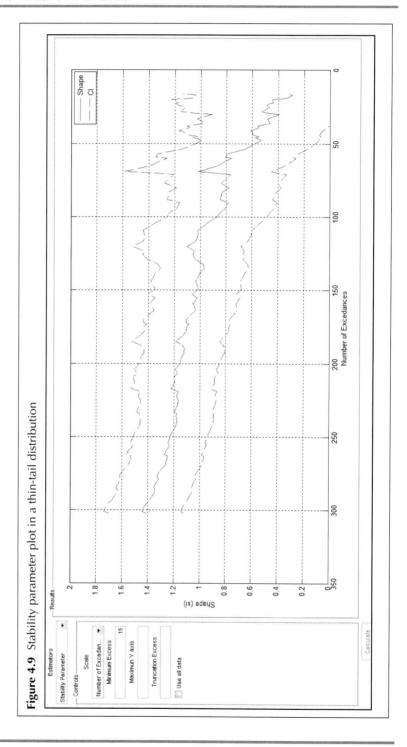

point where such a pattern changes is a candidate for being selected as the modelling threshold.

Figure 4.10 shows three lines: the wavy line is the tail plot of the empirical data being analysed, the actual tail plot; the top straight line is a Pareto distribution, which serves as a reference for fat-tail behaviour; and the bottom curved line is an exponential distribution to serve as a reference of light-tail behaviour. Clearly, the tail plot increases the slope indicating light-tail behaviour, similarly to the exponential reference line.

The tail plot in blue depicted in Figure 4.11 maintains its slope and replicates more closely the straight plot of the fat-tail Pareto distribution, clearly suggesting fat-tail behaviour.

Mean excess plot

The aim of the mean excess plot[4] is to assess tail behaviour, particularly fat tails in empirical data. It may also help to identify an optimal truncation point through the observation of changes in the slope of the plot. The BCSG-AMA explicitly mentions mean excess plot: "Other tools, such as … mean excess plots provide preliminary evidence on the type and shape of the probability distributions which better represent the data."

The mean excess is defined as the mean of the data after a truncation point, minus the value of that point. Mathematically, it can be expressed as follows:

$$E\left[X - t | X \geq t\right]$$

Figure 4.12 depicts a distribution of the empirical data for which the mean excess plot will be calculated. The mean excess for t=7 (truncation is equal to 7) would be the mean value of all observations of the distribution higher than 7 and subtracting from each observation the value of 7.

The mean excess plot (MEP) is created by plotting the mean excess for each of the subsamples versus the truncation, t. The bottom graph of Figure 4.13 represents the mean excess plot of a light-tail distribution, which later properly fitted a lognormal. It can be observed that it is convex and the slope of the MEP decreases as the severity increases. On the other hand, the MEP in the top graph of Figure 4.13 depicts a straight line with a constant slope, which suggests a fat-tail behaviour, as in a generalised Pareto distribution.

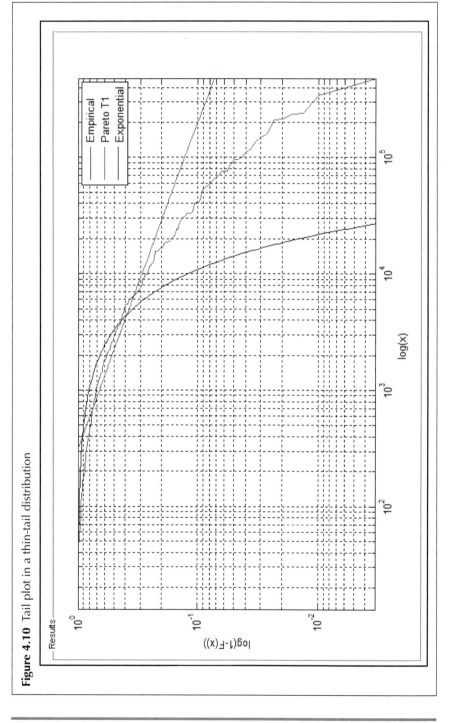

Figure 4.10 Tail plot in a thin-tail distribution

Figure 4.11 Tail plot in a fat-tail distribution

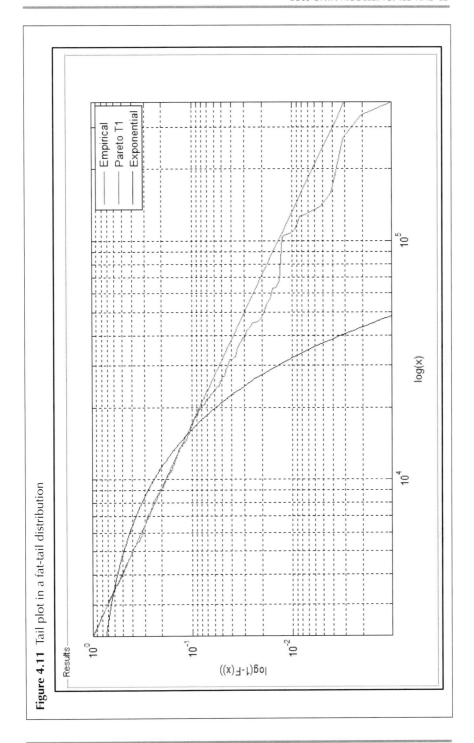

Figure 4.12 Mean excess plot representation

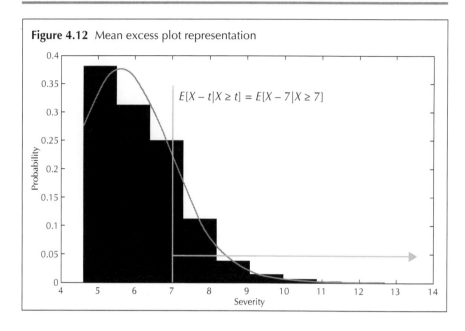

Finally, Figure 4.14 shows the MEP of an exponential distribution that has a very light tail and shows an almost horizontal MEP.

Hill estimator

The Hill estimator[5] seeks to identify fat-tail behaviour and is based on the estimation of the value of the tail index parameter ξ derived from EVT. The analysis is similar to that of the stability parameter, but the Hill estimator is determined by analysing the log of the exceedances, rather than fitting a Pareto distribution as in the former.

For a set of excess samples or excesses after a given truncation point, the Hill estimator is defined as the mean of the logarithms of the excesses less the logarithm of the truncation point, represented mathematically as follows:

$$HE(k) = E\left[\log(X)\middle| X \geq t\right] - \log(t),$$

such that, where the distribution underlying the excesses (or tail samples) follows a Pareto distribution, the Hill estimator implies a flat or slope-less straight line with constant value ξ. For fat tail distributions, the Hill estimator shows a curve that converges asymptotically to a ξ value other than zero, and for thin-tail distributions the Hill estimator shows a curve that converges to a ξ=0.

Figure 4.13 Mean excess plot in thin- and fat-tail distributions

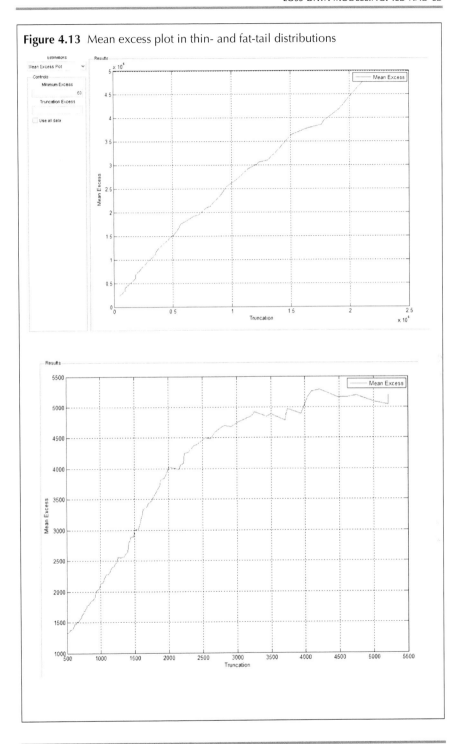

Figure 4.14 Mean excess plot in an exponential distribution

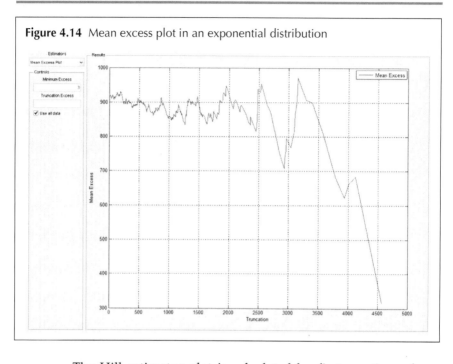

The Hill estimator plot is calculated by first creating a large number of tail subsamples. For each of the tail subsamples, the Hill estimator is calculated as the mean of the logarithms of the excesses less the logarithm of the truncation point. Then, the Hill estimator values are plotted versus the truncation point.

Figure 4.15 illustrates, in the graph on the right, a Hill estimator plot with fat-tail behaviour where the plot shows a constant slope around 0.8. The graph in the left shows the opposite case, where the Hill estimator plot tends to zero, suggesting light-tail behaviour.

Hill estimator extension

The Hill estimator extension[6] test derives from the Hill estimator and is designed to identify an optimal truncation point based on an optimal number K of exceedances. Such a number of exceedances (the number of samples after the threshold) will be the number at which the Hill estimator is more linear or more stable. Stability of the Hill estimator or tail parameter suggests fat-tail behaviour under EVT. Also, the threshold after which tail behaviour is stable is the threshold separating tail and body modelling under EVT.

The Hill estimator extension identifies the threshold by regressing

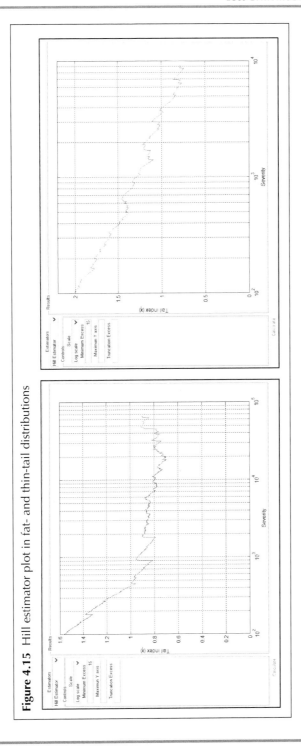

Figure 4.15 Hill estimator plot in fat- and thin-tail distributions

a horizontal linear function to the Hill estimator plot. Then the optimal threshold point would be that point at which the regression coefficient R^2 is maximised (or the squared errors are minimised):

❑ the Hill estimator plot is generated (as above);
❑ a regression with a horizontal line (slope 0, y=a+0x; y=a) is performed per threshold, considering only Hill estimator values higher than the thresholds; and
❑ the error is calculated as the sum of the square distances between the Hill estimator points calculated and the regressed line.

The number of excesses N for which the error is minimal is the number $N = K_{opt}$, where the Hill parameter extension is more linear and stable. This conclusion helps to establish an optimal K number of exceedances that implicitly mark an optimal truncation point.

Figure 4.16 shows the plot of the R^2 and squared errors following the Hill estimator extension analysis. The plot suggests several maxim of R^2 and minim of squared errors in order to select an optimal truncation point.

Capital stability by threshold plot

Capital stability by threshold analysis[7] refers to the analysis of the capital results and their stability, as a result of both selecting a specific modelling threshold and changes in the underlying fitting sample. A robust operational risk capital modelling should remain relatively stable given changes in the underlying fitting data. As operational risk capital is calculated periodically (not less than six months), new loss events are added to the existing fitting sample since the previous calculation, and capital results are therefore subject to change. Ideally, the modelling of operational risk should not change significantly unless the risk profile has really changed due to the materialisation of new losses, changes in the business environment, etc. Therefore, the selection of modelling assumptions should include the analysis of model stability given possible changes in the underlying data.

Capital stability by threshold analysis, as proposed in this section, allows for the analysis of three key characteristics of severity distributions, and the relationship between them, namely:

Figure 4.16 Huisman, Koedijk, Kool and Palm test plot

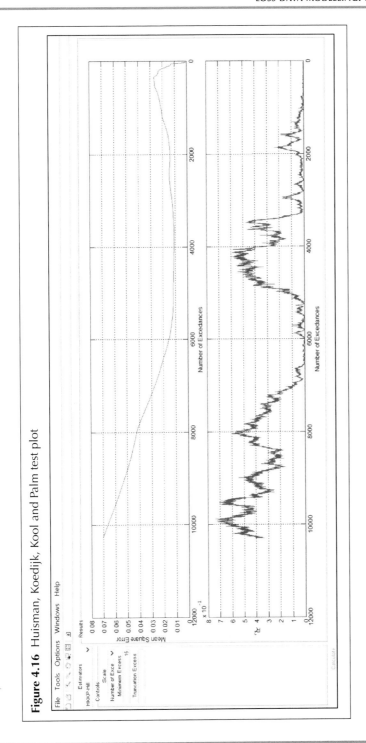

❑ truncation point for the tail fit;
❑ impact of the truncation point on the capital estimation; and
❑ stability of the capital estimations.

To perform the analysis, a sequence of truncation points is defined first and the corresponding tail subsamples are created. Each tail subsample is randomly resampled again, using either the jackknife or the bootstrap, to obtain a random "sub-subsample" of only a percentage of the size of the original. The lower the percentage, the more different the sub-subsamples would be, making the analysis more demanding. For instance, the sub-subsamples may be 70% of the size of the original subsample. This process is repeated n times to obtain an "n" number of random sub-subsamples from the same tail subsample. Each of these sub-subsamples is then used to perform a capital estimation. The capital is estimated first by using MLE to fit the selected distribution and then by using the single-loss approximation method for capital estimation. Since each sub-subsample is different, the corresponding capital estimation would be different as well. The results are provided in a box-plot graph representing the capital variability given changes in the underlying data, at that specific threshold. This process is repeated per tail subsample and the box plots are represented versus the tail subsample thresholds.

This resampling process replicates what theoretically happens in reality: fitting a distribution with different draws obtained from the same underlying loss distribution. With a stable loss-generating distribution in the institution, as time passes new losses are collected and added to the modelling sample each time the capital is recalculated. Each of the sub-subsamples actually represents a new capital calculation given new losses collected from the underlying operational loss distribution.

Figure 4.17 shows the results of this analysis on a sample of operational risk loss data. A lognormal distribution is fitted using MLE. A lognormal distribution was chosen through EVT analysis of the tail properties of the data sample. Thirty thresholds are defined and the analysis has been performed in each of the corresponding tail subsamples. Thirty sub-subsamples were generated per subsample of 70% of the size of the subsample and capital charge is estimated at the 99.9th percentile. The results show the possibility of obtaining the highest capital stability using more than 463 exceedances. Also,

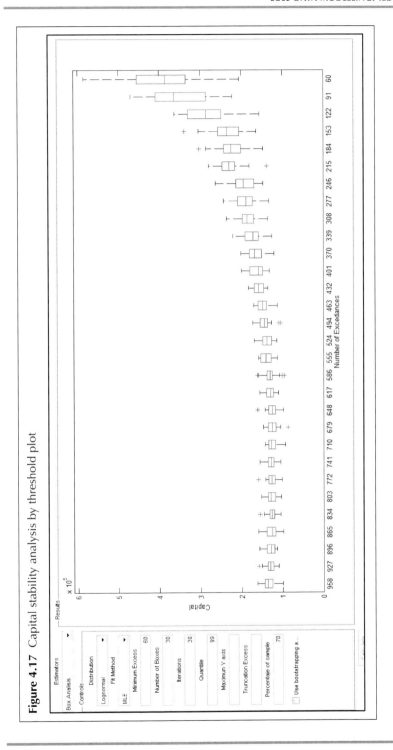

Figure 4.17 Capital stability analysis by threshold plot

results remain relatively stable if the threshold is decreased and more exceedances are added to the sample. As the number of exceedances decreases, fewer events are used for fitting the distributions and, as a consequence, capital estimations become unstable. It can be observed that, with fewer than 120 exceedances, capital estimations are really unstable.

GoF-by-threshold plot

The GoF-by-threshold plot allows the evaluation of GoF test values (see "Kolmogorov–Smirnov" and "Anderson–Darling" under "Goodness-of-fit evaluation" below) for different thresholds.

The rationale of the analysis is to identify truncation points providing a high significance on the fit. High significance implies that the data sample selected has homogeneous characteristics, allowing for robust modelling. Modelling internal loss data requires the consolidation of losses stemming from many different processes into single ORC, therefore, increasing the heterogeneity in the fitting sample. An important differentiation factor among losses pertaining to the same loss type and business unit is loss size. Small losses may stem from routine processes while large losses stem from other activities involving high amounts and critical processes for the institution.

The calculation process is simple. First, a set of truncation points is selected and the corresponding tail subsamples are generated. Second, a fit to a specific distribution is carried out for each of the truncation points, following the single-loss approximation method, and the significance under Anderson–Darling and Kolmogorov–Smirnov tests is calculated. These two values are plotted versus the truncation points, versus the truncation points in log scale or versus the number of exceedances.

Figure 4.18 represents the GoF-by-threshold plot of a fitting sample using a lognormal. The Anderson–Darling plot is represented on the top and the Kolmogorov–Smirnov on the bottom. It can be observed that a maximum of 550 exceedances is required to obtain a high significance in the Anderson–Darling tests. Also, the GoF becomes completely unstable with few exceedances.

The analysis of GoF by threshold can be combined with the capital-stability-by-threshold plot to determine a threshold providing high significance regarding the fit and stability of capital estimates. Figure 4.19 shows both analyses implemented over the

Figure 4.18 GoF-by-threshold plot

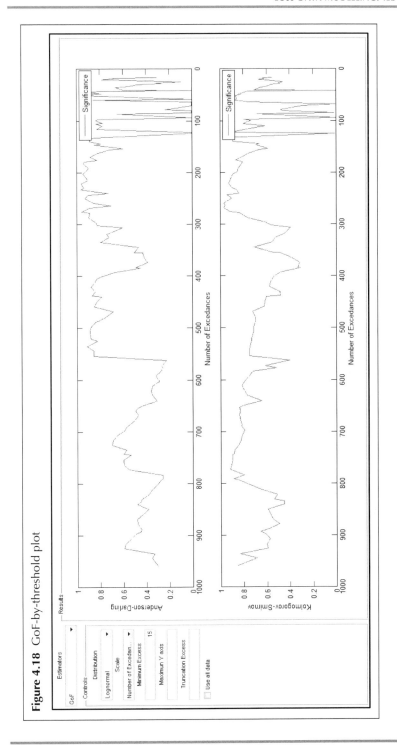

Figure 4.19 Combined analysis of GoF and capital stability analysis by threshold

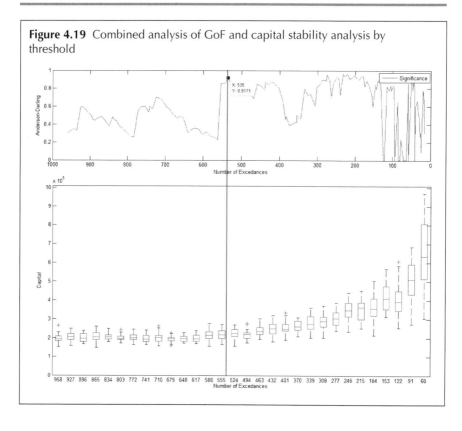

same loss sample. It can be observed that the threshold at 535 exceedances provides both high significance under Anderson–Darling and reasonable capital stability at the same point.

Splitting the distribution for modelling operational risk

As a result of the threshold determination, the ORC can be split into segments, mainly the body and the tail segments. Generally, the tail will be modelled with a fat tail shifted or left-truncated distribution (see "Shifted distributions" and "Truncated distributions" in Appendix 1), and the body with a light tail or empirical right-truncated distribution (see "Empirical distributions" in Appendix 1). It is also possible to split the distribution into various segments and have a low segment modelled with an empirical distribution, a middle segment for a light-tail double-truncated distribution (see "Truncated distributions in Appendix 1), and a high segment for a fat-tail left-truncated distribution.

Figure 4.20 shows a modelling of internal severity, where the low segment (between 1.000 and 79.789) was modelled with an empirical distribution, the medium with a light-tail lognormal with low σ and high μ, and the tail segment with a fat-tail Burr distribution.

SEVERITY DISTRIBUTION FITTING

Although observed losses could be directly used in a simulation process (see Appendix 1), the fitting of parametric distributions is required in order to correctly project from observed losses and estimate extreme tail losses determining operational risk capital. The BCSG-AMA states that, for selecting the probability distribution, "a bank should generally adhere to the following: Appropriate techniques for the estimation of the distributional parameters …" The section "Tail shape and threshold determination through extreme value theory" presents methods for determining an optimal distribution-fitting threshold and orienting the selection for either fat- or light-tail distributions. The analysis now turns into the proposed fitting methods to determine the parametric distributions that best correspond to the risk profile implicit in the empirical losses. The

Figure 4.20 Distribution split into several segments

Participation
Participation (%)   100

Currency   EUR

	Internal losses (low)	Internal losses (medium)	Internal losses (high)	Risk scenarios (medium)	Risk scenarios (high)	External data (medium)	External data (high)
Distribution #1	Lognormal	Lognormal	Burr				
Distribution #2	Undefined	Undefined	Undefined				
Mixture	1	1	1				
Parameter 1-1	7.971	5.489	0.007				
Parameter 1-2	2.072	1.503	1,311.896				
Parameter 1-3	0	0	1.371				
Parameter 1-4	0	0	0				
Parameter 2-1	0	0	0				
Parameter 2-2	0	0	0				
Parameter 2-3	0	0	0				
Parameter 2-4	0	0	0				
Frecuency	Poisson	Poisson	Poisson				
Parameter F-1	5,858	50.1	4.64				
Parameter F-2	0	0	0				
Sig A-D	0.957	0.007	0.683				
Sig K-S	0.994	0.452	0.921				

fitting methods should be applied consistently with the threshold and tail-weight conclusions derived from that section's analytical processes.

Also, the distribution choice should be suited to the quality and abundance of operational loss data. When loss data is abundant and of high quality, no prior assumptions of distribution type may be required and more distribution families are considered. In the case of limited data availability and/or quality, more restrictive assumptions should be taken using only the most common distribution in operational risk modelling (lognormal, Weibull and GPD, among others), and those with a limited number of parameters thus reducing the degrees of freedom in the modelling.

The distributions most typically used for operational risk modelling are parametric, truncated, shifted, mixtures and empirical. A detailed description of the characteristics and formulation of these distributions types can be found in Appendix 1.

The analysis now turns into the description of the fitting procedures for determining the most appropriate distributions and their parameters.

Moments method

The moments method allows us to determine the parameters of the distribution model by matching the moments from the observed losses. Generally, the moments of a parametric distribution can be expressed as a function of its parameters (see Table 4.3, which shows examples of moments expressed as a function of the distribution parameters). By calculating the moments from the observed losses, a system of equations can be defined from which to derive the distribution parameters.

It should be taken into consideration that the observed losses provide only a portion of the risk profile, often lacking the extreme events with which to truly model it. Therefore, moments calculated with observed losses will lack the information on such extreme events. It follows that the fitted distribution may also underestimate the potential losses faced by the institution and therefore the required capital. Additionally, the consistency between the distribution parameters and the moments derived from empirical losses is obtained only when the fitting threshold is zero. As explained earlier, modelling operational risk requires the definition of thresholds higher than zero.

Table 4.3 Summary of moments for relevant distributions in operational

Distribution	Mean	Variance	Skewness	Kurtosis
LogNormal	$e^{\mu+\sigma^2/2}$	$\left(e^{\sigma^2}-1\right)e^{2\mu+\sigma^2}$	$\left(e^{\sigma^2}+2\right)\sqrt{e^{\sigma^2}-1}$	$e^{4\sigma^2}+2e^{3\sigma^2}+3e^{2\sigma^2}-6$
Weibull	$\lambda\Gamma(1+1/k)$	$\lambda^2\Gamma(1+2/k)-\mu^2$	$\dfrac{\Gamma(1+3/k)\lambda^3-3\mu\sigma^2-\mu^3}{\sigma^3}$	$\dfrac{\lambda^4\Gamma\left(1+\frac{4}{k}\right)-4\gamma_1\sigma^3\mu-6\mu^2\sigma^2-\mu^4}{\sigma^4}$
Pareto	$\begin{cases}\infty & \text{for }\alpha\le 1\\ \dfrac{\alpha x_m}{\alpha-1} & \text{for }\alpha>1\end{cases}$	$\begin{cases}\infty & \text{for }\alpha\in(1,2]\\ \dfrac{x_m^2\alpha}{(\alpha-1)^2(\alpha-2)} & \text{for }\alpha>2\end{cases}$	$\dfrac{2(1+\alpha)}{\alpha-3}\sqrt{\dfrac{\alpha-2}{\alpha}}\ \text{for }\alpha>3$	$\dfrac{6\left(\alpha^3+\alpha^2-6\alpha-2\right)}{\alpha(\alpha-3)(\alpha-4)}\ \text{for }\alpha>4$

Figure 4.21 Representation of MLE fits

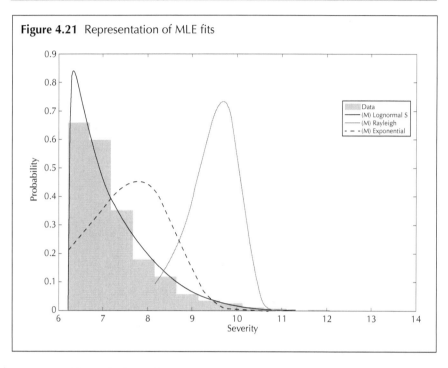

Nevertheless, the moments method results can be useful as a starting seed for mathematical optimisation-based fitting processes. If used, the optimisation converges more rapidly and the solution may be closer to an absolute maximum.

Maximum-likelihood estimator

Maximum Likelihood Estimation (MLE) is a statistical technique that allows obtaining the parameters of a parametric distribution that bets fit to a random sample of data. MLE proceeds to maximising a likelihood function as this in turn maximises the agreement between model and data. That is, it must be maximised:

$$L = \prod_{i=1}^{n} f(x_i \mid \theta),$$

where $f(x_i \mid \theta)$ is the probability density function and θ is the set of parameters. In practice, it is more efficient to maximise the log-likelihood function, since the product is transformed into a summation:

$$\log(L) = \sum_{i=1}^{n} \log(f(x_i \mid \theta))$$

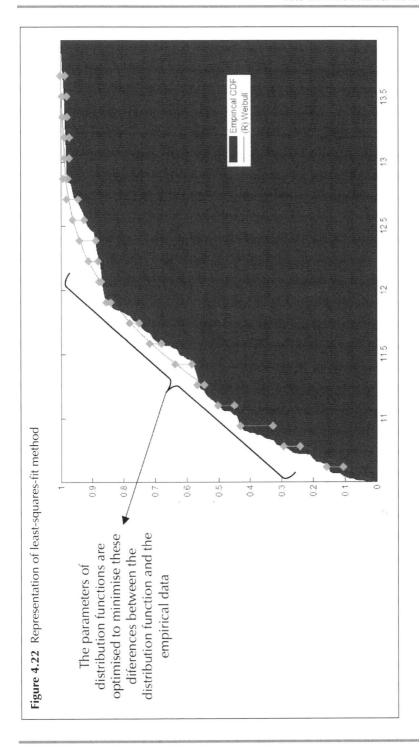

Figure 4.22 Representation of least-squares-fit method

The parameters of distribution functions are optimised to minimise these diferences between the distribution function and the empirical data

MLE requires the implementation of a mathematical optimization algorithm (see Appendix 3) to look for the parameters which maximises the L value.

Figure 4.21 illustrates a well-fitting lognormal distribution whose probability density function explains the majority of the histogram and maximises MLE product. On the other hand, the Rayleigh and exponential distribution probability density function can explain only a small portion of the histogram of the input data.

MLE presents desirable mathematical properties, including consistency, asymptotic normality, efficiency and second-order efficiency after correction for bias (see Schervish 1995).

Least squares
Least squares (LS) seeks to minimise the squared differences between the observed and theoretical distributions. The sum of the square differences will be minimal when the difference between the theoretical and observed distributions is also minimal. The fact that differences are squared makes the fit to focus on the large discrepancies.

Thus, the aim is to minimise (see Appendix 3) the value of the function:

$$\sum_{i=1}^{n}\left(F^*(x_i)-F(x_i)\right)^2,$$

where F is the theoretical cumulative probability function and F^* is the observed cumulative probability function. Figure 4.22 represents the differences between the theoretical, a Weibull distribution and the observed distributions represented as the blue area, which are minimised by the MS method while determining the parameters of the parametric distribution.

Probability-weighted least-squares-fit method
The probability-weighted least-squares-fit (WLS) method is a variant of the LS method. The variation is on the weightings of the differences between the observed and parametric distributions. These weightings vary according to how close the observation is to the distribution tail. The weight of the differences can be adjusted by changing the powers of the equation below. This procedure allows to better fit areas of the distribution selected by the user,

generally to focus the fit on tail observations determining capital requirements.

This method finds the distribution parameters minimising (see Appendix 3) the value of the following function:

$$\sum_{i=1}^{n} \frac{\left(F^{*}(x_{i}) - F(x)\right)^{2}}{\left(F^{*}(x_{i})\right)^{p} \left(1 - F^{*}(x_{i})\right)^{m}}$$

The weighting of the differences, $\left(F^{*}(x_{i}) - F(x)\right)^{2}$, can be regulated by adjusting the parameters "p" and "m" in order to increase the influence of data in the right or left tail or in the mid-range of the distribution, improving the fit at the distribution points most relevant for the desired calculations. Observe that the weights of the differences, $1/\left(F^{*}(x_{i})\right)^{p}\left(1 - F^{*}(x_{i})\right)^{m}$, are similar to those in formulation used in the Anderson–Darling goodness-of-fit test (see "Goodness-of-fit evaluation" below). However, in the probability-weighted least-squares method, powers are applied to the weighting to increase the focus on the tails as desired.

Figure 4.23 represents the differences between the theoretical cumulative probability function, a Burr distribution line, and the observed or empirical cumulative distribution function, the solid area. The figure on the left represents the weights to the differences as they increase based on p=0 and m=1, ie, $w_{i} = 1/\left(1 - F^{*}(x_{i})\right)$ set to focus the fit on the distribution tail.

The use of WLS can help to respond to the views expressed in the BCSG-AMA when it notes that a bank should generally adhere to: "Appropriate diagnostic tools for evaluating the quality of the fit of the distributions to the data, giving preference to those most sensitive to the tail."

Figure 4.24 shows how the WLS-fitted distribution enhances the precision of the fit in the tail data, while the MLE fit is further away from the perfect prediction line at the same points. It also shows how the absolute differences between the moments of the MLE and WLS distributions with respect to the data captured are minor.

A precise modelling of tail events is important, since these are the events that determine the capital required (as a general rule, it can be said that 1% of the events may determine up to 90% of the capital).

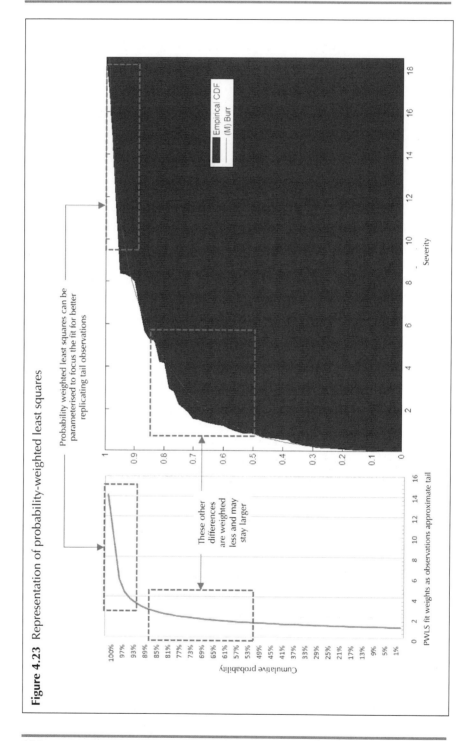

Figure 4.23 Representation of probability-weighted least squares

Robust least-squares (RLS) fit

The robust least-squares (RLS) fitting method (DuMouchel and O'Brien 1989) focuses the fit on those observations, better fitting the overall theoretical distribution, thus reducing the influence of those observations being potential anomalies. By the random nature of distributions, some observations, particularly those in the tail, may not fit the overall theoretical distribution, due to their random location, and may introduce distortions in the fitting process. Also, ORCs are the aggregation of losses stemming from heterogonous processes and some loss observation, coming from a low-frequency loss process, may have a different nature and fall out of the global model. RLS allows us to focus the fit into the global model, reducing distortions in the fitting optimisation process and providing us, in many instances, with a better fit as measured by a higher GoF.

BCSG-AMA explicitly mentions robust methods when it says, "Robust estimation methods (such as alternatives to classical methods as the Maximum Likelihood and the Probability Weighted Moments), proposed recently in operational risk literature, are reasonably efficient under small deviations from the assumed model."

The RLS method is an iterative process. It starts by giving all observations the same weight to obtain a first fitted distribution, ie, we use the standard LS approach. With the first fit, the initial differences between the fitted distribution and the empirical data are determined. A new fit is then produced by giving the fit errors, by observation, a weight inversely proportional to the errors determined in the first fit. The result is a new fitted distribution with new differences between the fitted distribution and the empirical data. Various iterations are performed until the fitting process converges and new iterations do not provide significant improvements to the fit.

Mathematically, the RLS method seeks to iteratively minimise the function:

$$\sum_{i=1}^{n}\left(F^{*}(x_{i}) - F(x_{i})\right)^{2} w_{i} \, ,$$

where w_i is inversely proportional to the fit error of the previous fitting iteration.

Figure 4.25, illustrates where RLS will focus the fit. Larger differences will be given a minor weight (inversely proportional to the

Figure 4.24 QQ plot differences between the WLS and MLE fits

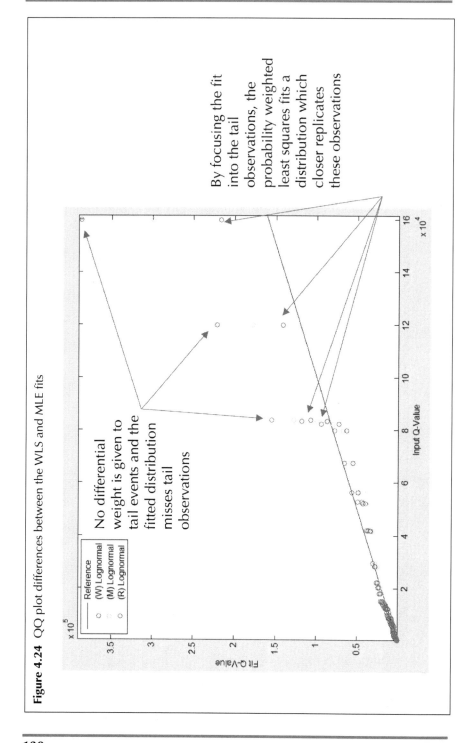

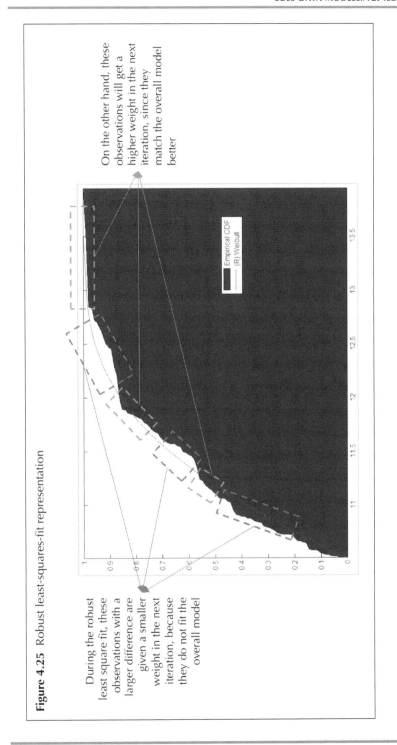

Figure 4.25 Robust least-squares-fit representation

During the robust least square fit, these observations with a larger difference are given a smaller weight in the next iteration, because they do not fit the overall model

On the other hand, these observations will get a higher weight in the next iteration, since they match the overall model better

Empirical CDF
(R) Weibull

error of the fit) to strengthen the fit of the observations that better fit the overall model.

RLS can be particularly useful in fat-tail distributions, when tails are scarcely populated. In fact, in these circumstances, the location of tail observations is mostly random and may distort the fitting results. Therefore, the p-value of the fit can be improved when it is concentrated in those parts of the distribution that match more precisely the overall data sample .

Figure 4.26 clearly shows how the RLS has increased the fit error on a tail observation that was presented as an outlier. However, the fit improved very significantly in the rest of the observations.

Time-weighted least squares

The modelling of operational risk internal data requires the use of loss data over several years. In fact, the Basel Committee mentions a minimum requirement of five years of data and an initial regulatory approval can be obtained only with three years of data.

However, note that, over a period of five years, the control infrastructure and business environment of an institution evolves, making the oldest internal loss data less relevant for the representation of the institutional current risk profile. Indeed, with the introduction and advance of the operational risk management programme, the size and frequencies of operational losses and the risk profile of the institution should change.

Therefore, a process for providing more influence to the newest, rather than the oldest, data could help to promote a more up-to-date risk profile model. In fact, supervisors frequently require institutions to adjust for age of data in the capital model.

This can be achieved by giving differential weights to the data, based on its age, for use in the calculation of cumulative probabilities. This is consistent with giving more probability to the more recent losses. The cumulative probabilities are then fed into the distribution fitting process to estimate the model accordingly.

The calculation of weighted cumulative probabilities may be performed as follows:

❏ Loss observations are ordered in size, from small to large.
❏ Loss observations are given a weight based on the relevancy of time periods. These weights should also take into consideration how loss frequencies evolve with time.

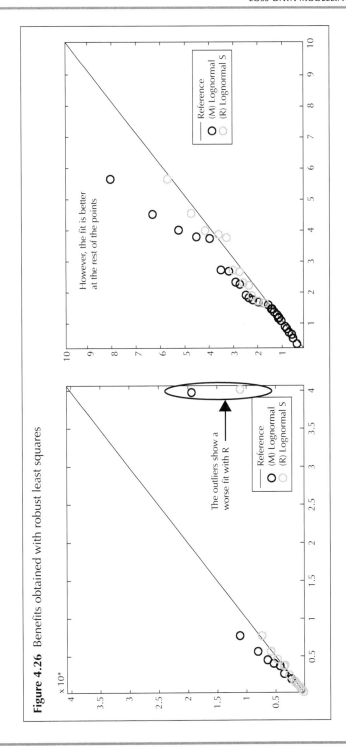

Figure 4.26 Benefits obtained with robust least squares

Table 4.4 Time-weighted least squares for discrete time periods

	Year of occurance	Distribution fitting data		Weight based on relevance	Probability of a random draw	
		Quantile	Percentile			
Historical loss 2	2012	0.02	6.67	1	4.44%	draw probability form 0.01 0.02
Historical loss 3	2011	0.08	8.89	0.5	2.22%	draw probability form 0.02 0.08
Historical loss 4	2011	0.09	11.11	0.5	2.22%	draw probability form 0.08 0.09
Historical loss 5	2011	0.24	13.33	0.5	2.22%	draw probability form 0.09 0.24
Historical loss 6	2012	0.63	17.78	1	4.44%	draw probability form 0.24 0.63
Historical loss 7	2012	0.77	22.22	1	4.44%	draw probability form 0.63 0.77
Historical loss 8	2011	0.91	24.44	0.5	2.22%	draw probability form 0.77 0.91
Historical loss 9	2011	0.91	26.67	0.5	2.22%	draw probability form 0.91 0.91
Historical loss 10	2011	1.08	28.89	0.5	2.22%	draw probability form 0.91 1.08
Historical loss 11	2012	1.22	33.33	1	4.44%	draw probability form 1.08 1.22
Historical loss 12	2011	1.73	35.56	0.5	2.22%	draw probability form 1.22 1.73
Historical loss 13	2012	3.19	40.00	1	4.44%	draw probability form 1.73 3.19
Historical loss 14	2012	3.43	44.44	1	4.44%	draw probability form 3.19 3.43
Historical loss 15	2011	4.93	46.67	0.5	2.22%	draw probability form 3.43 4.93
Historical loss 16	2012	5.04	51.11	1	4.44%	draw probability form 4.93 5.04
Historical loss 17	2011	6.72	53.33	0.5	2.22%	draw probability form 5.04 6.72
Historical loss 18	2012	7.12	57.78	1	4.44%	draw probability form 6.72 7.12
Historical loss 19	2011	8.12	60.00	0.5	2.22%	draw probability form 7.12 8.12
Historical loss 20	2011	8.55	62.22	0.5	2.22%	draw probability form 8.12 8.55
Historical loss 21	2012	9.35	66.67	1	4.44%	draw probability form 8.55 9.35
Historical loss 22	2012	9.76	71.11	1	4.44%	draw probability form 9.35 9.76
Historical loss 23	2011	10.63	73.33	0.5	2.22%	draw probability form 9.76 10.63
Historical loss 24	2012	11.89	77.78	1	4.44%	draw probability form 10.63 11.89
Historical loss 25	2011	13.09	80.00	0.5	2.22%	draw probability form 11.89 13.09
Historical loss 26	2012	22.16	84.44	1	4.44%	draw probability form 13.09 22.16
Historical loss 27	2012	23.49	88.89	1	4.44%	draw probability form 22.16 23.49
Historical loss 28	2011	26.23	91.11	0.5	2.22%	draw probability form 23.49 26.23
Historical loss 29	2011	32.44	93.33	0.5	2.22%	draw probability form 26.23 32.44
Historical loss 30	2012	38.35	97.78	1	4.44%	draw probability form 32.44 38.35
		Inf	100.00		2.22%	draw probability form 38.35 to Inf

❑ The percentile corresponding to each loss observation is calculated based on the assigned weights consistently with the method in Appendix A1, "Empirical distributions".

Table 4.4 includes 30 losses whose date of occurrence was either 2011 or 2012 ordered from smallest to largest. It is determined that losses from 2012 should carry twice as much influence in the fit. Therefore, losses from 2012 are given a weight of 1 and those from 2011 are given a weight of 0.5. Then, the percentiles for the losses are calculated following the percentile formula above and can now be fed into a fitting process, as explained earlier. If, following this procedure, a resampling of an empirical distribution is used (rather than fitting a parametric distribution), the resulting distribution will contain twice as many observations from 2012 as from 2011 and, again, losses from 2012 will have twice as much influence as those from 2011, as desired.

If loss samples from years 2011 and 2012 had different numbers of observations, adjustments proportional to that number of observations should be introduced into the weights, if the aim is that the sample from 2012 has twice as much influence in the fit as that of 2011. In this case, the weight of each sample could be calculated in the following way:

$$w_{2012} = \frac{Desired\ Influence\ for\ 2012\ Sample}{Number\ of\ 2012\ Loss\ Observations}$$

$$w_{2011} = \frac{1 - Desired\ Influence\ for\ 2012\ Sample}{Number\ of\ 2011\ Loss\ Observations}$$

This procedure can be generalised to k segments based, eg, on their age and desired influence, and weights can be calculated as follows:

$$w_i = \frac{Desired\ Influence\ for\ Period\ i}{Number\ of\ Observations\ in\ Period\ i}$$

$$\sum_{n}^{i=1} w_i = 1$$

For instance, Figure 4.27 illustrates a case with three periods. The set of data from 2012 is given 50% of the total weight in the fit. That from 2011 is given 30%. The rest of the weight is given to observations from 2010, 20%.

Figure 4.27 Time-weighed fitting example

		Severity	Date	Severity	Date	Severity	Date
Erase Data / >> Data 1	1	1983.909091	31/12/2012	1270.090909	31/12/2011	2080.210000	31/12/2010
Erase Data / >> Data 2	2	13447.823636	31/12/2012	769.172727	31/12/2011	581.378182	31/12/2010
Erase Data / >> Data 3	3	1335.454545	31/12/2012	552.315455	31/12/2011	607.845455	31/12/2010
Erase Data / >> Data 4	4	3824.300000	31/12/2012	1761.403636	31/12/2011	2920.559091	31/12/2010
Erase Data / >> Data 5	5	3680.590909	31/12/2012	545.454545	31/12/2011	677.229091	31/12/2010
Erase Data / >> Data 6	6	627.289091	31/12/2012	890.097273	31/12/2011	1024.414545	31/12/2010
	7	3401.272727	31/12/2012	11700.000000	31/12/2011	15667.272727	30/12/2010
Time Decay	8	1236.363636	31/12/2012	526.631818	31/12/2011	1941.090909	30/12/2010
☐ Use time decay	9	2132.175455	31/12/2012	1036.363636	31/12/2011	2096.287273	30/12/2010
Factor formulation	10	2375.149091	31/12/2012	581.818182	31/12/2011	5000.000000	30/12/2010
0.97^t	11	555.681818	31/12/2012	690.909091	31/12/2011	886.045455	30/12/2010
t (days)	12	856.247273	31/12/2012	6617.299091	31/12/2011	902.556364	30/12/2010
90	13	621.658182	31/12/2012	1910.127273	31/12/2011	1541.579091	30/12/2010

Probabilidades

Data 1	Data 2	Data 3	Data 4	Data 5	Data 6
0.5	0.3	0.2	0.0	0.0	0.0

Model Exit

This method allows for the use of a decay factor δ as a function of the age of the observations, as often used in market risk calculations of correlations and volatilities, adjusting the loss observation weights accordingly. Table 4.5 shows weights calculated with a decay factor of 0.97 to the power of the number of quarters (three-month period) since the date of the newest observed data. Generically, it can be expressed as δ^t, for $\delta \in [0,1]$ and t is the number of time periods since the last observed loss. The determination of an appropriate δ can be achieved through backtesting as explained in Chapter 9 under the heading "Operational risk backtesting", and identify δ values that maximise predictability. Decay factors used in market risk calculations are not valid references, as the risk level in capital markets may change much more quickly and unexpectedly than it does in operational risk.

Table 4.5 Time-weighted fitting with decay factor

	Date of Occurance	Distribution Fitting Data		Weight based on relevance	Probability of a random draw	
		Quantile	Percentile			
Historical loss 2	Apr-12	0.02	4.55	0.862	3.47%	sampling probability form 0.01 0.02
Historical loss 3	Mar-11	0.08	7.30	0.685	2.76%	sampling probability form 0.02 0.08
Historical loss 4	Nov-11	0.09	10.50	0.794	3.19%	sampling probability form 0.08 0.09
Historical loss 5	Dec-12	0.24	14.50	0.996	4.01%	sampling probability form 0.09 0.24
Historical loss 6	Apr-12	0.63	17.96	0.859	3.45%	sampling probability form 0.24 0.63
Historical loss 7	Sep-11	0.77	21.01	0.760	3.06%	sampling probability form 0.63 0.77
Historical loss 8	Jan-12	0.91	24.33	0.826	3.32%	sampling probability form 0.77 0.91
Historical loss 9	Nov-11	0.91	27.51	0.790	3.18%	sampling probability form 0.91 0.91
Historical loss 10	Jul-11	1.08	30.50	0.744	2.99%	sampling probability form 0.91 1.08
Historical loss 11	Oct-11	1.22	33.65	0.782	3.15%	sampling probability form 1.08 1.22
Historical loss 12	Feb-12	1.73	37.01	0.836	3.36%	sampling probability form 1.22 1.73
Historical loss 13	Jul-12	3.19	40.68	0.911	3.67%	sampling probability form 1.73 3.19
Historical loss 14	Oct-11	3.43	43.81	0.779	3.13%	sampling probability form 3.19 3.43
Historical loss 15	Jun-12	4.93	47.40	0.892	3.59%	sampling probability form 3.43 4.93
Historical loss 16	Jul-11	5.04	50.36	0.736	2.96%	sampling probability form 4.93 5.04
Historical loss 17	Mar-11	6.72	53.11	0.685	2.76%	sampling probability form 5.04 6.72
Historical loss 18	Feb-12	7.12	56.47	0.833	3.35%	sampling probability form 6.72 7.12
Historical loss 19	Dec-12	8.12	60.42	0.984	3.96%	sampling probability form 7.12 8.12
Historical loss 20	Jun-12	8.55	64.03	0.896	3.61%	sampling probability form 8.12 8.55
Historical loss 21	Nov-11	9.35	67.19	0.787	3.16%	sampling probability form 8.55 9.35
Historical loss 22	Jun-12	9.76	70.78	0.892	3.59%	sampling probability form 9.35 9.76
Historical loss 23	Jan-12	10.63	74.09	0.822	3.31%	sampling probability form 9.76 10.63
Historical loss 24	Nov-12	11.89	78.01	0.976	3.93%	sampling probability form 10.63 11.89
Historical loss 25	Dec-11	13.09	81.23	0.801	3.22%	sampling probability form 11.89 13.09
Historical loss 26	Aug-12	22.16	84.94	0.922	3.71%	sampling probability form 13.09 22.16
Historical loss 27	Dec-11	23.49	88.20	0.810	3.26%	sampling probability form 22.16 23.49
Historical loss 28	May-12	26.23	91.72	0.875	3.52%	sampling probability form 23.49 26.23
Historical loss 29	Mar-11	32.44	94.47	0.684	2.75%	sampling probability form 26.23 32.44
Historical loss 30	May-12	38.35	97.99	0.874	3.52%	sampling probability form 32.44 38.35
		Inf	100.00		2.01%	sampling probability form 38.35 to Inf

FREQUENCY DISTRIBUTION FITTING

The LDA, SBA and the HM in this document need a frequency estimation that represents the number of loss events that will happen
over the capital calculation time horizon. In high percentiles of fat-
tail-distributed events in a frequency–severity model, such as
operational risk, the most influential feature of the frequency distribution will typically be its mean. Other characteristics related to the
shape of the frequency distribution (such as skewness and leptokurtosis) have a lesser impact on high percentiles of the aggregate
distribution. In fact, the single-loss approximation capital calculation
(see Chapter 8) is based on the fact that only the mean frequency will
impact on capital estimates. Also, the BCSG-AMA expresses similar
views when it states, "The choice of frequency distributions has a
lesser impact on the final outcome."

Therefore, it is reasonable to simplify the modelling of the
frequency and use a Poisson distribution assumption (see Apendix 1
for other common frequency distribution assumptions). As the
Poisson distribution has a single parameter, it is particularly
appealing in cases in which the event data is not known and modelling is based on the assumption that there is a set of events that have
occurred over a period of time. Given the reduced relevance of aged
operational loss data, the information generally available for the
modelling frequencies is limited. Thus, it is common that the information available is only sufficient for estimating the frequency mean.

When sufficient loss frequency information is available, other
frequency distributions may be used, such as the negative binomial
and geometric.

Frequency distribution fitting process

The frequency distribution fitting can be done following any of the
methods presented in the section "Severity distribution fitting",
applied to frequency samples. Given the limited number of observations and the focus on the distribution mean, the distribution method
is a possibility, as well as the rest of distribution fitting methods
presented above. Finally, as the sample used for the frequency is
determined by the sample used for severity (see later in this section),
frequency truncations do not apply. This implies that there is consistency between the moments calculated for the empirical and
parametric distributions.

It is also possible to increase the number of observations for fitting other multiparameter frequency distributions, by time bucketing into shorter periods (days, weeks, months and so on), thus increasing the information on the distribution shape. However, this introduces an additional issue: the need to correct for seasonality effects with, again, a reduced number for yearly observations.

The frequency fit can be performed as follows:

❑ Sample selection for the fit: The sample used for determining the frequency fit needs to be consistent with that used for the severity fit. This implies that the same threshold used in the severity fit should also be used for the frequency fit. Therefore, the frequency distribution calculated is that of the specific loss sample used for the severity fit.

❑ A time-bucketing format: This is selected to determine frequency per period – days, weeks, months, quarters or years. When the focus of the modelling is on the frequency mean, the time bucketing has little impact.

❑ Occurrence date of the loss sample: Based on this, loss frequencies are calculated by the time-bucketing selected. For instance, frequencies are calculated 30 days periods as shown in Figure 4.27. We can observe how frequencies per month have been calculated. Also, the frequency calculation period should be adjusted to the observation period, particularly when low-frequency events are modelled, rather than just derived from the dates of the first and the observed losses. There might be some time buckets at the beginning or end of the observation period that do not have any observation due to the low frequency of the losses. If fact, this situation is typical of the modelling of tail observations that have a much lower frequency, and capital estimates are particularly sensitive to them. If frequency calculation initial and final dates are not adjusted to the observation period, frequency will be exaggerated with a corresponding increase in capital estimations.

❑ Frequency observations: Then, these are fed into a fitting process to derive a parametric distribution that best matches the observed data. Any of the fitting processes described in the section "Frequency distribution fitting" can be used to derive the frequency distribution. If a time-weighted least squares has been

Figure 4.28 Frequency fitting sample

	Initial date		10/05/2009
	Final date		06/05/2013

	Date	Data
1	05/2009	1
2	06/2009	6
3	07/2009	6
4	08/2009	6
5	09/2009	5
6	10/2009	13
7	11/2009	7
8	12/2009	13
9	01/2010	9
10	02/2010	11
11	03/2010	22
12	04/2010	12
13	05/2010	20
14	06/2010	19
15	07/2010	30
16	08/2010	21
17	09/2010	29

used to determine the severity distribution, it can also be used in the frequency determination for consistency. As explained, given the reduced size of the data sample generally available and the focus of the modelling, the moments method is also a possibility, in addition to the rest of distribution fitting methods presented above.

❏ Distribution parameters: These are rescaled, from the time-bucketing horizon, to the time horizon of the capital calculation.

Figure 4.29 shows the frequency fit for the Poisson, geometric and negative binomial distributions, although only the Poisson is represented in the histogram. The time bucketing was performed by month. All numerical and graphical GoF analyses described in the section "Goodness-of-fit evaluation" for severity fits (K–S, PP plot and so forth) apply to frequency fits. However, since the emphasis of the frequency fit is more focused on the distribution mean than on its shape, the GoF analysis is less relevant, as GoF focuses on the distribution shape.

Figure 4.29 Frequency distribution fitting

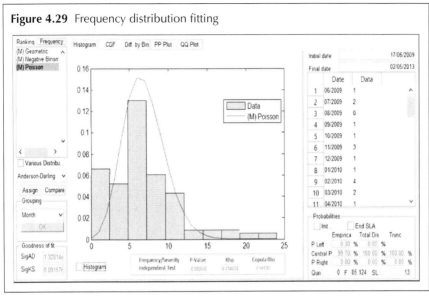

Figure 4.30 Frequency time trend analysis and projection

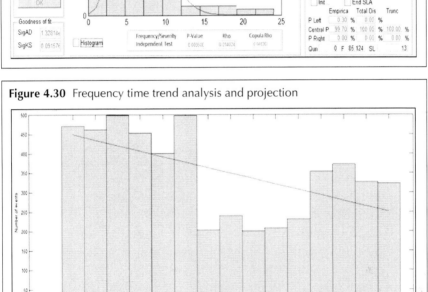

Projecting the time evolution of frequencies

Loss frequencies will be immediately sensitive to business factors, external environment, internal control effectiveness, etc. For instance, an increase in business activity may cause an immediate increase in the operational risk frequencies of the organisation. On the other hand, the implementation of a solid operational risk management framework should have an impact on the loss frequency levels. These changes in frequencies may have a direct impact on capital estimations.

Therefore, an analysis of the loss frequency evolution may add significant value to the modelling, helping to evaluate whether the frequency's long historical average represents the institution's current risk profile.

As an example, observe in Figure 4.30 a clear descending frequency level over a period of time. If the trend is robust, it may help to conclude that future operational risk loss frequency might also be lower. If adjustments are introduced into the modelling, frequency trends need to be analysed consistently with the thresholds introduced into the severity fitting.

GOODNESS-OF-FIT EVALUATION

Once a parametric distribution has been fitted to the empirical loss data, it becomes necessary to evaluate how well the fitted distribution replicates the empirical loss data. GoF is a measure of how closely the fitted distribution replicates the empirical data and should be one of the main criteria used in selecting the final modelling assumptions.

BCSG-AMA mentions the need to evaluate the adequateness of the fit when mentioning that "A bank should assess the quality of fit between the data and the selected distribution. The tools typically adopted for this purpose are graphical methods (which visualise the difference between the empirical and theoretical functions) and quantitative methods, based on goodness-of-fit tests. In selecting these tools, a bank should give preference to graphical methods and goodness-of-fit tests that are more sensitive to the tail than to the body of the data (eg, the Anderson–Darling upper tail test)."

GoF alone does not always provide the answer as to which distribution best describes the implicit risk profile in the empirical losses. In fact, it is frequently the case that there are several distributions with sufficiently high and similar GoF, making the selection of the final model far from obvious. In practice, GoF must be combined with other criteria (such as stability of capital results, realism of losses predictions and so forth, as explained below) to select the best modelling assumptions.

GoF numerical tests such as Anderson–Darling, Kolmogorov–Smirnov and Cramér–von Mises can be linked to a p-value, from 0 to

1. Note that the p-value provides us with an absolute measure of having an adequate fit, rather than simply ranking distributions from better to worse.

The p-value is the probability of finding a more extreme sample than the one being used to perform the hypothesis test, concerning:

❏ H_1: the fitted distribution is the function actually generating the losses; and
❏ H_0: the fitted distribution is not the function actually generating the losses.

The p-value is not strictly a measure of the similarities between two distributions but rather a measure of the likelihood of there being two identical distributions. In fact, when there is a high number of observations from two nonidentical but extremely similar distributions, an Anderson–Darling test can still deliver a low p-value. The reason for this is that the information contained in this high number of observations leads to the conclusion that the two distributions are actually not identical. Nevertheless, p-values may be used as one initial selection criterion to be later combined with other analysis, such as the QQ and PP plots and stability of capital results, for the final selection.

The GoF value will typically depend not only on the fit quality but also the amount of data on the sample. When operational risk data is not complete or the loss data collection criteria are not applied consistently across the organisation, it becomes difficult to obtain a high GoF. In fact, fitting distributions to the collected loss data may act as an *ex post* evaluation of the quality of the collection process. If the fitted parametric distributions do not deliver a high GoF, the completeness of the collection and implementation of a consistent operational loss definition should be reviewed across the organisation.

GoF numerical tests analyse the differences between observed ($F^*(x)$) and fitted distribution ($F(x)$) functions. Their formulation is based on the difference, $F^*(x) - F(x)$, at each of the available observed losses, as represented in Figure 4.31.

The following subsections describe the calculations used for the main GoF tests employed in operational risk modelling.

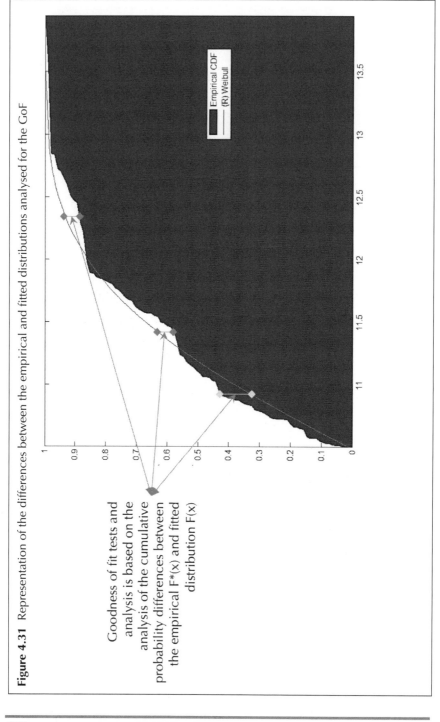

Figure 4.31 Representation of the differences between the empirical and fitted distributions analysed for the GoF

Goodness of fit tests and analysis is based on the analysis of the cumulative probability differences between the empirical $F^*(x)$ and fitted distribution $F(x)$

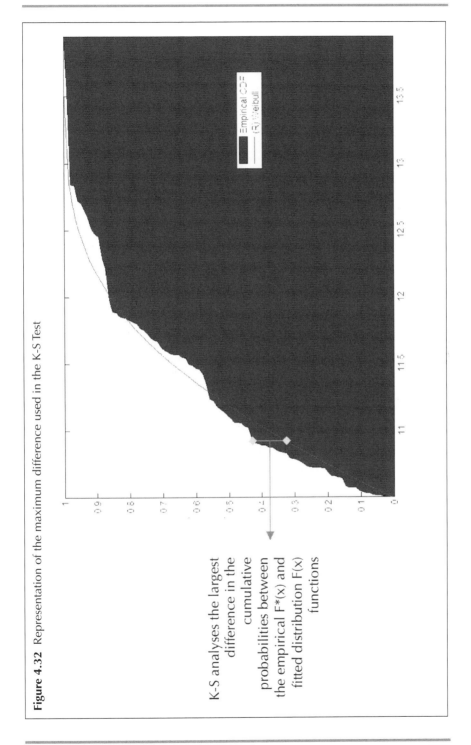

Figure 4.32 Representation of the maximum difference used in the K-S Test

K-S analyses the largest difference in the cumulative probabilities between the empirical F*(x) and fitted distribution F(x) functions

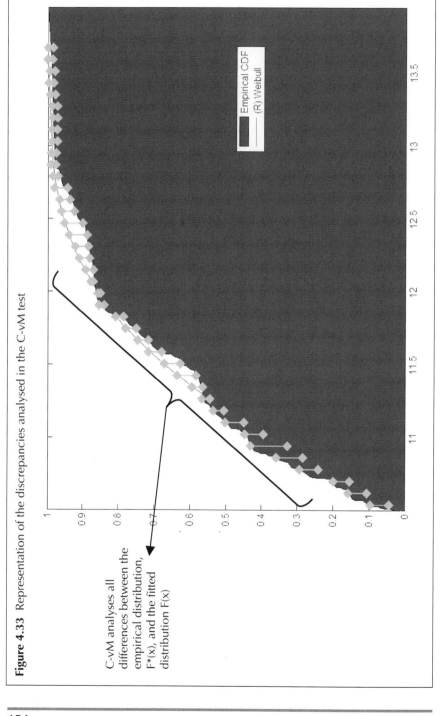

Figure 4.33 Representation of the discrepancies analysed in the C-vM test

C-vM analyses all differences between the empirical distribution, F*(x), and the fitted distribution F(x)

Figure 4.34 Representation of the discrepancies analysed by the A-D test

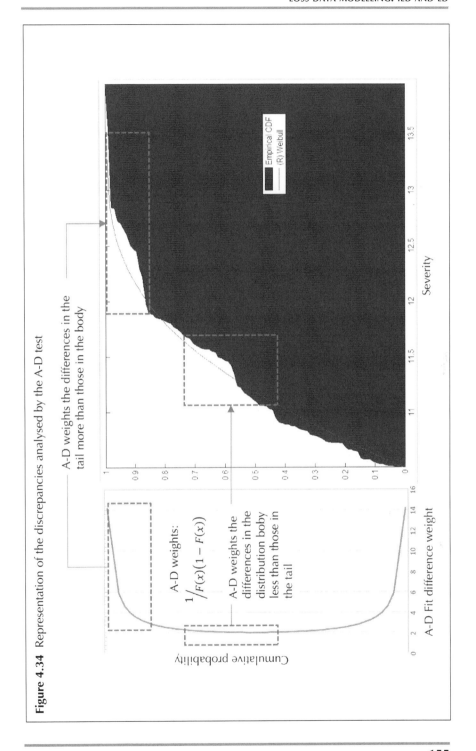

Kolmogorov–Smirnov (K–S)

The K–S test is based on the maximum difference between the cumulative observed and theoretical distributions in order to evaluate goodness of fit, ie:

$$K - S = Max\left(\left\|F^*(x) - F(x)\right\|\right)$$

As the maximum absolute difference tends to be in the mid-range of the distribution, the test focuses on the evaluation of the distribution body fit. In fact, the absolute value of cumulative probabilities in the tail is, by definition, small and unlikely to produce a significant absolute difference. Finally, as K–S is calculated based on the single largest discrepancy, it can be particularly sensitive to a single distribution anomaly, creating a large discrepancy between the fitted and observed distributions. Figure 4.32 represents the largest loss used by K–S to evaluate the GoF in an example.

The criterion is that a high K–S value indicates a high p-value (Corder and Foreman 2009), which means that there is no evidence to reject the null hypothesis. Observe that in our case, the null hypothesis is that the distribution of the fitting sample is not the one we are testing.

Cramér–von Mises

The C–vM is based on the square integral of the differences between the cumulative observed and theoretical distribution functions:

$$C - vM = \int_{-\infty}^{+\infty}\left(F^*(x) - F(x)\right)^2 dF(x)$$

This test considers all of the differences between the observed and theoretical distributions, instead of the maximal one, see Figure 4.33. The use of the square integral penalises the large differences. As with the K–S test, it tends to evaluate more the fit in the centre of the distribution and not in the tails, as the absolute cumulative probabilities discrepancies in the tail tend to be small. In practical terms, the C–vM and K–S tests provide very similar GoF results with similar p-values (Gibbons and Chakraborti 1992).

Anderson–Darling (A–D)

The A–D test weighs the differences based on proximity to the distribution tails, ie:

$$A - D = n \int_{-\infty}^{+\infty} \frac{\left(F^*(x) - F(x)\right)^2}{F(x)\left(1 - F(x)\right)} dF(x)$$

This test improves the evaluation of the tail adjustment, as the weighting of differences increases as a function of $1/F(x)(1 - f(x)$. A-D is mentioned by BCSG-AMA: "In selecting these tools, a bank should give preference to graphical methods and goodness-of-fit tests that are more sensitive to the tail than to the body of the data (e.g. the Anderson–Darling upper tail test)."

Figure 4.34 illustrates how the weight of the differences changes as it gets closer to the tail.

This test is generally more demanding than K–S or K–vM. A high value indicates a high p-value (Marsaglia and Marsaglia 2004) of rejecting the null hypothesis. Thus, the fitted distribution represents the observed losses well.

Other selection methods

When fitting a model it is relatively easy to increase the p-value by increasing the number of parameters in the model. However, doing so may result in overfitting problems. BCSG-AMA explicitly mentions similar concerns when it says,

> Moreover, the results of the goodness-of-fit tests are usually sensitive to the sample size and the number of parameters estimated. In such cases, a bank should consider selection methods that use the relative performance of the distributions at different confidence levels. Examples of selection methods may include the Likelihood Ratio, the Schwarz Bayesian Criterion and the Violation Ratio.

The Schwarz Bayesian criterion (SBC) provides an analysis of GoF, adjusted to the degrees of freedom of the distribution function and the number of data points in the fit. Its definition is:

$$SBC = n \times \ln\left(\sigma^2\right) + k \times \ln\left(n\right),$$

where n is number of data points used in the fit, σ^2 is their variance and k is number of parameters of the distribution function.

Although SBC cannot be easily linked to a p-value to evaluate whether to reject or not the null hypothesis, it can be used, in combination with other GoF tests, to rank the distributions. Those distributions with a reasonable p-value can be ranked according to SBC to select the final modelling assumptions.

Figure 4.35 Discrepancies and violation ratio

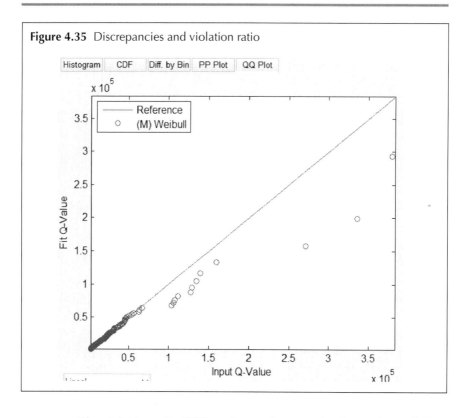

The violation ratio (VR) can be used as a method to evaluate GoF in different confidence levels of the distribution. It measures the difference between the expected number of occurrences in the fitted and empirical distributions. In principle, a perfect violation ration evaluation is 1, because in both cases there are the same numbers of events beyond the selected percentile, for both the empirical and the fitted distribution. When the ratio is above 1, it means that the fitted distribution is overestimating the empirical loss data and vice versa. The definition of the violation ratio is $VR = n_v/n$, where n is the number of expected violations and n_v are the actual number of violations.

However, the VR ignores the size of the over/underestimation and whether the violation is happening close to or far from the distribution tail, which is a main concern in capital modelling. In fact, it is perfectly possible to have a good violation ratio in a distribution that fits very well its body and systematically misses the tail. This situation is quite usual, as the fitting process minimises the overall differences and may compensate discrepancies in the tail with other discrepancies in the body. It is very common in ORCs to have a clearly differentiated tail behaviour and see that discrepancies are more common in the tail, and of a much larger size. Figure 4.35 shows an example of this circumstance where the dotted line of the QQ plot are below the straight, central diagonal line of perfect prediction. It can be observed how the Weibull distribution matches the perfect prediction line in the lower severity values of the empirical distribution. However, it shows an underestimation pattern of the severity values on the tail possibly resulting in an underestimation of capital requirements.

In fact, in the case above, the VR will generally suggest that the distribution is overestimating, as it ignores the size and location of violations. In fact, some large violations can be offset, during the fit, by multiple small violations of the opposite value.

For the measurement of the discrepancies in different confidence levels of the distribution, we also propose two other methods: the QQ error evaluation and the PP error evaluation. They are based on numerical analysis over the QQ and PP plots (see below), and can be used to compare the discrepancies of the distributions in the size of the discrepancies rather than on their frequency. A second advantage is that they permit us to focus the analysis above a specific percentile on the tail. These two tests can be applied in conjunction with A–D and K–S in order to further discriminate in distributions with a sufficiently high p-value.

The QQ error evaluation and the PP error evaluation analysis is performed by comparing the probabilities ($F^*(x_i)$ and $F(x_i)$) and quantiles (x_i and $F^{-1}(F^*(x_i))$) of the empirical and theoretical distribution, and focusing the analysis on the tail, which determines capital, thus evaluating the GoF at multiple confidence intervals. Indeed, we consider:

Evaluation of probabilities (p-p):

$$PP\_error = \sum_{i=M-N}^{M} \frac{1}{N}\left|1 - \frac{F^*(x_i)}{F(x_i)}\right|,$$

Evaluation of quantiles (q-q):

$$QQ\_error = \sum_{i=M-N}^{M} \frac{1}{N}\left|1 - \frac{x_i}{F^{-1}(F^*(x_i))}\right|,$$

where M is the total number of data observed, N is the threshold above which the differences will be evaluated, x_i is the i-th observed data ordered from small to large, and F^{-1} is the inverse of the cumulative probability function.

Figure 4.36 shows how the QQ error evaluation will measure the discrepancies and how can it be focused into a specific percentile of the distribution, to focus the analysis on the tail, determining the capital estimation.

These methods have problems when applied to data with few observations or when a very high percentile has been selected. In these cases, the amount of data may not be sufficient to provide a reliable result. For example, with few empirical observations available, any discrepancy in the violation ratio leads to a figure far from 1.

Finally, we mention the likelihood ratio. The likelihood ratio test (LRT) compares the likelihood function of the parameters estimated under a fit process with the likelihood function of the null hypothesis, and determines whether it is likely that the sample belongs to the population characterised by the true parameters. The LRT is defined as:

$$LR(x) = \frac{\sup\left(L(x;\theta_0)\right)}{\sup\left(L(x;\theta)\right)},$$

where sup indicates the supremum, L is the likelihood function, are the parameters under the null hypothesis and are the fitted parameters. The observed statistic LR(x) is always between 0 and 1. Values close to 0 of the likelihood ratio suggest that the observed results are less likely to occur under the null hypothesis; values close to 1 indicate that the observed outcome was nearly as likely to occur under the null hypothesis as compared with the alternative, and the null hypothesis cannot be rejected.

Graphical methods: differences by bin PP and QQ plots

In practice, a modeller gains additional insights combining numerical GoF analysis with graphical diagrams. As explained above, numerical GoF tests provide a one-figure evaluation summary for the fitting of all the observations. Also, while GoF tests such as A–D and K–S provide the likelihood of two distributions being identical, these tests do not provide a direct measure of their similarity and they should be complemented with other forms of analysis.

The opposite case is more typical in operational risk management, where low availability of loss observations might cause several

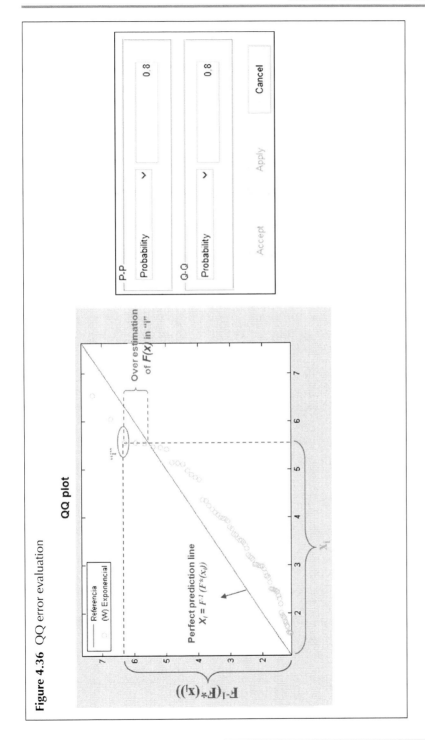

Figure 4.36 QQ error evaluation

parametric distributions to have a high p-value. Graphical analysis can help us to discriminate among distributions with a reasonable p-value by providing an intuitive representation of the fit discrepancy for all loss observations. These can be used to identify different behaviour along the distribution or systematic fitting discrepancies in a specific section of the distribution, mainly the tail. The identified systematic differences can be used to select distributions or structure the modelling, by splitting the distribution into segments for better tail modelling.

Let us remember the BCSG-AMA statement that refers to graphical methods: "A bank should assess the quality of fit between the data and the selected distribution. The tools typically adopted for this purpose are graphical methods (which visualise the difference between the empirical and theoretical functions) and quantitative methods, based on goodness-of-fit tests."

There are a number of graphical tests to evaluate GoF. Some of them are the joint representation of the observed losses versus the probability density function of the fitted distribution; the cumulative probability function of the observed losses versus the fitted distribution; the probability density differences by bin; the probability–probability plot; and the quantile–quantile plot.

Figure 4.37 illustrates three graphical figures for GoF analysis. The graph on the left compares the empirical distribution histogram and the probability density function of the fitted distribution. The middle one represents the differences between the empirical histogram and the probability density function of the fitted distribution. Finally, the one on the right provides a comparison between the cumulative probability of the empirical distribution and the cumulative probability function of the fitted distribution. These representations provide an initial view of how the fitted distribution fits the input data. More decisive insights can be obtained from an analysis of the quantile–quantile (QQ) and probability–probability (PP) plots.

The QQ and PP plots provide us with direct information on the GoF. The QQ plot charts the severity value of the empirical distribution versus that of the fitted distribution, given the same percentiles in both distributions. The diagonal represents the perfect prediction, where both values coincide. This permits a clear identification of over- or underestimation of observed losses by the fitted distribution. In fact, the differences in the QQ plot represent the actual

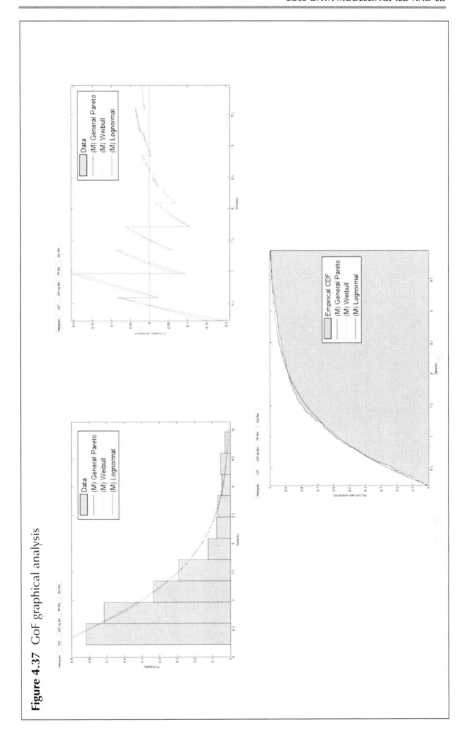

Figure 4.37 GoF graphical analysis

Figure 4.38 QQ plot

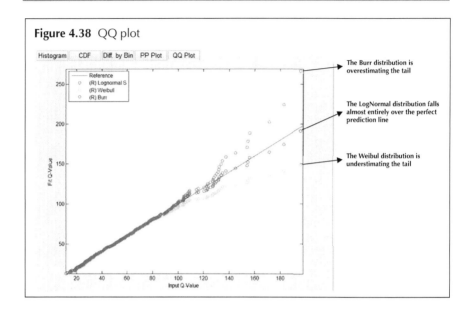

estimation error by percentile measured in loss monetary units, making this plot a fundamental tool for evaluating the GoF. The PP plot charts the percentile of the empirical distribution versus that of the fitted distribution, given the same quantile or severity loss. Differences in the PP plot represent the estimation errors on the probability of experiencing a given loss amount.

Figure 4.38 illustrates the QQ plot with three fitted distributions – lognormal, Weibull and Burr – over the same observed data. On the X axis, we represent the severity values of the observed distribution, x_i. On the Y axis we provide the values of the fitted distribution given the same percentile as in the observed distribution, $F^{-1}(F^*(x_i))$, for each of the fitted distributions. It can be seen how the lognormal actually replicates the input data quite well, how the Weibull underestimates the observed data severities and the Burr overestimates them. The three distributions had high p-values for their GoF tests.

Figure 4.39 shows a PP plot on the left. The X axis corresponds to the percentiles of the observed losses x_i, $F^*(x_i)$, and the Y axis corresponds to the percentile of the fitted distribution, given the same loss x_i, $F(x_i)$. It appears that the fit is well aligned with the perfect prediction line. The right-hand-side graph represents the % difference in the probability (of any loss being larger than x_i) assigned by the fitted

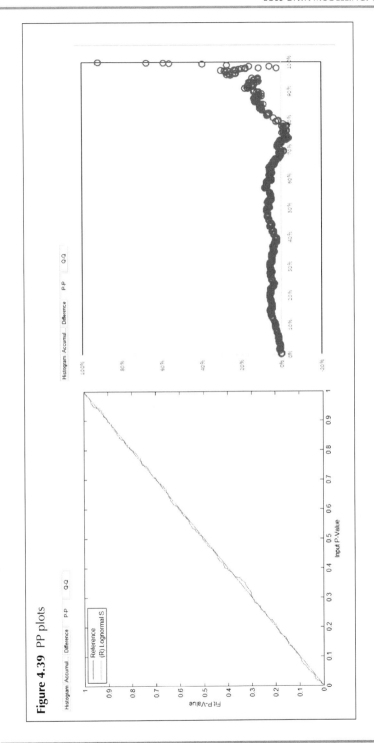

Figure 4.39 PP plots

distribution as compared with the implicit probability of the empirical distribution, as follows:

$$PP \text{ Differences} = \frac{\left(1-F(x_i)\right)-\left(1-F^*(x_i)\right)}{1-F^*(x_i)}$$

This method of comparing the probabilities of the empirical and fitted distribution allows for a better differentiation, particularly at very high percentiles that influence the operational risk capital calculation. It can be observed that differences are much emphasised in this format. Those differences close to the tail may be reasonable given the random nature and density of losses in the tail.

Distributions can be ranked and more informatively selected using QQ and PP plots by using the QQ error and PP error explained in the subsection "Other selection methods" above.

Practical decisions on goodness-of-fit determination

Each of the statistical tests and analyses entails many implicit assumptions, sometimes not completely consistent with each another. Also, some analysis provide us with an absolute measure of the goodness of fit, such as the p-values. Other analysis, such as the SBC, only provides us with a means to rank distributions. The K–S best evaluates the fit on the body, while the A–D is a better measure of the fit on the tail. Then, the SBC provides good information on overfitting given the number of parameters in the model, since it introduces a correction to the number of parameters in the model. Finally, a numerical test provides us with a single measure of the GoF for all the distribution, while the focus of the capital modelling should be on the high percentiles of the distribution-determining capital. Therefore, a graphical analysis such as the QQ and PP plots allows us to discriminate distribution fit per distribution (severity or frequency) segment, thus facilitating the identification of systematic biases in the upper percentiles of the distribution.

Therefore, a combination of all the different analyses would permit us to identify a distribution assumption that complies with all of the above-mentioned requirements. A practical distribution selection process may start with the selection of those distributions that fit the tail best and that, at the same time, provide us with a reasonable fit for the body. To illustrate an example, Figure 4.40 shows the selection, among multiple distribution modelling assumptions, that

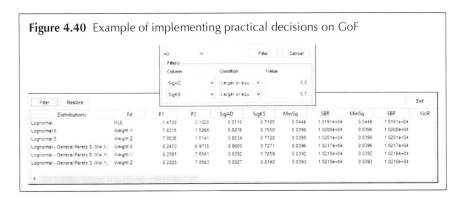

Figure 4.40 Example of implementing practical decisions on GoF

provides a minimum of 0.8 of p-value on the A–D and a minimum of 0.7 in the K–S.

Looking still at Figure 4.40, we can then select the distributions that, with a good fit at the tail (high A–D) and a reasonable fit on the body (reasonably high K–S), have the highest Schwarz Bayesian criterion, hence minimising the risk of overfitting.

The selection can now analyse the QQ plot at the high percentiles of the distribution for the selection of the distribution showing the closest fit in this visual graph. Alternatively, it can be based on the analysis of the QQ and PP error ratios, which provide a single figure of the QQ analysis and permit us to rank distributions (see "Other selection methods" above). In this last case, a ranking can also be established based on the numerical analysis of the QQ error ratio, to suggest a selection of modelling distributions.

Figure 4.41 provides an example of a distribution-fitting output and layout for the selection of the distribution assumptions that best replicates the underlying risk. The analysis to be used in the selection of the best distribution includes the A–D and K–S GoF tests; the severity-frequency independence test; the single-loss approximation estimation of capital under several confidence intervals; the possibility of including new losses in the fit to evaluate the stability of the fit; etc. Multiple distribution assumptions are generated to be compared, including mixtures, shifted and parametric, and all of them with a truncation and under different fitting methods (such as MLE, Robust, WLS). The distribution parameters should be analysed to determine the reasonability of the fit. All these methods, required for a solid distribution assumption selection, are described in detail below.

Figure 4.41 Example of operational risk fitting output and analytics

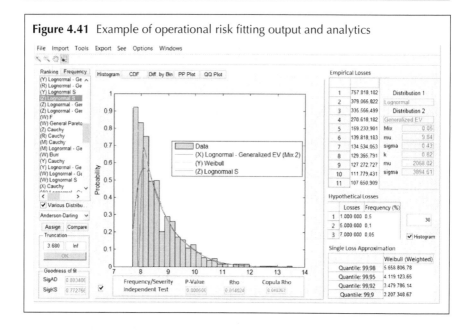

STABILITY ANALYSIS OF CAPITAL ESTIMATES, DISTRIBUTION PARAMETERS AND GOF

Operational risk capital estimations are periodically repeated, approximately every six months, during which time new losses are collected and added to the fitting sample. Because of this, capital estimates can significantly change. This is particularly true with fat-tail distributions, where tails tend to be lowly populated and tail parameters are sensitive to new observations. In turn, changes in tail parameters may have a significant impact on capital estimations.

Management issues result from such instability. The capital planning and management process needs stable estimates of capital requirement to allocate resources, plan financial needs, determine dividend payments and provide a reliable feed to the strategic plan definition. Also, instability of capital estimates can be interpreted as evidence of the underlying model being insufficiently robust, over-fitted, etc.

Therefore, the analysis of the operational risk capital estimates stability provides reliability to the model. The BCSG-AMA also mentions concerns on the variability and stability of capital estimates at various points such as when it says, "The bank should put in place methodologies to reduce estimate variability and provide measures of the error around these estimates" and "The techniques to determine the aggregated loss distributions should ensure adequate levels of precision and stability of the risk measures." Also, capital stability is becoming of increasing concern to supervisors.

The following subsections propose means with which to evaluate the capital estimates stability for selecting modelling assumptions.

The resampling method

The resampling method directly addresses the issue of instability of the capital model, given changes in the underlying modelling sample. The method is based on resampling over the fitting sample and evaluating the capital estimates obtained at each iteration, as presented in the subsection "Capital stability by threshold plot" above. The resampling implies that each of the capital estimates is performed with a different sample drawn from the same underlying loss distribution. This actually replicates what theoretically happens in reality: each operational risk capital recalculation is performed with a different dataset, which has been drawn from the underlying operational risk distribution of the institution. As time passes, new operational risk losses are collected and added to the fitting sample and capital estimates are repeated.

While the method in "Capital stability by threshold plot" above focused on identifying a modelling threshold providing stable capital estimates, the method now being described aims to identify, within that specific threshold, which is the distribution type and fitting method that delivers the most stable capital estimates.

Not only the distribution type but the fitting method can be selected to obtain a more stable fit. For instance, fitting methods such as RLS may deliver a better fit by reducing the weight on those observations that appear to be anomalies. When loss anomalies are drawn in one of the subsamples, the fit under the RLS method is more similar to that without anomalies because its weight is automatically reduced by the RLS process. This is also similar to what happens in reality. As the institution fitting sample grows with time, tails get more populated and a smaller percentage of loss observations appear as anomalies.

The process can be used not only to determine the stability of capital results but also to assess the stability in the goodness of fit under K–S and A–D, and the stability of the distribution parameters.

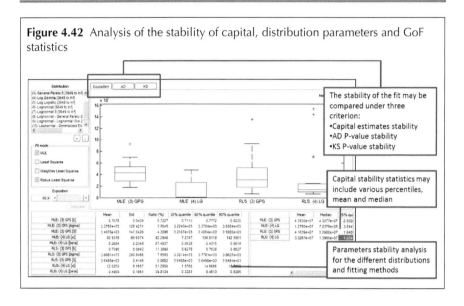

Figure 4.42 Analysis of the stability of capital, distribution parameters and GoF statistics

Figure 4.42 suggests a stability of GoF, capital and distribution parameters based on several modelling choices through different analyses and statistics. The box plot represents the capital stability according to different modelling assumptions. The data table on the bottom right-hand side represents the statistics of the capital estimates presented in the box plot. The data table on the left-hand-side corner includes the description of the parameters instability in terms of mean, standard deviation, and various percentiles. The same analysis can be done to analyse the stability of the GoF under the same method and evaluate the dispersion on the Anderson–Darling and Kolmogorov–Smirnov p-values.

Figure 4.43 shows an example of the analysis of GoF across different distribution assumptions. It can be seen how the mixture in the right-hand-side box plot is less stable, while the general Pareto, second to the right, provides the highest and model-stable fit.

The what-if? method
While the resampling method evaluates the stability of capital estimates based on what is already known from the loss distribution by resampling over the existing loss sample, the what-if? method evaluates the stability given new hypothetical losses different from those observed.

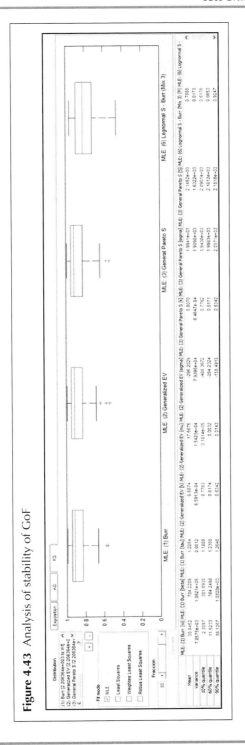

Figure 4.43 Analysis of stability of GoF

For instance, the capital modelling team may receive the information that other institutions have experienced losses of larger magnitude and/or different nature than those in the institution's modelling sample. Also, it is possible to have internally identified a potential loss scenario that is not captured by the loss modelling sample. Given these circumstances, the modelling team may want to evaluate the impact of these hypothetical losses on the institution's operational risk capital estimations and determine how well the current loss model would fit them.

For the introduction of new hypothetical losses into an existing data sample, we must follow a similar procedure to that above by introducing weights for the calculation of the empirical cumulative probabilities. In this case, the new losses would normally be in the distribution tail and are larger than any of the observed losses. The specific probability of the materialisation of the hypothetical loss can be considered also. If the probability is not specified, then it is implicitly assumed that the hypothetical losses will have the same probability as any other loss in the observed data sample. The weights of the hypothetical losses in the observed sample can be calculated as follows:

❏ Adjust the scenario probability to the annual frequency of the ORC. For instance, if the annual frequency of an ORC is 10, then 10 loss draws will be taken from the severity-distribution-per-year losses and, therefore, the scenario probability per draw should be approximately 10 times lower than its annual probability. This adjustment can be done as follows:[8]

$$P'_H = 1 - (1 - P_H)^{1/F},$$

where P_H is the desired annual probability of the hypothetical loss, P'_H is the adjusted annual probability, which considers the frequency of the ORC, and F is the frequency of the ORC. Observe that P'_H will be lower than P_H if the annual frequency of the ORC is higher than 1; it will be higher than P_H if the annual frequency is lower than 1, and, if $P'_H = P_H$, then the annual frequency will be equal to 1.

❏ Then, P_H is transformed into a weight within the rest of the losses to reflect the desired probability in a single draw from the total sample: Weight of hypothetical loss = P_H *Sample Size.

❏ Then, the cumulative distribution function with the assigned weight can be calculated consistently with the method presented in Appendix A1, "Empirical distributions".

Once the percentiles and quantiles are calculated, these are fed into a fitting process (MLE, robust and so forth) to determine the parameters of the distribution resulting from the addition of hypothetical losses. New capital charges are then estimated (following the single-loss approximation approach), with the new distribution resulting from the addition of new hypothetical scenarios. Capital stability can then be evaluated by comparing the capital charges from the original distribution with those of the distribution calculated with the inclusion of the hypothetical losses.

In Figure 4.44, the process for determining the new empirical cumulative probabilities for an ORC with 30 historical losses and an annual frequency of 10 is illustrated. Three additional hypothetical losses are added with severities of 150, 300 and 550 and annual probabilities of 0.01, 0.005 and 0.001, correspondingly. The table contains the calculations of the adjusted probabilities given the ORC annual frequency; the weight of each observation given the size of the

Figure 4.44 Introducing new hypothetical losses into an existing distribution

	Annual probability, $P{\downarrow}H$	Adjusted annual probability, $P{\downarrow}H$	Annual frequency		10
			Info into the fitting process		
			Quantile	Percentile	Weight
Historical loss 1			0.01	1.66	1
Historical loss 2			0.02	4.99	1
Historical loss 3			0.08	8.32	1
Historical loss 4			0.09	11.65	1
Historical loss 5			0.24	14.98	1
Historical loss 6			0.63	18.30	1
Historical loss 7			0.77	21.63	1
Historical loss 8			0.91	24.96	1
Historical loss 9			0.91	28.29	1
			...		
Historical loss 26			22.16	84.86	1
Historical loss 27			23.49	88.19	1
Historical loss 28			26.23	91.52	1
Historical loss 29			32.44	94.85	1
Historical loss 30			38.35	98.18	1
Hypothetical loss A	1.00%	0.1005%	150.00	98.28	0.030136
Hypothetical loss B	0.50%	0.0501%	300.00	98.33	0.015034
Hypothetical loss C	0.10%	0.0100%	550.00	98.34	0.003001

Figure 4.45 Analysing the impact of introducing hypothetical losses into an existing sample

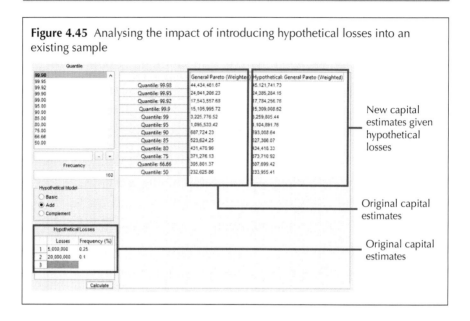

observed loss sample; and the resulting cumulative frequencies and quantiles to be fed into the fitting process.

Figure 4.45 illustrates, in a different example, the comparison of capital charges resulting from adding, to the observed losses, two hypothetical scenarios: a 5,000,000 loss with an annual probability of 0.005 and another one of 100,000,000 with an annual probability of 0.0005. The illustration shows the impact on capital charges with multiple percentiles calculated under the single-loss approximation method. In this example, original capital charges are actually slightly higher than those resulting from the addition of the hypothetical losses. This implies that the current modelling is consistent with the unobserved hypothetical losses.

This same procedure can be utilised to stress the loss distribution in the implementation of a modified LDA, for stress-testing purposes, as presented in Chapter 9 ("Stressing frequencies and severities").

Finally, the stability of capital can be evaluated by looking at the distribution parameter estimates volatility along time, as in the bottom graph of Figure 9.5, in Chapter 9. There, the fitting sample have been segmented in time buckets and a GPD has been fitted to each bucket. The resulting graph is used to evaluate the shape distribution parameter stability and pattern.

EVALUATING WHETHER THE CAPITAL ESTIMATES ARE REALISTIC

Operational risk modelling requires long projections from the observed losses and the use of highly sensitive fat-tail distributions. Due to the lack of observations on the tail, some distributions may exaggerate fat-tail behaviour and deliver unrealistic capital estimates. The opposite, an underestimation of capital, is also possible.

BCSG-AMA explicitly mentions the need to generate "a loss distribution with a realistic capital requirements estimate, without the need to implement 'corrective adjustments' such as caps". Caps are controls introduced during the Monte Carlo simulation of losses that limit the maximum size of losses produced by the distribution function sampling.

An evaluation of the realism of capital estimates can be introduced during the modelling process to confirm that the losses produced by the fitted distribution are commensurate with the loss-generation processes being modelled. When this is evaluated, then no caps or controls need to be introduced during Monte Carlo simulation. This can be achieved by calculating capital charges using the single-loss approximation (SLA), a short-time-consuming method for estimating capital. The SLA method provides (see Chapter 8) the single maximum loss that determines the capital charge in a very high confidence interval, while the Monte Carlo simulation provides the total capital charge of the summation of the losses in the loss scenario. In a fat-tail distribution, a single loss may explain up to 80–90% of the total capital charge, at a high confidence interval, and the other 10% or 20% can be explained by all other losses added. In fact, the use of a SLA provides information that is much easier to interpret, permitting us to evaluate whether that single major loss is actually realistic in the loss-generation process being modelled.

Figure 4.46 shows the evaluation of capital charges under SLA of a lognormal distribution under different fitting methods. The SLA is calculated for both high and low percentiles. The result in high percentiles provides an approximate estimation of capital charges for that percentile, as well as the size of maximum losses generated by the distribution function to evaluate that those losses are realistic. The SLA for low percentiles does not provide any approximate amount of the capital charge at that percentile. However, it shows the size of maximum losses at that lower percentile of the severity distribution, which could be used to evaluate the realism of the distribution in easier-to-observe events.

EXTERNAL DATA SCALING

We now look at external data (ED) scaling, which is a necessary transformation of ED prior to its modelling and integration into the institution's capital model.

ED is used in operational risk capital modelling to complement the risk profile captured in ILD. ED contains valuable information about potential losses that have materialised in peer institutions but have not necessarily been experienced by the institution. Given the operational loss characteristics of low-frequency and fat-tail behaviour, the ILD generally represents an incomplete vision of what operational losses may materialise in future. In fact, ILD in particular lacks extreme losses that characterise the fat-tail behaviour, determining real capital requirements, and ED can provide such information.

External data can be introduced into the modelling in several ways. One way is by providing information to the scenario analysis exercise in order to support the evaluation of potential impacts, as described in Chapter 3. A second method would be to create an ED model following processes similar to those described in Chapter 4, and introducing it into the hybrid model using any of the methods presented in Chapter 7.

To incorporate an ED model into a hybrid model, it is first necessary to perform a data scaling. The external losses of other institutions may have a different scale given their different activity levels, business nature, regulatory environment and so forth, and cannot be used directly without adaptation.

The Basel Committee shares similar concerns and its Supervisory Guidelines state, "A data scaling process involves the adjustment of loss amounts reported in external data to fit a bank's business activities and risk profile. Any scaling process should be systematic, statistically supported, and should provide output that is consistent with the bank's risk profile."

This section presents the following methods for scaling external data:

❏ the scale-and-shape method – a method based on creating ED distribution models with the scale of ILD and the shape of ED, based on the distribution moments;

❏ the tail parameter method – an alternative method to incorporate the tail shape in an ILD model, based on the distribution tail parameter; and

❏ the scaling factor method – a method that scales ED by determining a scaling factor derived from the analysis of the institution characteristics.

The scale-and-shape method

The scale-and-shape method addresses the issue that ILD may provide only sufficient data for the calculation of the low distribution moments and percentiles, and it is often insufficient for the calculation of the tail shape and higher moments, such as skewness and leptokurtosis. This method can be used to create an ED distribution model with the scale of internal loss data and the distribution tail shape as reflected in the skewness and leptokurtosis of the ED. The result is a distribution model with the scale of the ILD and the shape of the ED, which can be used for feeding the hybrid model.

The process consists of defining a distribution fitting process with optimisation constraints referred to both percentiles and distribution moments. Internal loss data percentiles and low moments are meant to provide the scale of the new fitted distribution. For instance, the internal loss data mean and percentiles 25, 50, 75 and 90 can be used to define the scale of the losses. The skewness and leptokurtosis of ED can be used to provide us with the shape of the loss distribution. This method may also help to reflect BCSG-AMA concerns when it states, "A bank should pay particular attention to the positive skewness and, above all, leptokurtosis of the data when selecting a severity distribution."

The proposed fitting process is designed to find the distribution family and parameters that best replicate the target percentiles and moments. The addition of distribution moments as constraints makes MLE hard to use and a least-squares-based method provides a solution. The algorithm minimises (see Appendix 3) the error function between the fitted distribution and the input goals constraint. The error function adopted is:

$$E(p) = \sum_{i=1}^{n} E_i(p),$$

where p are the distribution parameters, n is the number of fitting goals (including moments and percentiles), and E_i, the error function

Figure 4.46 Evaluating whether the losses produced by the distribution model are realistic

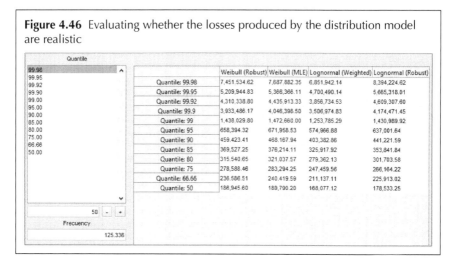

	Weibull (Robust)	Weibull (MLE)	Lognormal (Weighted)	Lognormal (Robust)
Quantile: 99.98	7,451,534.62	7,687,882.35	6,851,942.14	8,394,224.62
Quantile: 99.95	5,209,944.83	5,366,366.11	4,700,490.14	5,665,318.01
Quantile: 99.92	4,310,338.80	4,435,913.33	3,856,734.53	4,609,307.60
Quantile: 99.9	3,933,486.17	4,046,398.50	3,506,974.83	4,174,471.45
Quantile: 99	1,438,029.80	1,472,660.00	1,253,785.29	1,430,989.92
Quantile: 95	658,394.32	671,958.53	574,966.88	637,001.64
Quantile: 90	459,423.41	468,167.94	403,382.86	441,221.59
Quantile: 85	369,527.25	376,214.11	325,917.92	353,841.84
Quantile: 80	315,540.65	321,037.57	279,362.13	301,703.58
Quantile: 75	278,588.46	283,294.25	247,459.56	266,164.22
Quantile: 66.66	236,586.51	240,419.59	211,137.11	225,913.02
Quantile: 50	186,945.60	189,790.20	168,077.12	178,533.25

for the constraint i, which can be a percentile or a moment. E_i is defined through:

$$E_i(p) = \left(\frac{f(p,i) - O_i}{O_i} \right)^2 w_i,$$

where O_i is the objective and f can be any of the following functions depending on the fitting goal. The fitting goals can be:

❏ the inverse of the CDF function for parameters p and percentile i; or
❏ mean, variance, skewness or leptokurtosis for distributions with parameter p.

Finally, ω_i is the weight for the i-th constraint, which depends on the priority given to the different fitting goals. An equal weight to all fitting goals may be also perfectly justified as all fitting goals, if non-overlapping, explain different segments and characteristics of the distribution.

As described in "Severity distribution fitting process" above, the fitted distribution moments can be expressed as a function of the distribution parameters, permitting their use as an optimisation goal during the fit. When fitted distribution moments cannot be expressed as the distribution parameters (for instance, when the distribution has a threshold), moments can be calculated numerically

Figure 4.47 The scale and shape method for re-scaling ED

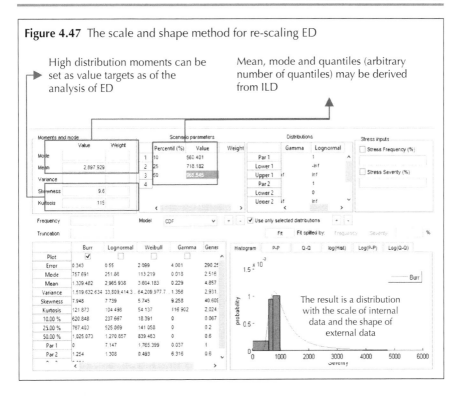

in each of the optimisation iterations. The resulting function can be used as a scaled ED distribution model or as the transformation function for scaling ED. For the last, the empirical cummulative probability of the ED observation, for instance, can be input into such transformation function which will return the scaled value of ED. This ED scaling function is more articulated than the standard scaling factor presented below.

Figure 4.47 illustrates the fitting process when the 10th, 25th and 50th percentiles and the mean have been derived from internal data analysis. The leptokurtosis and skewness have been derived from ED analysis. The results can be clearly seen as a distribution that has the scale of the internal loss data, which replicates the leptokurtosis and skewness of ED. The resulting distribution can be used as a scaled for ED model.

It is also possible to prioritise specific fitting goals during the fit, such as leptokurtosis or the high percentiles introduced as target values. In other words, the shape or scale can be prioritised during the fit. This can be implemented by giving higher weights, w_i, to the priority fitting goals. In Figure 4.48, leptokurtosis and skewness are given a priority weight 5, which means that difference in this constraint is multiplied by 5, increasing the optimisation focus. Note that this results in the leptokurtosis and skewness being much more closely replicated. This could also be considered as a hybrid model in which the shape characteristics of the ILD distribution have been assigned 0% of total credibility and are fully defined by ED (see Chapter 7).

However, sometimes high-distribution moments such as skewness and kurtosis can be hard to calculate if there is insufficient data, and such data has a strong tail behaviour. In these circumstances, the measures of skewness and kurtosis may be volatile and thus not useful to define the distribution tail. This can be addressed by establishing bounds into the shape parameters of the fitted distributions, as presented below. In fact, estimations of tail/shape distribution parameters are frequently less volatile than those of kurtosis and skewness.

The tail parameter scaling method

The tail parameter scaling method addresses the issue that the ILD does not contain sufficient information to determine the tail behaviour in an ORC. It can also be useful when the available ED is insufficient to determine stable values of skewness and/or kurtosis which get volatile in reduced samples with fat tails. In this case, the ED tail information can be used to bound/constrain the parameter that controls the tail/shape of the distribution, since the tail/shape parameters tend to be less volatile than skewness and kurtosis measures. ILD is also used for the determination of the scale of the scaled distribution model by introducing constraints, during the fitting process, referred to as its low percentiles and mean.

The method starts with the determination of the tail properties that the fitted distribution should have. The tail properties can be analysed by means of fitting distributions that incorporate a tail parameter. Alternatively, the tail behaviour can be determined with analysis such as the Hill parameter or the stability parameter, as explained in "Tail Shape and Threshold Determination through Extreme Value Theory" above.

Once the target tail properties for the ORC have been determined, they are introduced into the fitting process, by bounding the distrib-

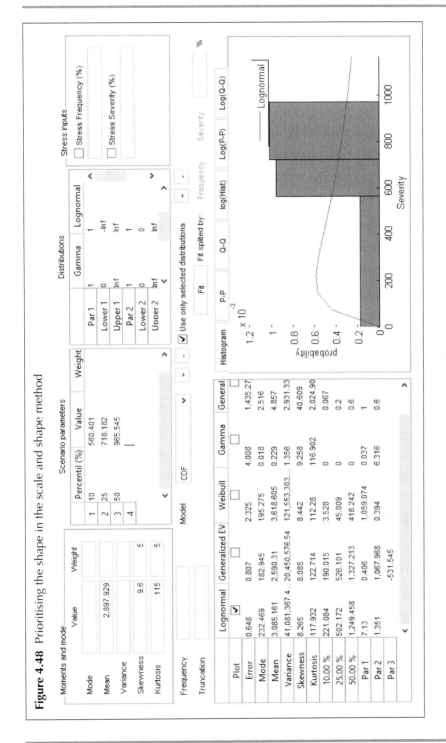

Figure 4.48 Prioritising the shape in the scale and shape method

ution tail parameter correspondingly. Indeed, many fat tail distributions incorporate a parameter that directly controls their tail/shape behaviour. The distribution function resulting from the fit can used as distribution model of scaled ED or as a transformation function for obtaining scaled values of ED, as explained above.

Figure 4.49 shows the fitting of a distribution based on the 25th, 50th and 75th percentiles and the mean from internal data. From the analysis of external data, it has been concluded that the tail parameter of the loss distribution should be approximately 0.7. This information is included in the fitting process by bounding the k parameter (after MatLab variable notation), the tail parameter of the GPD, between 0.65 and 0.75. An interval rather than a fix value is allowed to provide more flexibility to accommodate other fitting constraints. The result is a distribution with the fat-tail behaviour of external data but the scale of internal loss data. This distribution can be used as scaled ED, although it can be considered also already as a hybrid model in which the tail of the ILD has 0% credibility and is fully defined by ED see Chapter 7. As in the case of the scale-and-shape method, more weight can be given to different optimisation goals, such as the percentiles.

Multiple variants of this method can be implemented. More percentiles and low moments can be used to incorporate more characteristics of the internal loss data, when internal loss data is more abundant. For instance, skewness or higher percentiles (95, 99 and so on) from internal loss data can also be set as a fitting goal. The weights on the fit can be set to prioritise some fitting goals over others.

These methods may help to observe to BCSG-AMA's statement such as, "A bank should pay particular attention to the positive skewness and, above all, leptokurtosis of the data when selecting a severity distribution," since the tail parameter is directly linked to the leptokurtosis.

The scaling factor method

The scaling factor method is used directly to scale external data by multiplying ED by a scaling factor. The method focuses on the determination of the value of the scaling factor. It is based on the assumption that the size of operational losses is related to the size of the entity (Shih *et al* 2000).

The process is as follows:

1. identification of data categories in which external information is required;
2. analysis of the ED received from ORX to determine relevance and the process for scaling severity and frequency data so as to adapt the external information to the entity's circumstances (size of transactions, controls and business/social/internal environment and so on); and
3. determination of the severity and frequency distributions derived from ED.

The study of reference (Shih *et al* 2000) assumes that the relationship between operational losses and entity size is of the type:

$$L = R^a F(\theta),$$

Figure 4.49 The tail parameter method of scaling ED

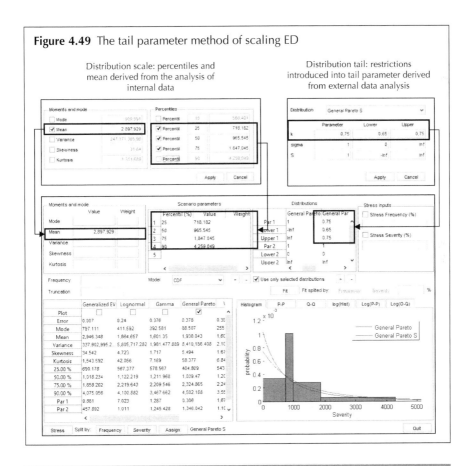

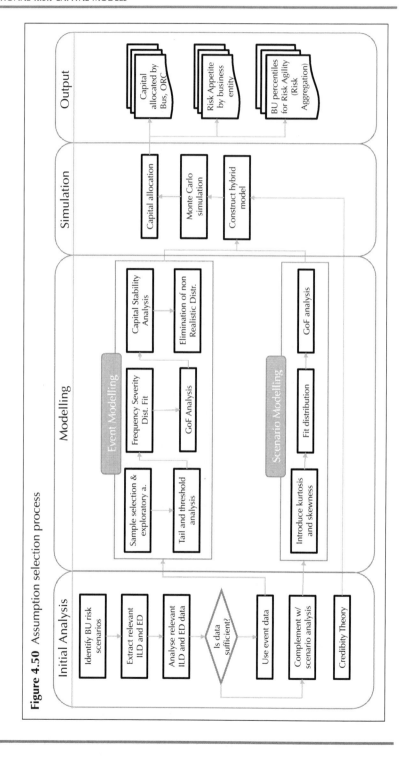

Figure 4.50 Assumption selection process

where L is the total size of the operational loss by business line, R is any indicator of the entity's size (eg, gross revenues by business line or subline), θ is the vector of all risk types that do not depend on indicator R, and $F(\theta)$ is a residual multiplier that does not depend on variance in indicator R. Consequently, "a" is the scaling factor or parameter to be estimated.

By taking logarithms at both sides and dividing by $\log(R)$, the above expression may be rewritten as follows:

$$y = a + bx + \xi$$

where

$$y = \frac{\log(L)}{\log(R)}, x = \frac{1}{\log(R)}, b = E\left[\log\left(F(\theta)\right)\right], \xi = \frac{\log\left(F(\theta)\right) - b}{\log(R)}$$

The estimation that may be viewed as a linear regression model obtained via WLS (weighted least squares) was $a \approx 0.23$, by Shih *et al* (2000).

In order to scale the ORX data, the same method is applied and the scaling factor a is estimated for the specific case of the institution and the available ORX data.

The data is therefore scaled as follows:

$$L_{esc} = L_{orig} \cdot \left(\frac{R_{int}}{R_{ext}}\right)^{a} \quad \text{Scaling Factor,}$$

where L_{esc} are the losses scaled to the institution's specific circumstances by business line, L_{orig} the original ORX losses by business line, R_{ext} the gross revenues from the external ORX data by business line, and R_{int} the institution's internal gross revenues by business line. Finally, and as commented, the a value can be assumed to be 0.23.

Although this method scales ED in the right direction, the criticism is that institution size is only one of the factors influencing the size of losses. The nature of the business – business environment, including jurisdiction and so forth – is the factor that probably has the largest influence in the loss amounts. On the other hand, the size of the firm has a clearer influence on the frequency of losses than on their average size.

Summarising, we have presented several methods to scale ED in order to make ED commensurate to the institution's risk profile permitting its coherent integration into the capital model. Using these methods, it is possible to use solid statistical means to address the issue of complementing ILD models with ED distribution tail and shape characteristics and to create ED models that can be used in the construction of a hybrid model. The benefits are the determination of capital estimates that reflect the potential tail behaviour of losses observed in peer institutions complementing those already observed by our institution and captured in the ILD.

DEFINITION OF THE LOSS DATA MODELLING PROCESS

In practical terms, the operational risk practitioner needs to establish a very specific modelling process and prove that it is consistently applied in all cases. It is important that the user should not direct/adapt the modelling to obtain a desired result. In fact, BCSG-AMA explicitly says, "The bank should follow a well specified, documented and traceable process for the selection, update and review of probability distributions and the estimate of its parameters."

Therefore, the capital modelling process should be clearly defined to guarantee that the same criteria are consistently applied to all units of measures and across time. The process should contain and connect all analytical processes described in this section and may incorporate practical decisions based on different views provided by the academic assumptions implicit in different tests and analysis.

In practice, institutions develop very detailed workflows incorporating all decisions from the analysis they perform. An example of a very high-level modelling process is illustrated in Figure 4.50, which shows all steps described in this chapter and the required decisions, from the input data to the capital results. The process in the figure shows three major steps with processes within them and the output report. Later, each of the different processes can be developed in more detail. Finally, the institution should demonstrate that modelling decisions are based on the strict adherence to the process defined.

CONCLUSION

We have reached the end of Chapter 4, where we have described methods to respond to the supervisory guidelines on loss data modelling and to construct realistic, updated and stable loss data models for operational risk capital. It is worth reminding that loss data issues can be effectively addressed with the proposed statistical methods, such as using older and newer data in the same model, leveraging time-weighted least squares; creating models with stable capital estimates; determining an optimal modelling granularity; scaling ED for its consistent integration into the capital model; modelling the distribution tail with precision; projecting frequencies for realistic capital estimates; and others.

1   The authors wish to thank José Ramón del Aguila Escobar for the research work performed in this section.

2   All graphs and calculations referring to capital modelling in this book have been performed using OpCapital Analytics, a software solution based on MatLab specifically designed for the calculation of operational risk capital requirements under advanced approaches.

3   Corporate finance; trading and sales: retail banking; commercial banking; payment and settlement; agency services; asset management; retail brokerage.

4   The mean excess plot is a popular analysis and it is mentioned in multiple references such as in Ghosha and Resnickb (2010). It is also mentioned in de Fontnouvelle, Rosengren and Jordan (2007).

5   The Hill estimator is a popular analysis and is mentioned in multiple references such as de Fontnouvelle, Rosengren and Jordan (2007).

6   The Hill parameter extension is based on the work published by Huisman, Koedijk, Kool and Palm (2001) on the analysis of tail index estimates in small samples.

7   A similar analysis was proposed in Mignola and Ugoccioni (2005).

8   The criticism of this method is that it requires independence between losses, which is a common assumption to the rest of the LDA model. See Chapter 8 for relaxing the independence assumption.

REFERENCES

Anderson, T. W. and D. A. Darling, 1954, "A Test of Goodness-of-Fit", *Journal of the American Statistical Association*, 49, pp. 765–9.

Beirlant, J, *et al,* 2005, *Statistics of Extremes: Theory and Application* (New York: John Wiley & Sons), p. 490.

Coles, S, 2001, *An Introduction to Statistical Modelling of Extreme Values* (London: Springer Verlag), p. 208.

Corder, G. W., and D. I. Foreman, 2009, *Nonparametric Statistics for Non-Statisticians: A Step-by-Step Approach* (New York: John Wiley and Sons).

de Fontnouvelle, Patrick, and Eric Rosengren and John Jordan, 2007, "Implications of Alternative Operational Risk Modelling Techniques", *The Risks of Financial Institutions*, National Bureau of Economic Research.

Dekkers, A., J. Einmahl, and L. de Haan, 1989, "A Moment Estimator for the Index of an Extreme-value Distribution", *Annals of Statistics*, 17, 1833–55.

DuMouchel, W. H., and F. L. O'Brien, 1989, "Integrating a Robust Option into a Multiple Regression Computing Environment", *Computer Science and Statistics: Proceedings of the 21st Symposium on the Interface*, American Statistical Association.

Ghosha, Souvik, and Sidney Resnickb, 2010, "A discussion on mean excess plots". *Stochastic Processes and their Applications* (London: Elsevier).

Gibbons, J. D., and S. Chakraborti, 1992, *Nonparametric Statistical Inference* (New York: Marcel Dekker).

Huisman, Ronald, Kees Koedijk, Clemens Kool and Franz Palm, 2001, "Tail-index Estimates in Small Samples", *Journal of Business and Economic Statistics*, 19, 208–16

Marsaglia, George, and John C. W. Marsaglia, 2004, "Evaluating the Anderson–Darling Distribution", *Journal of Statistical Software*.

Mignola, Giulio, and Roberto Ugoccioni, 2005, "Tests of Extreme Value Theory". Available at: http://db.riskwaters.com/data/operationalrisk/pdf/oct05_technical_evt.pdf

Pham, D. T., S. S. Dimov and C. D. Nguyen, 2004, "Selection of k in k-means clustering", *Mechanical Engineering Science*, 2004, pp. 103–19.

Rodriguez, Daniel, 2014, "kselection: Selection of k in k-means clustering", R package version 0.1.0.

Schervish, Mark J., 1995, *Theory of Statistics Springer Series in Statistics* (London: Springer).

Shih, Jimmy, Ali Samad-Khan, and Pat Medapa, 2000, "Is the Size of an Operational Loss Related to Firm Size?", *Operational Risk*, January.

5

Scenario Analysis Modelling

Rafael Cavestany

Having presented methods for loss data modelling in Chapter 4, we now examine scenario analysis (SA) modelling for its integration into the capital model, either the hybrid model or scenario-based approach. In fact, SA permits us to incorporate, into a capital model, institution-specific, high-impact risk information that can be obtained only from expert judgement due to its low frequency. This requires the translation of scenario results in distributions models that can be incorporated into the joint loss distribution for the derivation of capital estimates

On this topic, BCSG-AMA says, "A bank should thus ensure that the loss distribution(s) chosen to model scenario analysis estimates adequately represent(s) its risk profile." The process of choosing SA loss distribution that adequately represents the scenario risk profile can be performed through the following processes corresponding to this chapter:

❏ "Translating scenario analysis results into distribution characteristics";
❏ "Fitting a full distribution to scenario analysis";
❏ "Distribution shape control during the scenario distribution fit": this section describes how to arrive at a reasonable tail shape when fitting a distribution to scenario analysis results;
❏ "Goodness of fit in scenario analysis": in this section, we look at the methods for evaluating how the distribution model matches the scenario analysis input; and
❏ "Splitting scenario analysis into lower organisational entities":

in this section, we present methods for splitting scenario analysis models for capital allocation purposes.

TRANSLATING SCENARIO ANALYSIS RESULTS INTO DISTRIBUTION CHARACTERISTICS

Before the modelling starts, scenario analysis results are translated into distribution characteristics (percentiles, moments and so forth), which can be fed into a fitting process for the determination of the joint risk distribution. This process is specific to the elicitation method as shown in the examples proposed in Chapter 3, and it is based on determining distribution percentiles from the scenario analysis results.

The transformation for the worst-loss-by-time-horizon and frequency-by-severity-segments elicitation methods will be now presented.

Worst loss by time horizon

For the worst loss by time horizon, an expert is asked to suggest the severity of the largest loss observed over a certain period and the expected number of events in a year. It is implicitly assumed that the risk environment is constant over the time horizon, rather than evolving as it actually happens in reality. An example of this type of elicitation method is provided in Chapter 3.

The cumulative probability of event losses by time horizon can be calculated based on the annual frequency and time horizon and can be calculated through:

$$c_i = 1 - \frac{1}{fp_i},$$

where c_i is the cumulative distribution probability for loss i, f is the yearly event frequency, and p_i is the period of time between i loss events.

Table 5.1 shows an example of worst loss by time horizon, and the resulting implicit cumulative probability.

The worst-loss-by-time-horizon method may be justified as follows:

Definition
The quantile of order p of a distribution X is a value x_p such that,

$$P(X \leq Xp) \geq p \text{ and } P(X \geq Xp) \geq (1 - p)$$

Table 5.1 Results from scenario analysis

Number of events per year: 5

	Worst loss in the time horizon	Equivalent percentile
Worst loss in 2 years	US$10m	90.00
Worst loss in 5 years	US$25m	96.00
Worst loss in 10 years	US$45m	98.00
Worst loss in 20 years	US$75m	99.00

When no loss data is available (or when there is a desire to add qualitative information to the existing data), it is a common practice to try to qualitatively estimate the quantiles of the severity distribution, turning to expert opinion for the qualitative estimation of the quantiles.

The mathematical problem of fitting a distribution from a set of quantiles therefore arises. The problem is addressed by selecting a family of parametric distributions, and then estimating these parameters from the given quantiles.

Procedure: an expert is asked to estimate:

The expected numbers of events per year, n
The worst loss x in m years

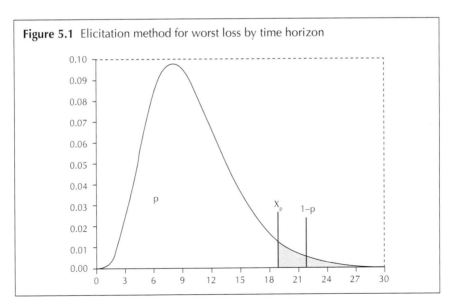

Figure 5.1 Elicitation method for worst loss by time horizon

It is then said that x is a quantile of order $1-(mn)^{-1}$ Justification – Hypothesis:

1. The distribution X is associated to the event of having a loss greater or equal to x.
2. It is stated that $n \cdot m$ such events occur in m years (from the expert opinion and assuming that the events come from independent and identically distributed random variables).
3. Let q be the probability of a loss event.
4. It is stated that X follows a distribution $B(n \cdot m, q)$, where B is a binomial, and q is estimated from the knowledge that a success has occurred (where success stands for a loss greater than x).

The method used to estimate q is the MLE. The likelihood, as a function of the parameter q, is:

$$L(q) = \binom{n \cdot m}{1} q^1 \cdot (1-q)^{n \cdot m - 1},$$

which reaches a maximum at:

$$\hat{q} = \frac{1}{n \cdot m}$$

Therefore, x is assigned to the quantile of order:

$$1 - \frac{1}{n \cdot m}$$

Frequency by severity bucket
In the frequency-by-severity-bucket (FSB) elicitation method the experts must suggest the number of expected events per severity segment. An example of this type of elicitation method is provided in Chapter 3.

The transformation into a CDF of the FSB method is performed by first calculating the cumulative number of events for the buckets, adding the number of events in the lower buckets to the higher ones. The distribution percentile is calculated by dividing the cumulative number of events by the total number of events. The quantile is the upper bound of the severity segment. This process can be described with the following expression, where the severity buckets are sorted by losses:

$$c_j = \sum_{i=1}^{j} \frac{n_i}{N} ,$$

where c_j is the percentile for the severity bucket j, n_i is the number of events for bucket i, and N is the total number of events, ie,

$$N = \sum_{i=1}^{j} n_i$$

Table 5.2 shows an example of the application of the FSB method. As an example:

$$C_2 = \frac{25+11}{40} = 0.923$$

The FSB method may be justified as follows. We consider K buckets, set p_i as the probability of having a loss in bucket i and n_i the number of suggested losses in bucket i_j, $i = 1, ..., k$. The stated n_i's may be viewed as an imaginary sample from a multinomial model M $(1, p_i, ..., p_k$. Then, the likelihood is:

$$L(p_i, ..., p_k) = \prod_{i=1}^{K} p_i^{ni} ,$$

and we may find that the MLE is:

$$\widehat{pi} = n_i / N$$

Then, we have that:

$$e_j = \sum_{i=1}^{j} \widehat{pi}$$

Another justification is as follows. Assume that $(p_1 ... p_k)$ ~Dir $(x_1 ... x_k)$ in a Dirichlet distribution with parameters $x_1 ... x_k$. We then have that $\widehat{pi} = E(p_i) = x_j / \Sigma x_i$, $i = 1, ..., K$. In N opportunities the expected number of events will be N E (p_i) = N* $x_i / \Sigma x_i$, if we match the moments we have N* $x_i / \Sigma x_i = n_i$. Simple algebra leads again to $\hat{p}_i = n_i / N$ and $e_j = e_j = \sum_{i=1}^{j} \hat{p}_i$.

FITTING A FULL DISTRIBUTION TO SCENARIO ANALYSIS

Once percentiles and quantiles are derived from the scenario results, these can be fed into any of the fitting processes described in Chapter 4.

Figure 5.2 is a screen grab that illustrates the fitting of a scenario

Table 5.2 Elicitation method, frequency by severity bucket

Severity Bucket	From US$100K to US$1m	From US$1m to US$10m	From US$10m to US$20m	From US$20m to US$50m	From US$50m to US$100m	More than US$100m
Annual frequency for severity bucket	25	11	2	0.6	0.3	0.1
Percentile of the distribution for the fit	64.10%	92.31%	97.44%	98.97%	99.74%	100%
Quantile of the distribution for the fit	US$1,000,000	US$10,000,000	US$20,000,000	US$50,000,000	US$100,000,000	Infinite

Table 5.3 Example of fitting distributions to scenario analysis results

Number of events per year: 2

	Worst loss in time horizon	Calculated percentile
Worst in 1 year	50	50
Worst loss in 10 years	120	95
Worst loss in 25 years	350	98

analysis that has been transformed into the percentiles and quantiles of the loss distribution. The scenario results and their transformation into percentiles and quantiles are summarised in Table 5.3. Also, weight has been introduced into the worst loss in 10 and 25 years to prioritise the fitting of those points in the distribution. These points can be prioritised based on the confidence on the expert estimations, or as means for focusing the fit in higher percentiles, for instance.

These percentiles and quantiles are used in the fit with the generalised extreme value, lognormal, gamma, and general Pareto distribution distributions,[1] whose parameters, moments and quantiles are shown in the bottom left data table. Then, the distributions are plotted on the bottom right histogram and pdf graph. We should observe that the worst losses by 10 and 25 years have been given

Figure 5.2 Fitting distributions to scenario analysis

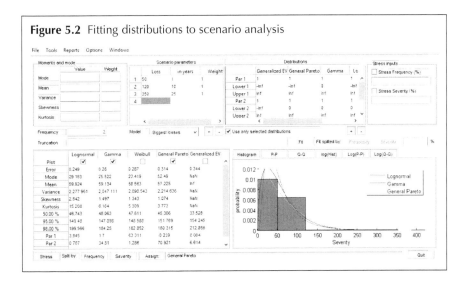

twice as much weight during the fit than the one for 1 year, as the top centre data box named "Scenario parameters" shows. This increased weight results in a better fit of these two inputs.

DISTRIBUTION SHAPE CONTROL DURING THE SCENARIO DISTRIBUTION FIT

Many scenario rating processes avoid asking questions about very infrequent events because experts generally have difficulty in evaluating events so far removed from their experience. The result of this is that questions in a scenario analysis may refer only to time horizons that can only be linked to low percentiles of the distribution not determining capital. These circumstances require a difficult projection of the distribution tail far from the fit input information, which may result in an arbitrary distribution. Also, even if the elicitation method includes questions about high percentiles, the answers are more subject to errors and imprecision than those referring to lower percentiles.

To prove the need for a control over the distribution shape during the scenario fit, Figure 5.3 represents a fit using low percentiles, as is done in scenario analysis, and the comparison between the moments of the fit. To be able to contrast the consistency of the moments, both percentiles and moments are derived from the same loss data sample. The fit is done with low percentiles including 90 and 95, as

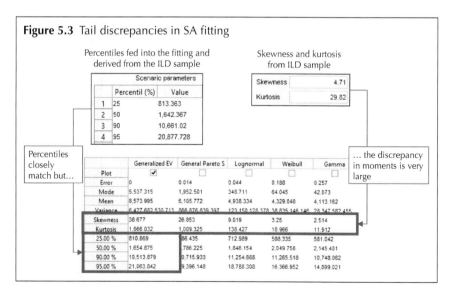

Figure 5.3 Tail discrepancies in SA fitting

Percentiles fed into the fitting and derived from the ILD sample

Skewness and kurtosis from ILD sample

	Scenario parameters	
	Percentil (%)	Value
1	25	813.363
2	50	1,642.367
3	90	10,661.02
4	95	20,877.728

Skewness	4.71
Kurtosis	29.82

Percentiles closely match but...

... the discrepancy in moments is very large

	Generalized EV	General Pareto S	Lognormal	Weibull	Gamma
Plot	✔	☐	☐	☐	☐
Error	0	0.014	0.044	0.188	0.257
Mode	5.537.315	1,952.501	348.711	64.045	42.873
Mean	8,573.995	6,105.772	4,938.334	4,329.048	4,113.162
Variance	6,427,682,530,711	866,876,839,397	123,150,128,378	38,835,146,146	28,347,582,455
Skewness	38.677	26.853	9.019	3.25	2.514
Kurtosis	1,866.032	1,009.325	138.427	18.966	11.912
25.00 %	810.869	86.435	712.989	588.335	581.042
50.00 %	1,654.875	786.225	1,846.154	2,049.758	2,145.481
90.00 %	10,513.879	0,715.933	11,254.668	11,265.518	10,748.062
95.00 %	21,063.842	9,396.148	18,788.308	16,366.952	14,899.021

would be done in the scenario fit. Then, the moments of the distribution fitted are compared to the moments of the original data sample. It can be observed that the discrepancy in the moments is very significant, even if the percentiles are almost perfectly matched.

The conclusion is that the scenario fit may be weak because of the difficulty in estimating the full distribution based solely in the low-percentile information. To address this issue, information on the distribution shape and/or tail from ED can be embedded into the fitting process. This can be achieved following the same procedure as explained in Chaper 4, "External data scaling", where moments are embedded as goals into the distribution fitting. In this case, the distribution percentiles would be derived from the scenario analysis and the moments would be derived from the analysis of a different data element, typically, external data.

Figure 5.4 illustrates the fitting results after the introduction of leptokurtosis and skewness estimations into the previous section example. It can be perceived that the introduction of stronger skewness and leptokurtosis reshapes the distribution into a tail-dominated distribution, thus reducing the body size. In the example,

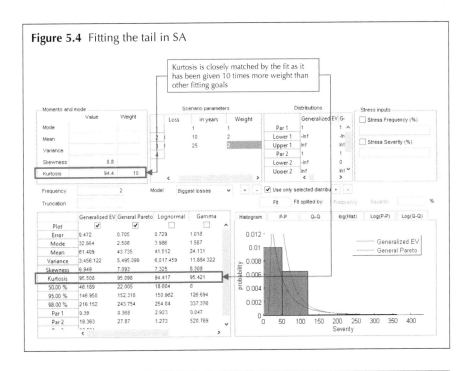

Figure 5.4 Fitting the tail in SA

the leptokurtosis has been given 10 times more weight than any of the other fitting constraints. As a result, it is closely replicated by the fitted distribution.

This type of fitting method for SA may help to address BCSG-AMA's concerns when it states, "A bank should pay particular attention to the positive skewness and, above all, leptokurtosis of the data when selecting a severity distribution."

However, sometimes high distribution moments such as skewness and kurtosis can be hard to calculate when only a low amount of data is available and the distribution of such data has a fat tail. In these circumstances, the measures of skewness and kurtosis may be volatile and thus not useful for determining the distribution shape. This can be addressed by controlling the scenario analysis tail fit establishing bounds/constraints into the distribution tail/shape parameter, similarly to the "The Tail Parameter Scaling Method" in Chapter 4, since the tail/shape parameters are generally more stable. The stability of kurtosis and skewness can be estimated as in the resampling method of Chapter 4, or by analysing their value along time as in figure 9.5 in Chapter 9.

GOODNESS OF FIT IN SCENARIO ANALYSIS

Performing a complete goodness-of-fit analysis for the scenario analysis distribution fit, as described for internal loss data in Chapter 4, may be not suitable given the few points of the distribution gener-

Figure 5.5 GoF in SA

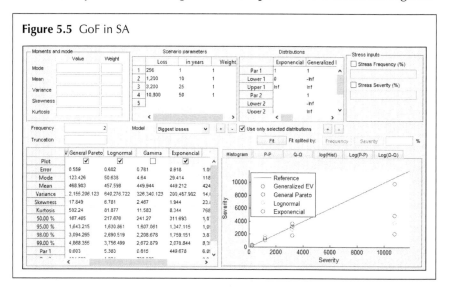

ally provided by the scenario analysis. Performing an Anderson–Darling or Kolmogorov–Smirnov with a reduced number of points will always deliver inconclusive results.

Therefore, the GoF analysis should be primarily focused on the graphical analysis of the PP and QQ plots and the ranking of the distributions based on the difference measurement on how each fitted distribution matches the input data.

Figure 5.5 shows the fitting in a four-point scenario. The fitting distributions are ranked from left to right based on the error minimisation described in Chapter 4. In the bottom right, the QQ plot graphically shows the differences between the distributions.

SPLITTING SCENARIO ANALYSIS INTO LOWER ORGANISATIONAL ENTITIES

In many instances, it is necessary to split a risk scenario into lower organisational units or legal entities. For instance, Solvency II requests capital to be reported at legal entity level and, therefore, modelling should be constructed at such level. When scenarios are defined at business unit level, they need to be split down into the legal entities of the business unit, when the business unit has more than one legal entity. The splitting could be also necessary for a more

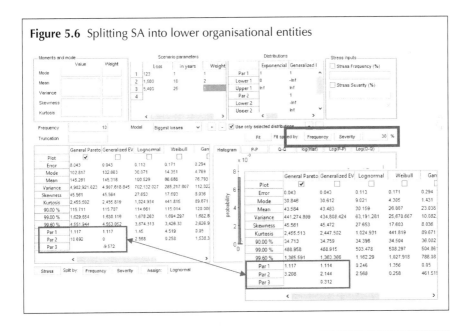

Figure 5.6 Splitting SA into lower organisational entities

granular capital allocation or for risk appetite cascading-down purposes.

Other examples are those scenarios that can be defined only at a very high level (such as the destruction of the company headquarters) and it is necessary to split them into lower organisational units for a granular and usable capital allocation. The split can be achieved by dividing the severity or the frequency of the scenario based on a materiality metric, depending on the nature of the risk. For instance, the materiality metric could be the asset size (in banking), number of policies (in insurance), number of employees, business volume and so on of the different legal entities. When severity is used to split the scenario impact, then the quantiles of the distribution need to be recalculated and the distribution refitted. When the scenario is split according to the frequency, the frequency that goes into the simulation is divided between the legal entities, but the derivation of percentiles is performed with the original frequency.

Figure 5.6 describes a process where a scenario has been split into two legal entities by 30% and 70%, respectively. The split of the scenario is done based on the severity. As a result, it can be seen that the shape or tail parameter of the Pareto distribution did not change, while the scale parameter did change significantly.

CONCLUSION

We have reached the end of Chapter 5, where we looked at the methods permitting a full, statistics-driven use of SA in the capital model. Moreover, the modelling process can incorporate tail-shape controls that allow for a more realistic SA distribution determination, in spite of the limited information typically available on tail behaviour from SA. These methods can also be used for allocating capital into granular organisation entities, permitting a detailed understanding of the operational risk profile and the impact of mitigation actions in such risk profile.

In summary, the SA modelling methods, together with SA collection framework presented in Chapter 3, make SA a high quality and robust input for capital modelling.

---

1   Most commonly used distributions in scenario analysis modelling are gamma, lognormal, weibul, GDP and Generalised EV

6

BEICFs Modelling and Integration into the Capital Model

Rafael Cavestany

After describing the modelling of ILD, ED and SA in Chapters 4 and 5, we now look at the modelling of business environmental and internal control factors (BEICFs), the fourth and last of the data elements of an operational risk capital model.

This chapter presents methods for the use of BEICFs in capital calculations. BEICFs are metrics (internal audit, RCSA, KRIs – see Chapter 3) that point to weaknesses permitting operational failures and hence they can provide a forward-looking character to the capital model. The benefits of the use of BEICFs are recognised by BCSG-AMA when it says, "BEICFs are operational risk management indicators that provide forward-looking assessments of business risk factors as well as a bank's internal control environment."

We introduced BEICFs and their use as an input into SA in Chapter 3, and, in the following sections, we present various methods for using BEICFs directly into the capital calculations:

❏ "*Ex post* capital adjustment driven by BEICFs": the use of BEICFs for the determination of capital add-ons to make capital estimates more forward looking and/or penalise/reward business units based on their operational risk management practices;
❏ "Modelling BEICFs": statistical analysis between BEICFs and operational losses, incidents, near misses and so on to determine an objective relationship for adjusting capital;
❏ "Qualitative and structured determination of correlations based

on BEICFs": the use of BEICFs-based factor models for the calculation of dependencies across ORCs; and

❑ "Capital attribution driven by BEICFs": the use of BEICFs in the attribution of the total operational risk capital to the BUs or ORCs.

EX POST CAPITAL ADJUSTMENT DRIVEN BY BEICFS

BEICFs are meant to provide a forward-looking character to capital calculation. Different BEICFs such as RCSA, KRIs and internal audit scores are designed to identify weaknesses that may lead to future losses. As operational risk management advances, weaknesses are identified and new controls and mitigation measures are implemented. This provides fresh information on the future operational risk profile, which, on the other hand, may take years to be reflected in the ILD and thus in corresponding ILD-based capital models.

Institutions may use the information from BEICFs to provide a more forward-looking character to the capital calculation. This information can also be introduced into capital estimations by establishing *ex post* adjustments. In fact, the BCSG-AMA says, "BEICFs are commonly used as an indirect input into the quantification framework and as an *ex post* adjustment to model output."

When introduced as an *ex post* capital adjustment, it should be validated that there is no double accounting if BEICFs are used in other ways in the capital model, such as if they are used as input into the scenario analysis. Most commonly, institutions introduce *ex post* adjustments through qualitative methods based on limited capital increase or decrease percentages. According to the AMAG survey on BEICFs, the common practice is to limit the impact on total capital to an increase or decrease such as 5%, 10%, 20% or 30%. This results in the BEICFs acting as a secondary factor in total capital estimation. When used, the introduction of BEICFs is designed to reflect considerations otherwise not taken into account and to provide capital estimations with a forward-looking character.

The BEICFs used to calculate capital adjustments generally differ by ORC or BU. For instance, staff turnover might be the only driver of capital adjustment in an ORC, while the number of corrections and incidents can be the basis of a different ORC capital adjustment. In addition, an ORC adjustment may be calculated with more than one indicator. This requires the integration of units with different scales, formats, signs and so on, which can be approached through the bucketing of indicator values and the standardisation of the bucket values for their consistent aggregation.

Figure 6.1 illustrates a method of creating a scorecard of indicators for this purpose. The indicator bucketing permits the standardisation of the indicator values facilitating the aggregation of very different scales, signs or unit indicators. The aggregation is performed based on assigned indicator weights. Finally, the total scorecard values are mapped to different levels of capital adjustment.

Figure 6.2 shows an example of implementation of *ex post* adjustments to capital estimations, following Figure 6.1. The adjustments are based on the results of internal control factors with a forward-looking character. RCSA and internal audit scores are used to increase capital charges. In fact, these indicators identify potential weaknesses in the processes and activities and may indicate that the risk profile is worse than reflected in the historical loss database.

On the other hand, the implementation of action plans for the mitigation of operational risk is used to decrease capital, as these represent an improvement of the risk profile. Improvements due to the implementation of action plans may not be reflected in the ILD database, and will not have a material impact on capital estimates for some years. In fact, this could discourage the mitigation of operational risk. The introduction of forward-looking adjustment into capital estimates allows us to reflect those improvements, encouraging the implementation of action plans.

In addition, capital add-ons can be implemented purely to encourage specific management behaviours, which may include incentives for the implementation of the operational risk framework in detail down to all business areas, processes, etc. Also, the institution may establish a target on total operational risk losses or frequencies and, if they are not met, the business unit or area is attributed a capital add-on for the additional implicit risk. Another example is capital add-on incentives to implement the scheduled action plans. A capital add-on attributed to such a unit implies that the business unit needs to obtain higher revenues to achieve the same percentage return on equity, which impacts on the performance evaluation of the business unit and its managers and, potentially, its managers' compensation.

Finally, capital adjustment driven by BEICFs can be used to influ-

Figure 6.1 Scorecard

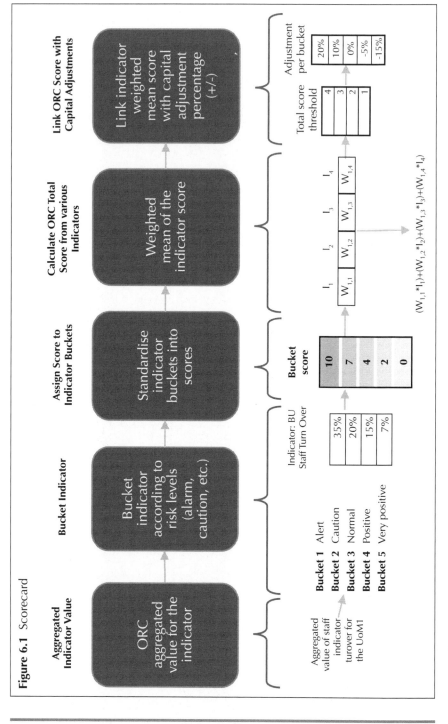

Figure 6.2 *Ex post* capital adjustments based on BEICFs

		Retail banking	Commercial banking	Merchant banking	Consumer finance	Sales and trading	Support	Payment and settlemens	TOTAL
Initial allocated capital		1203	956	311	492	555	150	297	3964
RCSA overall score	Score	91%	72%	82%	99%	79%	95%	90%	
	Adjustment	0%	10%	5%	0%	10%	0%	0%	167
Number and severity of audit non-conformities	Score	80%	81%	75%	91%	84%	50%	75%	
	Adjustment	5%	5%	10%	0%	5%	25%	10%	234
Implemented versus total action plans	% of completed	90%	50%	25%	95%	30%	45%	95%	
	Adjustment	-20%	0%	-10%	-25%	0%	0%	-25%	469

Total capital ExPost adjustment   68

Final OpRisk capital estimation   3,896

Figure 6.3 Example of capital add-ons to influence management

IMPLEMENTATION

	CIB Score	CIB Threshold % (<60 / 60–75 / >75)	CIB Capital add-on	PBB Score	PBB Threshold % (<60 / 60–75 / >75)	PBB Capital add-on	Africa Score	Africa Threshold % (<60 / 60–75 / >75)	Africa Capital add-on
Scenario	55%		20%	53%		20%	49%		20%
R&SCA	68%		0%	50%		20%	49%		20%
KRI	78%		-5%	61%		0%	57%		20%
Performance	71%		0%	58%		20%	54%		20%
Capital add-on	15%			60%			80%		

Op LOSS EVOLUTION

	CIB % chage from previous year	CIB Capital add-On	PBB % chage from previous year	PBB Capital add-on	Africa % chage from previous year	Africa Capital add-on
Total loss	-11%	-5%	9%	18%	-8%	-4%
Frequencies	-31%	-15%	-15%	-8%	3%	5%
Capital add-on	-10%		5%		1%	

TOTAL

	CIB	PBB	Africa
Final capital add-on	5%	65%	81%

ence management behaviour. Figure 6.3 shows the implementation of capital add-ons for penalising or rewarding the achievement of internal control factors' implementation goals and the reduction of operational loss frequency and total losses. Based on the degree of goal attainment, the different business units are given a positive or negative capital add-on. It can be seen that corporate and investment banking (CIB) is given first a 15% capital add-on because it has not completely achieved the implementation of internal control elements (such as scenario analysis and RCSA). However, given the good evolution of operational loss frequencies and severities, CIB is given a capital add-on relief.

MODELLING BEICFS

It is generally assumed that introducing BEICFs into the capital model via the use of statistical analysis is not feasible. However, institutions invest large amounts of money in internal audit reviews, KRIs, RCSA and other BEICFs, because it is actually believed that these indicators help in identifying weaknesses and preventing future operational failures. Hence, these types of metrics, at least collectively, should show operational loss prediction power.

A basic statistical modelling to identify a relationship between KRIs (after harmonising their frequencies), RCSA scores and so forth and basic capital model inputs such as loss frequencies, total loss amounts and frequency of losses above a specific severity threshold can be easily performed in order to shed light on the BEICFs' impact on capital. When a significant relationship is found, the relationship can be used to better project future capital requirements, identify root causes of operational losses or even create composite KRIs for early warning of increased losses (see also Chapter 12). The construction of this type of model and its application in the management of operational risk provides strong benefits to the organisation, creating an additional incentive for the collection of input data, BEICFs and ILD, with the adequate frequency and quality, as well as creating a clear link between the operational risk management, economic losses and the capital requirements.

The analysis can be performed first at an aggregated level (the entire institution or major business units) when determining the relationship between operational losses and high-level KRIs. In the case of internal audit or RCSA, the analysis can also be performed at a more disaggregated level, for instance lower business entities such as business areas, to increase the number of observations. Indicators potentially usable in this analysis include activity growth, scores from RCSA, staff turnover, near misses, internal audit number of nonconformities, IT incidents and bugs, overtime and number of mitigation plans implemented. These KRIs should be regressed to loss frequencies, total losses, frequency of large losses (above a specific threshold), mean loss of the period, etc. These regression models can be performed univariate, to understand the impact of individual factors, and multivariate, to create multifactor models.

Figure 6.4 describes a regression performed with BEICFs such as IT incidents, activity growth near misses and quarterly loss frequency against the existence of large events in the period (larger than €25,000). The results suggest a good model and significant variables. The number of observations has increased by segmenting the BEICFs data and corresponding loss sample by business unit and time.

Whenever a relationship is found between KRIs, such as activity growth and loss frequency, it can be used to obtain a more forward-looking and realistic capital estimation by projecting the model

Figure 6.4 Regression on BEICFs

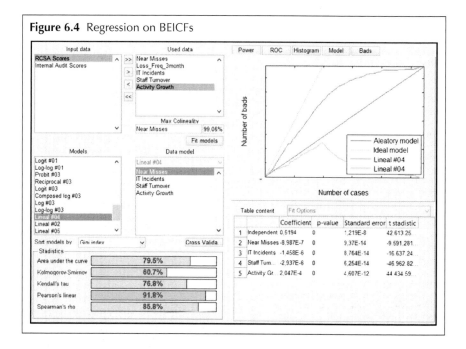

frequencies. Given the growth budgeted in the strategic plan of the institution, the frequencies of the corresponding business units and so on can be augmented into capital calculation.

The existence of a formal KRI database, generally supported by a GRC platform, and an appropriate interface with an analytical engine for regression analysis, would facilitate periodically carrying out this type of analysis as well as integrating BEICFs' predictive analytics into the daily risk management of the institution. In fact, this technology setup would eliminate large amounts of manual processes that would make the analytics hard to implement, and liberate analysts' time for value-added analytical tasks.

QUALITATIVE AND STRUCTURED DETERMINATION OF CORRELATIONS BASED ON BEICFS

Generally, the calculation of operational risk correlations presents multiple challenges if calculated with ILD (see Chapter 8 for the importance of operational risk correlations, the benefits of their internal calculation and a general calculation procedure). The reduced amount of ILD, the relevance of old data and the information lost during the extraction of seasonal effects make the calculation of robust correlations with ILD a challenge. The limited amount of data available gets even worse when the modelling is performed only with losses above high severity thresholds. If the model is based on SA, there are often very granular scenarios with low probability, making it almost impossible to calculate correlations based on ILD data for such low-frequency events.

BEICFs can be a useful input for the calculation of operational risk correlations by allowing for the implementation of qualitative structured methods based on KRIs and other business environmental factors. Indeed, business environmental factors allow for the development of a factor-based correlation model similar to those used in market and credit risk measurement such as those presented in Kealhofer and Bohn (1993), and adjusted as in Gupton *et al* (1997). These methods are based on the sensitivity of risks to factors and the correlations between such factors thus reducing the dimension of the correlation matrix from the number of ORCs to the much reduced number of factors. As a result, this method decreases significantly the correlation matrix in dimensionality and complexity and guarantees the consistency in correlation determination by providing a clear analytical framework. Such structure also facilitates a transparent justification of the correlations choices.

In this section, we present two methods for implementing the factor approach for a qualitative determination of operational risk correlations: a matrix multiplication approach and a composite index approach. Similar expert opinion driven approaches can be defined for the determination of the tail parameter of the t-Student copula.

A factor model for operational risk correlation determination can be implemented through matrix multiplication, as follows:

❑ Determine the factors that will drive the correlation determination. For simplicity, we shall consider the business environment factors described in Chapter 3. In practice, a factor model approach should be developed highly adapted to the institution idiosyncrasy. The business environment should be the main driver of dependencies across operational risk events, in our example. Alternatively, KRIs may also be used as the basis of qualitative estimation of correlations. Table 6.1 shows an example of business environment factors that may be used for the qualitative determination of an operational risk correlation matrix.

❑ Determine the correlation across the factors. This can be approached by using any of the methods proposed in Chapter 8. If a quantitative method is used, it is necessary to identify data series related to the factors from which to calculate the correlations. A qualitative method for determining the correlations across factors can also be implemented, following the processes described in this section. It can be assumed that the factors are independent and, thus, the correlation across ORCs would be driven only by the sensitivity to common factors. Table 6.2 shows an example of an operational-risk-factors correlation matrix, in which factors show positive dependencies. The values given to the pairwise correlations are based on expert perceptions on common drivers influencing factors.

❑ Elicitation method: the expert is asked to determine the sensitivity of the ORC to each of the risk factors. The sensitivity can be defined as the weight of each factor within the ORC. Generally, total factor weights should be less than 100% and the balance represents the idiosyncratic component of the ORC risk, which is independent of all risk factors. The idiosyncratic component

Table 6.1 Factors for operational risk correlation qualitative structured calculation

	Factor description	Factor short
Factor 1	The quality and ability of the institution´s employees, vendors and other resources	Employees-vendors
Factor 2	The complexity and riskiness of the business, products and processes they use to deliver them	Business complexity
Factor 3	The degree of automation of the product processes and capacity of the institution for automation	Automation
Factor 4	The legal and regulatory environment of the business	Legal environment
Factor 5	The evolution of the institution markets, including the diversity and sophistication of its customers and counterparties, the liquidity of the capital markets it trades in and the reliability of the infrastructure which supports those markets.	Market evolution

Table 6.2 Example of correlation across business environment factors

C=	Factor Correlations	Employees-vendors	Business complexity	Automation	Legal environment	Market evolution
	Employees-vendors	1	0.50	0.00	0.00	0.50
	Business complexity	0.50	1	0.50	0.50	0.75
	Automation	0.00	0.50	1	0.00	0.00
	Legal environment	0.00	0.50	0.00	1	0.50
	Market evolution	0.50	0.75	0.00	0.50	1

Table 6.3 Example of risk factor weighting for correlation factor model

		Weighting
Independent	I	0.0%
Very weak	VW	12.5%
Weak	W	25.0%
Weak-medium	WM	37.5%
Medium	M	50.0%
Medium-strong	MS	62.5%
Strong	S	75.0%
Very strong	VS	87.5%
Perfectly correlated	P	100.0%

211

represents the pure randomness (that is to say, good or bad luck) or things such as the mismanagement affecting only a specific ORC. Sensitivity to factors can be asked of experts using a free format or defining a sensitivity scale. An example of a sensitivity scale as illustrated in Table 6.3.

The analysis needed for the determination of the ORC sensitivity to common factors with other ORCs is possibly the most value-added activity in the qualitative determination of operational risk correlations, if linked to risk mitigation. This mitigation insight is probably not obtained calculating correlations using solely data series of historical data.

With these elements defined, the correlation matrix across the ORCs is then calculated[1] according to $W.\bar{C}.W$, where $\bar{C}$ is the matrix,

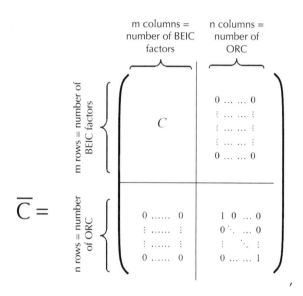

C is the business environment factor correlation matrix, described above, and W is the matrix of factor weightings (adjusted as in Gupton et al, 1997). In W, the columns, size n, represent the ORCs and the rows, size $m+n$, the different business environment factors plus the ORC idiosyncratic factors. Finally, W' is the transpose of W.

As an alternative to the method just described, the qualitative calculation of correlations can be implemented through the generation of composite indices, one per ORC based on the different factor sensitivities. Then, the ORC cross-correlations can be calculated directly from these ORC composite factors using any of the methods explained in "Operational risk correlations" in Chapter 8. The ORC composite factors can be generated as follows:

❑ A high number of business environmental factor replications, following a standard normal distribution and consistent with their cross correlations, C, are generated, for instance, 100,000 sets of correlated business factor replications. This can be completed using Monte Carlo simulation.
❑ An independent factor per ORC, also following a standard normal distribution, is generated, following the previous example, 100,000 replications. These series correspond to the independent/idiosyncratic factor component of each ORC.
❑ The ORC composite index is created as a linear combination of the business environmental factors, weighted to ORC sensitivity to each factor and to the independent factor component.
❑ Finally, correlations across ORCs are calculated numerically based on the ORC composite indexes.

Figure 6.5 represents the calculation of the correlation matrix for six ORCs based on composite indexes by ORC, as defined above. The final correlation is a function of the factor sensitivity and the correlation across factors. For instance, the correlation between failure of systems and failure of the ATM network is high with 0.27 because both risks have common sensitivities to factor: employees and vendors, business complexity and automation (see Table 6.1). Nevertheless, it is not perfect, since both ORCs have a significant weight on the independent factor. Then, the correlation between card-PIN security and fire-and-building destruction is very low at 0.06, since they have a very high idiosyncratic component. However, it is not 0, since the two risks share sensitivity to the employee and vendor factor. This method provides the means to justify correlations and guarantees consistency in correlation determination.

Comparing the matrix multiplication and the composite index-generation approaches, note that the top left matrix (with dimensions ORC by (Factors Sensitivity + ORC Idiosyncratic factor)) of Figure 6.5 is equivalent to the W matrix. The bottom left matrix

Figure 6.5 Example of operational risk correlations based on factor model

ORC	Factor sensitivity						ORC correlation matrix					
	Employees-vendors	Business complexity	Automation	Legal environment	Market evolution	ORC idiosyncratic component	Failure of systems	Failure of ATM networks	Fire & building destruction	Regulatory fines	Card pin security breakdown	Rogue computer programme
Failure of systems	0.10	0.10	0.20	0.00	0.00	0.60	1.00					
Failure of ATM networks	0.10	0.10	0.20	0.00	0.00	0.60	0.27	1.00				
Fire & building destruction	0.10	0.00	0.00	0.00	0.00	0.90	0.05	0.04	1.00			
Regulatory fines	0.10	0.10	0.05	0.20	0.10	0.45	0.29	0.29	0.06	1.00		
Card pin security breakdown	0.10	0.00	0.20	0.00	0.00	0.70	0.19	0.20	0.04	0.19	1.00	
Rogue computer programmer	0.20	0.05	0.05	0.00	0.05	0.65	0.19	0.20	0.06	0.25	0.14	1.00

Factors	Factor correlation matrix					
Employees-vendors	1.00					0.00
Business complexity	0.30	1.00				0.00
Automation	0.30	0.30	1.00			0.00
Legal environment	0.30	0.30	0.30	1.00		0.00
Market evolution	0.30	0.30	0.30	0.30	1.00	0.00

(dimensions factors x factors) is equivalent to the C matrix. And the top right matrix is the resulting ORC correlations.

In a factor-based approach for operational risk correlations, the values of the correlations are intuitive and easy to justify by analysing the sensitivity to common factors and the idiosyncratic component of the risk. Given the difficulties in obtaining a solid operational loss data series for correlation calculation, this method represents an attractive alternative and can provide a more easy-to-understand and acceptable correlation matrix. As mentioned before, the determination of correlations using this structured method also provides information on causes and dependencies, which can be a valuable insight for more efficient risk mitigation and increases the risk awareness in the institution.

CAPITAL ATTRIBUTION DRIVEN BY BEICFS

We refer to capital attribution as a non-statistical process of assigning total capital to ORCs. Capital allocation (see Chapter 8), differs from capital attribution in that the capital assignation process is derived from the implicit statistical characteristics of the capital model, such as the contribution of each of the ORCs to total standard deviation, expected shortfall, etc. Some institutions assign the total capital of the model to business units using a score or percentage approach rather than a statistical one. The reasons for using a score or percentage approach may include the lack of appropriate analytics or maturity of the operational risk models or the willingness to incentivise specific management behaviour.

These methods vary significantly and may take into consideration materiality metrics based on financial statements or business volume and internal control factors, such as RCSA, KRIs, internal audit results or some metrics of internal losses experienced. When multiple metrics drive the capital attribution, they are averaged using specific weightings, similar to the score-card method explained in the earlier section about *ex post* capital adjustments. The weightings are generally determined qualitatively, based on the relevance of each driver for capital consumption.

Figure 6.6 shows an example of a capital attribution to six business units based on both financial statements and internal control factors. The left-hand columns under the "Financial statements" label include both the revenue and three-year average gross margin values, which are used to calculate attribution percentages based on weightings (the three years' average is inspired in the standard and basic indicator approaches for operational risk capital models). The columns in the middle under the "Internal control factor" label are the scores coming from RCSA, KRIs and scoring of internal audits. These columns are weighted and averaged for determining the final percentage capital allocation by business unit.

BEICFs can also play a key role in the cascading-down of operational risk appetite (ORA), as presented in Chapter 11. Figure 6.7

Figure 6.6 Example of capital attribution based on BEICFs

Business units	Financial statements			Internal control factors				Attribution
	Budgeted revenue (figures in €m)	3 year avg gross margin (figures in €m)	Weighted average proportion	RCSA	KRI	Scoring of internal audit	Internal control factor weighting	% of total capital attributed
Weighting	70%	30%	100%	50%	30%	20%	100%	
Business unit 1	1,613	137.77	27.44%	34.0	5.7	17.4	22.2	41.22%
Business unit 2	2,263	54.33	29.56%	20.3	7.0	1.2	12.5	25.03%
Business unit 3	172	10.62	2.67%	28.6	4.9	-	15.8	2.85%
Business unit 4	717	55.29	11.82%	15.0	6.3	18.1	13.0	10.40%
Business unit 5	1,023	45.00	14.68%	29.0	4.0	9.3	17.6	17.47%
Business unit 6	286	163.97	13.83%	1.5	6.3	3.0	3.2	3.02%
	6,074	466.97	100.00%					

Figure 6.7 Using BEICFs in ORA cascading down

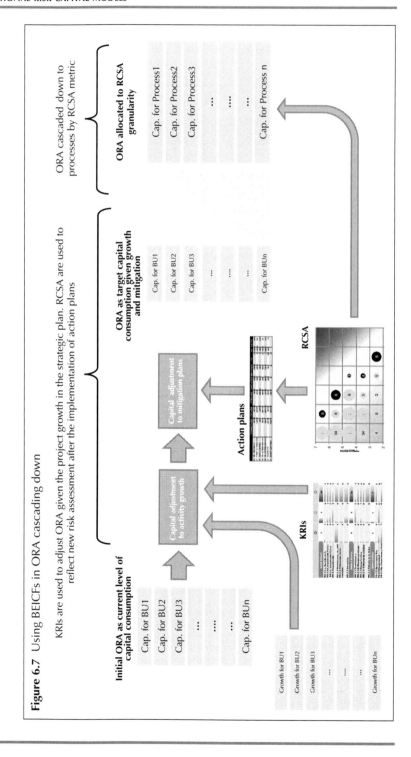

KRIs are used to adjust ORA given the project growth in the strategic plan. RCSA are used to reflect new risk assessment after the implementation of action plans

presents the high-level workflow of the ORA cascading down to very specific points for the monitoring of operational risk. In a first step, KRIs, including business volume, are used to adjust ORA to the projected growth in the strategic plan. Also, RCSA are used to adjust expected loss materialisations given the introduction of new action plans.

In a second step, RCSA results are used to cascade down ORA to business entities more granular than the capital model allocation. This permits us to monitor risk materialisation and identify specific processes that need to be improved, allowing a granular monitoring of the institutional risk profile. An RCSA metric can be based on the risk evaluations. Alternatively, the RCSA can be treated as scenario analysis fitting severity and frequency distributions and performing a Monte Carlo simulation to determine the total losses. These calculations can then be used as the metric to cascade down ORA.

CONCLUSION

BEICFs can play a major and high-value role in a capital model, adding institution-specific, forward-looking information about operational weaknesses and potential future failures. In fact, BEICFs can be used in many critical pieces of a capital model including capital *ex post* adjustments, capital allocation, model parameter statistical adjustment, the creation of management incentives and operational risk correlations in granular ORCs.

---

1   A detailed explanation of the logic and calculations in a factor model for determining correlation matrixes can be found in Gupton *et al* (1997), in the chapter "Estimating Asset Correlations", from the RiskMetrics Group.

REFERENCES

Gupton, Greg M., Christopher C. Finger and Mickey Bhatia, 1997, "The Benchmark for Understanding Credit Risk" CreditMetrics Technical. Paper presented by J.P. Morgan, New York, April 2.

Kealhofer, S., and Jeffrey R. Bohn, 1993, "Portfolio Management of Default Risk". Paper first published by KMV, San Francisco, California, November 15.

Hybrid Model Construction: Integration of ILD, ED and SA

Rafael Cavestany, Daniel Rodriguez, Fabrizio Ruggeri

Once the modelling of the four data elements has been performed, as presented in the last three chapters, we now look into the merger of these data elements into a hybrid model. The merger of data elements will result in a single loss severity distribution (or loss frequency distribution, if applied to frequencies) of the operational losses for the ORC incorporating different data elements.

Regarding the merger of different data elements, BCSG-AMA says, "A bank should carefully consider how the data elements are combined and used to ensure that the bank's operational risk capital charge is commensurate with its level of risk exposure."

This chapter presents credibility theory and various methods for merging the different data elements into a single loss or frequency distribution hybrid model, organised in the following sections:

❏ "Credibility theory: determining the weights for ILD, ED and SA in the hybrid model": In this section, we look at the different models for credibility theory that permit us to determine the weight of each data element within the hybrid model methods presented in this chapter.
❏ "The mixture approach": In this section, we present a method for hybrid models based on mixing the distributions of the different data elements during the Monte Carlo simulation given a specific weight to each data element.
❏ "The Bayesian approach": This section presents the use of Bayesian statistics to the construction of a hybrid model.

❏ "Tail complementing with external data losses": In this section, we look at how we enrich the distribution tail with additional observations from other sources such as external data.

❏ "Tail complementing with scenarios": This section presents a method of including SAs into the ILD fitting process, where the SAs are informed with a given probability of occurrence.

❏ "Mixing distribution properties from different data elements during the fit": Here, we look at a method for defining a hybrid model with distribution characteristics from different data elements, ie, low percentiles and mean from ILD, high percentiles from SA and kurtosis and tail from ED.

All these methods follow sound statistical processes, are based on widely accepted statistical principles and can help to comply with BCSG-AMA, which says, "The combination of data elements should be based on a sound statistical methodology."

CREDIBILITY THEORY: DETERMINING THE WEIGHTS FOR ILD, ED AND SA IN THE HYBRID MODEL[1]

The aggregation of different data elements (ILD, ED, SA ...) may require the allocation of weights to the different data elements, depending on the aggregation method. Examples of aggregation methods requiring weighted data elements are those presented in Chapter 7. Credibility theory provides a robust statistical framework for determining the weights for the different data elements, by determining the credibility of the available internal loss data, and has been widely used in many fields, mostly in actuarial science, but also in others such as engineering, climate change, etc.

In actuarial science, the term "credibility" is associated with the calculation of the appropriate risk premium for insurance policies by combining different sources of information. In this case, the sources of information are the specific historical data of the insured individual and the data of the group to which the individual belongs. An estimate of the risk premium based on a single data source, either aggregated (data from the corresponding to the group) or individual risk (the insured's own historical data), may produce a biased result. The rationale behind credibility theory is that it is possible to get a better estimate by combining two sources of information: collective and individual risk. The joint estimation is done using the weighted sum of the values of each source, giving greater weight to the more credible source of information.

In the area of operational risk, financial institutions wishing to use an AMA (advanced measurement approach) in Basel II/III and internal models for Solvency II for capital requirements have to implement a robust statistical models. At the same time, regulatory capital frameworks require the use of the four data elements (ILD, ED, SA and BEICFs) and their integration through a sound statistical methodology. The integration of the four data elements may require the challenging task of combining the frequency and severity distributions calculated from different data elements. ILD generally would have been collected by the entities over several years and usually contain few low-frequency, high-severity events, which are the most influential in the capital model. ED can be obtained through database consortia and external providers. These databases are particularly rich in low-frequency, high-severity events, since losses are recorded only above a specific severity threshold and the data is collected from multiple institutions. Finally, SA can provide us with the expert opinions on events due to new circumstances from which there is no experience.

The integration of different data elements in operational risk is a similar problem to the integration of individual data and insured group data in an insurance company, thus credibility theory can be used. In fact, the individual data can be assimilated to be ILD and the group data to be ED. This field is still in progress as the first models were presented by Bühlmann and his fellow authors (Bühlmann and Gisler 2005; Bühlmann, Shevchenko and Wüthrich 2007).

In Appendix 2, we introduce various credibility theory models – the classic models, the Bühlmann model and the Bühlmann–Straub models – and a discussion of how to apply the Bühlmann–Straub models in situations where there are losses with a difference of severity. Within the following sections, we present a summary of the application of these models and two examples of credibility theory implementation in operational risk measurement.

While the actuarial application of credibility theory is mostly applied to obtain an average (own-risk and group-risk data) of the most "credible" expected loss, in operational risk it is applied to complement the entity's ILD with ED and SA, as sources for extreme potential losses and a more updated risk profile. An approach is to use the credibility weight obtained from credibility theory, z (see Appendix 2) to weight ED and SA when constructing the HM methods in this chapter.

Table 7.1 presents a summary of the possible implementations of credibility theory under the different methods later discussed in more detail in Appendix 2.

Also, it is possible to use credibility theory to calculate a weighted average of the distribution function parameters, stemming from the modelling of the different data elements (see the final section below). This type of model was featured in a 2005 article by Bühlmann, later developed in detail by Agostini (Agostini, Talamo and Vecchione 2010). This section uses the Bühlmann–Straub credibility models for the integration of estimates from different sources, such as internal data and scenario analysis is applied.

We start the presentation of this method, by defining the credibility equation (see Appendix 2) of the posterior distribution:

$$\overline{xy} = z \times x + (1 - z) \times y,$$

where x and y are two different data elements and z and $(1 - z)$ are the weight of each data element in the posterior distribution.

The proposed method requires that both distribution parameters, x for ILD and y for SA, be consistent. This means that both estimates are built using the same parametric distributions family with equivalent parameters.

The following sections present two examples of this approach (similar to Agostini *et al*): the calculation of frequency is based on the determination of the λ parameters of Poisson distribution from two different data elements; the determination of the severity is based on the tail parameter of the generalised Pareto distribution (GPD) of ILD and SA. Nevertheless, other approaches can also be implemented deriving the credibiity of the available data from the analysis of ED.

Integrating frequency distributions

In this example, the volatility of the frequency distribution parameter is determined by analysing samples of frequency taken in different periods of time. The loss frequency distribution of losses is modelled through Poisson distribution that depends only on a parameter, usually denoted as λ. The value of this parameter can be estimated as the average number of losses observed by time period,

Table 7.1 Summary of operational risk credibility implementations

Model	Formulation	Uses and limitations
Classical model – complete credibility	$$N \geq \left(\dfrac{q_i - \dfrac{\alpha}{2}}{k} \right)^2 \left(\dfrac{\sigma_X}{\mu_X} \right)^2$$	Indicates the amount of data needed to ensure that severity has complete credibility. Calculated under assumptions of normality. It will probably be insufficient for the tails.
Classical model – partial credibility	$$z = \dfrac{k}{q_1 - \dfrac{\alpha}{2}} \dfrac{\mu_X}{\sigma_X} \sqrt{N}$$	Provides the proportion needed from other sources to supplement ILD. It requires the underlying data to be normally distributed, which is uncommon in operational risk loss data. Could be used for frequency distribution of high frequency.
Bühlmann	$$z = \dfrac{N}{N + \dfrac{\mu_{PV}}{\sigma_{HM}^2}}$$	Permits the relaxation of the normality distribution. It is more appropriate for operational risk data. It can be used to determine the weight to mix two different data sources, the weight to average the distribution parameter (eg, tail parameter, shape parameter), and so on. It can be used for modelling severity and frequency distributions. Nevertheless, it requires that the variance in the data sample be constant in time.
Bühlmann–Straub	$$z = \dfrac{m_s}{m_s + \dfrac{\mu_{PV}}{\sigma_{HM}^2}}$$	It permits us to relax the assumption of constant variance along time in the data sample. However, it still requires the behaviour of large losses to be a linear combination of small losses.
Bühlmann–Straub (for large and small losses)	$$z = \dfrac{m_s}{m_s + \dfrac{\mu_{PV}}{\sigma_{HM}^2} + \dfrac{m_s(l + l_s)^2}{\sigma_{HM}^2}}$$	It permits us to relax the assumption that the behaviour of large losses is a linear combination of small losses. It is the most complete model for credibility for operational risk modelling.

ie, the sampling frequency. Assuming that available N observation periods in each of these observations were recorded, X_i is the sample frequency:

$$\lambda_m = \frac{1}{N} \sum_{i=1}^{N} X_i$$

We may consider λ as the variable to be estimated by Bühlmann–Straub credibility model. Thus, you have to estimate the corresponding values of μ_{pV}, σ^2_{HM} and m_s. The average value is given by the value of λ, while the variance of the process is given by λ / N, which can be identified with σ^2_s with λ and m_s with N. Bühlmann–Straub's running as:

$$\mu_{pV} = E(\lambda) = \lambda_m$$
$$\sigma^2_{HM} = \mathrm{var}(\lambda)$$

Applying these terms to the credibility factor, we get:

$$z = \frac{N}{N + \dfrac{\lambda_m}{\mathrm{var}(\lambda)}}$$

Integrating severity distributions

This section presents a method for merging ILD and SA through the weighted average of the GPD tail parameter. The necessary tail parameter volatility estimation is obtained from the answers of different experts to the SA forms. Finally, the tail parameter of the severity distribution is obtained as a z weighted average of that derived from ILD and SA.

As mentioned earlier in this work, the GPD function is defined by three parameters: the location, μ; the scale, σ; and the tail, ξ. The most determinant parameter is ξ, which, in the presented method, is calculated as a weighted average from the results of the ILD fit and the SA. Then, the other two parameters of the GPD will be derived from a fitting process in which ξ is fixed and μ and σ are optimised to match the ILD.

The method starts with a scenario analysis, where M experts are given questions on the severity distribution of an ORC following any of the elicitation methods explained in Chapter 3, "Scenario rating". From there, M estimations of the ξ parameter are obtained following the methods presented in Chapter 5. These ξ_i estimates, from Bühlmann–Straub credibility parameters, are calculated as follows:

$$\mu_{pV} = \sum_{i=1}^{M} \frac{l(\xi_i)}{M}$$

$$\sigma^2_{HM} = \sum_{i=1}^{M} \frac{(\xi_i - \bar{\xi})^2}{M-1},$$

where I (ξ_i) is the Fisher information index or the covariance matrix and $\bar{\xi}$ is the average of the estimates ξ_i obtained from the answers of each of the experts, ie:

$$\bar{\xi} = \sum_{i=1}^{M} \frac{\xi_i}{M}$$

Now, the final ξ parameter for the ORC will be a weighted average of the results of the ILD and SA analysis:

$$\xi_{xy} = z\bar{\xi} + (1-z)\xi_s,$$

where ξ_{xy} is the final, or posterior, tail parameter for the ORC, ξ_s is the prior tail parameter derived from ILD, $\bar{\xi}$ is defined above, N is the number of observation periods and z is the credibility factor:

$$z = \frac{N}{N + \dfrac{\mu_{pV}}{\sigma_{HM}^2}} = \frac{N}{N + \dfrac{\sum_{i=1}^{M} \dfrac{I(\xi_i)}{M}}{\sum_{i=1}^{M} \dfrac{\left(\xi_i - \bar{\xi}\right)^2}{M-1}}}$$

For the severity, we have used the expert evaluations to estimate the credibility factor. ILD can be used to estimate the actual risk in the distribution tail, but does not give us the information we need to estimate the uncertainty associated with the estimate. The scenarios are, however, a way to assess the risk class in a subjective way, but complete, covering all potentially dangerous events that relate to the ORC.

A similar approach can be implemented by deriving the implicit uncertainty on the parameter estimates, by analysing ED from consortia such as ORX. This can be performed by defining consistent criteria for segmenting the ED from which to derive the volatility estimates. Using ED will provide a more implementable and objective process for the calculations, is more doable by the operational risk modelling team independently, does not require the involvement of multiple experts.

THE MIXTURE APPROACH
The mixture approach is widely implemented because it is simple and direct. The underlying principle is creating a hybrid distribution model through the mixing, during the Monte Carlo simulation, of

the distributions from different sources of information or data element (ILD, ED and SA), weighted by the credibility factor, z, of each of the elements. It allows the merging of an unlimited number of data elements (different ED sources, SA, etc), provided they have been previously modelled into distributions and that a weight is assigned to each data element. The weight of different data elements can be determined using credibility theory as earlier. Then, the hybrid distribution will be the result of losses generated by the mix of the different distribution models of the individual data elements, given the weight of each element. This process can be applied to both the severities and frequency distributions.

Below in the numbered list is the description of the process required to merge two severity distributions from two different data elements, ILD and ED. In a simple case, with only one distribution segment, the ILD and ED thresholds are coordinated, as in Figure 7.1. In the illustration, it can be seen that the ILD severity distribution has a 1,000 threshold, while the ED has a 10,000 threshold. The frequency is 100 annual events. Finally, it has been determined that the credibility of an ILD for the threshold above 10,000 corresponds to a weight, z, of 30% and 70%, $1 - z$, for ED. For the mixing of both severity distributions, it is necessary to divide the ILD distribution into two segments, below and above 10,000. Only in the segment above 10,000 will the ILD and ED be mixed. The segment below 10,000 will include only internal losses.

1. A distribution model for each of the data elements is created as well as external data scaled as presented in Chapter 4. Also, a weight, z, for each of the information sources should have been determined, given their credibility.
2. Coordination of the threshold of the different data element models: most commonly, each of the data elements is modelled with a different threshold. Internal loss data is modelled with a threshold specific to the characteristics of the data sample. External data generally has an implicit threshold of the ED provider data collection thresholds.[2]
3. The loss frequency is split between both segments. The frequency split would be proportional to the cumulative probability at the threshold. Therefore, for the severity segment below 10,000, the frequency will be $100 \times F(10,000) = 100 \times 89.19$

= 89.19 annual events, where F(10,000) is the cumulative distribution function with which the ILD severity distribution has been modelled. The frequency of the segment above 10,000 would then be 100x (1 – F(10,000)) = 10.81 annual events. Alternatively, the frequency split can be derived from the empirical distribution, if it is considered to be sufficiently populated around the threshold.

4. Then, two truncated distributions are defined for each of the segments. In this case, the segments above and below 10,000 in the ILD distribution. These segments will be defined as F(x | 1,000 <X<10,000) and F(x | x≥10,000), as explained in Appendix 1.

5. A Monte Carlo simulation creates the hybrid distribution: for each of the losses, there should be a 0.8919 probability that the sample value will come from F(x | 1,000<X<10,000). Consequently, there should be a 0.1081 probability that the loss will be taken from the other segment above 10,000. Given the loss is from the segment above 10,000, then there is a 0.3 probability, z, that the loss will be taken from the ILD model, and 0.7 probability, $1 - z$, that the loss will be taken from the ED model. The result is a hybrid tail distribution above the 10,000 mark, which is made up of 30% of losses from the ILD model and 70% from the scaled ED model.

More complex systems can be created with multiple distribution segments and information sources (various ED sources, scenario analyses, etc) which can be resolved by applying the steps described above. Also, the system can include mixtures of frequency distributions if different data elements for frequency are used. Alternatively, the mixte can be bilt based on joint loss distributions, rather than on severity and freqency distribution. Figure 7.2, shows a modelling where internal loss data, external data and scenario analysis have been parameterised. In the example, the severity distribution was modelled in three segments. In the low segment, 100% is ILD and is simulated with a nonparametric or empirical distribution of 5,868 frequency. The medium segment is simulated with a mixture of scenario analysis and ILD. Scenario analysis was assigned 30% of the weight and ILD the rest. The high-severity segment is modelled with the three information sources, where ED is 50%, scenario analysis is

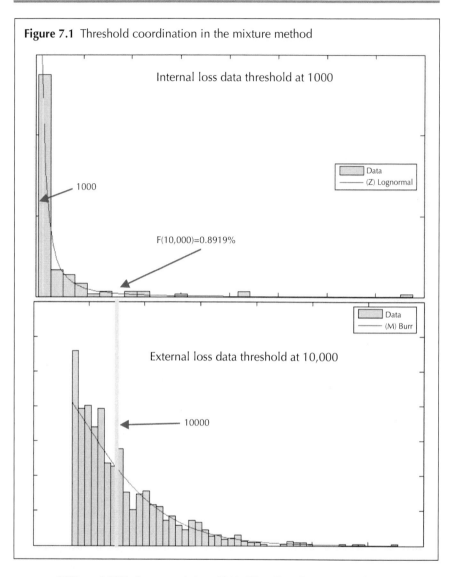

Figure 7.1 Threshold coordination in the mixture method

30% and ILD the remaining 20%. The distribution model of the ILD changes in each of its three segments. The low segment is a nonparametric distribution, the medium segment or body is a lognormal and the tail is a Burr distribution. The frequency by segment is 5,858 in the low segment, 50.1 in the body and 4.642 in the tail.

Figure 7.2 Example of mixture method implementation

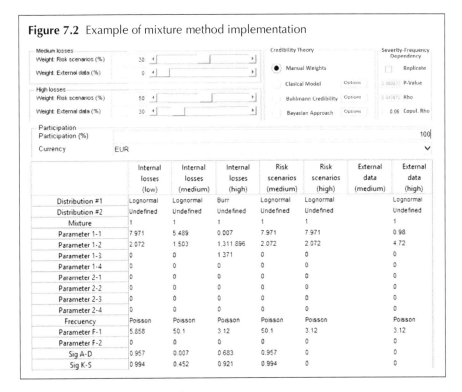

THE BAYESIAN APPROACH[3]

Proper estimation of tail behaviour is one of the most important and challenging aspects when considering operational risks. It refers to events that are very rare but may be very disruptive for a financial institution or a company. There is therefore the need for a sound approach that allows the use of all possible sources of information and is based on solid scientific grounds. The Bayesian statistical approach[4] provides a robust answer to this question, which allows for the formal combination of available data about the problem at hand and available knowledge provided by experts and/or data from past, similar cases. The combination is provided by the Bayes Theorem, whose simplest form is given by:

$$P(A|B) = P(B|A)P(A)/P(B), \text{ with } P(B) = P(B|A)P(A) + P(B|\bar{A})P(\bar{A})$$

We can think of three possible events:

❏ A = The new fraud detection system is able to prevent major frauds occurring in an institution.

229

❏ $\bar{A}$ = In spite of the new fraud detection system, major frauds still occurr in an institution.

❏ B = After one year the antifraud system was successfully implemented: the institution's IT is, in a timely manner, providing all the required inputs; the personnel managing the system were adequately trained; and the procedures associated with the system's alerts were mandated in policies and procedures and timely executed by the antifraud department.

The final goal is to estimate the posterior probability $P(A\,|\,B)$ of the institution being able to identify and avoid all fraud attacks, if it has successfully implemented the antifraud system. The probability is called posterior because it refers to the probability of the event of interest, A, after observing another one, ie, B. It differs from the prior probability $P(A)$, which corresponds to the opinion that the institution had, prior to observing B, on preventing all major fraud attacks. This is the stage in which past data and bank security experts' experience intervene. If we consider for a moment just the second source of information (banks' expertise collected through SA), the prior probability is based on the institution's past experience on fraud, the external fraud environment/levels, the fraud type and experience with fraud in similar cases, to name just some. The elicitation of such probability is not, in general, a simple task, since the security experts have to look, not only to information about the antifraud system, but also about the propensity of the bank to risk, possibly overestimating or underestimating the success probability. This aspect, whose description is beyond the scope of this book, relates Bayesian statistics with decision analysis.

The probability of not suffering a major fraud attack, $P(\bar{A})$, comes from just the basic laws in probability, ie, $P(\bar{A}) = 1 - P(A)$. The other two probabilities, $P(B\,|\,A)$ and $P(B\,|\,\bar{A})$, could come from historical fraud data and the experience in implementing systems. They represent the probability of a successful implementation of an antifraud system for those situations where the antifraud system was able or not able to avoid major fraud attacks.

As an example, suppose that $P(A) = 0.7$, $P(B\,|\,A) = 0.4$, $P(B\,|\,\bar{A}) = 0.2$. In this case, we have:

$$P(B) = P(B\,|\,A)P(A) + P(B\,|\,\bar{A})P(\bar{A}) = 0.4 \times 0.7 + 0.2 \times (1-0.7) = 0.34 \text{ and}$$
$$P(A\,|\,B) = P(B\,|\,A)P(A)/P(B) = 0.4 \times 0.7 / 0.34 \approx 0.8235$$

Therefore, the knowledge about the antifraud system's implementation after one year increases the probability of avoiding all major fraud attacks from 0.7 to 0.8235.

This is definitely a very simple case, but very instructive about the possibility of using the same approach when interested in the tail behaviour of operational risks. The Bayesian approach is getting more and more popular, especially over the last 20 or so years after the development of algorithms – and the advent of cheap computational power – mainly those known under the general name of Markov Chain Monte Carlo (MCMC) methods, which made computation of posterior probabilities and quantities of interest easier with respect to the past. Bayesian statistics is nowadays flourishing not only from a foundational and methodological viewpoint, but also in terms of applications in finance, economics, engineering, medicine, genomics, life sciences, environmental sciences, actuarial sciences and social sciences, to name just a few. The interested reader can find many books on Bayesian statistics, requiring different levels of knowledge. A relatively easy book is Bolstad (2007).

In the context of operational risks, there are quantities that can be hard to estimate using current data, especially the ones that are very rare or, using statistical jargon, are extreme events. We will concentrate on them, since their estimation and forecast are very critical in this context. As an example, we could think of an insurance company interested in fraudulent claims exceeding €10,000,000.

First of all, a statistical model is necessary to describe the size of the fraudulent claims. The choice is actually done at two different stages: *a priori*, the selection of a model is justified by known properties of the observed quantity (eg, claim size); whereas, *a posteriori*, after performing a statistical analysis, models are compared in terms of their skill in describing the observed data (using, eg, goodness-of-fit tests, Bayes factors). For simplicity, we use exponential distribution to describe the claim size, assuming that larger claims are always less likely than smaller ones (fat-tail distributions can be implemented but have been omitted in the explanation due to the implicit complex algebra required). If there are reasons to exclude many very small claims, then a gamma distribution (or a lognormal one) could be chosen, since there are sizes that are more likely than smaller and larger ones. After performing the statistical analysis, exponential, gamma, lognormal or fat-tail distribution models could be compared in terms of goodness of fit with respect to the observed data. It is an iterative process, which requires software able to suggest models *a priori* compatible with users' knowledge and compare them *a posteriori*, suggesting the most adequate one.

This description of the choice of an adequate model applies to both the Bayesian approach and its main competitor, ie, the frequentist one. The peculiar thing about the Bayesian approach is the choice of the prior distribution.

For simplicity, let us suppose that claim sizes in an insurance company can be described by an exponential distribution with only one parameter λ, ie, if X is the random variable denoting the claim size, then its continuous density function (CDF) is:

$$f(x \mid \lambda) = \lambda e^{-\lambda x}, x > 0$$

Given a sample of claim sizes, X_1, ..., X_n, then the frequentist approach estimates the parameter λ using the maximum-likelihood estimator (see Chapter 4). In the Bayesian approach, λ is considered a random variable whose distribution allows for the incorporation of an expert's and past knowledge. First of all, it is worth observing that $1/\lambda$ is the expected claim size EX (from properties of the exponential distribution) and λ equals $1/EX$. The expert has some knowledge about EX and the statistician's job consists of extracting as much information as possible from the expert to find an adequate model (a prior distribution) to describe it. *Ad hoc* software is very valuable at this stage, both in acquiring information from the expert and showing them the prior distribution obtained by the statistician. The expert could provide information on λ (actually on EX) in terms of, eg, the most likely value, upper and lower bounds, median or other quantiles. The information could be obtained through graphical displays, questionnaires, physical meetings, training sessions. The software, properly used, should provide different choices of distributions (eg, gamma or lognormal) fitting the expert's input, and statistician and expert should work together, interactively, until an acceptable distribution is found. The final goal of the training process would be to provide the expert with the skill to perform alone all the tasks, and a very user-friendly software program would be necessary to achieve it.

A gamma distribution could be deemed useful to model prior knowledge on λ and the expert could provide three quantiles for it (ie, three values of λ such that the probability of being less than them equals three given values, eg, 0.25, 0.50, 0.75). Two quantiles are sufficient to find the two parameters α and β of the gamma density:

$$f(x \mid \alpha, \beta) = \beta^{\alpha} x^{\alpha-1} e^{-\beta x} / \Gamma(\alpha), x > 0,$$

whereas the third one is used to assess the compatibility of the three values, adjusting them until the gamma density fits them reasonably well.

Another possibility for the choice of α and β is provided by two other quantities: mean and variance. For the gamma distribution, the former is given by α/β, whereas the other is α/β^2. The expert could provide their opinion on the mean through a value, providing another one on the variance as a measure of their belief on the assessed value on the mean (small variance corresponds to strong belief on the assessed values, unlike a large variance). The software should allow for different choices in the selection of the parameters of a distribution when its functional form (eg, gamma) has been chosen.

So far, parameters have been estimated based on an expert's opinions but, as we saw earlier, past data could be used, eg, mean sample sizes from the past could be transformed into assessment on λ, remembering that $\lambda = 1/\text{EX}$. We would have a "sample" on λ whose mean and variance could be equated to the gamma mean and variance, ie, α/β and α/β^2, respectively, using the method of moments.

Once both the statistical model for the fraudulent claim size X and the prior distribution on λ have been chosen, then inferences on λ and forecasts on future claim sizes are possible. The posterior distribution, obtained through the Bayes Theorem, is the key element for both inferences and forecast. It is possible to estimate the parameter λ using, eg, the posterior mean, ie, the mean of the posterior distribution (this choice has a justification from Bayesian Decision Analysis, based on the search of the value minimising an adequate expected loss). In the previous example, it is possible to see that the posterior distribution on λ is still gamma with parameters $\alpha + n$ and $\beta + \Sigma X_i$, so that the posterior mean is $(\alpha + n)/(\beta + \Sigma X_i)$. Simple computations lead to the posterior predictive density of a future claim size Y, after observing the sample $X_1, ..., X_n$:

$$f(Y \mid X_1, ... X_n) = (\alpha + n) \times (\beta + \Sigma X_i)^{(\alpha+n)} / (\beta + \Sigma X_i + Y)^{\alpha+n+1}$$

Figure 7.3 illustrates a conceptual workflow for the derivation of the hybrid distribution under the Bayesian approach, using SA and ILD. We have three distributions in the workflow: the frequentist distribution, the prior distribution and the posterior distribution. In a first step, a frequentist approach is used to derive the severity frequentist distribution, for instance, an exponential distribution, $f(x; \lambda)$, fitted to ILD using MLE. Under the Bayesian approach, the λ parameter is not assumed to be constant but to follow a specific distribution, the prior distribution, and thus, in a second step, SA is used to raise additional information on the distribution of the λ parameter, by providing various percentiles of λ. In our example, the prior distribution is assumed to be a gamma distribution $f(\lambda; \emptyset; k)$. A fitting process thus is implemented to determine the parameters of the prior distribution, where the inputs are the mean of the distribution from the frequentist approach, and various percentiles of the λ derived from SA. Different techniques could be used to combine these two sources of information. A mathematical one could consist of considering a mixture of two cumulative distribution functions (CDFs), $f_1(\lambda; \theta_1)$ and $f_2(\lambda; \theta_2)$, obtained from the past data and the expert's opinion, respectively. The two CDFs would be joined in considering a unique CDF given by:

$$f(\lambda;\theta_1,\theta_2,\varepsilon)=(1-\varepsilon)f_1(\lambda;\theta_1)+\varepsilon f_2(\lambda;\theta_2), 0 \leq \varepsilon \leq 1,$$

where ε denotes the relative weight given to the two sources. A large (small) value of ε denotes that the expert's opinion is deemed more (less) important than the information provided by past data (credibility theory, as presented earlier, provides a statistical method to determine the weight of each source). It is possible to rely completely on either the past data or the expert's opinion, just taking $\varepsilon = 0$ or $\varepsilon = 1$, respectively. This technique might not be very effective since we expect that the two CDFs will have, for example, different means and the sum of two gamma CDFs with different means results in a density function with two modes (two "peaks" in the graphical display), and that result would be hardly acceptable, since we should not expect, in general, to have two "most likely" values. An alternative approach could consist of considering a unique CDF whose parameters are obtained by merging the parameters of the two CDFs. If both CDFs are gamma, then it might be possible to consider a unique gamma CDF, whose mean is just the weighted mean of the

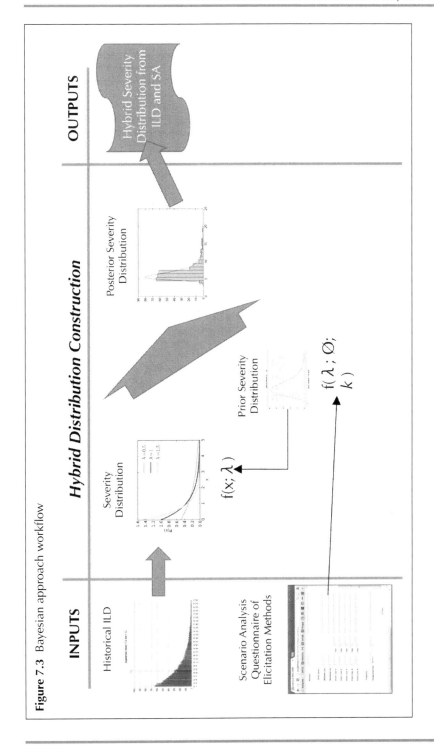

Figure 7.3 Bayesian approach workflow

means of the two CDFs (with the weight ε playing the same role as before). The variance could be again determined based on how strong the expert believes in the obtained mean, as discussed earlier. This procedure is based on the interaction between expert and statistician, helped by adequate software capable of showing the results of the merger of the different sources and used until a satisfactory (from the point of view of the expert) CDF is obtained.

Finally, we generate the posterior distribution, which is the result of the exponential distribution with a λ provided by the prior distribution, the gamma $f(\lambda; \emptyset; k)$. The posterior distribution represents the hybrid model distribution.

Therefore, there is the need for software that gives the possibility of using past data, assessing quantities and choosing priors interactively for a broader class of problems, including the ones of interest in this book. As we saw earlier, operational risks are often determined by rare events and extreme-value distributions, such as GEV (generalised extreme value) and GPD (generalised Pareto distribution), which are the proper statistical models to describe their behaviour and forecast them. Assessment of prior distributions on the parameters of such models is not an easy task, although it could be useful in this software implementation of the method proposed in Gaioni, Dey and Ruggeri (2010).

It should be noted that ILD distribution models, ORCs, are developed, most often, aggregating many different risk-generation processes rather than a single loss origin. This implies that, although there might be an evolution in the risk profile (new controls introduced, processes automated, activity growth, etc), most of the loss-generation processes remain completely unchanged and ILD remains highly relevant.

The method presented here allows for incorporation of different sources of information and represents a robust alternative since it is based on sound statistical principles.

TAIL COMPLEMENTING WITH EXTERNAL DATA LOSSES

Tail complementing addresses the issue concerning the ILD distribution tails typically being underpopulated to obtain robust tail modelling. This issue is addressed by complementing the tails with external data (ED should be scaled, as in Chapter 4), without increasing the total probability in the distribution segment where the new data is added. A simple data refilling would completely distort the distribution, arbitrarily increasing the likelihood of events added.

The method is based on the calculation of cumulative probabilities after the determination of each loss observation weights (see Chapter 4 for methods for the determination of cumulative probabilities based on weights[5] given to loss observations). Then, the cumulative probability is fed into any of the fitting methods (as presented in Chapter 4). The process can be performed as follows:

1. Determination of the threshold above which to complement data: A threshold is chosen above which the internal loss data distribution is underpopulated and requires additional data. The cumulative probability of the threshold, $F^*(x)$, is determined, based on the observations in the empirical distribution.
2. Then, the rest of the probability, $1 - F^*(x)$, is recalculated with the CDF resulting from the mixture of the two datasets by recalculating the cumulative probability distribution above x. The number of observations per data sample should be taken into consideration for establishing the credibility for the ILD. If the ED set has twice as many observations as the ILD, and it is determined that both data elements have the same credibility, $z=50\%$, then the ED loss observations should be given half of the observation weight in the determination of the cumulative probabilities. The credibility of each of the data samples can be determined through credibility theory, as explained earlier in this chapter, and calculating the z credibility factor. Figure 7.4 illustrates a histogram of the ILD observations, and it has been decided to complement data above x=2000, T1, where it is clearly underpopulated for robust tail modelling. From the empirical distribution, it has been calculated that the cumulative probability to T1 is $F^*(2,000) = 0.89$. Above T1 data from scaled ED is added to better populate the distribution above T1 and the remaining cumulative probability, 0.11, is split based on the total data sample.
3. This process can be repeated when several sources of ED or SA exist by defining new thresholds. Figure 7.5 illustrates a case in which a second source of ED has been added above the threshold T2. The result is a cumulative probability with more

detail on the tail. As in the previous example, it is only the probability above F**(T2) that is split among the new data sample created by pooling together ILD and ED. As a result, the distribution ensures that the body's cumulative probability is still F*(T1)=0.89, and that the tail probability is still F**(T2)=0.02.

Figure 7.6 illustrates an example of implementing the observation complementing method with three data sources. The weight or z credibility factors given are 0.5 for the first data sample, 0.3 for the second and 0.2 for the third.

TAIL COMPLEMENTING WITH SCENARIOS

This method allows for the addition of scenarios into the ILD data distributions, when scenarios are defined as one specific single possible outcome, such as taking as reference the losses observed in other institutions and incorporating as such into the distribution fitting.

This complements the information on the tail, above a specific threshold or cumulative probability. It is similar but not identical to

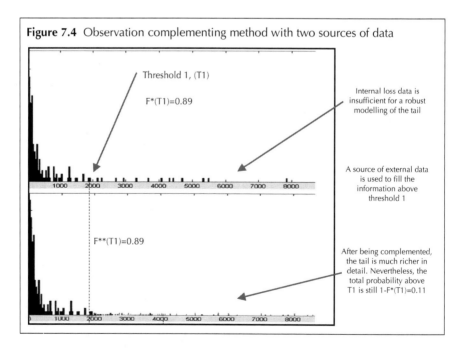

Figure 7.4 Observation complementing method with two sources of data

Threshold 1, (T1)

F*(T1)=0.89

Internal loss data is insufficient for a robust modelling of the tail

A source of external data is used to fill the information above threshold 1

F**(T1)=0.89

After being complemented, the tail is much richer in detail. Nevertheless, the total probability above T1 is still 1-F*(T1)=0.11

Figure 7.5 Observation complementing method with three sources of data

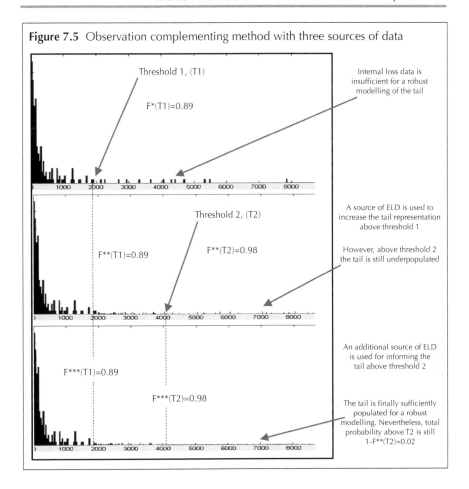

the method explained in the "what-if? method" in Chapter 4. The difference is that, in that method, new losses are added to the ILD sample, shifting the whole cumulative probabilities. In the method described in this section, no new losses are added to the fitting sample, meaning that cumulative probabilities up to the threshold remain unchanged. However, above the threshold, additional information from the scenario analysis is used to inform us as to how the tail progresses above the threshold where no data is available. This is illustrated in Figure 7.7, which shows the ILD threshold before which cumulative probabilities remain unchanged, and after which information is added from scenario analysis.

The process can be executed as follows:

Figure 7.6 Example of tail data complementing implementation

Erase Data	>> Data 1		Severity	Date	Severity	Date	Severity	Date
Erase Data	>> Data 2	1	1983.909091	31/12/2012	1270.090909	31/12/2011	2080.210000	31/12/2010
Erase Data	>> Data 3	2	13447.823636	31/12/2012	769.172727	31/12/2011	581.378182	31/12/2010
		3	1335.454545	31/12/2012	552.315455	31/12/2011	607.845455	31/12/2010
		4	3824.300000	31/12/2012	1761.403636	31/12/2011	2920.559091	31/12/2010
		5	3680.590909	31/12/2012	545.454545	31/12/2011	677.229091	31/12/2010
		6	627.289091	31/12/2012	890.097273	31/12/2011	1024.414545	31/12/2010
		7	3401.272727	31/12/2012	11700.000000	31/12/2011	15667.272727	30/12/2010
		8	1236.363636	31/12/2012	526.631818	31/12/2011	1941.090909	30/12/2010
		9	2132.175455	31/12/2012	1036.363636	31/12/2011	2096.287273	30/12/2010
		10	2375.149091	31/12/2012	581.818182	31/12/2011	5000.000000	30/12/2010
		11	555.681818	31/12/2012	690.909091	31/12/2011	886.045455	30/12/2010
		12	856.247273	31/12/2012	6617.299091	31/12/2011	902.556364	30/12/2010
		13	621.658182	31/12/2012	1910.127273	31/12/2011	1541.579091	30/12/2010

Probabilidades
Data 1: 0.5 Data 2: 0.3 Data 3: 0.2

Model   Exit

Figure 7.7 Example of tail complementing with scenarios

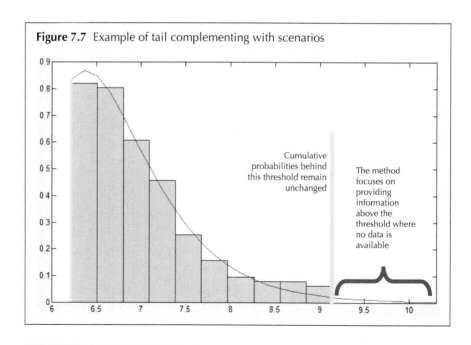

Cumulative probabilities behind this threshold remain unchanged

The method focuses on providing information above the threshold where no data is available

❏ Define the scenarios to be used for complementing the information concerning the tail behaviour. These scenarios need to be
defined with a single specific value loss or by ranges (scenario
loss to be between x and y) and with a specific probability of
occurrence, P.

❏ Transform the annual probability of each of the scenarios, P_{annual},
into the probability of a draw, P, for its incorporation into the
cumulative probabilities of the severity distribution. If the
annual frequency is, for instance, 10, then the draw probability
should be approximately 10 times smaller. The scenario probability calculation is as follows:

$$P = 1 - \left(1 - P_{annual}\right)^1 / Frequency$$

❏ The draw probabilities are used to complement the tail and
compute the cumulative probabilities, for each loss scenario xi:

$$Percentile_i = 1 - \sum_{i=1}^{s} P_i,$$

where s is the number of scenarios, P_i is the probability of the
scenario and x_i is the loss of the scenario, $P_i < P_{i+1}$ and $x_i > x_{i+1}$.

❏ Finally, the percentiles calculated together with the corresponding quantiles are included in the ILD cumulative
probability for the distribution fitting process.

This method does not require us to define a weight of the data
elements, since the probability of occurrence of the scenario already
determines its influence in the fitting process.

Figure 7.8 illustrates the calculation of the distribution resulting
from complementing the tail beyond the observed data with three
scenarios of severities of 3,157.37, 5,000 and 10,000 with annual probabilities of 0.1, 0.005 and 0.001 correspondingly. The annual
probability has been transformed into sampling probabilities, given
the 12 annual frequencies, of 0.0087, 0.00041 and 0.0000833. These
have been transformed into percentiles of the distribution 99.0757%,
99.9499% and 99.9916% and added to the rest of the percentiles for
the distribution fitting.

Figure 7.9 shows the results of complementing tail data with four
scenarios. The scenario losses are 2,000,000, 5,000,000, 10,000,000 and
50,000,000 and their probabilities are 0.05, 0.01, 0.005 and 0.0005
respectively. It can be seen that the capital charge calculated under

Figure 7.8 Tail scenario complementing calculations

	Annual frequency		12	

	Fitting input		
	Quantile	Percentile	
Historical loss 1	0.01	1.14	1
Historical loss 2	0.02	3.41	1
Historical loss 3	0.08	5.68	1
Historical loss 4	0.09	7.95	1
Historical loss 5	0.24	10.23	1
Historical loss 6	0.63	12.50	1
Historical loss 7	0.77	14.77	1
...			
Historical loss 40	146.63	89.77	1
Historical loss 41	181.02	92.05	1
Historical loss 42	276.35	94.32	1
Historical loss 43	516.39	96.59	1
Historical loss 44	821.87	98.86	1

	Annual probability			Draw Probability
Scenario loss A	10.00%	3,157.37	99.08	0.87416110%
Scenario loss B	0.50%	5,000.00	99.95	0.04176246%
Scenario loss C	0.10%	10,000.00	99.99	0.00833716%

the single loss approximation has gone up from 29 million to 37 million, at the 99.9% confidence interval. The loss percentiles of the distribution are less impacted on by scenarios that complement only the information above the tail.

MIXING DISTRIBUTION PROPERTIES FROM DIFFERENT DATA ELEMENTS DURING THE FIT

These are very similar analytical processes to those described for scaling ED in Chapter 4, but they are applied to create a hybrid model rather than to scale ED. The most relevant difference is the target values of the distribution shape and tail parameters. For the hybrid model construction, this information is not solely derived from the ED, but uses a weighted average of the parameters used as fitting constraints by applying credibility theory as presented earlier.

The process of creating a hybrid model consists of selecting distribution characteristics percentiles, moments and tail parameter from a mix of internal loss data, external data and scenario analysis and feeding all this information into a fitting process directed towards

Figure 7.9 Analysing results from the tail scenario complementing method

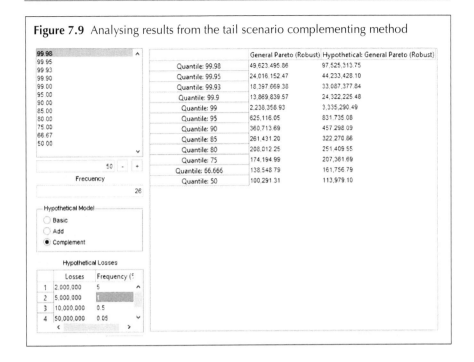

	General Pareto (Robust)	Hypothetical: General Pareto (Robust)
Quantile: 99.98	49,623,495.86	97,525,313.75
Quantile: 99.95	24,016,152.47	44,233,428.10
Quantile: 99.93	18,397,669.38	33,087,377.84
Quantile: 99.9	13,869,839.57	24,322,225.48
Quantile: 99	2,238,358.93	3,335,290.49
Quantile: 95	625,116.05	831,735.08
Quantile: 90	360,713.69	457,298.09
Quantile: 85	261,431.20	322,270.86
Quantile: 80	208,012.25	251,409.55
Quantile: 75	174,194.99	207,361.69
Quantile: 66.666	138,548.79	161,756.79
Quantile: 50	100,291.31	113,979.10

finding a solution that matches all inputs. The resulting distribution is a hybrid model of all the data sources used: ILD, ED and SA.

CONCLUSION

We have finally reached the end of the chapter, which presents several methods of creating a hybrid model using different data elements, including the means to determine the weight of each data element in the hybrid model. These methods follow solid statistical principles, as requested by supervisors, allowing a robust justification of the hybrid model and, eventually, permitting the integration, into the capital model, of all available relevant information. In fact, the hybrid model enables the incorporation of highly distinctive and necessary information from different data elements for a complete description of the institution's risk profile.

1 This section has been contributed by Daniel Rodriguez.
2 The scenario analysis may also have a specific threshold for the determination of the frequencies. Sometimes, the scenario analysis frequency questions are given with a severity threshold such: "What's the frequency of losses larger than €1,000,000?"
3 This section has been contributed by Fabrizio Ruggeri.

4 A Bayesian approach for combining different data elements was also proposed in Cope (2012).

5 Please note that, in this section, we use the term "weight" to refer to two different things: one is loss-observation weight, which is used to determine the cumulative probabilities from an empirical distribution; the other is the credibility weight, which is the z credibility factor used to average different data elements.

REFERENCES

Agostini, A., P. Talamo and V. Vecchione, 2010, "Combining Operational Loss Data with Expert Opinions Through Advanced Credibility Theory", *Journal of Operational Risk* 5(1), pp. 3–28.

Bolstad, W. M., 2007, *Introduction to Bayesian Statistics*, 2nd edn (New York: John Wiley & Sons).

Bühlmann, H., and A Gisler, 2005, *A Course in Credibility Theory and its Applications* (New York: Springer Verlag).

Bühlmann, Hans, Pavel V. Shevchenko and Mario V. Wüthrich, 2007, "A Toy Model for Operational Risk Quantification using Credibility Theory", *Journal of Operational Risk* 2(1), pp. 3–19.

Cope, Eric W., 2012, "Combining scenario analysis with loss data in operational risk quantification", *Journal of Operational Risk* 7(1), pp. 39–56.

Gaioni, E., D. Dey and F. Ruggeri, 2010, "Bayesian modelling of flash floods using generalized extreme value distribution with prior elicitation", *Chilean Journal of Statistics* 1(2), pp. 51–68.

8

Derivation of the Joint Distribution and Capitalisation of Operational Risk

Rafael Cavestany and Daniel Rodriguez

Having described in Chapter 7, the methods for creating severity and frequency distribution hybrid models with different data elements, we now look at the derivation of the joint distribution and capitalisation of operational risk, using hybrid or single-data-element models.

The process described in Chapter 7 delivers a single severity or frequency distributions per ORC, incorporating all the operational loss information contained in ILD, ED and SA. This input is then used for the determination of the joint distribution and capitalisation of operational risk. BCSG-AMA says, "The techniques to determine the aggregated loss distributions should ensure adequate levels of precision and stability of the risk measures," also suggesting, "As such, simulation, numerical or approximation methods are necessary to derive aggregated curves (e.g. Monte Carlo simulations, Fourier Transform-related methods, Panjer algorithm and Single Loss Approximations)."

The final output of this process represents the operational risk profile main metrics utilised in the use test for integrating the capital results into day-to-day risk management.

In this chapter, we present methods for the derivation of the joint distribution in the following sections:

❏ "Monte Carlo simulation": A joint distribution for the ORC is created by the convolution of its frequency and severity distributions. The convolution can be done through Monte Carlo simulation or following an analytical method such as single-loss approximation.

❏ "Single-loss approximation, analytical derivation of the loss distribution": As an alternative to Monte Carlo simulation, we present this analytical method to derive the joint distribution.

❏ "Operational risk correlations": In this section we look at the key considerations and methods for the determination of the correlations across the different ORCs and the dependency between severity-frequency correlation.

❏ "Using copulas for replicating operational risk dependencies": Here, we look at the implementation of copulas for the determination of the joint total operational loss distribution for the institution with correlations. It also presents copulas for the replication of the severity-frequenccy dependence.

❏ "Capitalisation of operational risk": This section presents the methods for deriving the operational risk capital from the joint loss distribution: different percentiles (such as 99.9, 99.95 or 99.98), expected shortfall, different moments (such as the expected loss, variance, leptokurtosis).

❏ "Allocation of operational risk capital": Here we look at different methods for the allocation of the total capital to each of the ORCs of our model.

❏ "Operational risk profile measurement": Finally, we present the metrics, derived from the joint distribution that can be used for the description of the risk profile that is used in the use test.

MONTE CARLO SIMULATION

Monte Carlo simulation is used for the determination of the joint distribution by convoluting the hybrid model frequency and severity distributions. This is done per ORC. Later, each of the ORC total operational loss distributions is fed into the copula process to be aggregated and correlated (see "Using copulas for replicating operational risk dependencies" below) for the determination of the total aggregated operational loss, which represents the operational risk distribution for the institution.

The Monte Carlo aggregation process consists of the following steps:

❏ a random number, λ, from the frequency distribution is generated to determine the number of operational losses occurring in the scenario;

❏ λ random numbers are generated from the severity distribution, representing the value of each of the losses in the scenario;

❏ the total operational loss of the scenario is calculated as the sum of the λ losses drawn from the severity distribution; and

❏ a large number of replications are generated to fill the joint distribution, particularly to fill the distribution tail, by iterating the previous three points; with operational risk fat-tail distributions, the number of replications required to achieve convergence can be very high, up to several million.

The same process can be used for the generation of losses from multiple segment severity distributions. This is slightly more complex because each operational event loss may be generated from any of the segments of the distribution and uses the composition method. The process is explained using a two-segment severity distribution, as follows:

❏ The two segments of the severity distribution are defined thus:
  ○ low losses are modelled using a distribution with bottom and top truncation points: the bottom truncation, T1, represents the data capture threshold; the top truncation, T2, is the tail modelling threshold (determined as in Chapter 4) used to separate the body and the tail; and
  ○ high or tail losses are modelled with a different distribution with a bottom truncation equal to T2.

❏ The cumulative probability of each of the two severity distribution segments is determined. This can be obtained from the empirical loss distribution and by calculating $F^*(T2)=P$. Alternatively, it can be calculated by fitting a parametric to all unsegmented data, $F(x)$, and calculating the cumulative probability by $F(T2 \mid x>T1)=P$. The first segment of the distribution has P as total cumulative probability and the second segment has $(1 - P)$.

❏ For each of the losses generated, there should be probability P that it will be generated from the low segment distribution and

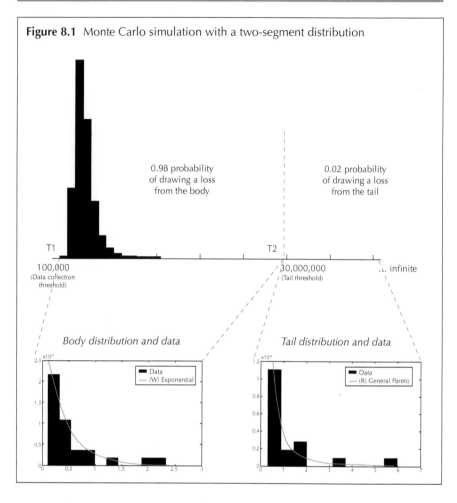

Figure 8.1 Monte Carlo simulation with a two-segment distribution

(1 – P) that it will be generated using the distribution in the second segment.

Figure 8.1 shows the split of a severity distribution into two segments. The body segment is modelled using an exponential distribution between T1=100,000 and T2=30,000,000. The tail segment above 30,000,000 is modelled with a Pareto distribution. The cumulative probability above the tail threshold is 0.02.

The same case is generalised to n segment severity simulations, where the cumulative probabilities are split between n sections and the losses are generated accordingly from the n segments.

Figure 8.2, illustrates a three-segment-distribution Monte Carlo

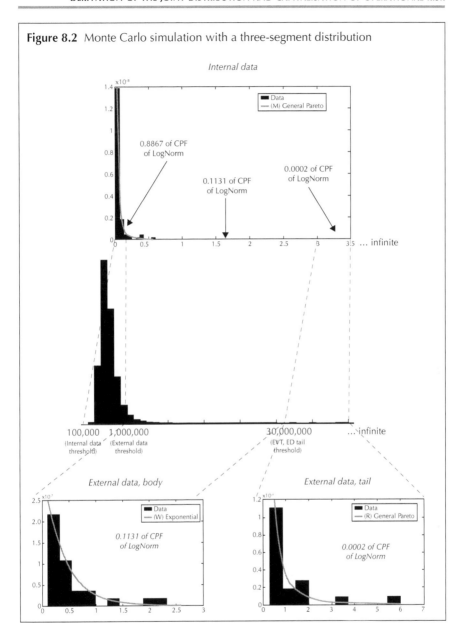

Figure 8.2 Monte Carlo simulation with a three-segment distribution

simulation setup. The lower segment is performed with an empirical distribution, which takes 0.9167 of the cumulative probability. The middle segment is modelled with a lognormal distribution and takes 0.063 of the total probability. And, finally, the tail segment is modelled with a generalised Pareto distribution, which takes 0.0203 of the probability.

The Monte Carlo simulation will typically require a large number of replications to achieve a stable capital estimate. The number of replications required for stability of total capital estimates depends on many characteristics of the modelling, which include the frequency (the lower the frequency, the larger the number of replications), the weight of the distribution tails (the higher the weight, the larger the number of replications), the number of ORCs (the fewer ORCs, the larger the number of replications) and the dominance of a few ORCs on the overall total risk profile (the greater the dominance, the larger the number of replications).

Also, in addition to these, there are factors that influence the stability of the capital allocation (see "Allocation of operational risk capital" below), requiring additional replications, which include the allocation methodology (for instance, Euler allocation or incremental allocation requires more replications than the volatility contribution or expected shortfall contribution allocations) and the dominance of a few ORCs over the total risk profile.

Therefore, it is hard to estimate but it is very common to see Monte Carlo simulations performed with more than 10,000,000 replications. It is even harder to estimate the computation time as, in relation to all the factors above, the frequency of the models and distribution types have a major impact as well. Some distribution types require up to 1,000 times more computational effort for the generation of random numbers. Needless to say, hardware and software will have a major impact as well.

SINGLE-LOSS APPROXIMATION: ANALYTICAL DERIVATION OF THE LOSS DISTRIBUTION

Analytical methods for determining the joint distribution, such as the Panjer Algorithm and Fourier Transform-related methods, are generally far less computationally intensive than Monte Carlo simulation. Nevertheless, these methods may get too complex to implement, when using less standard distribution families, splitting the distribution into segments or aggregating different data elements.

The single-loss approximation (SLA) method is an attractive approximation, as it is computationally simple, results are obtained almost instantly and it provides an easy interpretation of results. It can be used also for the evaluation of the realistic loss magnitude generated by the fitted distributions at different percentiles, including those used for capital determination (see Chapter 4).

The SLA method is based on the estimation of the largest individual loss from the joint distribution percentile determining capital. For instance, if capital is calculated at a 99.9% confidence interval, this method will estimate the largest individual loss in the 99.9th percentile of the total operational loss distribution. The method is based on the principle that, with fat-tail distributions, there is a single loss determining the large majority of the high-percentiles value of the joint distribution. In some instances, up to 90% of the total percentile value can be explained by a single loss, and the addition of the rest of the losses makes up the other 10%. Therefore, SLA provides a good first evaluation of the capital charge and can be calculated almost immediately.

The SLA is consistent with what happens in reality. There have been institutions that were bankrupted following a single event, such as Baring Brothers (*The Economist* 1995), or had their capital base seriously damaged, again by a single event, such as Société Générale (*Financial Times* 2008). All other operational risk losses were normally absorbed by these institutions' capital.

The SLA method can be used for a quick evaluation of capital charges such as in the resampling method for capital stability analysis (see Chapter 4). Also, as opposed to the methods based on Monte Carlo simulation or Panjer Algorithm, which calculate the value of total losses, the SLA method is easier to interpret because it provides the value of a single (largest) loss, and can be used directly to evaluate the realism of the losses generated by the fitted distributions (as in Chapter 4).

When the SLA method is used in low percentiles (99, 95, 50, etc), the results can be very far from the real total capital charge, as, in these percentiles, the value of total losses is driven more by a high loss frequency than by a single very large loss. Nevertheless, the analysis is still useful as a means of evaluating the size of the individual losses and, thus, for the evaluation of the realism of a distribution fit.

Given a fitted distribution, the SLA can be calculated based on two parameters:

❏ a percentile, p, defining the confidence interval for which capital requirements are determined; and

❏ a frequency, f, which stands for the expected number of events of the ORC.

The SLA for operational risk capital can be calculated as follows:

1. the confidence interval is transformed into the number of years that the capital should be higher than the losses, computed as:

$$\frac{1}{1-p};$$

2. the losses to produce the largest loss given the percentile p, can be expressed as:

$$\frac{f}{1-p};$$

3. the percentile of the severity distribution, say p', can be expressed as:

$$p' = 1 - \frac{1}{f/(1-p)}; \text{ and}$$

4. the single loss from the severity distribution defining the capital estimation can be expressed as:

$$SLA = F^{-1}\left(1 - \frac{1}{f/(1-p)}\right),$$

where $F^{-1}(x)$ is of the CDF of severity.

For example, if the fitted severity distribution is a lognormal, $\mu=8$ and $\sigma=2$, the confidence interval for capital calculation is 99.95%, and the annual loss frequency is 11 loss events, then:

❏ the probability of having a larger annual loss than the capital, given the confidence interval for the capital calculations is (1 − 99.95%) = 0.0005;

❏ the number of years required for such an event to materialise given the above probability is 1/0.0005 = 2,000;

❏ the number of individual losses given the annual frequency is 2,000*11 = 22,000;

❏ the percentile of the severity distribution for the worst loss in 22,000 losses is $1 - (1/22,000) = 99.9954\%$; and
❏ the size of the worst loss in 22,000 losses is SLA = INV.LOGNORMAL $(99.9954\%; 8; 2) = 7,433,834$.

The figure 7,433,834 is the size of loss that would determine the large majority of the capital at a 99.95% confidence interval, given the severity and frequency distributions of this hypothetical ORC.

OPERATIONAL RISK CORRELATIONS

Operational risks show clear dependencies arising from common drivers on the risk factors that manifest in correlations across the frequencies and severities of the different ORCs. These include the business and control environment (IT, people or common processes) and external factors such as fraud tendencies and macro economy. Also, it is plausible to have dependencies between severity and frequency within the same ORC, which, at least, should be verified to identify whether the dependence is significant. Therefore, a solid quantification of operational risks requires the consideration of all these dependencies.

BCSG-AMA recognises the possibility of using internally determined correlations when it says,

> The bank may be permitted to use internally determined correlations in operational risk losses across individual operational risk estimates, provided it can demonstrate to the satisfaction of the national supervisor that its systems for determining correlations are sound, implemented with integrity and take into account the uncertainty surrounding any such correlation estimates (particularly in periods of stress).

If internally determined correlations are not used in the capital model, then the perfect correlation assumption should be used for regulatory capital reporting. In fact, internally calculated correlations represent an opportunity to reduce the capital charges.

When modelling operational risk dependencies, the first step is to determine which of the different elements of the model are to be correlated, and how. There are three dimensions to correlate in operational risk: frequency and severity within the ORC, cross-ORC severity and cross-ORC frequency. The last two can be captured indirectly by estimating cross-total-loss correlations (as the joint result of frequencies and severities). The correlation model should be complete and avoid overlaps or double counting of dependencies.

To implement an operational risk correlation model, there are two potential generic approaches:

1. Full dimension correlation model or correlating severities and/or frequencies across ORCs: The correlation of frequencies across ORCs is relatively simple, and can be implemented directly using copulas. The correlation of severities across ORCs is more complex, but it can be implemented following the common latent factor similar to that explained under "Using copulas for replicating operational risk dependencies" below. The determination of cross-ORC frequencies can be achieved by creating time series as explained below. The determination of correlations across ORC severities can be estimated using an optimisation process for determining the common latent factor component such that the observed values of severities are replicated.

    Even if frequencies and severities are correlated across ORCs, the correlation model would still be incomplete, missing the correlation between severity and frequency, which multiplies the dimensionality of the model. Although it is possible to envision a statistical model to handle the fully dimensional correlation model, it would be extremely complex with high dimensionality, and almost impossible to obtain robust results from, given the limited operational loss data availability. In these circumstances, a correlation model approach focused on reducing the dimensionality of the correlation model would provide much better results.

2. Nested or stepped correlation model: Distributions are correlated in various steps, decreasing very significantly its dimensionality. In a first step, each ORC total loss is generated independently, convoluting frequency and severity. No cross-ORC correlation of frequencies and severities is considered at this stage. In a more developed approach, the frequency and severity distributions can be also correlated as explained in "Copula for the dependency between frequency and severity" below.

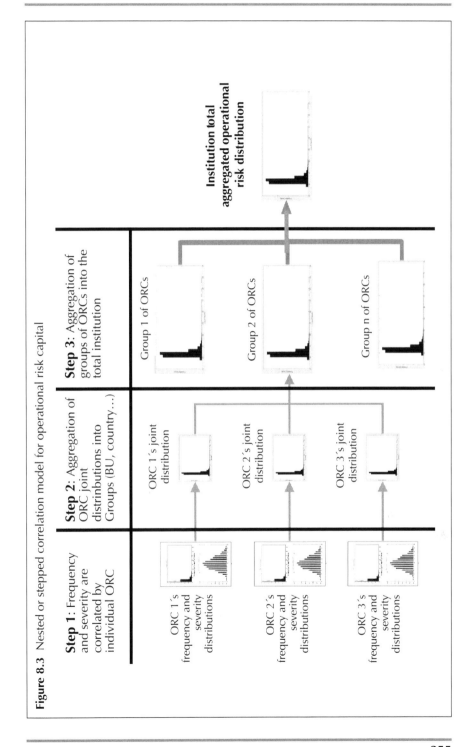

Figure 8.3 Nested or stepped correlation model for operational risk capital

In a second step, the total losses across ORCs are aggregated using copulas and total loss correlations. Using total loss correlations, the cross-dependencies between severities and frequencies of different ORCs are captured by a single correlation matrix of total loss. Total-losses correlations can be calculated as explained below.

If required, it is possible to establish a third step and create groups of ORCs for a progressive aggregation, as explained in "Consecutive copulas for a robust aggregation of a large number of ORCs" below, and decrease the dimensionality of the correlation model.

Figure 8.3 presents a high-level conceptual workflow of the three steps of the stepped correlation model. The frequency and severity of ORCs 1, 2 and 3 are aggregated in Step 1 (using three correlation matrices of 2x2, which represents the dependence between severity and frequency) to generate their joint distributions; In Step 2, these ORCs are aggregated into ORC Group 2 (using 3x3 correlation matrices), which may correspond to the ORCs of a business unit, country, activity or other. The same is supposed to be done with the other ORC groups. In Step 3, the different ORC group distributions, 1 through n, are aggregated into a single-loss distribution for the institution as whole. The total aggregated operational risk distribution will be used to derive the capital requirements and allocate total capital down to the original ORCs. Using the approach, the dimensionality of the correlation matrices used decreases significantly.

This work focuses in the stepped correlation model, as it is probably the only feasible model given the data generally available, if a complete correlation model incorporating the three dimensions is to be implemented.

In the following sections, we propose methods for a robust calculation of operational risk dependencies for the progressive model, which include the following:

❏ data series preparation – describes how to set up the data sample and eliminate seasonal effects;
❏ numerical calculation of correlations;
❏ multivariate MLE calculation;
❏ qualitative method calculation;
❏ positive semi-definitive transformation; and

❏ testing the independence and determination of the correlation between severity and frequency.

Data series preparation

Operational risk loss data comes in the form of individual losses with their own date. This implies that the raw ILD does not have the time structure permitting a direct correlation calculation. Therefore, operational risk data should be previously prepared for correlation calculations. Especially, the existence of seasonal patterns in the data should be analysed, which may artificially exaggerate or cancel correlations. If there are seasonal effects, they should be removed from the data sample.

Arranging the operational risk data should be consistent with the way in which the copula will be applied later. In "Analysing severity and frequency dependence" below, we explain how to set up operational risk data to determine the dependency between frequency and severity. We shall describe now how to set up loss data as time series to determine operational risk total loss correlations, which is consistent with the copula aggregation process later described. This copula process aggregates total losses of the different ORCs to obtain the total operational loss distribution.

The data series preparation process can be implemented as follows:

❏ Establish the actual start and finish dates of the loss observation period, rather than deriving them from the earliest and latest dates of the available data. This is particularly important if short time buckets, such as weeks or days, are used to create the time series, and/or when a high threshold is used for the modelling. It is possible that, during the first and last time buckets of the observation, no losses occurred and a zero should be used for the time bucket of the series. If this is ignored, the correlation would most likely be exaggerated.
❏ Establish time buckets for the creation of the operational risk time series of total losses. Ideally, time bucketing should be annual, as the time horizon for operational risk is annual, and the correlation structure will be applied to annual losses. However, annual bucketing is not possible given the scarcity of data and the loss of relevance of the older data. Therefore, a higher-

frequency time bucket is selected, such as monthly or quarterly bucketing. For instance, if three years of data will be used in the calculations and monthly time bucketing is used, 36 six-monthly periods will be used to count total losses over those 36 months.

❏ Per time bucket and ORC, total losses experienced are calculated, resulting in a time series of total operational losses per ORC. The result is a matrix with a size equal to n ORCs times the number of time buckets (36 in our example). Operational risk total-losses correlations across ORCs can be calculated based on this matrix.

❏ Seasonality effects are taken out of the total-loss time series. Operational risk losses may present clear seasonality patterns. If these seasonality patterns are not withdrawn from the time series, this may result in a correlation exaggeration and eventually an overstatement of capital needs. Sources of operational risk loss seasonality are driven generally by activity cycles and external factors, which relate to vacation periods, weekday activity patterns, financial results' recognition deadlines and budget planning. Even certain fraud activities are more typical in some seasons than others. Similarly, particular care must be taken when events have been reported manually and an exaggerated amount appears around the time of exercise closures.

Since time bucketing of less than a year is required to obtain a minimum length in the operational risk time series, seasonality patterns should be expected and removed for a robust correlation calculation. Methods for seasonality adjustment include such as ARIMA (Box and Jenkins 1971), which can be applied according to the data availability and characteristics.

Once loss data has been set up into total loss data series and seasonal effects have been subtracted, they can be used to determine operational risk correlations as in the following sections.

Numerical calculation of correlation coefficients: Pearson, Spearman's Rho and Kendall's Tau

Calculating correlation coefficients based on the operational risk time series created in the previous section is straightforward. There are several variants of the correlation coefficient that can be implemented depending on the different characteristics of the time series.

Table 8.1 Correlation coefficients for operational risk dependencies modelling

Formulation	Comments
Pearson: $$\rho_{X,Y} = \frac{\sigma_{XY}}{\sigma_X \sigma_Y} = \frac{E\left[(X - \mu_X)(Y - \mu_Y)\right]}{\sigma_X \sigma_Y}$$	It is a measure of the strength and direction of the linear relationship between two variables (x, y) that is defined as the (sample) covariance of the variables divided by the product of their (sample) standard deviations. Given the strong non-normality of operational risk distributions, other coefficients such as Spearman's Rho and Kendall's Tau are usually considered more appropriate to correlate operational risk.
Spearman's Rho: $$\rho = 1 - \frac{6\Sigma D^2}{N(N^2 - 1)}$$	Spearman is a rank-order correlation and is calculated by substituting the values for their order in the sample. It is less sensitive than Pearson's coefficient when there are extreme values in the sample, because the value is limited to their order in the sample. Also, when both time series have an identical order, even though they had very different distribution shapes, Spearman will still provide a perfect correlation while the Pearson coefficient will not. Therefore, it is able to better gauge dependencies between very differently shaped distributions. For this reason, it is more consistent for its application into copulas than the Pearson coefficient, when distributions of ORC present more differences. In fact, copulas do a rank ordering of individual distributions.
Kendall's Tau: $$\tau_{X,Y} = \frac{2}{n(n-1)} \sum_{i<j} sign\left((X_i - Y_j)(X_j - Y_i)\right) ,$$ where n is the number of time buckets, Xi is the number of events in the first dataset at time i, Yj is the number of events in the second dataset at the time j and the sign(x) is 1, 0, or -1 where z is positive, zero or negative. When all Kendall's tau parameters have been calculated, the correlation matrix is calculated using the expression (Perkins and Lane 2003): $$M = \sin\left(\tau \frac{\pi}{2}\right)$$	Kendall's Tau is a measure of the correlation between two variables based on the number of concordant movements. When the two variables increase or decrease simultaneously, the coefficient adds one unit without requiring that increase to be represented by a linear relationship. When the movement is opposite, then it subtracts one unit. Its interpretation is more direct than the other correlation coefficients. For example, in a population with t = 1/3, two sets of observations are twice as likely to be concordant than discordant. Its intuitive interpretation can be leveraged for its application into qualitative determination of correlations (in this case correlations are determined one by one, as described below) and can be used to structure the analysis and questions for the experts.

Figure 8.4 Example of calculating operational risk correlations based on coefficients

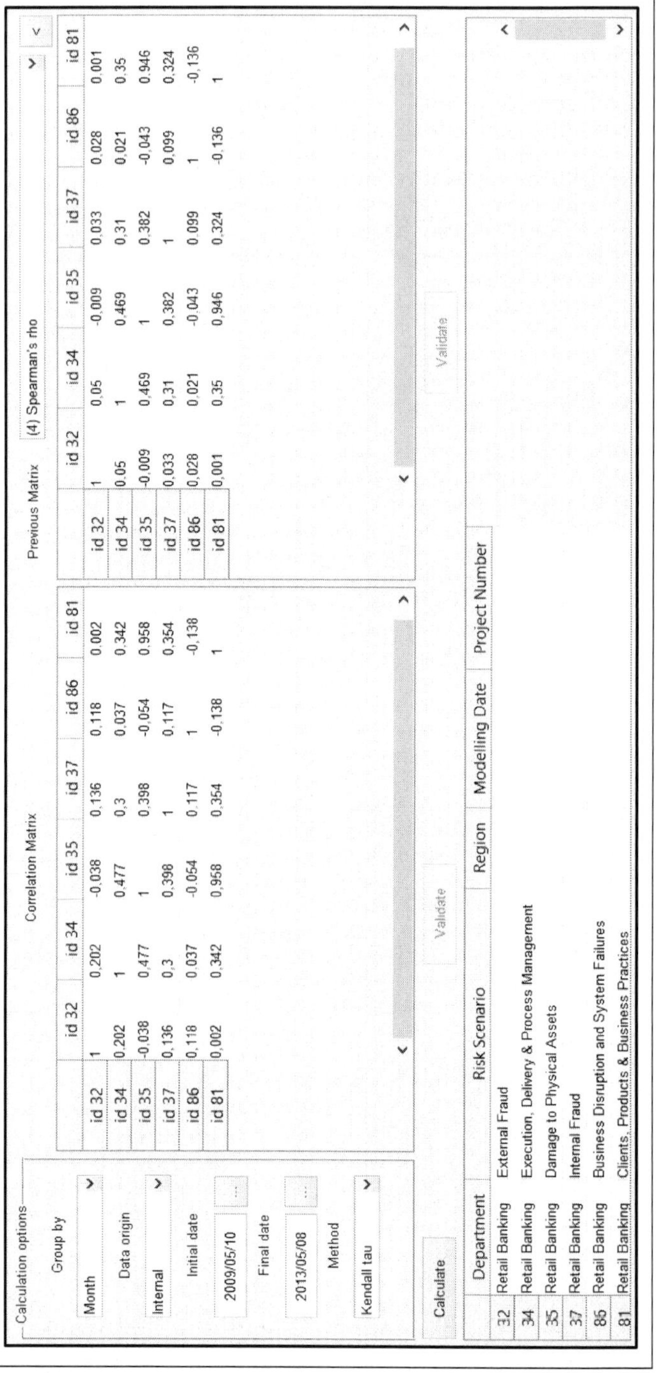

Figure 8.4 shows the calculation of operational risk correlations using the procedure explained within this section, for six ORCs by risk type within the retail banking business unit. The observation's initial and final dates were set at 2009/05/10 to 2013/05/08. The time bucketing used was monthly, which means a sample size of 48 was used in the calculations. The correlation matrix on the left has been calculated with Kendall's Tau and that on the right with Spearman's Rho. Some of the correlations may look very high, which could be due to the limited number of observations in the ORC.

Multivariate MLE applied to operational risk correlation calculation

The use of multivariate MLE for the determination of operational correlations is an attractive option. This method estimates the parameters of all correlations using an MLE optimisation process, which calculates the correlations to fit all parameters of the copula simultaneously. This constitutes a significant difference from the methods presented earlier, which derive the correlations pairwise independently.

The multivariate MLE method (Bouye *et al* 2000) for calculating the correlation matrix requires one vector with the number of ORC grouped using the same time buckets as explained in "Series data preparation" above. The time periods used for all risks must be the same for all ORCs, which limits the analysis to the minimum observation period. This list of vectors is the input to an MLE algorithm that looks for a matrix that best fits a multivariate normal cumulative distribution function (Gaussian copula) or a multivariate *t*-Student cumulative distribution function (*t*-Student copula). In the case of the *t*-Student copula, the output also includes the corresponding tail parameter.

This process generates a valid correlation matrix for a Gaussian or *t*-Student copula – positive, semi-definite (PSD) – and it is not necessary to transform it using a process like that proposed by Jaeckel and Rebonato (1999), as used for the Kendall's Tau approach.

Figure 8.5 shows the correlations calculation for the same dataset, but using multivariate MLE. The matrix on the left has been fitted with the *t*-Student copula, whereas the matrix on the right has the Gaussian one. It can be seen that the numbers are much more

Figure 8.5 Example of calculation of operational risk correlations based on multivariate MLE

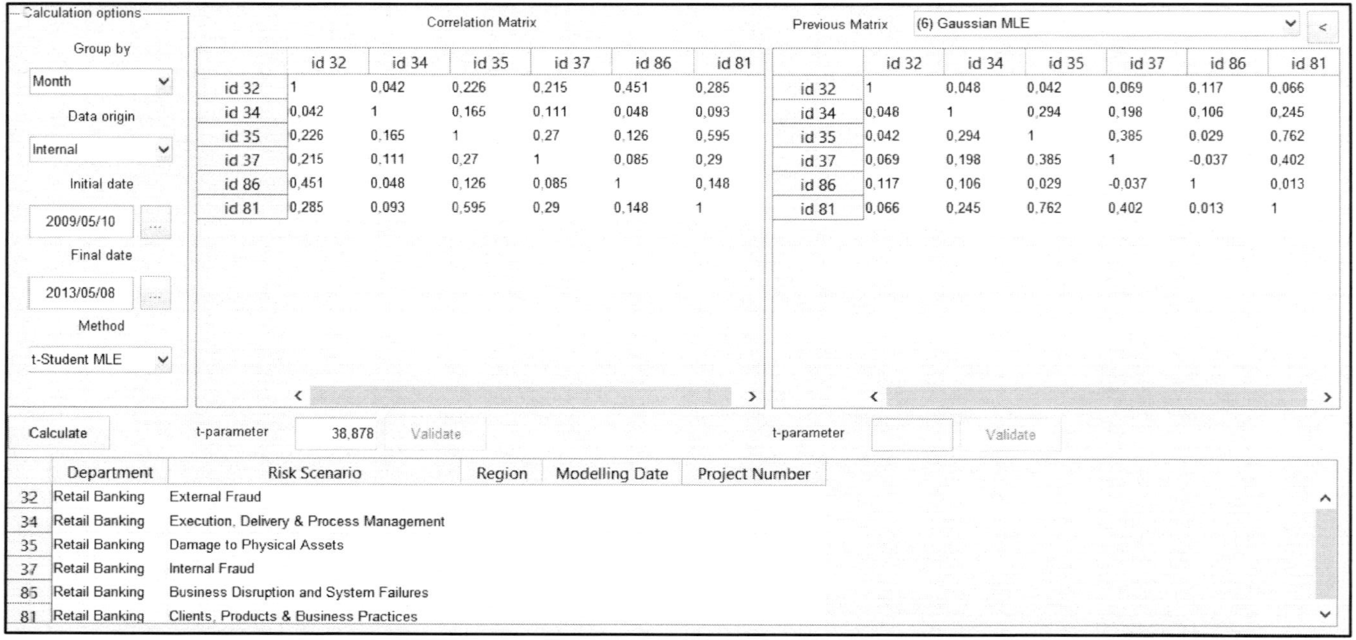

Calculation options

Group by	Month
Data origin	Internal
Initial date	2009/05/10
Final date	2013/05/08
Method	t-Student MLE

Correlation Matrix

	id 32	id 34	id 35	id 37	id 86	id 81
id 32	1	0.042	0.226	0.215	0.451	0.285
id 34	0.042	1	0.165	0.111	0.048	0.093
id 35	0.226	0.165	1	0.27	0.126	0.595
id 37	0.215	0.111	0.27	1	0.085	0.29
id 86	0.451	0.048	0.126	0.085	1	0.148
id 81	0.285	0.093	0.595	0.29	0.148	1

Previous Matrix (6) Gaussian MLE

	id 32	id 34	id 35	id 37	id 86	id 81
id 32	1	0.048	0.042	0.069	0.117	0.066
id 34	0.048	1	0.294	0.198	0.106	0.245
id 35	0.042	0.294	1	0.385	0.029	0.762
id 37	0.069	0.198	0.385	1	-0.037	0.402
id 86	0.117	0.106	0.029	-0.037	1	0.013
id 81	0.066	0.245	0.762	0.402	0.013	1

t-parameter 38.876 Validate

t-parameter Validate

Calculate

	Department	Risk Scenario	Region	Modelling Date	Project Number
32	Retail Banking	External Fraud			
34	Retail Banking	Execution, Delivery & Process Management			
35	Retail Banking	Damage to Physical Assets			
37	Retail Banking	Internal Fraud			
85	Retail Banking	Business Disruption and System Failures			
81	Retail Banking	Clients, Products & Business Practices			

consistent and less extreme, and there are fewer negative values. This is due to the joint determination of all dependency parameters, rather than the pairwise calculation performed earlier.

Qualitative methods for estimating operational risk correlations

As we saw earlier, the calculation of correlation matrices based on ILD presents significant challenges: a limited amount of data available and information possibly lost during the elimination of time series seasonality. When implementing a scenario-based approach (SBA), there are additional issues, including the data unavailability for low-frequency events and insufficient ILD for the typical detailed SA segmentation (a standard SBA may imply more than 50 scenarios for the institution, many of them of very low frequency).

In fact, BCSG-AMA mentions similar concerns when it says, "On the other hand, a bank modelling correlations that use a high number of ORCs might have difficulty finding statistical means to validate correlation assumptions due to minimal loss data for each ORC."

Under such circumstances, a qualitative method for determining operational risk correlations may be a reasonable option. In addition, calculation methods with expert judgement input have the advantage of developing a deeper understanding of the cross-risk links, dependencies and so forth, thanks to the required analysis in the determination of such qualitative inputs. It also increases the risk awareness among those who participate in the qualitative determination of the correlations. The analysis can be also be leveraged for the identification of more efficient risk-mitigation strategies. In fact, the BCSG-AMA observes, from the results of LDCE and Range of Practice Paper, "Expert judgment (40%) is the primary means used to estimate dependence."

One approach can be to manually determine each of the pairwise correlation. However, this method may pose significant challenges again, such as maintaining consistency across correlation evaluations and justifying the correlations selection. Also, when a high number of scenarios is involved, it could be very time-consuming and laborious to implement and maintain. For instance, a model with 100 risk scenarios requires the determination of nearly 4,900 correlation numbers. Also, it is likely that, if correlation determination is not consistent across ORCs, it will require the transformation of the correlation matrix into a PSD matrix, thus changing the original evaluation.

An alternative method is to implement a correlation calculation based on a factor approach. Correlation factor models are widely used in risk management, for both market and credit risk, to reduce sampling errors and permit the calculation of correlations of lowly traded assets, or even with non-observable prices. In operational risk, a factor model may be based on BEICFs such as business environment factors and KRIs. Then, the sensitivity of each ORC is qualitatively defined to permit the determination of the correlation matrix of the ORCs. A detailed description on the implementation of a BEICFs-based operational risk correlation can be found in Chapter 6. Similar issues can be found in the determination of the tail parameter of the t-Student copula and a qualitative approach simular to those described in this section can also be implemented.

Positive semi-definitive transformation

Given the limited amount of data, the characteristics of such data and the dimensionality of the correlation matrix, it may happen that the correlation matrix resulting from the calculation methods presented above is not PSD. In other words, the correlation matrix does not represent a logical and cross-consistent dependency structure and cannot be used to generate correlated random numbers. When this happens, it is necessary to transform the matrix using a process such as that described in detail by Jaeckel and Rebonato (1999).

Figure 8.6 shows the transformation of the matrix on the left, which is not a PSD, to the matrix on the right, which is. The method used is the spectral method, as in the work referenced above.

This type of transformation can be applied to the numerical and

Figure 8.6 Example of PSD transformation

Correlation Matrix				Previous Matrix	(9) Validate		<
	id 37	id 32	id 87		id 37	id 32	id 87
id 37	1	0,8	0,8	id 37	1	0,632	0,632
id 32	0,8	1	-0,3	id 32	0,632	1	-0,201
id 87	0,8	-0,3	1	id 87	0,632	-0,201	1

qualitative correlation methods, when they do not provide a PSD correlation matrix.

Analysing severity and frequency dependence

The LDA model relies on the assumption that frequency and severity are independent. If this assumption does not hold, the joint distribution needs to be derived with the corresponding dependence between the severity and frequency distributions being taken into account. This represents an additional computational step corresponding to Step 1 in Figure 8.3. This issue is becoming relevant to supervisors who demand that institutions perform a validation-of-independence assumption between severity and frequency and so that they guarantee consistency.

Dependence between severity and frequency is indeed a plausible hypothesis in many contexts. A weakness in a fraud-detection system may both increase the number of successful attacks and their size. An over-relaxed control environment may lead to the same effect in process execution errors and there are many other systematic factors that can induce a dependence between severity and frequency (such as HR policy, providers and technology environment). Therefore, the validation of independence is necessary. To test it, we need first to arrange the data series for that analysis.

Arranging severity and frequency data for independence test

Testing the independence has the challenge that there is a single frequency observation per a variable number of severity observations. We present two methods to address this issue, a direct one in Figure 8.7 and a more developed one in Figure 8.8.

In Figure 8.7, each value of a severity observation is linked with the corresponding value of the frequency value. This will permit us to test whether high frequencies tend to produce high severities. In a second step, the frequency and severity values are substituted for their rank order (as in Spearman's Rho's rank-order correlation), to address the nonlinearity of the frequency and severity. The series can then be fed into the analysis of "Running of the independence test and determining the level of dependence" below.

In the example in Figure 8.7, there are four observation periods with 3, 4, 3 and 2 losses respectively. The setup of the series is illustrated in the columns on the right by pairs of severity and frequency. Columns in Step 1 can be used to calculate Spearman's Rho, as

Figure 8.7 Setting up operational risk losses for testing independence of severity and frequency

| | Step 1 | | Step 2 | | | | |
| | Frequency-severity pair | | Frequency-severity rank pairs for independence test | | | | |
Period frequency	Period frequency	Loss severity	Frequency mean rank	Severity mean rank	i	W$_i$
Period 1 — 3	3	€4,954	5.5	12	1	0.333
Period 2 — 4	3	€539	5.5	7	2	0.333
Period 3 — 3	3	€15	5.5	1	3	0.333
Period 4 — 2	4	€2,152	10.5	9	4	0.250
	4	€2,633	10.5	10	5	0.250
	4	€1,007	10.5	8	6	0.250
	4	€39	10.5	3	7	0.250
	3	€19	5.5	2	8	0.333
	3	€312	5.5	5	9	0.333
	3	€48	5.5	4	10	0.333
	2	€2,814	1.5	11	11	0.500
	2	€448	1.5	6	12	0.500

Loss severity per event (Step 1):
- Period 1 (frequency 3): €4,954, €539, €15
- Period 2 (frequency 4): €2,152, €2,633, €1,007, €39
- Period 3 (frequency 3): €19, €312, €48
- Period 4 (frequency 2): €2,814, €448

explained elsewhere in this section. In Step 2, the data series have been transformed into rank order to address the nonlinearity. This data arrangement is consistent with the copula process to replicate the dependence explained later.

If the data series of step 1 are to be used directly to estimate their dependence, Pearson's coefficient will not be appropriate, given the non-normality of the frequency and severity distributions. A rank order, such as correlation in Spearman's Rho, is more appropriate and consistent with standard practices in modelling operational risk dependencies and with the copula process reproducing such dependencies.

However, the method illustrated in Figure 8.7, although intuitive and direct, has caveats. Those periods with higher frequency will be overstated and the opposite will happen with low-frequency periods. Given the limited-frequency data availability, the overstatement of some periods may entail distortions within the correlation calculations.

To avoid the over- or understatements because of period frequency, we can introduce weights into the correlation calculation, inversely proportional to the frequency of the scenario, as in the correlation weighted to period frequency of "Running of the independence test and determining the level of dependence" below.

Alternatively, we propose an arrangement of data series based on the period's severity mean rank and the frequency rank (see Figure 8.8). We use the rank-order values rather than the base values because of the nonlinearity of the frequency and severity distributions. This is again consistent with the factor approach to correlations and the Gaussian copula method we shall see later in the section titled: "Copula for the dependency between frequency and severity". Under this method, the severity and frequency values are explained through a common factor and an independent factor, both following a Gaussian distribution, later transformed into the corresponding frequency and severity distributions. The independent factor is random and its mean is zero, and the correlation is determined only by the sensitivity of severity and frequency to the common factor. By averaging over severity rank, the independent component of severity tends to its mean (zero in the Gaussian distribution), allowing us to focus the correlation over the common factor. Also, the aggregation of severity values from each period into their rank mean avoids the over-representation of the high-frequency periods into the correlation calculation. Finally, we use the mean of the rank rather than the rank of the means (the rank of the mean severity of the periods) in order to mitigate the nonlinear behaviour before computations. In fact, the use of the mean in skewed distributions will typically overstate the actual dependence, as the mean of a skewed distribution is higher than its median. In high-frequency periods, the rank of the means increases

Figure 8.8 Setting up operational risk losses for testing independence of severity and frequency

Step 1:	Loss frequency	Severity per loss			
Period 1	3	€4,954	€539	€15	
Period 2	4	€2,152	€2,633	€1,007	€39
Period 3	3	€19	€312	€48	
Period 4	2	€2,814	€448		

		Severity rank				Step 3:	Data series for test	
Step 2:	Frequency mean rank						Period frequency mean rank	Period mean severity rank
Period 1	2.5	12	7	1			2.5	6.7
Period 2	4	9	10	8	3		4	7.5
Period 3	2.5	2	5	4			2.5	3.7
Period 4	1	11	6				1	8.5

(as it gets closer to the distribution mean), distorting the analysis by adding fake positive correlation.

Figure 8.8 illustrates a more developed arrangement of the data series for independence testing. In Step 1, it is identical, as illustrated in Figure 8.7. In Step 2, we calculate the mean rank order of the frequency (as in Spearman's Rho) and the rank order of the severity (or mean rank, if severity values are repeated). Finally, in Step 3, we calculate the mean rank for the severity period, which is aligned with the frequency rank for the independence test calculation.

The periods that have no losses (loss frequency equal to 0) should be eliminated from the sample, since they will show a perfect correlation between frequency and severity (same minimum rank for both

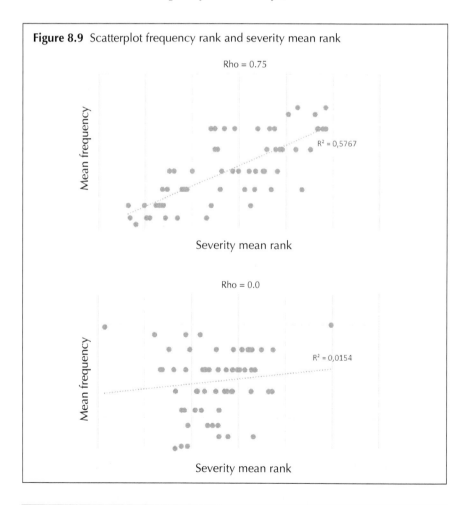

Figure 8.9 Scatterplot frequency rank and severity mean rank

severity and frequency), but this correlation is not due to dependency. Also, it is hard to imagine circumstances *a priori* that could induce seasonality over the severity and frequency dependence.

Once the operational loss data arrangement is described, the analysis now turns into running the test and determining the dependency degree.

Running of the independence test and determining the level of dependence

For testing the independence between frequency and severity, standard graphical and numerical tests can be implemented. In relation to graphical tests, a scatterplot is proposed. Figure 8.9 shows a scatterplot of frequency rank and severity mean rank, where the graph on the left has 0.75 of Spearman's Rho and the graph on the right is independent with a 0 of Spearman's Rho. This analysis helps in identifying dependencies that are nonlinear.

Concerning numerical tests, Kolmogorov–Smirnov test one relevant option. These tests provide us with a probability of the independence of severity and frequency distribution, but do not provide a measure of the degree of the dependence, which can later be used to replicate dependencies.

An approach for the determination of the degree of dependence between loss frequency and loss severity is to fit a regression model between them.[1] The output of the regression will provide us with an estimate of such dependency and its significance. Linearity issues have been addressed by setting up the data according to their rank order (following the same principles as in Spearman's Rho rank-order correlation), as explained in the previous section.

Figure 8.10 shows the output of such a regression analysis performed with five years of monthly observations on an ORC arranged as described above. The regression output suggests a low dependence degree, Multiple R = 0.0264, and a high significance of fit being purely by chance, Significance F=0.839.

Data grouping of multiple ORCs should be considered when determining dependence between severity and frequency. Grouping allows for the use of more complete data series and provides us with an average dependence for the grouped ORCs. If the dependence analysis suggests a material and statistically significant correlation, the dependence should be modelled into the joint distribution derivation as described later.

Figure 8.10 Frequency severity independence and dependency degree determination

Regression statistics	
Multiple R	0.026433370
R squared	0.000698723
Adjusted R squared	-0.016238586
Standandard error	1396.124011
Observations	60

ANOVA					
	df	SS	MS	F	Significance F
Regression	1	80409.739	80409.7397	0.04125348	0.83974827
Residual	59	115000573	1949162.25		
Total	60	115080982			

	Coefficient	Standard error	t stat	P-value
Intercept	4979.39288	390.117804	12.76381858	1.27E-18
Severity	-0.06367625	0.31350696	-0.20310954	0.839748270

Finally, as mentioned in the previous section, the correlation between severity and frequency can be also calculated with the dataset of Figure 8.7, by introducing weight into the correlation calculation in order to avoid the over- or understatement of periods because of the period frequency. A correlation weighted to period frequency of the period can be calculated as:

$$\rho_{Frequency-Severity} = \frac{Cov_{Frequency-Severity}}{\sigma_{Frequency}\sigma_{Severity}},$$

where

$$Cov_{Frequency-Severity} = \frac{1}{\sum_{i=1}^{n} w_i} \sum_{i=1}^{n} \left(\lambda_i - \bar{\lambda}\right)\left(S_i - \bar{S}\right) w_i;$$

$$\sigma_{Frequency} = \sqrt{\frac{1}{\sum_{i=1}^{n} w_i} \sum_{i=1}^{n} \left(\lambda_i - \bar{\lambda}\right)^2};$$

$$\sigma_{Severity} = \sqrt{\frac{1}{\sum_{i=1}^{n} w_i} \sum_{i=1}^{n} \left(S_i - \bar{S}\right)^2};$$

$$\bar{S} = \frac{1}{\sum_{i=1}^{n} w_i} \sum_{i=1}^{n} w_i S_i;$$

$$\bar{\lambda} = \frac{1}{\sum_{i=1}^{n} w_i} \sum_{i=1}^{n} w_i \lambda_i;$$

$$w_i = \frac{1}{Period\ frequency\ of\ pair\ i};$$

n is the number of loss events, λ_i is the frequency mean rank of the frequency–severity pair i, and S_i the severity mean rank of the frequency–severity pair i (see Figure 8.7).

USING COPULAS FOR REPLICATING OPERATIONAL RISK DEPENDENCIES

A copula simulation is used to generate correlated random numbers from distributions where there is no other easy way to define the dependencies across them. Sklar's Theorem (Sklar 1959) states that any multivariate joint distributions can be written in terms of univariate marginal distribution functions and a copula that describes the dependence structure between the variables. Copulas are widely used in statistics and finance[2] since they permit the definition of a dependency structure, given individual distributions.

There are many parametric copula families available (Gaussian, t-Student, Archimedean, etc), which have different parameters that control the strength of dependence. This section describes those copulas most typically used in operational risk modelling and their applications in defining the dependencies between ORCs, in the aggregation of large number of ORCs and to reproduce the dependency between severity and frequency.

Correlating ORCs with Gaussian and t-Student copulas

The correlation of operational risk ORCs (Step 2 in Figure 8.3) represents the typical case whereby copulas are required to reproduce the dependencies across ORCs. An ORC is the result of a multistep model, starting with the convolution of severity and frequency, plus a hybrid model joining several sources of information. There isn't a direct way, otherwise, to generate correlated values across groups of ORCs in this type of multistep model. A copula is useful since it can correlate the final vector of total loss resulting from the whole ORC model execution.

Gaussian copulas and especially t-Student multivariant copulas are used in operational risk quantification. A Gaussian copula can be implemented more directly and simply, and its computational requirements are less. However, the t-Student copula permits a more detailed modelling of the joint distribution, because, in addition to the correlation matrix, it has a tail parameter for modelling the tail behaviour of operational risk losses. Generally, supervisors expect institutions to model their operational risk dependencies using copulas permitting a tail modelling, such as the *t*-Student copula. The parameters of the copula can be estimated using the methods proposed in "Operational risk correlations" above.

The Gaussian copula can be used to acquire an intuitive understanding of how a copula process works, because of its simplicity. The Gaussian copula can be implemented in the following steps to correlate a number *n* of ORCs:

❏ The individual *n* ORCs are generated independently, following the steps in "Monte Carlo simulation" above. This process results in a vector with all the total losses of the Monte Carlo simulation, for each of the ORCs. We call this the ORC independent distribution.

❏ The desired dependency structure for the ORCs is defined. This can be done following any of the methods described in "Operational risk correlations". Logically, this will be a correlation matrix size *n* x *n*, which we name C.

❏ A standard normal multivariate simulation of *n* distributions with a correlation structure, as in C: for instance, 1,000,000 replications for *n* variables following a standard normal distribution and correlated after C. The result is a matrix of size *n* x 1,000,000, which we name the Gaussian distribution sample matrix.

❏ Each of the numbers in such a matrix is transformed into the corresponding percentile of the standard normal distribution. The result is a matrix-size *n* x 1,000,000 containing percentiles of the correlated standard normal simulation. The *n* columns correspond to each ORC and the 1,000,000 correspond to the number of replications in the simulation. We name it the Gaussian distribution rank matrix.

❏ Each of the *n* ORC vectors of the Gaussian distribution rank matrix is transformed into the corresponding ORC independent distribution. This is done by using the percentiles distribution to derive the quantile from the ORC independent distributions of first point in the explanation.

❏ The result is a matrix of size *n* x 1,000,000, where each of the vectors is distributed as the ORC independent distributions and they are cross-correlated, as is C.

Figure 8.11 Calculations in a Gaussian copula

| UoM1 & UoM 2 correlation | | | | | | | | 0.85 | |

Simulati on iteration	UoM original distribution		Correlated gausian simulation		Gaussian simulation percentile		Copula final value	
	UoM 1	UoM 2	UoM 1	UoM 2	UoM 1	UoM 2	UoM 1	UoM 2
1	187.2	32.1	0.8925	1.0604	81.39	85.55	338.3	69.4
2	140.0	1.7	-0.6194	-0.6159	26.78	26.90	76.0	1.6
3	76.0	1.6	0.7203	2.1703	76.43	98.50	335.6	474.3
4	194.1	0.8	-0.0565	0.4441	47.75	67.15	166.9	16.3
5	97.3	8.4	0.0037	0.2355	50.15	59.31	166.9	8.4
6	338.3	1.6	0.3504	-0.2280	63.70	40.98	194.1	1.7
7	439.1	17.8	0.2869	0.0946	61.29	53.77	187.2	8.1
8	54.9	1753.6	-0.8141	-0.2567	20.78	39.87	54.9	1.7
9	10.1	0.4	-0.3317	-0.2322	37.01	40.82	97.3	1.7
10	421.1	8.1	-0.6385	-1.2404	26.16	10.74	76.0	0.8
11	166.9	16.3	-0.8344	-0.1438	20.20	44.28	54.9	1.7
12	335.6	69.4	-1.0211	-1.1568	15.36	12.37	11.2	0.8
13	11.2	1.0	0.5860	0.5603	72.11	71.24	335.6	17.8
14	481.7	474.3	-1.8982	-1.9888	2.88	2.34	10.1	0.4

The process for all other copulas is similar to the one above. The major difference would be that of the first correlated simulation, which we named the Gaussian correlated distribution matrix. For the *t*-Student copula, these correlated random numbers are generated also with the desired tail parameter of the *t*-Student distribution, in addition to the correlation structure.

Figure 8.11 shows the definition of the dependence between two ORCs using a Gaussian copula. A reduced number of replications, 14, and an overly high correlation of 0.85 are used, permitting an easy tracking of the copula process and its effect over the ORCs' dependency. Using the correlated Gaussian numbers, the original ORC individual distributions are given the desired dependence structure. As we can easily observe, the high values of ORC 1 also tend to be high in the same replication. This can be observed in both the simulation's final values and the Gaussian simulation's percentiles. The dependency is most notorious in replications 1, 2, 5, 12, 13 and 14.

Consecutive copulas for a robust aggregation of a large number of ORCs

The aggregation of operational risk presents a challenge, particularly when the capital model has a large number of ORCs, the model includes multiple countries or financial institutions. The aggregation also becomes challenging when the model incorporates several of the four elements – for instance, ILD and SA – and there is not a perfect granularity matching between them. For example, ILD is generally modelled at business line and Risk Type I. However, SA may have a very different grouping. Sometimes, the scenarios are defined at institution level rather than at a specific business unit. In other cases, the scenarios are defined at a Risk Type II level, representing a mismatch with the ILD modelling, which is most commonly modelled at the less granular Risk Type I. Finally, the existence of a high number of ORCs represents a challenge for the correlation matrix determination, because, given the matrix dimensionality, it requires a long historical time series for its robust determination.

These issues can be addressed using stepped copulas (Step 3 in Figure 8.3), which are the consecutive application of copulas in various aggregation phases. For instance, in a first step, the risk type ORCs are aggregated by business unit to obtain a joint distribution per business unit. Later, an additional aggregation is performed to aggregate each of the business units' joint distributions into a single global joint distribution.

Figure 8.12 illustrates a simple stepped copula example, with 13 Risk Type I ORCs from three business units. The ORCs are first aggregated by business unit to create a total operational risk distribution for each of the business units (commercial, retail and support business units). In a second phase, the three business unit distributions are aggregated into a single-institution total operational risk distribution. The stepped copula permits the use of a much more reduced dimension correlation matrix, facilitating its robust calculation. In fact, the largest correlation matrix used in the example below is 6x6, corresponding to 36 elements, clearly down from the 13x13 and 169 elements required for the aggregation in a single phase. In fact, correlations can be calculated with aggregated loss data from multiple ORCs and are more robust.

Other circumstances in which stepped copulas resolve common problems are those in which the granularity of each of the four elements is different. It is very frequent for SA to be collected at a very different granularity from ILD. SA can be collected down to business area or process level (as in the example illustrated on the left-hand side in Figure 8.13) or down to Risk Type II. On the other hand, ILD is modelled at Risk Type I and business unit. This requires

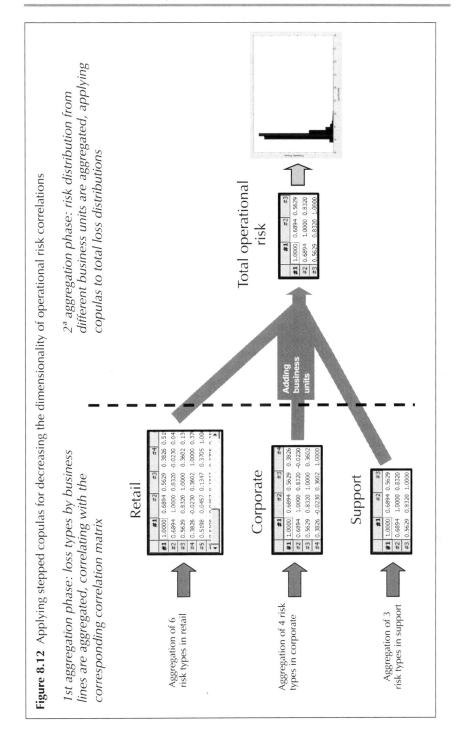

Figure 8.12 Applying stepped copulas for decreasing the dimensionality of operational risk correlations

1st aggregation phase: loss types by business lines are aggregated, correlating with the corresponding correlation matrix

2ª aggregation phase: risk distribution from different business units are aggregated, applying copulas to total loss distributions

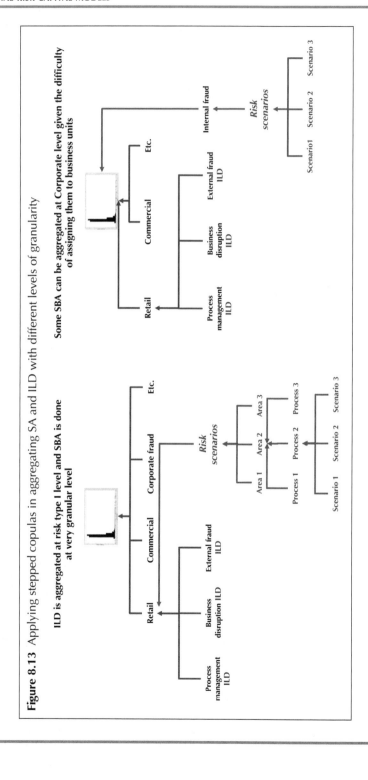

Figure 8.13 Applying stepped copulas in aggregating SA and ILD with different levels of granularity

a previous aggregation of risk scenarios for a later aggregation of both sources of information. The opposite scenario is also possible, as in the example on the left-hand side of Figure 8.13, below which is shown the definition of risk scenarios from internal fraud at corporate level. In this case, internal fraud cases were rare and difficult to assign to specific business units and had to be aggregated at the highest level.

The difference in granularity of the four elements can be generalised for the use of ILD, ED and SA and in different levels of granularity by business unit, risk type, etc. Stepped copulas can resolve these aggregation issues by enabling multiple and flexible aggregation phases to accommodate the different formats of the AMA elements.

The stepped copula implementation is conceptually simple and may be performed by the following steps:

❑ ORCs are grouped according to a specific criterion, most commonly, by an organisational unit: business unit, business area, product, etc. Other grouping criteria may include grouping Risk Type II scenarios into Risk Type I.
❑ Each ORC group is aggregated independently, applying the process described in the previous sections of this chapter. This includes the application of copulas to correlate the different groups of ORCs, as we saw earlier. The result is the joint distribution per ORC group (a business unit, say, or area). The joint distribution of the ORC group is described by a vector containing all the values of the scenario total losses per group. Each vector can be assimilated into the nonparametric joint distribution of the ORC group.
❑ A second copula is applied to aggregate the ORC groups. The aggregation follows the same process as explained earlier, but applied to a nonparametric distribution (see Appendix 1). The result is the total distribution of all of the ORC groups.
❑ Additional steps can be added by applying copulas to nonparametric distributions for aggregating different groups of ORCs and designing of the full aggregation tree as desired.

The definition of a perfectly adapted aggregation tree may require the implementation of multiple aggregation nodes. For some nodes, the distributions are integrated to create a joint distribution. In others, they are mixed into, for instance, a hybrid model.

Copula for the dependency between frequency and severity

Independence between the frequency and severity distributions is a requirement for the consistency of assumptions on the modelling of capital (see "Analysing severity and frequency dependence" above). In case there is a material and significant relationship, the dependence should be modelled for the joint distribution derivation for consistency. In fact, dependence between frequency and severity is of increasing concern for supervisors and, at a minimum, a validation test is requested.

Although this would be a first step (as Step 1 in Figure 8.3), in the operational risk aggregation model it has been placed last in the book, because it would only be part of a highly developed operational risk capital model.

The frequency–severity dependence can be easily replicated by implementing a copula process with a common latent factor, for both severity and frequency, driving the first simulation of the Gaussian copula. The common factor will be the same per replication, both in the frequency random number and in all severity random numbers for that replication. Frequency and severity distributions will be generated by a combination of their own independent factors plus the common factor. The dependence between severity and frequency is determined by the weight of the common factor into the severity and frequency. The weight of the common factor is derived from the analysis described in "Analysing severity and frequency dependence" above.

Figure 8.14 shows the representation of five replications of a Gaussian copula, replicating a dependence between frequency and severity. The correlation used in the example, 0.75, is overly high to show clearly the effect with the use of only a reduced number of Monte Carlo replications. The simulation replication numbers are shown in the left column. There are as many lines as loss events in the simulation replication. For instance, there are five lines for Replication 4, because that replication loss frequency was equal to five; and there were five losses generated from the severity distribution. The severity distribution is a lognormal $\mu=5$ and $\sigma=1.5$ and the

Figure 8.14 Generating correlated numbers of the frequency and severity distributions

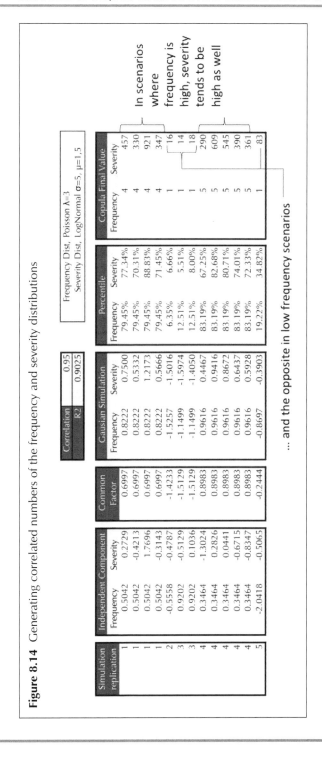

frequency distribution is a Poisson $\lambda=3$. It can be seen clearly that severity is higher when the frequency is higher.

As in any Gaussian copula, the simulation starts with the generation of normally distributed random numbers with the desired correlations. A common factor between severity and frequency is used to replicate the desired dependence between severity and frequency.

This common factor remains unchanged for the simulation replication and it is the same for all severity numbers generated at each replication. However, the independent component of the severity distribution changes for every loss generated. This implies that, if the frequency was high due to the common factor, the severity numbers would tend to be high as well, unless the independent factor gets an opposite direction. For instance, Replications 1 and 4 are high-frequency and also high-severity ones, as can be seen in the two right-hand columns. Also, Scenarios 2, 3 and 5 are low-frequency and low-severity. This method for reproducing dependence between frequency and severity is consistent with the method used to test and determine dependence between frequency and severity described in "Analysing severity and frequency dependence" above.

As we can observe, creating dependence between severity and frequency is, within the nested or stepped correlation model, the process with the lowest dimension and simplest statistics.

Figure 8.15 shows the normalised values of severities and frequencies and the corresponding correlation coefficient, generated following the copula model presented in this section. It can be seen how frequency and severity have more coordinated normalised values as dependence increases.

Finally, we need to estimate the weight of the common factors in the severity and frequency and the Gaussian copula's latent factors, allowing for the replication of the observed dependence. Given the very significant differences between the marginal distribution functions (severity-and-frequency distribution) and the copula's latent factors (Gaussian distributions), the correlation coefficient applied in the copula's latent factors should be adjusted for reproducing the observed dependence between the severity and frequency, generally upwards. The correlation of the Gaussian copula's underlying latent factors can be easily adjusted through a simple optimisation process, since its relationship with the correlation of the severity and frequency is strictly monotonic.

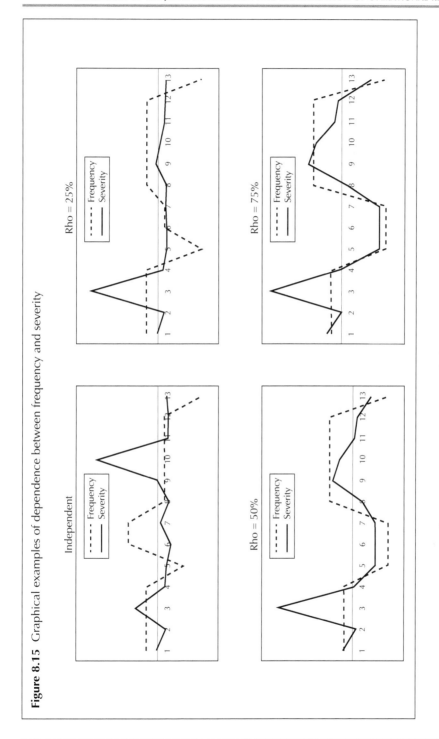

Figure 8.15 Graphical examples of dependence between frequency and severity

CAPITALISATION OF OPERATIONAL RISK

The process described in "Monte Carlo simulation" above provides the total aggregated operational loss distribution, from which to derive the total capital figure. Capital is determined so as to guarantee the institution solvency with a specific confidence interval. In other words, the capital is calculated so as to be sufficient to absorb losses with a specific probability. This concept is also known as capital-at-risk.

Operational capital-at-risk is the amount of capital required, beyond the anticipated average operational loss that could be lost due to operational events, at a certain confidence level and over a specific time horizon, given the operational risk profile of the institution during such time horizon.

The time horizon is determined by the capital-raising schedule of the institution. A financial institution will generally not be willing to raise additional capital more than once a year, and capital-at-risk is most commonly calculated with a minimum time horizon of a year. In fact, the regulatory frameworks of Basel II/III and Solvency II are based on a one-year time horizon. In operational risk terms, this implies that loss frequencies of the ORC are calculated as annual frequencies. In credit risk, an annual time horizon implies that probabilities of default are also calculated as annual probabilities. In market risk, it implies that the volatility of the portfolio is calculated as annual volatility or that the VaR is adjusted to reflect an annual volatility. Larger time horizons can be used to calculate longer-term capital needs, as an input to the medium-to-long-term capital-planning process. In operational risk, the use of a time horizon longer than one year typically entails the scaling of the loss frequency distribution.

The amount required to support operational losses is derived from the total aggregated operational loss distribution, which links the amount of total operational losses with their probability of occurrence. Capital-at-risk is calculated so that the probability of exhausting the capital by the institution's operational losses is less than, or equal to, the probability of default corresponding to the desired agency rating by the institution. For instance, if the institution desires an A rating, which has an annual default probability of 10 basis points (0.0010), then the operational capital-at-risk should be above operational losses of 99.9% $(1 - 0.0010 = 0.999)$ of the potential circumstances being faced by the institution within the next year. This means that the capital requirements can be derived from the 99.9th percentile of the total aggregated operational loss distribution, subtracting the mean of the distribution, or expected loss, which represents the anticipated operational loss average, used to determine reserves. In fact, capital requirements for Basel II/III and Solvency II are calculated based on Rating A and a 99.9% confidence interval.

Referring to the holding period and confidence interval for capital calculation, BCSG-AMA says, "Whatever approach is used, a bank must demonstrate that its operational risk measure meets a soundness standard comparable to that of the internal ratings-based approach for credit risk (i.e. comparable to a one year holding period and a 99.9th percentile confidence interval)."

Figure 8.16 illustrates the calculation of capital-at-risk from the aggregated loss distribution. The table in the top right-hand corner shows the target rating, the corresponding confidence interval for the capital calculation and the annual default probability (or the probability of the operational losses exceeding capital) from which the confidence interval has been derived. The histogram shows the representation of the total aggregated operational loss distribution and the percentile from which capital needs have been derived.

The calculation of the overall distribution of losses allows other information to be extracted, in addition to the above-mentioned economic capital. The capital required to cover the entity's operational losses can provide us with the following metrics:

❏ Expected loss or anticipated average loss. It is the mathematical hope of the operational loss distribution. It is typically calculated as the mean of the replications resulting from the joint loss distribution simulation, although sometimes the trimmed mean, median or other variation is proposed. It is used as the basis for calculating the required reserves for operational risk and passed annually in the profit-and-loss statement. In fact, BCSG-AMA also mentions expected loss as one the outputs to be obtained from an operational risk capital model when it says, "A bank should also gather information on the expected loss. Due to its high sensitivity to extreme losses, the arithmetic mean can cause an inaccurate picture for the expected losses. In light of this, the

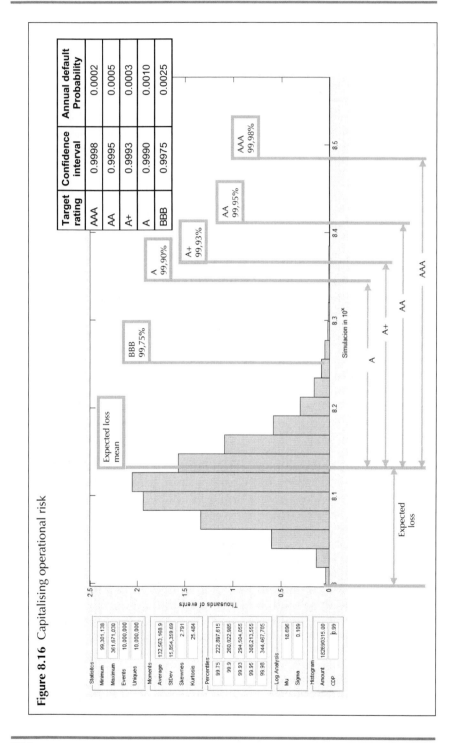

Figure 8.16 Capitalising operational risk

use of statistics that are less influenced by extreme losses (eg median, trimmed mean) is recommended, especially in the case of medium/heavy tailed datasets."

❏ Loss volatility, defined as the standard deviation of the joint distribution. It is used to estimate the capital multiple as the ratio of the capital divided by the loss volatility. The capital multiple is used to compare the tail behaviour with that of the normal distribution, which is a light tail distribution.

❏ Capital for unexpected losses, value-at risk, defined as the difference between the percentile of the distribution at a specified confidence level corresponding to the entity's target rating and the expected loss.

❏ Losses based on qualitative descriptions: these include the typical loss (50th percentile or the distribution mode), large loss (percentile 90), very large loss (percentile 99), extremely large loss (percentile 99.9, which can also be used for the capital-at-risk), etc.

❏ Expected shortfall: average losses above a specific threshold. This provides information regarding the mean event given a specific probability of its happening.

Figure 8.17 shows the representation of the calculation of the expected loss based on the mean, the trimmed mean (between the 5th and 95th percentiles) and the median, as compared with the percentile 99.95 for capital determination. Depending on the kurtosis and skewness of the total aggregated loss distribution, the differences between the mean, trimmed mean and median maybe less significant.

In practice, operational capital-at-risk is calculated under several parameterisations of the model, in order to compare results and evaluate the sensitivity of the model to different inputs and factors. The capital requirements may be calculated first based on a hybrid model with four elements (ILD, ED, etc); then, based only on ILD, or with any of the combinations of the four elements. Different correlation assumptions can then be used to evaluate their impact over total capital (perfect correlation, stressed correlation, etc). Finally, the impact of insurance on capital versus the absence of insurance can also be estimated to assess the effectiveness of the insurance. All this requires multiple runs of the model.

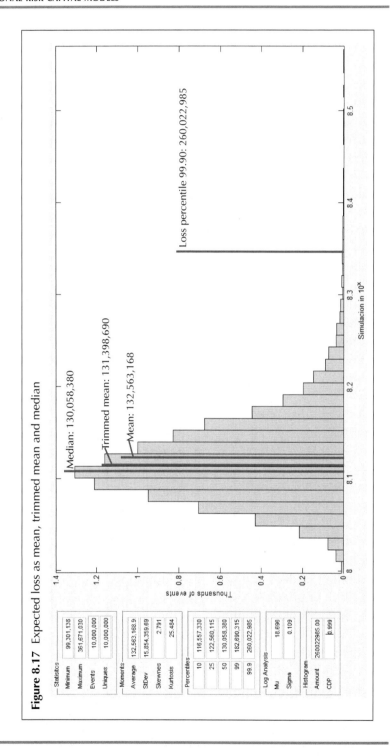

Figure 8.17 Expected loss as mean, trimmed mean and median

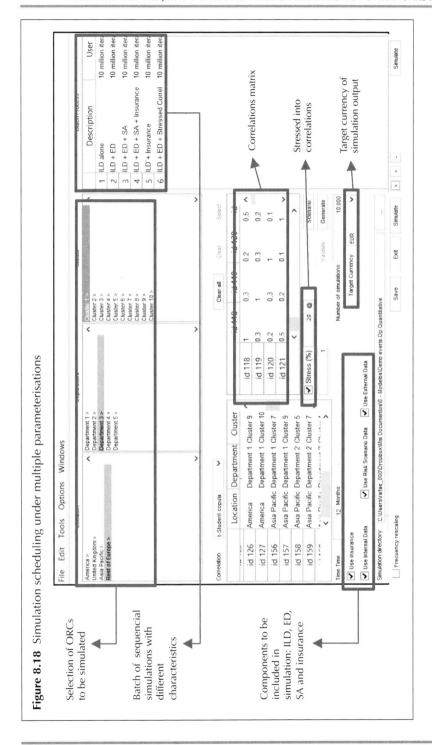

Figure 8.18 Simulation scheduling under multiple parameterisations

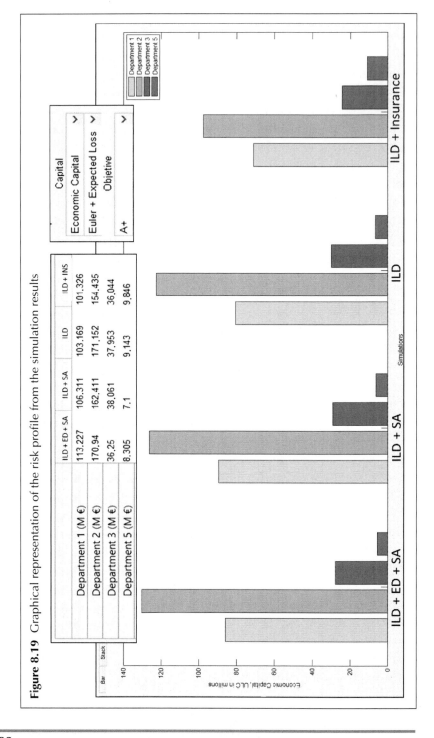

Figure 8.19 Graphical representation of the risk profile from the simulation results

	ILD + ED + SA	ILD + SA	ILD	ILD + INS
Department 1 (M €)	113.227	106.311	103.169	101.326
Department 2 (M €)	170,94	162,411	171.152	154.435
Department 3 (M €)	36,25	38,061	37.953	36,044
Department 5 (M €)	8.305	7.1	9.143	9,846

Capital

Economic Capital

Euler + Expected Loss

Objetive

A+

Department 1
Department 2
Department 3
Department 5

Figure 8.18 represents the scheduling of the model runs. It shows the consecutive batch process for the calculation of operational risk capital under different parameterisations: with and without insurance, with and without ED, with and without SA, different correlation matrices, possible different target currencies, etc.

Figure 8.19 shows the representation of some of the capital calculations from the previous batch calculation setting. We can observe the impact of the components and data elements in the calculation, which represent different visions of the risk profile. The consideration of mitigation, SA and ED produces an impact on the total capital obtained and its allocation by department. The capital has been calculated for an A+ solvency standard and allocated based on Euler allocation (see below).

ALLOCATION OF OPERATIONAL RISK CAPITAL

While total capital derived from the operational risk capitalisation process is used to evaluate the institution's solvency, capital allocation is required for integrating the capital estimations into many processes of the daily management and the use test of the institution. An institution is managed business unit by business unit and risk mitigation is implemented according to risk exposure. Capital allocation helps in this task by demonstrating how each of the business units and risk exposures contributes to the overall capital consumption/use. Capital allocated to business units, exposures, scenarios and so forth permits us to understand how an organisational unit contributes to total capital and the corresponding cost of the capital.

We refer to capital allocation as the process of assigning total capital down to the ORC using statistical processes that capture implicit model characteristics, including the diversification level and distribution characteristics (such as types and tail behaviour). Capital allocation is thus different from capital attribution, which uses qualitatively defined criteria to assign the total capital to the different business units, etc.

Capital allocation permits the embedding of risk measurement into the daily management of the financial institution's risk beyond the capital adequateness evaluation. The allocation of capital to specific business units, exposures or even managers can be used for the estimation of the return on equity (ROE) achieved by business units and all other measures of risk-adjusted performance (risk-adjusted return on capital, economic value added, embedded value, etc); the cascading down of risk appetite and limit control; the evaluation of the risk profile change from risk-mitigation measures; and the identification of the largest individual exposures as well as those business units with the most extreme risk profile, resource allocation, risk-adjusted compensation, etc.

BCSG-AMA mentions capital allocation in several parts of the document, such as when it says, "Capital allocation to internal business lines should be a factor when choosing ORCs, as these ORCs may be used as part of the capital allocation process."

There are various techniques in the bibliography to allocate capital, each of which responds to specific management issues. Table 8.2 summarises these methods and explain their different properties.

In the following sections we will describe the calculation methodology of these processes except for the non-diversified allocation, due to its simplicity.

Euler allocation

Euler allocation is the theoretical answer to how much capital is consumed by each ORC. It is the capital figure in each ORC given the percentile of the total aggregated loss distribution when an extremely high number of replications have been produced resulting in a perfect filling of the tail. For instance, if the capital is derived from at the 99.9% confidence interval of the total aggregated loss distribution through 10 billion replications, the 99.90000000th percentile would be made up of the addition of other percentiles from the individual ORCs. Those values of the individual ORCs, adding up to the 99.90000000% of the total aggregated loss distribution, would be the answer to capital allocation by ORC. The assumption is that the 10 billion replications provide a perfect filling of the tails.

Since generating a sufficient number of replications to obtain a stable Euler capital allocation is computationally very expensive and lengthy, Euler allocation is calculated with the mean of a specific number of replications around the capital allocation percentile of the ORCs. For instance, the 10 replications above and below the target percentile are averaged to determine an approximate and stable value of the Euler allocation.

The calculation process can be executed as follows:

Table 8.2 List of capital allocation methodologies

Methodology	Application
Non-diversified allocation	This is the simplest approach as it provides pure standalone results of the capital of the individual ORCs. It assumes perfect correlations across ORCs and is used for estimating regulatory capital from advanced models when no diversification benefits are allowed by the supervisor.[3]
Euler allocation	It provides the theoretical answer to capital allocation, although it is difficult to apply in practice, as it requires a very large number of replications to achieve a precise solution, particularly when fat-tail distributions are used.
Contribution to expected shortfall	This method responds to which ORCs have strongest potential extreme losses and to what ORCs increase more capital requirements. It is determined based on the contribution to tail risk or on how each ORC contributes to the expected shortfall of the joint distribution.
Contribution to total volatility	This method allocates more capital to those ORCs with highest volatility of losses or with high probability for losses in the medium term. This method attributes capital to where there is a higher probability of experiencing an increase of losses in the short to medium term. Allocation is based on the contribution of each ORC to the total operational risk distribution.
Incremental capital analysis	This method answers the question of how much capital would be saved if the ORC risk is transferred by the sale of the business line, interruption of an activity or outsourcing of a process, etc. This is appropriate for analysing the impact on operational risk of whole business lines and estimating the impact of closing their activities. The allocation is based on the analysis of the capital difference of excluding each of the ORCs from the calculation.
Standalone allocation	This is an intuitive attribution based on the standalone contribution to risk. Its calculation is also simple and more easily accepted by business units, but it does not take into consideration the diversification benefits.
Capital attribution	The total operational risk capital is attributed based on factors external to the statistical model. Accounting figures and internal control factors (such as RCSA and KRIs) are frequently used to attribute total capital to ORCs. Sometimes, capital add-ons (positive or negative) are also attributed to the different organisational units for incentivising desired management actions or penalising others. Capital attribution is explained in Chapter 6.

❏ A Monte Carlo simulation is generated, and the replications of losses from the different ORCs are ordered based on the total aggregated loss distribution percentiles. The total capital is calculated for a specific percentile, for instance, the 99.9th percentile.

❏ The loss value of individual ORCs, which add up to the 99.9% of the total aggregated loss distribution, would be the Euler allocation, if an extremely high number of replications had been generated in the Monte Carlo simulation.

❏ To approximate the value of the attribution with a reasonable computational effort, the 10 replications of the ORCs above and below are averaged together with the 99.9th percentile as an approximation for the Euler allocation. If the Monte Carlo simulation had been generated with 1,000,000 replications, the average would be calculated with the ORC values corresponding to the following percentiles of the total aggregate loss distributions: 99.9890, 99.9891, ..., 99.9898, 99.9899, 99.900, 99.9901, 99.9902, ..., 99.9909 and 99.9910.

❏ If the sum of the allocation (the averages of the ORC surrounding the percentiles) is not equal to total capital to be allocated (the 99.9% of the total aggregated loss distribution), these values are standardised to equal exactly the capital to be allocated.

Figure 8.20 provides a graphical representation of Euler allocation. The column labelled "quantile" on the left shows the total aggregated loss distribution values by the percentiles, as in the next column to the right, in which the percentiles are ordered from low to high. The columns below the ORCs (1 through 5) represent the loss value of the ORC, which is added to the total aggregated loss for calculating the total aggregated loss percentile. Logically, these are ordered following the sequence of the percentiles of the total aggregated loss distribution. The greyscale in the ORCs is proportional to how large the loss is for the scenario in ORCs. Observe the positive correlation across the ORCs as they get darker in the highest percentiles at the bottom of the columns. The white thick square is the Euler allocation, if there were infinite replications generated, for the 95th percentile. The total aggregated risk capital at a 95% confidence interval would be 942 and, if a very large number of

Figure 8.20 Calculation for Euler allocation

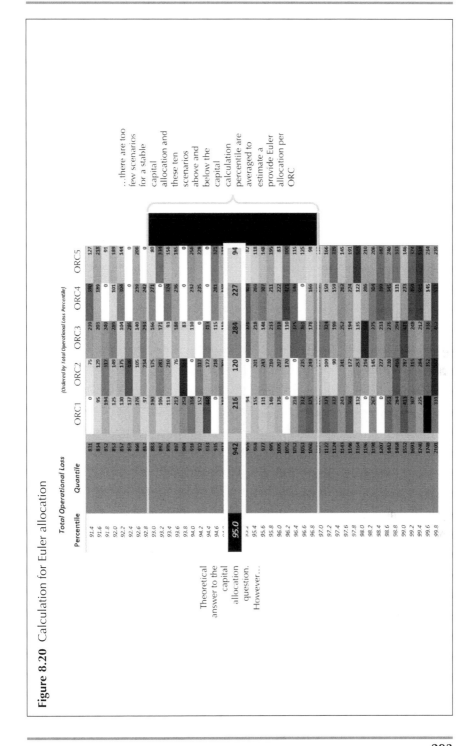

replications had been generated, it would have been allocated as 216 to ORC 1, 120 to ORC 2, 284 to ORC 3, 227 to ORC 4 and 94 to ORC 5. Since replications are insufficient to fill the tail and produce a stable allocation, 10 replications below and above the 95th percentile are also used to calculate the ORC average, which is used for the capital allocation. The scenario-averaging process produces the final capital allocation as 188 for ORC 1, 191 for ORC 2, 198 for ORC 3, 215 for ORC 4 and 150 for ORC 5. When the averaged values do not add up to the total capital, the allocation values are normalised.

Contribution to expected shortfall

This method allocates capital based on the contribution of each ORC to the expected shortfall of the total aggregated risk distribution. The "expected shortfall at q% level" is the expected loss in the worst q% of the cases. It is the mean value of the operational loss distribution above a specific percentile, q%. The expected shortfall is a coherent measure of risk, which means it is subadditive. This means that the addition of the expected shortfall contributions of each of the units of measure is equal to the total expected shortfall of the portfolio.

The contribution to the expected shortfall allocation can be calculated as follows:

❏ A Monte Carlo simulation of the ORCs is generated, and the replications of the losses from different ORCs are ordered based on the total aggregated loss-distribution percentiles. The total capital is calculated for a specific percentile, for instance, the 99.9th percentile. For simplicity in the explanation, it is assumed the simulation is generated with 10,000 replications.
❏ The mean of the loss values of the ORCs distributions is calculated corresponding to the total aggregated loss distribution percentiles 99.90, 99.91, ..., 99.99 and 100. These are the existing replications above the 99.9th percentile of the total aggregated loss distribution. If the simulation had been performed with 100,000 replications, then 100 rather than 10 replications would exist above the 99.9%.
❏ The total capital at the 99.9th percentile of the total aggregated loss distribution is allocated to the ORC proportionally to the means calculated above.

Figure 8.21 Calculations for expected shortfall allocation

Percentile	Quantile	ORC1	ORC2	ORC3	ORC4	ORC5
92.4	859	137	436	288	0	0
92.6	886	176	105	140	239	206
92.8	867	97	234	253	242	0
93.0	883	190	175	166	271	80
93.2	892	106	281	171	0	328
93.4	895	113	210	93	324	156
93.6	897	212	76	188	236	185
93.8	904	258		83	0	0
94.0	916	318	0	110	212	256
94.2	932	152	317	0	235	228
94.4	933	448	172	313	0	321
94.6	935	0	218	115	281	
94.8	937	190		110	168	188
95.0	**942**	**216**	**120**	**284**	**227**	**94**
95.2	955	94	0	178	403	82
95.4	959	155	201	218	366	118
95.6	977	131	243	148	307	148
95.8	995	146	210	233	211	195
96.0	1095	176	207	318	222	83
96.2	1052	0	170	110	475	300
96.4	1062	216	0	175	346	115
96.6	1063	332	235	361	0	125
96.8	1060	375	243	178	166	98
97.0	1094	222	177	319	257	118
97.2	1122	373	109	124	150	166
97.4	1124	337	90	159	159	339
97.6	1143	243	241	252	262	145
97.8	1146	366	172	194	224	191
98.0	1164	132	253	135	122	320
98.2	1196	0	216		206	210
98.4	1198	267	145	275	304	206
98.6	1207	0	227	233	399	347
98.8	1442	351	230	276	345	240
99.0	1658	284	416	294	131	332
99.2	1562	413	287		233	146
99.4	1669	307	315	248	456	374
99.6	1740	225	284	212		326
99.8	1748		352	305	145	234
100.0	**2101**	**335**		**452**	**515**	**239**

In the expected shortfall allocation, the scenarios above the capital percentile of each ORC are averaged to allocate capital. The addition of the ORC means is equal to the mean of the scenarios above the same percentile on the total operational loss distribution

295

The contribution to expected shortfall, at quantile t of the i-th ORC can be defined using the following expression:

$$L_{ES}^i(q) = \left(L(q) - \bar{L}\right)\frac{E\left[l^i \mid q\right]}{E\left[L \mid q\right]},$$

where $L(q)$ is the loss at quantile q, $\bar{L}$ is the mean of losses, $E[l^i \mid q]$ is the expected value of the losses of $ORC\ i$ over the quantile q, and $E[L \mid q]$ is the expected value of the total losses over the quantile q.

Figure 8.21 provides a graphical representation of the expected shortfall contribution allocation method. The red column on the left is the total aggregated loss values by the percentiles as in the next column to the right, which are ordered from low to high percentiles. The columns below the ORCs 1 through to 5 represent the loss value of such ORCs, which are added to the total aggregated loss distribution for calculating the total aggregated loss percentile. Logically, these are ordered following the sequence of percentiles of the total aggregated loss distribution. The greyscale in the ORCs corresponds to how large the loss is for the scenario in the ORCs. Observe the positive correlation across the ORCs as they get darker, and note the highest percentiles at the bottom of the columns. The total operational risk capital at a 95% confidence interval would be 942 and its expected shortfall contribution to the ORCs is 216 for ORC 1, 120 for ORC 2, 284 for ORC 3, 227 for ORC 4 and 94 for ORC 5, respectively.

Contribution to total volatility

This method allocates capital proportionally to the contribution that each ORC makes to the standard deviation (σ) of the total aggregated risk distribution. This method is most frequently used in market risk, where risk distributions are closer to normal and multiples of the standard deviation can be used to estimate percentiles and capital.

In fat-tail operational risks, the volatility contribution is less meaningful. It can be interpreted as an allocation based on how likely it is to witness losses in the medium term. The variance or σ^2 is a low-distribution moment, and it becomes higher in those distributions with large loss values in the medium percentiles (between the 75th and 95th percentiles) but it is less sensitive to high but low likelihood losses of fat tails.

Capital is allocated based residual OpRisk, which is the risk or volatility that is not diversified within the group of ORCs of the capital model. It is calculated following the principle of the contribution made to the total operational loss volatility by each type of operational loss, using the following formula:

$$Residual\,Operational\,Risk_i$$

$$\equiv Vol\left(Operational\,Loss_i\right)\frac{\partial Vol\left(Total\,Operational\,Loss\right)}{\partial Vol\left(Operational\,Loss_i\right)}$$

$$\equiv Vol\left(Operational\,Loss_i\right)\frac{\sum_{j=1}^{n}\partial Vol\left(Total\,Operational\,Loss\right)\rho_{i,j}}{\partial Vol\left(Operational\,Loss_i\right)},$$

where,

$$Operational\,Loss_i\ \text{refers to the}\ ORC_i,$$

Residual Operational Risk$_i$ is the non-diversified risk of an ORC$_i$ within the group of ORCs of the capital model. It is defined as the contribution to the standard risk or deviation made by the total operational risk of Operational Loss$_i$.

Vol (Operational Loss$_i$) is the estimated standard volatility or standard deviation of ORC$_i$, which may be calculated based on the operational loss replications resulting from the simulation of the severity and frequency of ORC$_i$.

Vol (Total Operational Loss) is the volatility or standard deviation of the group of ORCs of the capital model, which may be calculated based on the simulation of all the ORCs of the capital model.

When operational losses are assumed to be independent, the residual risk formula may be simplified as follows:

$$Residual\,Operational\,Risk_i \equiv \frac{Variance\left(Operational\,Loss_i\right)}{Volatility\left(Total\,Operational\,Loss\right)}$$

Having calculated residual risk, the capital multiple can be calculated. The capital multiple is defined as the number of standard deviations of operational losses necessary to cover economic capital. The capital multiple in a normal distribution will be 3.09 for a confidence interval of 99.9% and 1.65 for a confidence interval of 95%. For asymmetric distributions, such as operational risk distributions, the capital multiple is significantly higher than in a normal distribution. The following formula is used to calculate the capital multiple:

$$\text{Capital Multiple} = (\text{Total Operational Risk Capital} / \text{Volatility of Operational Risk})$$

Finally, capital is allocated to each operational loss as follows:

$$\text{Allocation of Capital to Operational Loss}_i$$
$$= \text{Capital Multiple} * \text{Residual Operational Risk}_i,$$

where *Allocation of Capital to Operational Loss$_i$* is the capital allocated to a type of operational loss "i" within a business line.

The advantage of using this capital allocation methodology is that the sum of the allocated capital numbers equals the total capital.

Incremental capital analysis

Incremental capital analysis allocates the total capital proportionally to the capital reduction as it removes each ORC from the total aggregated risk distribution. It is more meaningful when the ORC corresponds to an operational risk that can be completely transferred (via insurance, say). It actually represents the incremental capital required, as it bears the risk rather than transferring it. It is really meaningful when the analysis is done with full business units or activities that could be outsourced, sold or interrupted. When the ORC corresponds to a risk that is more difficult to be disentangled from the business of the institution or from the business unit and cannot be hedged, the meaning of the allocation is harder to interpret.

The calculation process can be executed as follows:

❏ The total capital is calculated as the percentile of the capital calculation minus the total expected loss.
❏ The total operational risk is calculated without one of the ORCs (percentile of capital calculation minus the expected loss). The result is subtracted from the total operational risk calculated with all the ORCs and can be interpreted as the incremental capital consumption for ORCs.
❏ The same process is repeated for each ORC and the incremental capital consumption per ORC is calculated.
❏ The total operational risk capital is allocated proportionally to the capital incremental consumption of each ORC.

Mathematically, the incremental capital analysis can be expressed as follows:

$$L^i_{inc}(q) = \left(L(q)-\bar{L}\right)\frac{\left(L(q)-\bar{L}\right)-\left(l^i(q)-\bar{l}^i\right)}{\sum_{j=1}^{n}\left(\left(L(q)-\bar{L}\right)-\left(l^j(q)-\bar{l}^j\right)\right)},$$

where $\bar{l}^i$ is the expected loss for the ORC i.

Standalone allocation

The standalone allocation is a simple and direct capital allocation approach. Total capital is proportionally allocated to the ORC based on the standalone capital calculated with the same percentile as the total capital.

It has the significant caveat that specific ORC cross-dependencies are ignored and may lead to decisions that increase total operational risk correlation. However, it produces an intuitive result that is more easily accepted by the business units, at least at the beginning of the integration of the capital calculations into the performance measurement of the business units.

The proportional allocation can be defined using the following expression:

$$L^i_{sa}(q) = \left(L(q)-\bar{L}\right)\frac{l^i(q)}{\sum_{j=1}^{n}l^j(q)}$$

OPERATIONAL RISK PROFILE MEASUREMENT

The operational risk profile is the amount of operational risk that an institution faces, at a point in time. It can be measured using the operational risk capital model described in this book and its measurement is the main input into the use test, as illustrate in Figure 8.22. The operational risk profile measurement typically includes the metrics derived from the overall operational risk distribution (see "Capitalisation of operational risk" and "Allocation of operational risk capital" above), such as:

❏ operational risk capital at different confidence intervals;
❏ capital allocated to business units and other organisational entities;
❏ measures of risk such as extreme losses, high losses, likely loss;

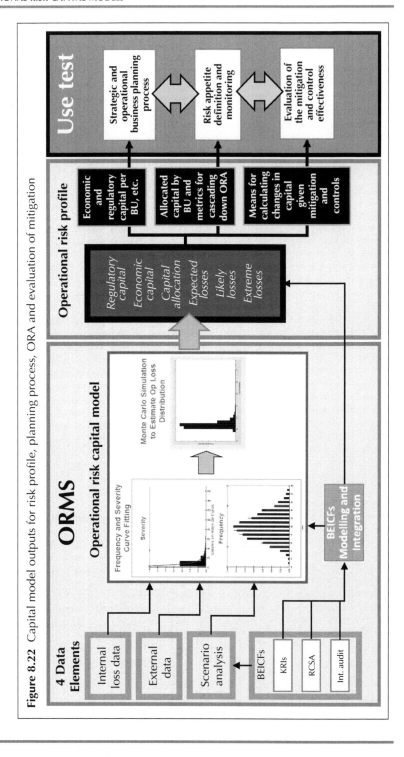

Figure 8.22 Capital model outputs for risk profile, planning process, ORA and evaluation of mitigation

❏ expected losses; and
❏ the risk profile metrics calculated under different than expected circumstances, such as stressed scenarios, or the risk profile resulting from the implementation of mitigation plans.

The measurement of the operational risk profile may also include other metrics from the operational risk measurement system (ORMS), such as KRIs, RCSA and other BEICFs. These capture aspects of the operational risk profile that are more difficult to translate into a capital figure but frequently represent important attributes of the risk profile in need of thorough management.

All in all, the operational risk profile is measured in metrics, in units and formats, and with the characteristics for facilitating risk profile integration into the day-to-day risk management of the institution.

Figure 8.22 summarises the process for estimating the risk profile and its integration into the main risk-management processes: strategic and operational business planning process, operational risk appetite and evaluation of the effectiveness of controls and mitigation.

CONCLUSION

This chapter has presented the consecutive processes for the derivation of the joint distribution and capitalisation of operational risk. These permit detailed measurement of the operational risk profile. In fact, the presented processes allow for the consideration of all relevant characteristics of operational losses, including dependencies, in addition to providing detailed insights into the capital consumption from the different risk types and organisational entities through the allocation process.

As a result, the operational risk profile metrics can be better used in the day-to-day risk management of the institution, as requested by supervisors. In fact, since capital can be allocated to very granular organisational entities and risk types, the integration into management can be applied to highly specific mitigation actions and controls evaluations.

---

1 The criticism of this method is that it measures only the linear dependence between the data series but will not capture other, more complex, dependencies. Nevertheless, the amount of

relevant data generally available for operational risk modelling is much reduced and makes the determination of more complex dependencies hardly feasible.

2   For instance, in risk/portfolio management, copulas are used to perform stress tests and robustness checks that are especially important during "downside/crisis/panic regimes", where extreme downside events may occur. In credit risk, the Merton Default Model responds to a copula process, when applied to portfolio management. Default correlations are determined by the correlation of the debtor's assets, whose returns can be assumed to be normally distributed. The normal distribution of asset returns is then translated into a binomial distribution, default or non-default, when the asset value falls below the total debt (in a simplified explanation). More complex approaches have been developed, such as CreditMetrics, where the distribution is not binomial but has as many states as rating grades.

3   Given its calculation simplicity, no specific subsection was written to describe this allocation methodology.

REFERENCES

Bouye, E., *et al*, 2000, "Copulas for Finance: A Reading Guide and Some Applications", working paper, Groupe de Recherche Operationnelle, Credit Lyonnais.

Box, George E. P. and Gwilym Jenkins, 1970, *Time Series Analysis: Forecasting and Control.* (San Francisco: Holden-Day).

Economist, The, 1995, "A Fallen Star", March 4, pp. 19–21.

Financial Times, 2008, "SocGen postmortem", January 25.

Jaeckel, P., and R. Rebonato, 1999, "The most general methodology for creating a valid correlation matrix for risk management and option pricing purposes", *Journal of Risk* 2(2), Winter.

Perkins, Peter, and Tom Lane, 2003, "Monte-Carlo Simulation in MATLAB Using Copulas", *MATLAB News & Notes*, November.

Sklar, A., 1959, "Fonctions de répartition à n dimensions et leurs marges", Institut de statistique de l'Université de Paris 8: 229–231.

Backtesting, Stress Testing and Sensitivity Analysis

Rafael Cavestany and Daniel Rodriguez

So far, we have described an end-to-end statistical process of estimating capital requirements for operational risk. In this chapter, we look at the backtesting and stress testing of such models, in order to provide a quality control and validation of the completeness of the operational risk capital model. The backtesting represents an *ex post* validation of the accuracy of the modelling and compares the new experienced operational risk losses with those predicted by the models used during the capital estimation. This helps to validate whether the capital model was actually over or underestimating the risk profile. On the other hand, stress testing estimates the potential losses of severely adverse operational risk scenarios and serves as an additional capital adequateness validation.

OPERATIONAL RISK BACKTESTING
Backtesting is a necessary analysis in any risk estimation and provides us with an *ex post* evaluation of the precision of the calculations. Backtesting of operational risk capital estimations involves the challenge of backtesting risk estimations performed for a one-year time horizon and a high confidence interval of generally 99.9%. This implies that more than 1,000 yearly observations of total operational losses would be required for the direct backtesting of operational risk capital, which is clearly not possible.

This issue is also common to market and credit risk capital estimations, which are done with the same time horizon and confidence interval, also requiring a similarly large number of yearly observations, for a direct backtesting of capital estimations.

In market and credit risks the issue is addressed by performing the backtesting with a shorter time horizon and low percentile to validate models. This significantly reduces the observations needed for the backtesting. If this backtesting is passed, it is assumed that the model is then good enough for the capital requirement estimations performed at a higher confidence level and longer time horizon. For instance, in market risk, the backtesting is done with the value-at-risk (VaR) used for investments management, which is calculated, for instance, as 10 days VaR at 95%. Later, this VaR figure is rescaled to the time horizon and confidence interval of the capital requirements. Credit risk backtesting is frequently based on the evaluation of the expected values of EAD, PD and LGD, rather than the extreme cases that define capital.

In operational risk, a similar approach can be used for the backtesting of capital estimates. The severity and frequency distribution models used for estimating capital requirements can be compared with the new yearly losses experienced by the institution, to evaluate whether there is an overestimation or an underestimation by the distribution models.

BCSG-AMA mentions validation and verification guidelines, which can be addressed via backtesting: "The validation process of the ORMS [Operational Risk Measurement System] should provide enhanced assurance that the measurement methodology results in an operational risk capital charge that credibly reflects the operational risk profile of the bank."

Backtesting of the severity of the year

The backtesting can be performed as an *ex post* goodness-of-fit (GoF) analysis, leveraging on similar techniques to those explained in Chapter 4. For the backtesting, the two distributions compared are the new collected losses and the parametric distributions used in the capital estimates. Similarly, new losses experienced by the institution can be compared with the losses used to model the capital or experienced prior to the modelling date. This will tell us how past operational risk losses are actually predictive of future losses. The comparison of actual losses from different time periods can also be used for evaluating the evolution of the institution's operational risk profile with time.

The distributions can be tested through visual analysis of PP plot,

QQ plot, difference by bin, and histograms versus probability density function, or by using numerical analysis such as A–D or K–S. In Figure 9.1 we can see the evaluation of the backtesting of a severity Burr model used in the capital model for 2012 H2 of an ORC. QQ and PP plots comparing the Burr model with the new losses experienced is illustrated. It can be observed the Burr model replicates well the new losses in the body distribution but does not match well new extreme losses experienced. The QQ plot suggests overestimation of capital requirements, as the model is predicting higher losses than the actual experience. Observe, also, the AD, which between the Burr model and the new losses is too low to reject the null hypothesis. It should be then analysed as to whether this is due to a change in the risk profile or an error in the modelling, which can be done by comparing the loss empirical distributions from different years.

Figure 9.2 represents the QQ plots comparing the empirical distributions of the new losses' posterior to the capital modelling, in year 2013, with that loss dataset used for the modelling and the losses from 2012, 2011 and 2010. It can be clearly observed that the new losses from year 2013 were overestimated also by the empirical loss models from any of the previous years, suggesting a potential change in the risk profile, which results in lower-severity losses. The root causes of this change should be analysed when constructing the new severity model in order to justify increasing the weight of these lower-severity losses in the new capital model (see Chapter 4).

Backtesting of annual frequency

The backtesting of severities is implemented using the numerous annual severity observations and their comparison with the parametric distribution used in the severity model. However, in the case of frequency, there is only one annual observation for the frequency, making it impossible to backtest following the same procedure as in the severity distribution.

The number of observations for the backtesting of frequencies can be increased by segmenting the analysis into the ORC.[1] For instance, if the capital model has 15 ORCs, we do have 15 observations to test the frequency. The frequency observations of the ORCs can then be backtested using the following process:

❏ Every ORC has a different frequency distribution, making the standard validation test of comparing multiple observations to a

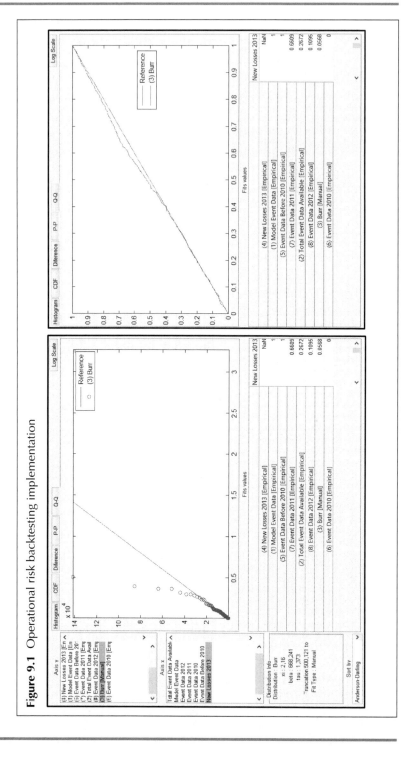

Figure 9.1 Operational risk backtesting implementation

Figure 9.2 Analysing a potential change of risk profile in losses

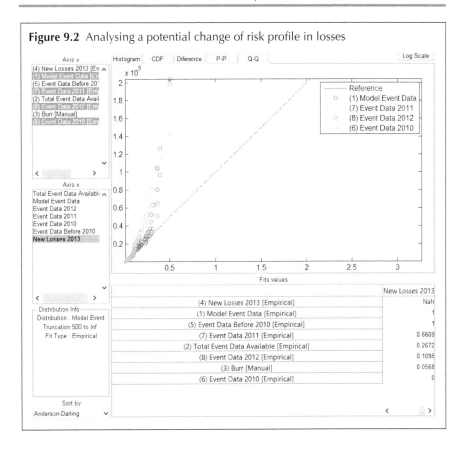

parametric distribution impossible. This can be resolved by calculating the cumulative probability of each of the actual observations with the frequency distribution used for the capital projection for each ORC:

$$CP_i = F^{-1}(x_i),$$

where "i" is the number of ORC, F^{-1} is the inverse of the frequency distribution used for the modelling, CP_i is the calculated frequency cumulative probability of ORC "i" and x_i is the annual loss frequency observations of the ORC "i".

❑ If the frequency projection was perfect, then the vector of CP for each of the ORC "i" would follow a flat distribution defined between 0 and 1. Therefore, a GoF test can be used to validate the frequency modelling. The result of the analysis gauges the capital model overall precision of the frequency estimation.

❏ QQ plots comparing the CP of the observed frequencies versus that of the flat distribution can also be used to evaluate the over- or underestimation of frequencies across the ORCs.

However, it is possible that the frequency modelling was focused mainly on the frequency mean rather than on the shape, as explained in Chapter 4. In this case, the analysis can be simplified by determining in which ORC the observed frequency falls above or below the projected frequency distribution 50th percentile. By counting how many times the frequency observation falls below or above the ORC projected 50%, an evaluation of the over- or underestimation of frequencies can be obtained. This method is similar to the violation ratio presented in Chapter 4. The violation ratio analyses the number of times the observations are supposed to be above and below the prediction model. Basically, we would expect the observations of frequency to be 50% of the time above the frequency used in the model. If the actual observations' ORCs frequency is above 50%, then model is underestimating the real frequency and vice versa.

A more sophisticated approach directed at obtaining a p-value can be constructed by translating the frequencies of the ORC into a binomial distribution, 0 being below the projected 50% and 1 being above. Then, this distribution is compared with a parametric binomial with P=0.5, which represents the perfect prediction, and a GoF test can be performed.

Alternatively, the analysis can be done using the frequency expected mean, which provides a more intuitive answer. This analysis is more appropriate when frequencies used in capital modelling are high (above 20). In this case, the Poisson distribution would be very close to symmetrical and the mean and the median will be very close, thus making the analysis just described more relevant. Also, this analysis will work better when the number of ORCs is high compared with the ORC frequencies. In this case, the observed loss frequencies can be expected to be sufficiently high to permit the statistical analysis of the mean.

Backtesting of annual total losses

The backtesting of total losses has the same issue as the annual frequencies, where there is only one annual total loss observation. Again, it can be resolved following the same segmentation into ORCs to increase the number of observations, using these steps:

❏ The joint distribution for each of the units of measure is used to derive the corresponding cumulative probability. This is a nonparametric distribution made of a vector containing the total losses of each of the replications of the Monte Carlo simulation. The cumulative probability is derived as follows:

$$CP_i = F^{-1}(x_i),$$

where "i" is the number of ORC, F^{-1} is the inverse of the joint distribution resulting from the Monte Carlo simulation, CP_i is the calculated joint cumulative probability of ORC "i" and x_i is the annual loss joint observations of the ORC "i".

❏ If the joint projection was perfect, then the vector of CP for each of the ORC "i", would follow a flat distribution defined between 0 and 1. Therefore, a GoF test (see Chapter 4) can be used to validate the overall total loss modelling.

❏ QQ plots comparing the CP of the observed ORC joint distribution with that of the flat distribution can also be used to evaluate the over- or underestimations of total-loss modelling across the ORCs.

❏ The violation ratio concept can also be applied into this analysis. The analysis of how many times the ORC total losses are above or below the 50th percentile of the joint distribution used to model the ORC capital allows an analysis of the over- or underestimation of the model.

Operational risk sensitivity analysis and stress testing

The purpose of operational risk stress testing is an evaluation of the institution risk profile and capital adequateness under more extreme situations. BCSG-AMA mentions the need for stress testing and sensitivity analysis when it says, "Moreover, a bank should perform sensitivity analyses and stress testing (e.g. different parameter values, different correlation models) on the effect of alternative dependence assumptions on its operational risk capital charge estimate." The analysis can be performed using a sensitivity or what-if analysis or just by testing the impact of specific events on into the capital base.

Supervisors have increased the emphasis of stress testing for capital adequacy analysis. Example includes the US Federal Reserve's "Comprehensive Capital Analysis and Review" (CCAR), "Stress and Scenario Testing CP08/24" in the EU, or "Annual Industry-Wide Stress Testing Exercise" in Singapore. The stress testing under these regulatory frameworks also includes the impacts of scenario operational risk.

One of the largest benefits of stress testing probably comes from the analysis required during the definition of risk scenarios and the evaluation of the potential vulnerabilities of the institution. The understanding gained regarding the interactions and causal relationship between risks, losses, indicators, RCSA and so forth provides a valuable insight for more effective and focused risk mitigation.

The sections below describe the modelling techniques that can be used in the sensitivity analysis and stressing of frequencies and severities, as well as the case for stressing correlation.

Stressing frequencies and severities

In this section, several standard methods for operational risk stress testing are presented, which include:

❏ the stressed scenario analysis;
❏ regression methods;
❏ modified LDA;
❏ shifting the distribution moments (kurtosis);
❏ distribution tail stress;
❏ focusing the fitting process into the tail observations;
❏ shifting modelling parameters; and
❏ introducing stressed losses into the ILD distribution fitting.

Operational risk stress testing is often considered a specific case of scenario analysis, for the more extreme cases. Under this approach, the scenario analysis inputs, severities and frequencies can be directly stressed by a specific percentage and the model is refitted.

Figure 9.3 represents the stressing of a scenario frequency and severity by 30% and the refitting of the distributions to determine the new scenario loss. The new capital estimate given the new fitted distribution can be determined via single-loss approximation. The size of the stress can be defined by expert judgement by analysing

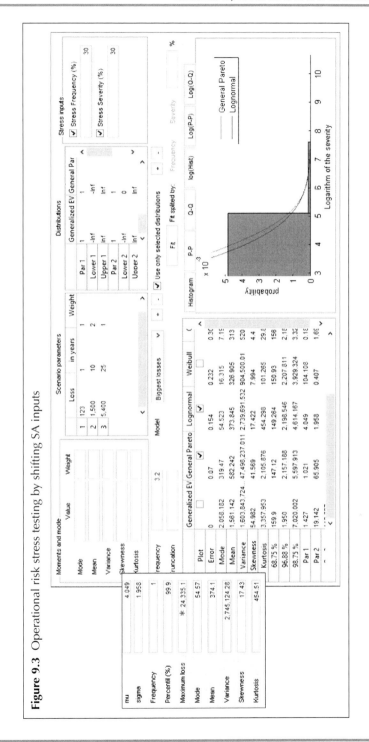

Figure 9.3 Operational risk stress testing by shifting SA inputs

external data, publicly available data, risk scenarios, etc. Highly valuable information for the mitigation of operational risk can be obtained by the discussions among experts, during the workshops for stress scenario determination, causes and drivers.

The stressed severity can be introduced by increasing the corresponding loss estimate provided in the elicitation method and feeding it to the fitting process again. The stressed frequency should be used only to estimate the new total loss distribution by the SLA or Monte Carlo, but the fit of the scenario should be performed with the original frequency. If the stressed frequency is used in the fit, for instance, in the worst-loss-by-time-horizon-elicitation method, it is equivalent to having the same level of losses with a higher frequency. This actually means that the severity profile is decreased.

The severity and frequency of shocks should be determined according to the type of stress scenario. Stress testing (Federal Reserve 2013, 2014) refers many times to macroeconomic or financial market scenarios affecting credit, market and operational risks, in particular those scenarios proposed by supervisors for the analysis of capital adequacy.

For instance, a decrease in GDP may affect the credit cycle, financial markets and operational risk. Operational risk can be affected in various ways:

❏ activity may fall and thus the number of low-severity events;
❏ a major financial/economic crisis may stress other processes in the organisation (due to pressure for results or staff layoffs resulting in higher workloads and loss of trained personnel, or even cost reduction affecting the control environment) and trigger high-severity losses;
❏ large movements in financial markets may reveal valuation errors (model risk) or hidden losses from rogue trading;
❏ a negative credit cycle may bring to light erroneous loan granting or credit evaluation processes (execution, delivery and process management); and/or
❏ changes in the housing markets cycle may reveal erroneous assumptions around housing market behaviour; similar scenarios include rises in unemployment, drops in equity prices and increases in interest rates.

Operational risk in insurance activities may also be impacted on by macroeconomic variables: a long-lasting economic crisis, for instance, increases external fraud through fake claims achieved by simulating fires or robberies to cash in insurance payments.

Regression analysis can be used for determining the frequency and severity shocks, given macroeconomic, market or credit stress scenarios. Examples on how to determine the statistical relationship between operational loss frequency and severity and macroeconomic indicators, KRIs or any other business environmental factors using regression analysis can be found in Chapters 6 and 12. Also, Figure 9.4 shows an example of macroeconomic factors, such as local GDP growth, unemployment and equity prices regressed to total operational losses. The resulting model can be used to estimate a level of operational losses under a stressed environment.

In addition to regressions, analysis of the historical behaviour of losses during stress periods, both ILD and ED, can be used for determining the shocks on severity and frequency distributions. The ILD and ED mean loss severity, the tail parameter of the GPD fit, the sigma and mu parameters of the lognormal fit, or distribution moments such as variance, skewness and kurtosis can be analysed during normal and stress scenarios. Alternatively, expert judgement may be used to determine the shocks in the model parameters or total operational losses.

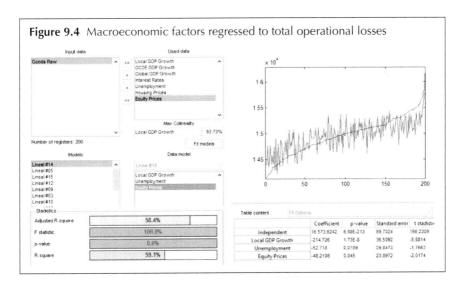

Figure 9.4 Macroeconomic factors regressed to total operational losses

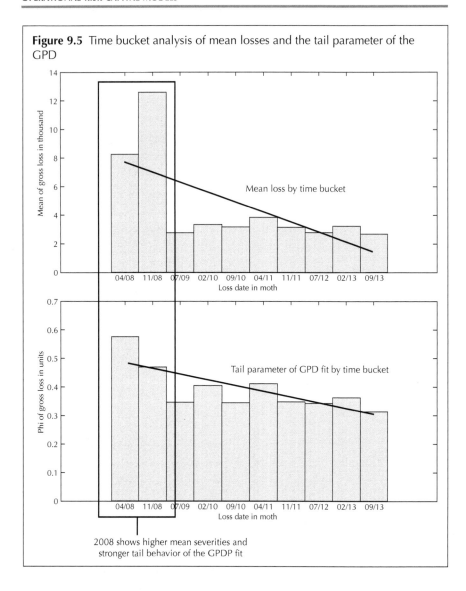

Figure 9.5 Time bucket analysis of mean losses and the tail parameter of the GPD

Figure 9.5 shows the time bucket analysis of the mean severity of the losses and tail parameter of the GPD fit. It can be appreciated that the year 2008 has stronger values for these two metrics. Next, it should be verified whether this behavioural change is due to the financial crisis. The same analysis is much more robust if performed using ED as a larger loss base, and multiple institutions would be involved.

The observed differences on these parameters during historical stress periods can be used to modify the modelling and evaluate the impact of stress scenarios. For instance, an increase of tail parameter or a distribution moment can be introduced in the model, as presented in Chapter 4. An observed increase in the mean severity or frequency is illustrated in the example in Figure 9.3.

Once the model parameters are stressed, a modified LDA method can be applied. This method consists of generating the total aggregated loss distribution with stressed model parameters and using a percentile lower than 99.9 to determine the scenario losses. For example, the 70th percentile is commonly used for a stress scenario and, for a severely adverse scenario, the 98th percentile. Alternatively, modified SBA or hybrid models can also be applied following the same principles, depending on the approach of the original operational risk model.

The same process to stress the capital model can be done when modelling ILD. When fitting an ILD, it is possible to incorporate fitting goals that look for specific values of distribution moments, as explained in Chapter 4 (see "The scale-and-shape method"). This method permits the incorporation of stressed values of leptokurtosis or skewness (stressed by a specific percentage) into the fitting process, maintaining the value of the known distribution percentiles derived from historical data. Similarly, hypothetical losses representing stressed scenarios can be introduced into the ILD distribution fitting process, to allow for the stress scenarios in the joint distributions. Examples of methods that permit us to incorporate hypothetical losses are the what-if? method in Chapter 4, which provides a new capital/loss estimate given the addition of hypothetical losses into the fitting sample, and the tail complementing method of Chapter 7, which allows us to stress the tail of the distribution.

Figure 9.6 presents the stressing of an ILD-based model. Four additional hypothetical losses have been added (10,000,000 with a 0.01 annual frequency, 25,000,000 with 0.0025 annual frequency, 75,000,000 with 0.0005 annual frequency. As a result, capital analysis shows an increase on the loss percentiles of the distribution (the 98th percentile and 70th percentile representing the stress and the severity adverse scenario under the modified LDA go up to 4,363,119 and 560,296 respectively), which is consistent with the increase in kurtosis from 437 to 1,064.

Figure 9.6 Stressed ILD-based model

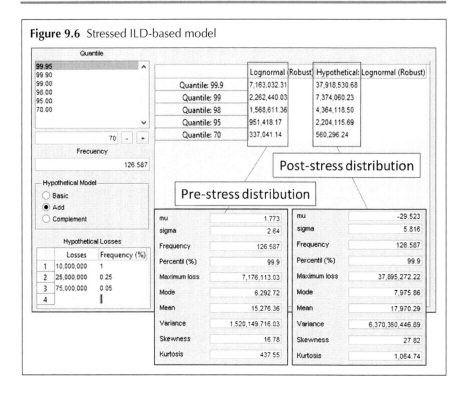

A different way to perform sensitivity analysis is by leveraging on the probability-weighted least-squares fit, as in Chapter 4. This fitting process permits an increase in the focus of the fit into the tail observations by adjusting the powers of the formulation. This results in a more precise tail fitting than the rest of the distribution. The question this exercise answers is, "What if the true loss distribution is better represented by the observations in the tail than by those in the rest of the distribution?"

Figure 9.7 shows the fitting of a Weibull distribution using different values for the parameters m and n in the weightings as

$$1\Big/\left(F^*(x_i)\right)^n\left(1-F^*(x_i)\right)^m$$

of the probability least-squares fit. The distribution on the left was fitted with n=0 and m=3; the distribution in the middle, n=0 and m=6; and the distribution in the right, n=0 and m=12. These values of m progressively increase the focus of the fit into the tail. The result is

Figure 9.7 Operational risk stress testing by emphasising the fit on the tail region

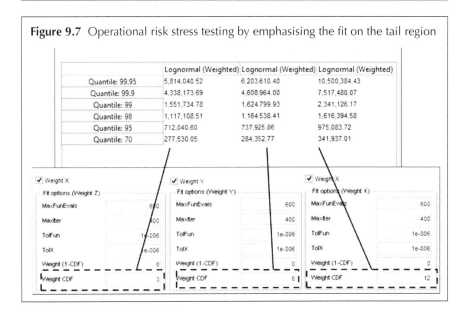

	Lognormal (Weighted)	Lognormal (Weighted)	Lognormal (Weighted)
Quantile: 99.95	5,814,040.52	6,203,610.40	10,500,384.43
Quantile: 99.9	4,338,173.69	4,608,964.00	7,517,480.07
Quantile: 99	1,551,734.78	1,624,799.93	2,341,126.17
Quantile: 98	1,117,108.51	1,164,538.41	1,616,394.58
Quantile: 95	712,040.60	737,925.86	975,083.72
Quantile: 70	277,530.05	284,352.77	341,937.01

☑ Weight X		☑ Weight Y		☑ Weight X	
Fit options (Weight Z)		Fit options (Weight Y)		Fit options (Weight X)	
MaxFunEvals	600	MaxFunEvals	600	MaxFunEvals	600
MaxIter	400	MaxIter	400	MaxIter	400
TolFun	1e-006	TolFun	1e-006	TolFun	1e-006
TolX	1e-006	TolX	1e-006	TolX	1e-006
Weight (1-CDF)	0	Weight (1-CDF)	0	Weight (1-CDF)	0
Weight CDF	3	Weight CDF	6	Weight CDF	12

that capital charges, calculated under the SLA, increase as the fit weight in the tail is increased.

This approach may also be useful to comply with BCSG-AMA when it says, "Appropriate diagnostic tools for evaluating the quality of the fit of the distributions to the data, giving preference to those most sensitive to the tail."

A different approach is to analyse parameter volatility estimation resulting from the fit. This volatility represents a level of incertitude as to what is the real parameter of the distribution. The parameter volatility can be used for stressing capital charges by estimating the capital, given a specific percentile of the parameters. Also, the stress can be calculated by shifting the parameter by a multiple of its standard deviation. The estimation of the parameter volatility can be performed using the method explained under "The resampling method" in Chapter 4, which permits us to derive the parameter volatility and percentiles resulting from the different fits. Alternatively, the stress can be derived directly from the capital volatility as a result of the resampling process of the resampling method and calculating the capital using SLA. This method presents the advantage that the capital volatility incorporates the volatility of all the distribution parameters following their joint distribution.

Figure 9.8 shows the volatility of capital and distribution parame-

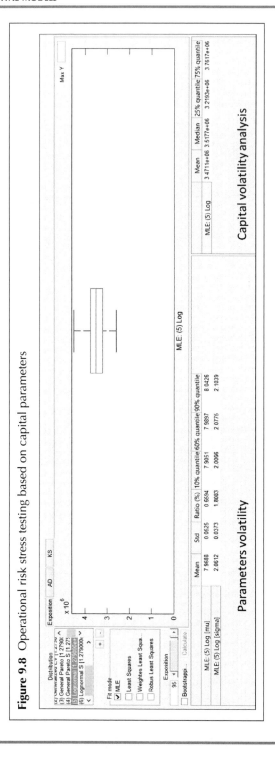

Figure 9.8 Operational risk stress testing based on capital parameters

Figure 9.9 Operational risk stress testing by shifting the model parameters

	Original frequency: 239.4	Original frequency: 250	Original frequency: 275	
Original tail parameter: 0.734	k 0.734 sigma 154.798 Frequency 239.743 Percentil (%) 99.9 Maximum loss * 1,873,932.44 Mode 146.71 Mean 511.9 Variance 5,961,943.74 Skewness 25.9 Kurtosis 949.51	k 0.734 sigma 154.798 Frequency 250 Percentil (%) 99.9 Maximum loss * 1,932,457.00 Mode 146.71 Mean 511.9 Variance 5,961,943.74 Skewness 25.9 Kurtosis 949.51	k 0.734 sigma 154.798 Frequency 275 Percentil (%) 99.9 Maximum loss * 2,072,503.59 Mode 146.71 Mean 511.9 Variance 5,961,943.74 Skewness 25.9 Kurtosis 949.51	* Resulting capital from sensitivity analysis
Original tail parameter: 0.75	k 0.75 sigma 154.798 Frequency 239.4 Percentil (%) 99.9 Maximum loss * 2,233,696.54 Mode 156 Mean 534.75 Variance 7,236,124.13 Skewness 26.89 Kurtosis 1,011.84	k 0.75 sigma 154.798 Frequency 250 Percentil (%) 99.9 Maximum loss * 2,367,385.94 Mode 156 Mean 534.75 Variance 7,236,124.13 Skewness 26.89 Kurtosis 1,011.84	k 0.75 sigma 154.798 Frequency 275 Percentil (%) 99.9 Maximum loss * 2,478,377.38 Mode 156 Mean 534.75 Variance 7,236,124.13 Skewness 26.89 Kurtosis 1,011.84	

ters. Percentile 75 of the capital can be used as a stressed value of the risk profile. Also, the volatility of the parameters can be used to shift the distribution parameters and to calculate the new risk-profile-given stressed values.

Finally, the stress testing can be analysed by shifting the distribution parameters such as shape parameter and frequency. Figure 9.9 shows the analysis of shifting the tail parameter of the distribution and the frequency. The new capital estimation is performed under SLA under the 99.9% confidence interval. It can be observed how capital charge increases with the shifts of the parameters, from the original 1,873,932 to 2,478,377. The capital increases, given frequency shifts, are more dramatic for the cases where the tail parameter has already been shifted.

Stressing operational risk correlations

Correlations should also be part of the stress testing of the operational risk capital model. Generally, a robust calculation of operational risk correlations is challenging given the data scarcity and the rapid evolution of the risk profile. Therefore, sensitivity analysis with stressed correlations adds robustness to the calculation of correlations.

The sections below describe the methods used for stressing corre-lations including an additive shift (increase correlations by "X" amount), a proportional shift (modify the correlations by "X"%) and a Bayesian approach based on a stochastic shift (uncertainty about the correlations). The shift is introduced into the diversification index of the joint distribution of the units of measure.

We discuss the problem of increasing correlations by "X" amount when we use it as a diversification index of the joint distribution of the units of measure:

$$\ell pat = \frac{\sum_{I=1}^{N}\sum_{J=1}^{N} UL_i \times UL_j \times \ell_{ij}}{\sum_{I=1}^{N}\sum_{J=1}^{N} UL_i \times UL_j},$$

where ℓ_{ij} is the correlation between the ith and j^{th} units of measure and ULi is the standard deviation of the ith ORC. We have that $\ell_{ij}\varepsilon\lfloor-1,1\rfloor \forall ij$ and $UL_i > 0$:

Note that we may call and rewrite

$$\ell pat = \Sigma_i \Sigma_j w_{ij} \times \ell_{i,j}$$

with

$$\Sigma_i \Sigma_j w_{ij} = 1$$
$$w_{ij} \geq 0$$

Finally, since ℓ_{ij} and ℓ_{ji} and $w_{ij} = w_{ji}$ and $\ell_{ij} = 1$, we may write this in the more convenient formula:

$$\ell pat = \sum_{I=1}^{N} w_{ii} + 2\Sigma_{i>}\Sigma_j w_{ij} \times \ell_{i,j}$$
$$= R + 2\Sigma_{i>}\Sigma_j w_{ij} \times \ell_{i,j}$$

with

$$R_z \sum_{r=1}^{N} w_{il}$$

Since the request "Increase correlations by "X" amount" is not precisely defined we shall provide several answers. Because correla-tions can be positive or negative, we replace "increase" with "modify" and answer accordingly.

Figure 9.10 represents the stressing of a correlation matrix by 0.2, as explained in the section above. Every number in the correlation

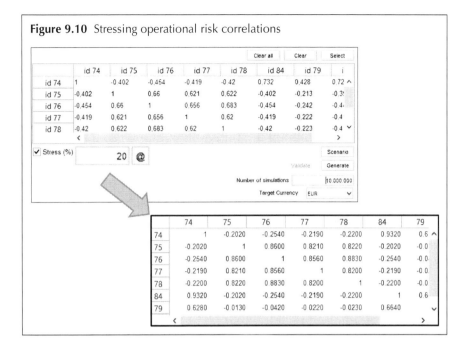

Figure 9.10 Stressing operational risk correlations

matrix except for those in the central diagonal has been increased by 0.20.

Modify the correlations by "X"% whenever possible and see the maximum and minimum impact on the diversification index.

Since $\ell_{i,j}\varepsilon[-1,1]$, we cannot freely modify it. In particular, $\ell_{ij}=1$, thus we first interpret perturbating $\ell_{i,j}$ by "X"%, as follows:

If $i = j$, we leave it as it is.

If $i \neq j$, then we understand that $\ell_{ij}\varepsilon\lfloor a_{ij},b_{ij}\rfloor$ with:

$$b_{ij}\min\left[1,\ell_{ij}\left(1+\frac{x}{100}\right)\right]$$

$$a_{ij}\max\left[\ell_{ij}\left(1-\frac{x}{100}\right),-1\right]$$

and compute the maximum and minimum index value when $\ell_{ij}\varepsilon\lfloor a_{ij},b_{ij}\rfloor$ that is, if we call:

$$T_P = R + 2\Sigma_i\Sigma_j w_{ij} \times \ell_{i,j}$$

with

$$\ell = \left(\ell_{11}, \dots \ell_{nn} \right)$$

We want to compute:

$$R_1 = \max T\left(\ell \right)$$
$$s.t.$$
$$\ell_{ij} \varepsilon \left[a_{ij}, b_{ij} \right]$$
$$R_2 = \min T\left(\ell \right)$$
$$s.t.$$
$$\ell_{ij} \varepsilon \left[a_{ij}, b_{ij} \right]$$

This is easily accomplished, since $w_{ij} > 0, \forall ij$:

$$R_1 = R + 2\Sigma_{i>}\Sigma_j w_{ij} \times b_{ij}$$
$$R_2 = R + 2\Sigma_{i>}\Sigma_j w_{ij} \times a_{ij}$$

From this, we easily get percentages of increase and decrease, and so we can say, $\ell pat\, \varepsilon \left[R_2, R_1 \right]$.

Study the impact of our uncertainty about the correlations by "X"% over the diversification index.

In this case, we assume uncertainty over the incumbent range, whenever relevant. A typical assumption would be $\ell_{ij} \sim \beta(a_{ij}, b_{ij})$ (this includes $\ell_{ij} \sim U(a_{ij}, b_{ij})$). Then we would use a simulation approach, as follows:

$$\text{For } K = 1 \text{ to } K$$
$$RHO_K = R$$
$$\text{For } j = 1 \text{ to } N$$
$$\text{For } j = i+1 \text{ to } N$$
$$\text{Generate } X \sim \ell_{ij}$$
$$RHO_K = RHO_K + 2w_{ij}x$$

We would then display $\{RHO_K\}_{k=1}^{K}$, summarise it and go on.

We want to identify how much we need to modify the correlations so as to increase the diversification by "X". (A similar approach holds if we want to reduce the diversification index.)

We assume a procedure similar to that described above, which for a given Y computes the corresponding b_{ij}, which we call b_{ij}^{Y} and the corresponding R_1, which we call R_1^{Y}.

We have a procedure, let us call it CHECK(Y), which computes

$$\frac{R_1^v - \ell pat}{\ell pat}.100$$

and divides if it is greater than "X".

We have to do a binary search method (like bisection, golden section methods or similar).

Then the procedure essentially goes as follows:

$$K = 1$$

Until check (K_x) true

$$K = K + 1$$

Comment: once we have stopped, we know that we have to search between $[(K - 1)X, K_X]$ to identify "Y".

Once we have finished, we could report the vectors:

$$l_{ij} b_{ij}^Y$$

CONCLUSION

Capital models can be thoroughly backtested and stress-tested, as credit and market risk models are. These processes provide additional trust on operational risk capital estimations and allow for operational risk modelling to be used in the stress testing required by the financial supervision authorities.

---

1   A way to increase the number of observations is to additionally segment the analysis into shorter time periods. For instance, the frequencies could be segmented into quarters, so that the number of observations of frequencies would be multiplied by four.

REFERENCES

Federal Reserve, 2013, "Capital Planning at Large Bank Holding Companies: Supervisory Expectations and Range of Current Practice", Board of Governors of the Federal Reserve System, August.

Federal Reserve, 2014, "Comprehensive Capital Analysis and Review 2014 Summary Instructions and Guidance", Board of Governors of the Federal Reserve System.[1] A way to increase the number of observations is to additionally segment the analysis into shorter time periods. For instance, the frequencies could be segmented into quarters, so that the number of observations of frequencies would be multiplied by four.

10

Evolving from a Plain Vanilla to a State-of-the-Art Model

Rafael Cavestany

Previous chapters have described the components of a state-of-the-art operational risk capital model. However, institutions generally start with much simpler models and progressively evolve by adding the analytics required for much more realistic and forward-looking capital estimates. In this chapter we look at the progressive steps that an institution may take to evolve the model from plain vanilla to fully developed.

The process of building a state-of-the-art operational risk capital model that accurately reflects a forward-looking risk profile has various phases, which include an initial regulatory approval of the capital model. Although there is no equal case in how an institution arrives at a fully developed capital model, Figure 10.1 represents a common path.

Along the implementation of a mature operational risk capital model, institutions pass by different typical model development stages, which are summarised in this chapter and are based on the experiences of the authors. The capital model enhancement drivers are the understanding and automation of the required analytical processes, as well as the integration of the capital results into daily management. The last in turn incentivises the calculation of a more forward-looking and realistic operational risk profile.

MODEL PREPARATION

During the model preparation stage, the institution implements the processes required for the collection of the capital model primary

Figure 10.1 Example of progress in the implementation of an operational risk capital model

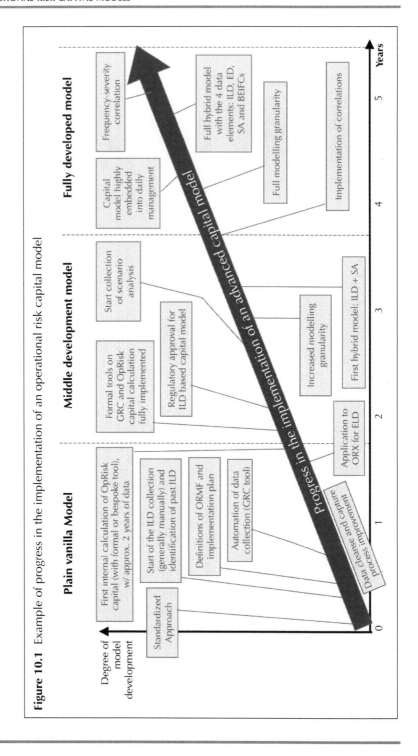

inputs. Banks will generally put the emphasis on ILD to build a model based on this data element. Guaranteeing sufficiency of observations and appropriate ILD quality (completeness, consistency with accounting, establishment of loss collection processes and audit trail and data certificates) is the focus of this stage (see Chapters 1 and 2). It may be necessary to cleanse any old operational risk data that is used in order to comply with the standards of capital modelling.

In general, an insurance institution will start with a focus on scenario analysis, as ILD is less abundant than in banks. The scenario analysis starts with the identification of the major risks to analyse by business unit. An adequate process for collecting scenario analysis with the necessary quality should be established – and it may require several loops.

During this stage, the institution will also ensure the availability of external data, either by acquiring a commercially available database, or by joining a consortium. The latter case requires the implementation of specific procedures for capturing ILD defined by the consortium and sharing a number of losses above a specific threshold that satisfies the collection procedures defined by the consortium.

This stage represents the foundation of a capital model and will determine the maximum accuracy and realism the capital estimations will have, as the quality of a model cannot exceed that of its inputs.

INITIATION MODEL

Institutions generally first construct a model based on a single data element. A bank's common approach is to implement an ILD model first, although, many banks have also started with a scenario analysis model. This requires the implementation of many of the processes described in Chapter 4 – at least those processes for modelling ILD severities, frequencies and evaluation of the model goodness of fit. With the adequate technological solution, processes for the evaluation of capital stability, or that capital estimations are realistic, can also be introduced into the initiation model.

On the other hand, insurers most commonly create an SBA (scenario-based approach) capital model first, given the generally less abundant ILD availability. This requires the implementation of the processes in Chapters 3 and 5, at least those processes for the modelling of the scenario analysis answers and the evaluation of the model goodness of fit. When an SBA is implemented, institutions should put a major focus on using the scenario workshops and analysis to identify the most effective mitigation strategies.

Once the single data element is modelled for the different ORCs, the results need to be aggregated into the ORC's joint distribution and the aggregated loss distribution. This can be performed by implementing some of the processes in Chapter 8, at least the processes for the determination of aggregated operational loss distribution for determining capital charges by ORCs.

With the implementation of an initiation model, an exhaustive documentation of the modelling process should be created. An example method for this documentation can be found in Chapter 4. As a result, the institution seeks initial regulatory approval for its advanced operational risk capital. This also depends on the institution's relevant jurisdiction.

HYBRID MODEL CONSTRUCTION

After the consolidation of an initiation model, institutions generally proceed to incorporate additional data elements to produce a more realistic capital estimation. At this stage, an institution will incorporate ED into the model, and either SA or ILD, to complement the initiation model. The main ED issue is to scale it in order to make it relevant for the risk profile of the institution. For this purpose, the processes described in Chapter 4 can help an institution in the ED scaling process.

The creation of a hybrid model requires the aggregation of the information of different data elements into a single loss distribution per ORC. This can be achieved following the methods described in Chapter 7. The hybrid model also requires the determination of the weights of the different data elements within the final ORC loss distribution. Data elements' weights can be determined using expert judgement, although a statistically driven method is more appropriate. A statistical methods can be implemented through credibility theory as presented in Chapter 7 and Appendix 2.

CORRELATED MODEL

Once a proper hybrid model is implemented, the model is evolved into incorporating dependencies across ORCs, to allow for the diversification benefits and a more realistic capital estimation.

The major issue on the calculation of operational risk correlations is the availability of relevant ILD for its robust calculation. Generally, only a portion of ORCs will have sufficient ILD for a data-driven correlation calculation. This can be achieved implementing the correlation calculation methods presented in Chapter 8. The dependencies of ORCs with insufficient ILD for a data-driven correlation calculation or low-frequency risk scenarios can be calculated using qualitative methods, as presented in Chapters 6 and 8. The determination of operational risk correlations through qualitative methods provides a unique opportunity to analyse common drivers for defining a better mitigation strategy definition.

The calculation of capital allowing diversification benefits represents a sufficiently realistic figure to be more easily accepted for the day-to-day risk management of the institution. Together with the model correlations, the availability of loss data and the maturity of the risk measurement processes allow for an increase in the modelling granularity. With this, the institution achieves a more accurate operational risk profile, capital allocation to more specific organisational entities and improvement in the impact analysis of mitigation plans and controls into such risk profiles.

CAPITAL RESULTS EMBEDDED IN DAY-TO-DAY OPERATIONAL RISK MANAGEMENT

Once operational risk capital numbers are perceived as realistic, they can be more easily accepted and integrated into critical management processes such as strategic and operational business planning. Also, in this stage, institutions integrate operational risk into the risk appetite framework and the necessary evaluation of the impact controls and mitigation plans. These methods are presented in Part III.

At this stage the institution integrates the operational risk capital into their stress-testing programme for capital adequacy analysis.

INCORPORATION OF BEICFS

Once the institution has incorporated capital model results into the day-to-day risk management, it becomes more aware of the need for a more forward-looking and realistic capital estimation. This represents a strong stimulus for continuing the development of the capital model with the incorporation of BEICFs into the capital calculations.

BEICFs such as KRIs, RCSA, controls and evaluations provide information on controls and root causes of risks, which anticipate future losses and can be used to estimate a more forward-looking capital requirement. The implementation of these processes can be achieved following the methods presented in Chapters 3 and 6.

FULLY DEVELOPED MODEL

The benefits of a solid operational capital model with a forward-looking character and the integration into management of the capital results leads to a further development of an operational risk capital model and a more precise determination of capital requirements.

In this stage, the model can be enhanced by introducing methods for replicating dependencies between severity and frequency, better modelling of insurance, or operational risk prediction analytics adding precision to capital estimations (see Chapters 7, 8 and 12). Additional processes may be implemented to backtest the capital modelling and perform stress-test analysis to gain trust in the results (see Chapter 9). Finally, modelling granularity is increased in order to capture very specific idiosyncrasies of the institution, which also benefits the integration of capital estimates into the daily risk management of the institution.

At this stage, the institution will have a state-of-the-art capital model.

CONCLUSION

The process of creating a fully developed capital model may take several years as the institution collects the required information and advances in the modelling learning curve. The benefits from the model will increase with its granularity and forward-looking character. This, in turn, further incentivises its effective integration into the day-to-day risk management of the institution, creating a virtuous risk management circle.

We have reached the end of Part II, where we have examined how to create a robust capital model that permits a precise and detailed calculation of the operational risk profile. In Part III, we will introduce risk management that uses calculated risk profiles and specific examples on how to integrate the capital model output into an institution's daily management. This will permit us to illustrate the high value that an advanced capital model can provide in an institution.

Part III

Use Test, Integrating Capital Results into the Institution's Day-to-Day Risk Management

After describing in Parts I and II the construction of an operational risk capital model, we now look into the integration of this model's outputs into the day-to-day risk management of the institution, the so-called use test under Basel and Solvency regulatory frameworks.

The use test is a critical piece of a capital model when used to communicate the solvency of the institution to external parties. It helps to prove that the results of the capital model are internally trusted so as to be used in daily risk management. In addition, it shows the degree to which the institution has implemented an integrated risk management process to effectively mitigate all risks.

In fact, an advanced measurement system of operational risk requires thorough research and data collection for obtaining the required deep understanding of risk exposures, dependencies, weaknesses, potential impacts and so forth to adequately model the operational risk profile. This understanding of the risk profile will provide the largest benefits from an advanced measurement capital model when used for risk mitigation, permitting a more effective and efficient rationalisation of the operational risk profile and increasing risk awareness. It also permits the focus of risk management into the risk–reward relationship, rather than the traditional one-sided threat-and-loss analysis.

Using capital inputs and results in risk mitigation, incentivises a deeper analysis of risk exposures, which improves, in turn, the quality of the capital model inputs. Also, as many additional areas – such as process improvement, control, insurance, critical infrastructure protection, internal audit and financial planning (see Chapter 12) – are impacted on by and feed into the operational risk measurement system (ORMS), the inputs and outputs of the operational risk capital model are validated from different perspectives, having a positive effect on the quality of the whole operational risk management and measurement process. In fact, the advanced approach for capital calculation together with the use test creates a strong virtuous circle for robust operational risk mitigation.

Under a standardised approach for operational risk capital, the motivation to search for such information and understanding of the risk profile is much lower and, in practice, few institutions actually implement the required efforts to obtain this information, making their risk mitigation less proactive and efficient.

BCSG-AMA captures similar concerns to those mentioned above when it says,

> The bank should incorporate the following guidelines in its assessment of an AMA's use and embeddedness: (a) The purpose and use of an AMA should not be solely for regulatory compliance purposes; (b) As the bank gains experience, an AMA should reflect evolving risk management techniques; (c) An AMA should support and enhance the bank's operational risk management policies and practices; and (d) An AMA should benefit a bank in the management and control or mitigation of operational risk.

Part III presents several of the means of integrating the operational risk measurement system within day-to-day risk management of the institution, including the capital results, the use of the model to analyse the sensitivity of the mitigation measures and the use of the capital model inputs into risk mitigation strategies.

For this purpose, Part III is structured as follows:

❏ Chapter 11, "Strategic and Operational Business Planning and Monitoring", examines the integration of the operational risk profile into the business planning and GRC reporting, and an operational risk appetite framework for monitoring the implementation of the risk business plan.
❏ Chapter 12, "Risk–Reward Evaluation of Mitigation and Control

Effectiveness", presents examples of how to evaluate, from the risk–reward perspective, the impact into the risk profile of different controls and mitigation plans to be used for adjusting ORA, risk limits, etc.

11

Strategic and Operational Business Planning and Monitoring

Rafael Cavestany, Lutz Baumgarten and Brenda Boultwood

We now look at the embedding of the risk profile, calculated as presented in Part II, into the strategic and operational business planning and its monitoring. We have structured this chapter into the following sections:

- ❏ "Integrating the operational risk profile into the strategic and operational planning": In this section, we examine the means and key considerations when integrating the operational risk profile into the strategic and operational business planning process.
- ❏ "Integrating capital results into the GRC risk reporting": Here, we look at the integration of the capital results into the overall reporting of the GRC.
- ❏ "ORA for monitoring the strategic and business plan": This section introduces the a framework for operational risk appetite – or ORA – and its use in the monitoring of the operational risk profile in accordance with the business plan.

INTEGRATING THE OPERATIONAL RISK PROFILE INTO THE STRATEGIC AND OPERATIONAL PLANNING[1]
Introduction
Since the onset of the financial crisis in 2007, the industry has moved in the direction of a more integrated (or holistic) approach towards planning. This development was triggered by a mix of explicit regu-

latory requirements and increased volatility, leading to significant changes in the risk profiles and associated financial impacts.

Regarding operational risk regulatory requirements, the BCSG-AMA says,

> A bank's strategic and business planning processes should consider its operational risk profile, including outputs from the ORMS (Operational Risk Measurement System). Potential material changes to the operational risk profile resulting from strategic and business planning change should be appropriately reviewed, considered, reported and monitored.

Integrating a forward-looking view of an institution's risk profile with the planning and budgeting processes is not a simple and straightforward task, as a multitude of processes is typically run in a siloed manner. Some of the key challenges arising from this are:

❑ rolling out risk strategy setting from the group to BUs and subsidiaries, in particular the cascading of risk appetite into BU-relevant elements;
❑ building up risk planning and forecasting capabilities at BU level in dialogue with the group;
❑ realigning the positioning of strategic risk within the organisation (ie, overcome the siloed risk-type management approach);
❑ introducing KPIs that are relevant to risk appetite into performance;
❑ realigning the risk reporting structure to the levels of cascaded risk appetite and risk budgets; and
❑ raising the profile of "integrated risk managers" at group level and below with a combination of skills in the areas of risk and capital management as well as business planning and controlling.

This section provides a brief overview of how financial institutions can integrate operational risk profile (calculated as presented in Part II) considerations into their planning process. It first considers how risk profile targets are set in terms of risk appetite and other risk-related targets. Following from that, it looks at how these targets are integrated into the planning process. Finally, it concludes by discussing a few of the challenges financial institutions are faced with when better integrating risk profile into their planning.

Risk profile, risk appetite and other risk-related targets

Risk profile is the measure of the amount of risk an institution is exposed to at a specific point in time. The risk profile is calculated using risk models per risk type (ie, the operational risk profile is determined using the models and methods presented in Parts I and II). Risk appetite in the planning and budgeting context forms a hard limit where a clear ceiling exists, ie, the maximum risk capacity, and regulatory intervention is triggered if the risk position exceeds the risk capacity. To integrate with planning and budgeting processes, the risk appetite should be set in close conjunction with strategic considerations, ie, targeting a certain price-to-earnings or price-to-book range implies the willingness to expose the organisation to a certain amount of risk. Provided that there is typically a more concrete financial target set as part of the planning process, a corresponding targeted level of risk should be stipulated via risk targets.

In the absence of industry-wide standards or a regulator-prescribed definition, it is key to establish a common terminology across the organisation. Figure 11.1 illustrates one possibility.

The incorporation of the risk profile reporting in a cascading manner permits its integration into the day-to-day management of the institution. The risk profile should be reported at all levels of the organisation in adequate levels of granularity. Operational risk is one element of the risk profile and it is provided by the operational

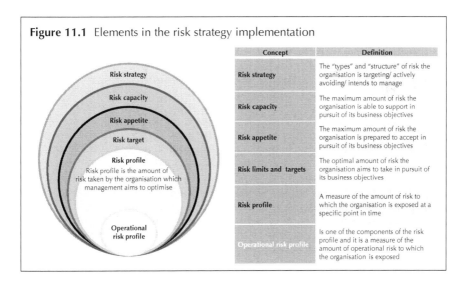

Figure 11.1 Elements in the risk strategy implementation

Concept	Definition
Risk strategy	The "types" and "structure" of risk the organisation is targeting/ actively avoiding/ intends to manage
Risk capacity	The maximum amount of risk the organisation is able to support in pursuit of its business objectives
Risk appetite	The maximum amount of risk the organisation is prepared to accept in pursuit of its business objectives
Risk limits and targets	The optimal amount of risk the organisation aims to take in pursuit of its business objectives
Risk profile	A measure of the amount of risk to which the organisation is exposed at a specific point in time
Operational risk profile	Is one of the components of the risk profile and it is a measure of the amount of operational risk to which the organisation is exposed

risk measurement system (ORMS). The ORMS includes the advanced capital models, and all its inputs (determined as presented in ILD, ED, SA and BEICFs) are allocated by activities, BUs, products or other organisational entities (see Chapter 8). This measurement is integrated into all other risk metrics of the organisation (economic capital, regulatory capital, earnings at risk, liquidity) and embedded into the corresponding reports to the board-level committees, management-level committees and BU-level committees, as represented in Figure 11.2.

The risk targets are formulated to optimise the institution's usage of its risk capacity in accordance with its risk strategy and appetite. The day-to-day execution of the operational risk plan requires the implementation of an operational risk appetite (ORA) framework. ORA represents the maximum amount of operational risk the organisation is prepared to accept in pursuit of its business objectives and in line with its performance targets. For the execution of the operational risk plan in BUs and lower organisational entities, the ORA is broken down into operational risk metrics and cascaded down to the specific points in the organisation (eg, BUs, processes, activities and other organisational entities) where the operational risk mitigation is implemented. This permits establishing a link between the group risk appetite and BU-level targets and to ensure the adherence to the risk limits by generating alerts and prompting mitigation actions and escalation procedures. Later in this chapter we present methods for the implementation of an ORA framework, including its cascading down, definition of limits and limit monitoring, using operational risk metrics from the ORMS.

Integration of risk profile into planning

An organisation's risk appetite and targets cannot be set in isolation, since unintended conflicts can arise. A fully integrated planning process requires good coordination between capital risk, funding/liquidity and strategic elements in parallel rather than sequentially. Figure 11.3 illustrates all the desired interactions between these elements during the planning phases: the overall strategy definition, high-level plan and challenge, and detailed plan and budget approval.

During the planning process, the impact of strategic aspects, such as growth per BU, should be reflected in the operational risk profile,

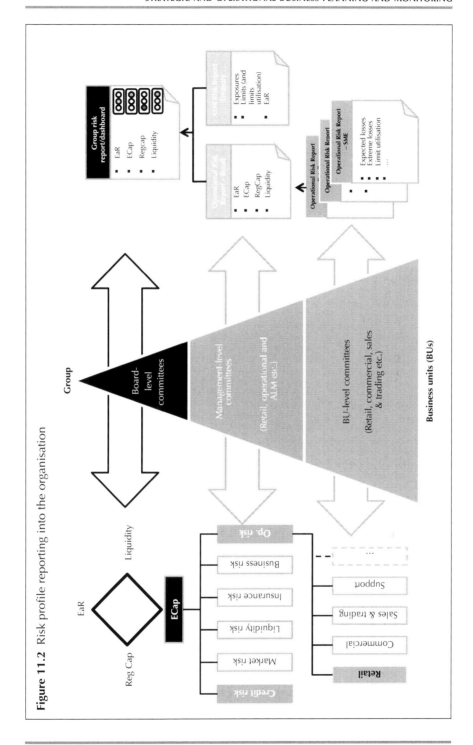

Figure 11.2 Risk profile reporting into the organisation

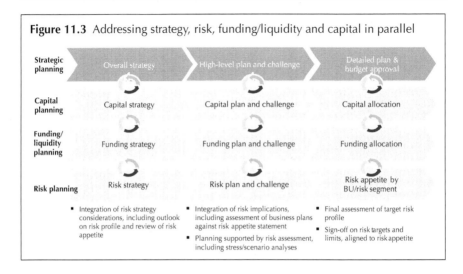

Figure 11.3 Addressing strategy, risk, funding/liquidity and capital in parallel

and budgeted for accordingly. Also, the impact of the planned actions for the mitigation of the operational risk profile should be evaluated. Such actions include insurance programmes, additional controls, process improvements, automation, critical infrastructure protection policies and the implementation of audit recommendations, for example. Chapter 12 introduces examples of how to estimate the impact on the risk profile of such mitigation actions.

Figure 11.4 provides an example of how the planning is done where there are frequent feedback loops and checks and balances to ensure compliance of plans with risk appetite.

Challenges when integrating the operational risk profile into the planning

Frequently, institutions that have established an ORMS (measurement of capital, KRIs, RCSA, SA and so forth), have not integrated their ORMS into the institution's day-to-day risk management and, hence, they do not have the tools for establishing the necessary link between their operational risk profile and its business planning and risk strategy. In fact, institutions face significant challenges when integrating the risk profile into the strategic and operational planning, as we outline:

❏ Calculation of a realistic operational risk profile: difficulties in reflecting the potential extreme events that determine the real

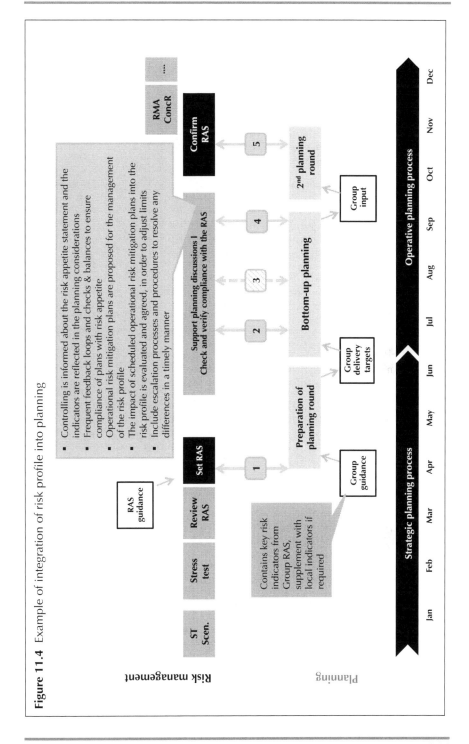

Figure 11.4 Example of integration of risk profile into planning

operational risk profile, which can be achieved only through advanced capital models (see Part II). In fact, standard models produce risk profile measurements that are less realistic and tend to be ignored during the operational and strategic planning of the institution.

❏ Defining metrics that permit cascading down and monitoring operational risk at BU, process and lower levels, allowing a more specific accountability (see below).

❏ Linking operational risk metrics with escalation procedures and actions and establishing the monitoring processes ensuring that such actions achieve the defined goals (see below).

❏ Linking the operational risk quantification and operational risk management in a joint process that provides the business case for the operational risk mitigation actions (see Chapter 12).

❏ Aligning risk reports to management structure, including current risk position and outlook on risk profile.

❏ Defining processes that permit us to evaluate the impact of controls and mitigation actions in managing the operational risk profile (see chapter 12).

❏ Moving from an operational risk minimisation perspective (ie, essentially working against operational or business units) to a perspective that seeks to balance operational risks with the costs of their mitigation and/or the potential upside in the associated activities (eg, partnering with operational or BUs).

Addressing these challenges will enable the institution to move from a lagging into a leading operational risk management framework.

INTEGRATING CAPITAL RESULTS INTO THE GRC RISK REPORTING[2]
What the capital number means for an organisation
Organisations primarily work with several capital numbers: balance sheet, economic and regulatory. The economic capital number is an internal figure that banks track but do not generally report. In contrast, the regulatory capital number represents the minimum amount of capital that banks must keep on hand to satisfy regulatory requirements.

But what does the regulatory number actually mean for an organisation? Institutions often attempt to maintain regulatory capital numbers that are low, with an eye towards satisfying the minimum requirements. Regulatory capital, however, provides financial institutions with an important safety net that may in some circumstances present the last bastion of security in the context of tumultuous market conditions. If recent history is any guide, events such as the subprime credit crisis of 2008 have made regulatory capital more important than ever.

Against this backdrop, rather than simply trying to maintain the bare minimum, it is imperative for organisations to think beyond the baseline regulatory requirements and develop capital numbers that are dynamic and correspond to their changing risk appetites. While organisations with a higher risk appetite will hold a lower regulatory capital number, a lower risk appetite will correspond to a higher amount of regulatory capital.

The role of operational risk management in ERM

Financial institutions comprise a diverse number of risk profiles. In addition to operational risk, organisations face credit, market and liquidity risks as well as risks related to their HR, IT and legal departments. What is more, in today's increasingly globalised world, businesses face risks that extend throughout their supply chain, from the back of the house to third-party vendors and their entire customer ecosystem.

In comparison with credit and market risk, operational risk is a fairly new category, emerging only in the wake of the Basel II accords, which created a formal separation between these various risk types (BIS 2001). Though the tendency has often been to treat different risk categories as distinct, the current risk reality makes it clear that a sound and strategic risk management framework requires an appreciation of the ways in which diverse types of risk overlap and intersect. Enterprise risk management (ERM) is an approach that takes seriously the interconnected nature of today's risk environment, treating risk management as a holistic process with direct implications for larger business goals.

Operational risk exists at the centre of this new reality, making it a core component of any effective ERM framework. Understanding this, however, requires looking beyond just the numbers. For instance, while the value-at-risk (VaR) numbers for credit and market risk will most likely be significantly higher than the VaR level for operational risk, what the difference in VaR fails to capture is the way in which market and credit risk losses are deeply entwined with failures related to operational risk.

Take, for example, the case of unauthorised trading. Though many organisations would be apt to characterise this as market risk, in truth, the core part of the failure that allows unauthorised trading to take place is most likely linked to operational risk factors – systemic breakdown, the absence of strict oversight and governance, or the lack of a risk-aware culture that fosters accountability and encourages whistleblowers. Ultimately, operational risk bears on the overall health of an organisation precisely because of its direct impact on all other risk profiles.

As the risks organisations face have become increasingly complex and interdependent, the role of operational risk management has grown in importance. Operational risk has a central role to play in ERM frameworks due to the fact that multiple parts of an organisation interact with and relate to operational risk functions on a daily basis. As such, operational risk can act as a centralised point of integration for risk data from diverse business units and departments. In this regard, an operational risk profile actually provides a holistic and comprehensive view of an organisation's overall strategic risk position and can offer important insight into specific aspects of organisational efficiency.

This type of holistic integration is essential for developing the pervasive governance, risk and compliance framework (GRC) that the current risk environment demands. Where organisations once saw operational risk management as a burden, content to perform the bare minimum to satisfy regulatory requirements, there is now a growing consensus that operational risk can play a critical role in organisational decision making. From vendor selection to product design, more and more corporate boards and executives are seeking tactical input and counsel from operational risk managers in order to better understand the inherent risks associated with key business decisions. This trend will most likely continue in the face of an evolving risk landscape and an increasingly complex web of regulatory requirements.

ORA FOR MONITORING THE STRATEGIC AND BUSINESS PLAN[3]

After presenting the integration of the risk profile in the strategic and business planning process, we now examine an ORA framework for the daily monitoring of the plan implementation. In this section, we describe ORA cascading down, the definition of limits and thresholds and the monitoring of the adherence to risk appetite.

The final goal of an institution's operational risk management programme is to mitigate operational risks, thus decreasing its costs, protecting the institution's earnings and eventually creating value for the shareholders. Risk mitigation may require significant investments, the introduction of controls, process changes and automation – all with the implicit consumption of resources that can hardly be achieved without the strong mandate of the institution's management. The management mandate on the desired levels of operational risk is reflected in the strategic and business plan.

The institution's management exercises its mandate by first establishing the operational risk maximum acceptable levels and then being closely involved in the operational risk mitigation, monitoring the materialisation of events. This implies that the top management (board of directors or its delegated bodies, such as the CRO) should receive communications and alerts when unexpected levels of operational risk are materialised in order to protect earnings, or when there are significant changes in the risk profile of the institution. These communications should trigger the necessary corrective actions at very specific points and processes in the organisation, to comply with the institution's risk strategy. In turn, business units, activities and processes may have different inherent and residual levels of operational risk implicit in their activities. Thus, the acceptable and expected level of operational risk may be different by business unit, activity, process, etc.

In these circumstances, the responsibility over the operational risk of the institution's management represents a challenge requiring specific management tools. This challenge can be addressed by implementing a framework for operational risk appetite (ORA). ORA (Reiner 2012; Society of Actuaries in Ireland 2011) can be defined as the maximum amount of operational risk the organisation is prepared to accept in pursuit of its business objectives. The day-to-day management of the ORA is exercised by attributing ORA, defining limits and monitoring these across different business units, activities, process and so on, delegating the responsibility of the detailed operational risk management to the corresponding risk and process owners. Risk appetite can thus be seen as the "lever" top management uses to enforce its mandate relating to operational risk management, as determined in the strategic and business plan. It provides the top management with the understanding of key risk exposures (avoiding surprises), efficient communication on changes in the risk profile and the means to trigger the necessary mitigation actions to bring operational risk into the defined maximum amounts.

The BCSG-AMA incorporates concerns on ORA by saying,

> A bank's board of directors should approve and review a clear state-ment of operational risk appetite and tolerance. Risk appetite and tolerance statements should: account for all relevant risks, including the bank's current financial situation and strategic direction; encap-sulate various risk tolerance and/or threshold levels; and detail how the board of directors will monitor and manage adherence to the risk appetite and tolerance statement. The board of directors and senior management performance assessment should reflect and measure adherence to the risk appetite and tolerance statement and be applied and monitored across all business entities.

An ORA framework should be closely adapted to the idiosincracy of each institttion. Figure 11.5 presents a high-level workflow example of risk appetite determination and attribution (or cascading down) to the business units which is later developed in this section. The input to the risk appetite framework is the economic capital, which accounts for all relevant risks and reflects the current risk profile. As opposed to market and credit risks, where capital can be allocated down to specific assets and adjusted through investments and divestments, operational risk capital is derived from the overall busi-ness unit operations and can be managed only by the introduction of controls, automation of processes, outsourcing, etc. Therefore, the current level of capital requirements can be taken as a basis of the risk appetite definition or pre-ORA as illustrated in Figure 11.5.

Capital is an ideal metric to refer to and control ORA, because, in addition to representing the actual risk profile, from AMA, it is the base for the performance evaluation (ROE etc) and can be linked to the risk–reward analysis. Also, it can be linked to the available finan-cial resources of the institution and adjusted to reflect the institution's current financial situation and implicit risk capacity.

Then, the institution's pre-ORA is allocated to business units and limits are hence established, in order to monitor and manage adherence to the risk appetite and tolerance statements of all business entities. The allocation reflects the current required capital needed to absorb losses for the desired solvency standard, given the implicit current operational risks in their activities and business processes. This total required capital is calculated as explained in Parts I and II of this book. In the proposed ORA approach, the total required capital is allocated to business units using the methods explained in Chapter 8 (see "Allocation of operational risk capital", which also reflects the risk profile of the ORC).

Then, the limits should be adjusted to reflect the current strategic direction: expected growth in business (based on the strategic plan). The projected business growth and the corresponding increase in capital consumption are determined in accordance with the financial situation of the institution and availability of financial resources. Here, the limits' adjustment can be calculated as a function of KRIs related to activity, volumes, etc. It is important to note that the control of operational risk should not be directed at limiting the levels of activity of the institution, but to orient the risk mitigation, permitting the development of the institution's business at acceptable levels of operational risk in relation to return opportunities or the cost of operational risk mitigation.

After the business growth adjustment, the limits are again adjusted to the projected mitigation actions included in the business plan. If new controls and mitigation plans are implemented, the expected level of operational risk losses should be lower and, thus, the limits should be decreased accordingly. For the implementation of the mitigation adjustment, methods such as those in Chapter 12 can be used to evaluate the risk level before and after the introduction of the mitigation plans.

Finally, the ORA is cascaded down to very specific monitoring points where the operational risk events materialise, as described below. This last step allows us to assign the risk management ownership and responsibilities to specific managers and business entities where the mitigation actions are actually implemented.

Thus, the implementation of this ORA framework requires the generation of metrics monitoring different dimensions (see list below) of the institution's operational risk profile consistently with the ORA definition process presented in Figure 11.5.

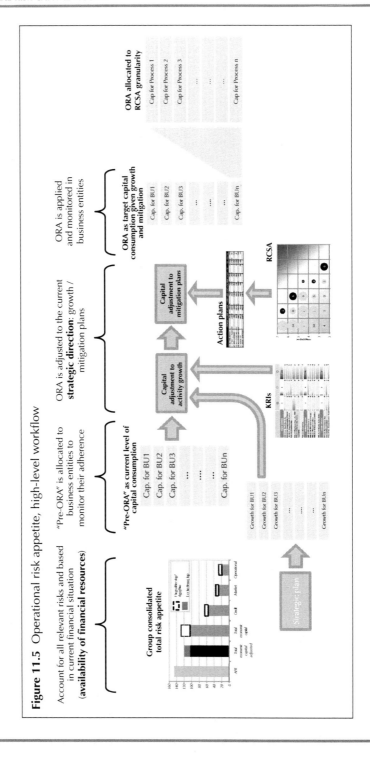

Figure 11.5 Operational risk appetite, high-level workflow

❑ Use of financial resources dimension: Metrics on loss materialisation (total frequencies and frequencies above specific thresholds) and earnings-at-risk monitoring (total-losses materialisation indicators for very specific points in the business entities, in order to protect the earnings of the institution).

❑ Strategic direction dimension: This includes the control over business activity, which can be controlled with activity KRIs (volumes, number of transactions, etc), and the implementation of mitigation plans, which can be measured via the degree of success in the implementation of the scheduled mitigation plans.

❑ Hard-to-quantify aspects of operational risk: KRIs on matters such as staff turnover, fraud level and cyber-attacks are hard to statistically link to losses and capital but are critical for operational risk control. A dashboard of KRIs can be used to monitor this aspects of risk, which could be referred to any of the above-mentioned dimensions.

The practical implementation of an ORA framework requires the definition of processes for ORA cascading down for the monitoring of the specific points (organisational entities, processes, etc), where the operational events materialise; ORA thresholds and limits for risk monitoring and triggering of corresponding action; and adherence to ORA, including escalation and action procedures based on limit monitoring. In the following sections, we present an approach to implementing these processes.

ORA cascading down

The mitigation of operational risk is performed in very specific points and processes of the organisation and, thus, the monitoring and control should also be performed at such points and processes. Similarly, ORA should be cascaded down to the same monitoring and mitigation level whenever possible. In practice, cascading down ORA needs the use of the mathematical allocation methods of the capital model, qualitative adjustments based on negotiations with risk owners and simple attribution methods when cascaded to the necessary low-level monitoring points beyond the capital model allocation.

Figure 11.6 summarises the process for cascading down ORA and the levers that ORA provides to the board of directors to execute its mandate over the operational risk management of the institution. The fact that ORA is measured in capital units implies that the allocation methods of the capital model are insufficient for the more granular cascading needed to monitor the points where operational events are materialised. In fact, ORC capital models are generally referred to business units and risks, but not to granular entities such as processes and business areas. Thus, cascading down ORA requires use of a metric different from capital model output to attribute it to the required mitigation and monitoring points. Examples of these metrics include scores from self-evaluations, RCSA results and KRIs such as number of employees, business volume and so on, which can be used to proportionally attribute the capital to lower levels of risk control and monitoring.

The final amount of ORA assigned also requires negotiations and acceptance by the different business units, as it limits their activity and frequently entails the implementation of risk mitigation measures. Business units may negotiate for more capital given their expansion plans, available budget and capacity to implement mitigation plans, etc. The result is the final ORA attributed to the business units, and business units take clear ownership of the monitoring and mitigation of operational risk.

Figure 11.7 summarises the workflow to cascade down ORA. First, the capital is cascaded down via mathematical allocation methods (see Chapter 8). Later, it is adjusted to the strategic plan and mitigation actions, using KRIs and negotiations with business units. Finally, ORA is cascaded to the lowest granular level using BEICFs (ie, scores obtained from RCSA) permitting an attribution to business areas, processes, etc.

ORA threshold levels and limit monitoring

Next, ORA should be monitored at different risk thresholds defined within an operational risk limit structure and linked to different escalation and action procedures as described later in this section.

Total risk appetite thresholds are established based on the institution's total risk capital capacity, as determined by its financial resources (capital available and earnings) and risk strategy (type and structure of the risks the institution intends to assume). Figure 11.8 shows a conceptual representation of how total risk appetite (including market, credit, operational) is monitored based on the risk

Figure 11.6 ORA cascading methods

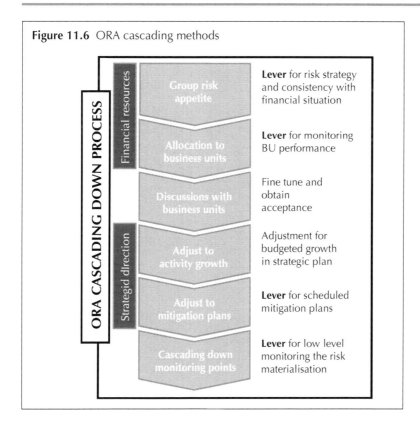

profile. The central, light grey, square represents the risk appetite limits, with early warnings (the upper and lower triggers) and the upper and lower risk appetite limits. When the triggers are exceeded, the "breach" is escalated for corrective action to be considered. If the risk appetite is breached, then corrective actions need to be taken. If risk exposure increases and surpasses the institution's risk capacity, then the institution is no longer viable and should enact its recovery and resolution plan, change its target rating, raise additional capital, divest from specific businesses, transfer risk, etc.

These upper and lower limits and triggers and risk capacity of the total risk appetite structure are replicated for operational risk, after allocating total capital to operational risk capital and defining ORA accordingly. The monitoring and definition of thresholds and limits is done in each of the ORA monitoring dimensions consistently with the ORA definition process: use of financial resources, strategic direction and hard-to-quantify aspects of the operational risk profile.

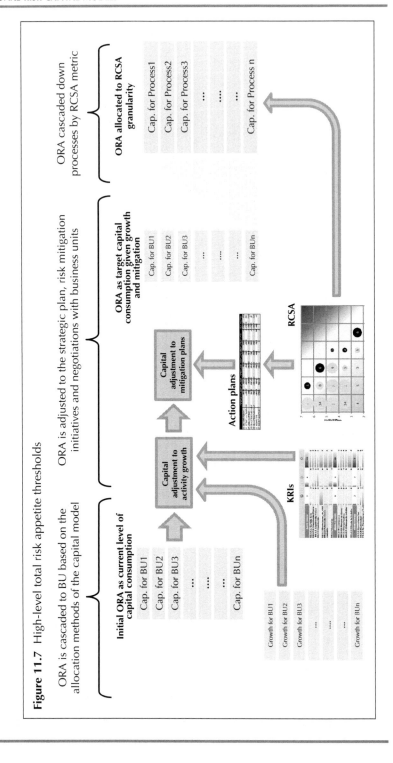

Figure 11.7 High-level total risk appetite thresholds

Financial resources dimension

The financial resources dimension is challenging to measure with precision, as no metric exists that is directly proportional to operational risk capital usage.[4] However, loss materialisation indicators and earnings-at-risk monitoring can be set up to provide an indication of capital usage such as frequency of high losses (losses above a specific severity threshold).

As we saw earlier, high losses result in higher capital requirements. A ratio of annual high-loss frequency (those used to estimate the capital requirement inputs of ORA), or other similar metrics, to target ORA (see "Reference for target ORA" in Figure 11.8) can be used to translate the loss materialisation into capital usage and compare ORA thresholds and limits. This can be analysed in quarterly frequencies of large losses to prompt early alarms. If the frequency of high losses increases, then it is assumed that the organisational entity is in need of more operational risk capital and the limits are closer to being breached. Alternatively, mitigation actions as, for instance, additional controls, can be implemented to make sure that the operational risk profile is under control.

Additionally, a measure of earnings-at-risk monitoring and potential capital depletion can be implemented. Figure 11.9 illustrates the impact of potential losses on the institution's capital and the corresponding thresholds related to earnings and dividends (90%), rating change (99% to 99.9%) and capital depletion onwards. These thresholds can be replicated at the business entity level to which ORA has

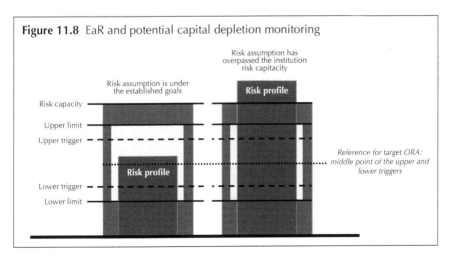

Figure 11.8 EaR and potential capital depletion monitoring

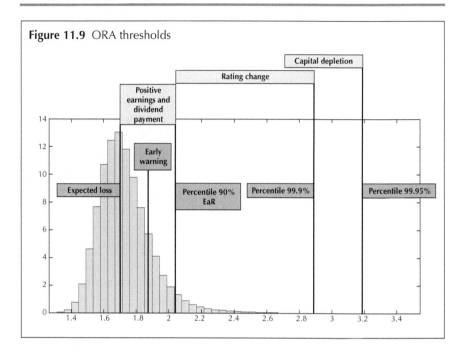

Figure 11.9 ORA thresholds

been cascaded down and monitored against materialised losses. When the different thresholds are breached, the corresponding escalation or mitigation actions should be taken as explained in "Monitoring adherence to ORA" below.

These thresholds can be derived from the distributions of losses of the ORC or business units generated by the Monte Carlo simulation of the capital model. These thresholds are the result of the distribution shape for each ORC and can be cascaded down to low, very specific monitoring points (processes and so forth) by the use of other BEICFs such as RCSA and KRIs.

Strategic direction dimension
The strategic direction dimension monitors both the business growth and the implementation of mitigation plans.

Business growth can be monitored with business-activity KRIs, such as business volumes, providing us with an approximate level of capital consumption, given increased activity. To gauge the limit consumption, a ratio of target ORA to the initial value of the KRI can be calculated to link capital usage and activity growth. Also, regression analysis between losses and activity growth can be performed as described in Chapter 12, in order to determine a closer relationship between growth and losses. As the business activity grows, capital usage is assumed to change in direct proportion to the KRI multiplied by the ratio. It should be noted that the relationship between business activity and operational risk capital is not typically linear, as it also happened in the case of the financial resources dimension.

Nevertheless, limiting the activity levels, to reduce operational risk exposure is most of the times not feasible, as the activity supports the real business that actually generates the income for the institution: lending, financial services, etc. Therefore, the intervention and monitoring of operational risk due to activity growth should be directed at fixing processes with mitigation actions rather than limiting or stopping the institution's activity.

The second leg of the strategic direction dimension is the adjustment given the mitigation actions scheduled in the business plan. The monitoring of such plans in the ORA framework is the lever of the top management to incentivise the actions for risk mitigation. As mentioned before in this chapter, the implementation of mitigation plans decreases the tolerated risk level in the ORA determination, as the implementation should decrease the level of losses experienced. Therefore, when the scheduled mitigation plans are not implemented, the initially assumed risk reduction should be added and the actual risk profile be pushed up accordingly, while leaving the limit unchanged (note that the limit was set assuming a reduction in risk levels). This adjustment plays the double role of both projecting a more realistic representation of the risk profile and penalising the noncompliance with the mitigation plan schedule.

The ORA reduction, given the planned mitigation actions or, when the scheduled mitigation plan fails to be implemented, risk increase, can be estimated following the methods explained in Chapter 12.

Hard-to-quantify aspects of operational risk profile
Indicators monitoring hard-to-quantify aspects of operational risk should be complementing the above dimensions. Issues related to HR, technology, fraud and providers are certainly critical for operational risk management in the long term. However, KRIs around these issues are difficult to link with capital consumption, often due

to insufficient quantity and quality of the data used to determine a statistical relationship and the time lag between the KRIs and loss materialisation.

Nevertheless, a dashboard of KRIs on aspects such as staff turnover and satisfaction, staff training, technology issues, number of fraud events, number of lawsuits against the institution and so on should be created and used to monitor ORA.

Monitoring adherence to ORA

Finally, the limit breaches need to be escalated based on their relevance to inform higher levels of management up to the board of directors of the circumstances of the operational risk materialisation and/or changes to the risk profile. Also, limit breaches may trigger action plans, investigations, reviews, etc.

Figure 11.10 shows an example of the organisation of the corresponding action plans and escalation procedures given different limit breaches. It contains three axes. The first one corresponds to the severity of the limit breach. The second corresponds to the aggregation of losses and limits cascading down, where, in the example, the lowest level is process, the medium one is business line and the third is the corporate level. Finally, there is a time axis, which considers whether the limits may have been breached, for instance, for the whole year or only for the quarter. The time axis will be particularly necessary for those monitoring points of high loss frequency.

Based on the structure of limits and thresholds, the board of directors should receive timely reports on major limit breaches, or

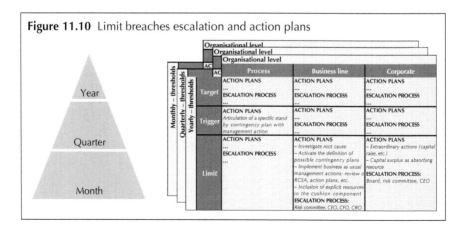

Figure 11.10 Limit breaches escalation and action plans

periodically receive summaries of losses materialised or of other minor limit breaches within the organisation.

With the matrix of escalation and action plan procedures in Figure 11.10, we close the circle in the operational risk capital model and management. The capital model is used to better understand risk exposure. Based on the capital figures, an ORA framework can be established to control the levels of risk materialisation and ensuring that the risk business plan is executed to comply with the institution's risk strategy.

CONCLUSION

The operational risk profile can be effectively embedded into the institution's business planning and GRC reporting. The implementation of the business plan can then be monitored in a timely and granular manner, using the ORA framework. These elements facilitate adherence to the mandate from the upper management on the institution's risk strategy, in accordance with the established limits and risk capacity.

1   This section has been contributed by Lutz Baumgarten.
2   This section has been contributed by Brenda Boultwood.
3   This section has been contributed by Rafael Cavestany
4   In market and credit risk, there are clear exposure metrics that can be linked to capital consumption almost proportionally, such as loan amounts and the market value of securities.

REFERENCES

BIS 2001, "Consultative Document Operational Risk: Supporting Document to the New Basel Capital Accord", Basel Committee on Banking Supervision.

Reiner, Eric, 2012, "Firm-wide Risk Appetite and Risk Aggregation", Leland-Rubinstein Retirement Conference, November 17.

Society of Actuaries in Ireland, 2011, "Constructing a Risk Appetite Framework: an Introduction", March.

12

Risk–Reward Evaluation of Mitigation and Control Effectiveness

Rafael Cavestany and Javier Martinez Moguerza

In Chapter 11, we introduced the integration of the operational risk profile into the business plan and the monitoring of the plan execution using an operational risk appetite framework. Here, we examine examples of the evaluation of controls and mitigation plans that have an impact on the risk profile, which can be used for measuring the consumption of, and/or adjusting the risk limits defined by, the ORA framework.

The impact of the mitigation and controls on the risk levels, ORA, limits and so on should be evaluated, as they change the risk profile of the institution, which is measured by the operational risk capital model. Far too often, the operational risk analysis is single-sided, evaluating only the threats and potential losses. In this chapter we examine various examples of joint analysis of the risk impacts and the benefits of their mitigation.

The chapter is structured into the following sections, describing the risk–reward evaluation of the mitigation actions that can be included in an operational risk business plan:

❑ "Insurance programmes: evaluation of their mitigation impact";
❑ "Risk–reward evaluation of the mitigation impact of action plans";
❑ "Internal audit nonconformities evaluation":
❑ "Process improvement: Six Sigma and operational risk";
❑ "Operational loss predictive analytics"; and

❑ "Adversarial risk analysis: linking risk measurement with optimal mitigation":

In addition, the determination of operational risk capital requirements entails the collection of information on risk exposures, scenarios, potential impacts, dependencies, causes, historical impacts, etc. All this information is highly valuable for the mitigation of operational risk and may provide the means to rationalise the operational risk profile and improve the control environment. The evaluation of the risk impact together with the benefits of its mitigation focuses the analysis into the risk–reward relationship, creating an incentive for the expert involvement in the risk analysis and a more comprehensive identification of the consequences of the risks to be mitigated.

In fact, BCSG-AMA includes similar propositions when saying,

> The ORMS elements should provide a key input into the assessment and ongoing monitoring of the control's effectiveness in relation to the risk appetite and tolerance statement. For example, during the stressing of the control environment in a scenario workshop (as a result of a loss event or from monitoring of indicators), weaknesses within the control environment may be detected.

The analysis now turns into presenting implementation cases of the above activities and how to evaluate their impact on the risk profile might be evaluated. Also, we present examples for leveraging the operational risk capital inputs into the mitigation of operational risk.

INSURANCE PROGRAMMES: EVALUATION OF THEIR MITIGATION IMPACT

One of the most direct instruments for risk transfer is insurance programmes. An insurance programme will reimburse the institution for the events suffered, provided specific conditions are met, cancelling partially or totally the loss suffered.

However, the estimation of the impact of insurance loss mitigation will not typically be simple. Insurance programmes may include deductible and maximum-coverage conditions, affecting the claimed amounts, decreasing their effectiveness in protection from large losses and, thus, in capital saving. These deductibles and maximum coverages may refer to individual or total losses, or even to both. Also, insurance contracts may get very wordy, may cover several legal entities but not all, include exceptions, etc, introducing difficulties for their precise modelling.

Finally, some insurance programmes may have recourse to excess loss – also called layered insurance – whereby an additional limit is set up once the initial loss limit is surpassed. These layers of insurance may be referred to for very specific loss events, also adding requirements to the standard insurance modelling.

The consideration of all these insurance features is required to evaluate the true mitigation potential of the insurance hired. Figure 12.1 shows a simple example comparing two insurance programmes to demonstrate how effectively they save capital, according to the original capital requirements. Each of the coloured bars represents the risk profile from an insurance programme. The dark grey bar is the resulting risk profile from not hiring insurance. The medium dark grey bar is the risk profile from buying an effective insurance programme with a sufficiently high maximum coverage. The light grey bar represents the risk profile resulting from buying insurance with a low maximum coverage.

The risk profile is analysed at several confidence levels of the joint distribution – the expected loss (EL), 95%, 99%, 99.90%, 99.95% and 99.97% – to evaluate the effectiveness of the insurance programmes for different solvency standards. Both programmes are equally effective in mitigating EL and the low percentiles of the distribution, including the 99th, which corresponds to a low solvency standard. However, for the regulatory solvency standard, 99.9%, the light grey bar insurance programme will actually be far less effective than the full coverage programme in dark grey, which permits twice as much capital saving. Indeed, for the highest solvency standard at the 99.97% confidence interval (AA+ or AAA), the light grey bar insurance mitigation is very close to not being insured, while the dark grey bar programme still provides an effective protection, permitting a very significant capital saving.

Nevertheless, both capital and insurance policies have costs, sometimes very significant, and the capital saved by an insurance programme should be compared with the cost of the policy to support the business case of the insurance purchase. Potentially, it can be more rational, from an economic point of view, to self-insure the risk rather than to acquire an insurance policy (see Figure 12.7 in risk–reward evaluation of the mitigation impact of action plans).

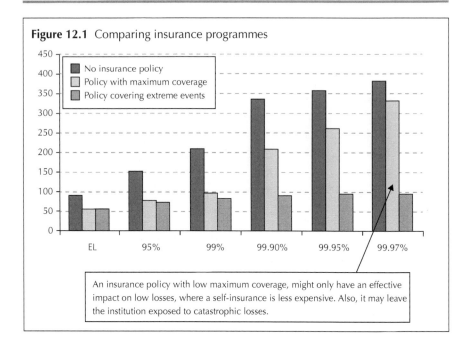

Figure 12.1 Comparing insurance programmes

An insurance policy with low maximum coverage, might only have an effective impact on low losses, where a self-insurance is less expensive. Also, it may leave the institution exposed to catastrophic losses.

Figure 12.2 shows the derivation of the business case for insurance acquisition. The top histogram represents the operational risk joint distribution without insurance, where the loss at the 99.9% percentile is US$198 million and the EL US$96 million. The insurance policy has no maximum coverage, a deductible of US$126 million and costs US$10.5 million. As a result of the insurance policy loss coverage, the loss at the 99.9th percentile goes down to the deductible US$126 million and the EL down to US$92 million. These capital and expected-loss savings, minus the annual cost of the policy, represent an expected net saving of US$3.7 million for the institution.

An adequate evaluation of the insurance mitigation impact requires modelling mitigation during the generation of the joint distribution. The insurance features can be modelled as follows:

❏ Deductible and maximum coverage of individual events: These should be modelled during the generation of the random number from the severity distribution by adjusting each individual loss to the deductible and maximum coverage.

❏ Deductible and maximum coverage of total losses: These should be modelled during the generation of the random number from

Figure 12.2 Insurance business case

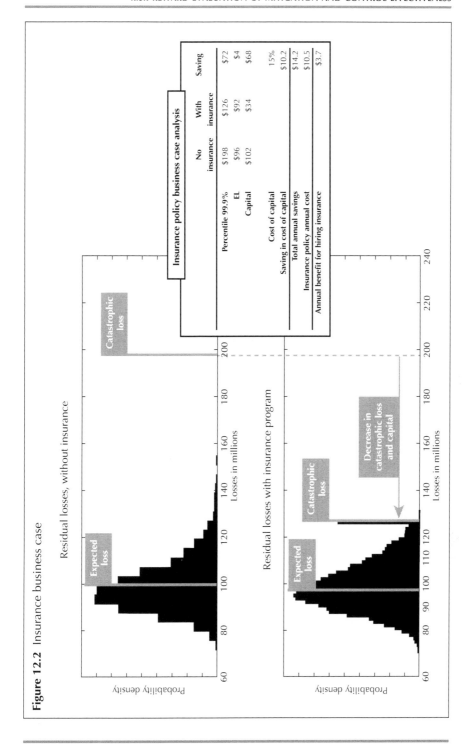

Insurance policy business case analysis

	No insurance	With insurance	Saving
Percentile 99.9%	$198	$126	$72
EL	$96	$92	$4
Capital	$102	$34	$68
Cost of capital			15%
Saving in cost of capital			$10.2
Total annual savings			$14.2
Insurance policy annual cost			$10.5
Annual benefit for hiring insurance			$3.7

Residual losses, without insurance

Catastrophic loss

Expected loss

Losses in millions

Probability density

Residual losses with insurance program

Catastrophic loss

Expected loss

Decrease in catastrophic loss and capital

Losses in millions

Probability density

the joint distribution. As in individual loss coverage, total scenario loss should be adjusted to the maximum coverage and deductible of the policy.

❏ Exceptions to the coverage: Insurance policies include exceptions, with the result that the coverage may not apply to the materialised losses, under several different circumstances. The exact modelling of exceptions requires the creation of two different ORCs, one for the events complying with the policy and a second ORC for those events that do not comply. This approach needs ILD to be sufficient for the creation of the two ORCs, which is unlikely to be possible due to data unavailability. Thus, the original ORC can split into the two ORCs and modelled through the probability of coverage, determining whether each individual loss would be covered or not by the insurance policy. The probability of coverage can be informed by SA/expert opinion.

❏ Maximum number of risk events insured annually: It can be modelled by introducing a control on the number of events, as generated by the frequency distribution, to which the insurance programme can be applied. Once the total number of events has been reached, the insurance will not be applied to the additional events generated during the Monte Carlo replication.

❏ Layered insurance: although the use of layered insurance policies is unfrequent in the financial industry, they are common practice in non-financial companies

❏ Joint insurance and new controls risk impact impact analysis, see example of Figure 12.9. It is frequent that insurers condition the price of the insurance prime or even its granting to the existance of specific controls. This is particularly true for the most extreme risk events.

Figures 12.3 and 12.4 show the analysis of the impact on the loss distribution of insurance programmes. First, in Figure 12.3, the impact of a 200 deductible and 10,000 maximum loss coverage at individual losses is tested, resulting in a decrease on the expected loss from 243.65 to 133.77, saving 109.88 annually. Also, the loss percentiles below the 99.9th have gone down very significantly, almost by a tenth of the original value. Nevertheless, the percentiles for a high confidence interval, 99.98, which is a solvency standard

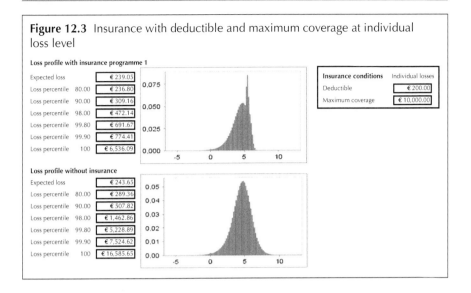

Figure 12.3 Insurance with deductible and maximum coverage at individual loss level

pursued by AAA banks, is still high at 6,539. The impact of the insurance policy in the loss distribution histogram is notorious, significantly cutting the distribution tail.

In Figure 12.4, the insurance programme incorporates an additional coverage for total losses deductible of 450 and maximum coverage of 3,000. The percentile of the joint distribution at 99.98 goes down from 6,536 to 3,725, while the EL is also decreased from 133.77 to 109.65, equivalent to a saving of 24.12 annually. The risk is perfectly hedged in the percentiles 98%, 99.8% and 99.9%, where it is limited to

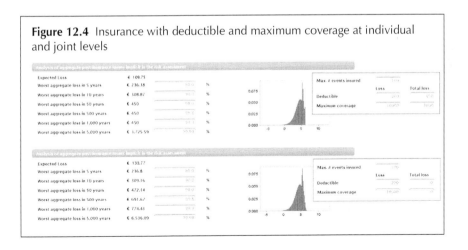

Figure 12.4 Insurance with deductible and maximum coverage at individual and joint levels

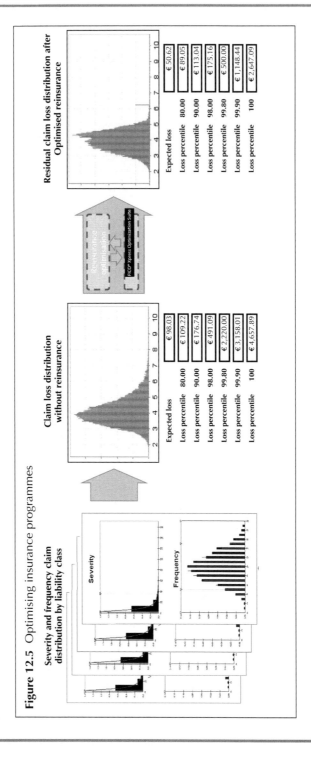

Figure 12.5 Optimising insurance programmes

the deductible. The distribution histogram shows a clear sharper cut on the losses. These capital and expected loss savings should be compared to the insurance cost as illustrated in Figure 12.4.

These savings in capital requirements and expected losses should then be compared with the cost of the different insurance programmes to determine the business case for the insurance policy. Insurance programmes can be potentially optimised to obtain the desired risk profile at an acceptable pricing as compared with the risk cost savings. The insurance conditions, given maximum coverage and deductible, can be determined to obtain the most advantageous insurance programme, given the different exposures to different risks. Figure 12.5 represents the process of optimising insurance and shows the risk distribution before and after insurance optimisation. Restrictions can be established for maximum capital savings allowed by the supervisor, on a regulatory basis, for accounting for saving from capital costs.

RISK–REWARD EVALUATION OF THE MITIGATION IMPACT OF ACTION PLANS

The modelling of operational risk losses permits the linking of risk management with the actual cost of assuming, mitigating or transferring risk. By understanding how the risk profile changes given the introduction of specific action plans, we can determine the cost savings in capital and EL and compare them with the cost of implementing the plan, similarly to the evaluation of the insurance shown earlier. In the case of an investment, the analysis compares a one-off investment with the multiannual savings.

In Figure 12.6, a first example illustrates how to evaluate the mitigation impact of a fingerprint scanner to authorise trading transactions. This control is evaluated for the mitigation of rogue trading and data input mistakes in the trading room. Fingerprint scanning for authorising transactions permits the trading control mechanisms to work effectively, as authorisation passwords will not be shared among the traders, and the specific trading limit of each trader is truly enforced. Through scenario analysis, we determined that the number of limit breaches resulting in major losses will be halved and the severity of those breaches will also be much more reduced, approximately one quarter, close to the limits of lower-rank traders. As in the risk aseessment, the evaluation of the mitigation impact should considerer both

Figure 12.6 Risk profile impact given the introduction of fingerprint scanning in the trading room

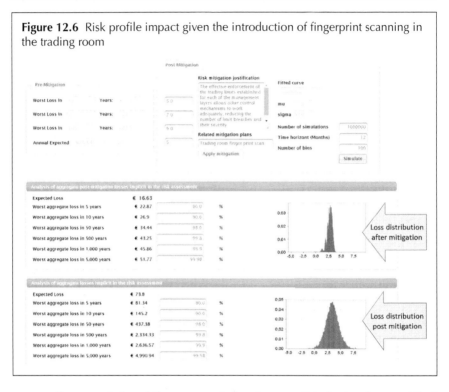

the expected and the unexpected outcomes. It is far too frequent that experts focus primarily or even solely on expexted outcomes.

Recalculating capital requirements under the new situation, results in a reduction of capital at 99.95% from a massive €4.99 billion – similar to those suffered in the worst rogue trading cases – to €51.7 million. This amount should be translated into a significant overall capital saved on a diversified basis. The EL also goes down from €73.8 million to €16.63 million, an annual saving of €57 million. The savings in capital cost and EL should be compared with the cost of introducing and enforcing the fingerprint authorisations, to decide on the investment.

These risk profiles of before and after the implementation of the mitigation plan can be used to evaluate the economic business case for the strong investments required in the implementation of a new trading system with fingerprint scans to approve transactions. Based on the EL and capital saved, even a large investment of €25 million can be easily justified by an important positive net present value

Figure 12.7 Business case calculation for investment

Cost of capital	10%
Diversification	85%
WACC	6%

Years for investment	5		Raise issue

	Business case for mitigation plan (amounts in millions)				
Year	1	2	3	4	5
Raw capital saved	€4,881.69	€4,881.69	€4,881.69	€4,881.69	€4,881.69
Diversified capital saved	€732.25	€732.23	€732.25	€73.23	€732.25
Cost of capital saved	€73.23	€73.23	€73.23	€57.48	€73.23
Expected loss saved	€57.48	€57.48	€57.48	€0.10	€57.48
Other cost reductions	€0.10	€0.10	€0.10	€2.00	#0.10
Annual fixed cost	€2.00	€2.00	€2.00		#2.00
Investment	€25.00			€128.81	
Net profit	€103.81	€128.81	€128.81	€105.04	€128.81
PV of NP	€100.82	€118.03	€111.34		€99.10
NPV of mitigation plan	**€534.33**				

obtained of €543.33 million, as illustrated in Figure 12.7, over a period of five years.

This type of analysis can be applied to any IT decisions (duplication of data center, new antifraud systems, enhanced passwords and others). Figure 12.8 shows the analysis of investing to increase the availability of fraud detection systems in credit cards and ATMs. Different scenarios of fraud levels, both for frequency and severity, were defined, given different levels of downtime in the fraud detection system. Incrementing the fraud detection system availability entailed a direct investment and maintenance costs. On the other hand, the increased availability reduces fraud costs, as more fraudulent transactions will be avoided. There are highly notorious decreasing returns on the system availability investment. Fraud cost reductions are much more significant with the initial increases of system availability, while they are marginal when the availability is close to maximum. This analysis can be used to identify the optimal investment threshold where additional investments will not provide a positive utility and the investments will be larger than the cost reductions obtained.

The implementation of mitigation plans such as that of Figure 12.8 can be evaluated jointly with insurance programmes. The analysis can be used for the negotiation of insurers explaining the impact of

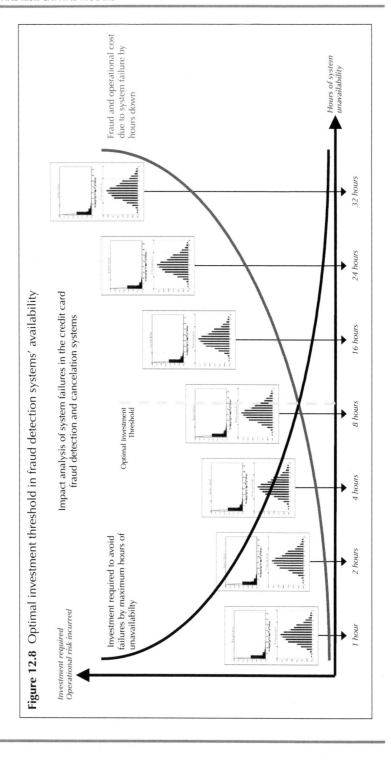

Figure 12.8 Optimal investment threshold in fraud detection systems' availability

Impact analysis of system failures in the credit card fraud detection and cancelation systems

Investment required
Operational risk incurred

Optimal Investment Threshold

Investment required to avoid failures by maximum hours of unavailability

Fraud and operational cost due to system failure by hours down

Hours of system unavailability

1 hour   2 hours   4 hours   8 hours   16 hours   24 hours   32 hours

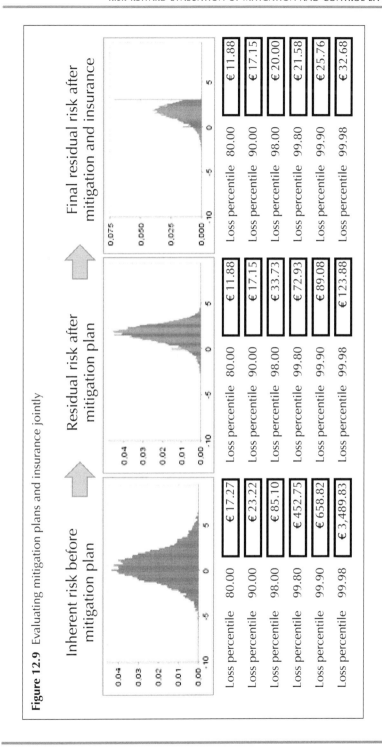

Figure 12.9 Evaluating mitigation plans and insurance jointly

mitigation plans and evaluating the real benefits of insurance protection. In fact, it is frequent that an insurer conditions the prime price or even its granting to the implementation of specific controls, particularly for those most extreme risk events. The process consists of first generating the loss distribution prior to the implementation of the mitigation plan, and then the loss distribution after the implementation. Then, this second loss distribution is adjusted to the deductible and maximum coverage and other insurance characteristics to compute the final loss distribution, as described in Figure 12.9.

In conclusion, the proposed analysis creates a direct link between the risk analysis and the corresponding reward. This should not only increase the involvement of the experts, but increase the comprehensiveness of the risks that should be mitigated, creating a virtuous circle that benefits both the mitigation and the risk evaluation.

INTERNAL AUDIT NONCONFORMITIES EVALUATION

An institution's internal audit function generally identifies a large number of nonconformities referring to system vulnerabilities, fraud threats, process errors, etc. The number of nonconformities can be very significant and these may have different natures, such as pure inefficiencies and material risks. Within the material risks, potential risk impacts comprise overtime, reputational impacts, economic loss, etc.

The nonconformity risk evaluations from internal audit are often based on a simple traffic-light scale, rather than on a structured and robust evaluation of the material risks in which both the occurrence probability and expected and worst-case-scenario impacts are analysed. Therefore, many nonconformities may have a risk evaluation not reflecting a realistic occurrence probability and/or potential impact. Often, the nonconformity recommendations and priority do not consider whether the implicit economic effort is justified, given the actual risk exposure.

Addressing, managing and mitigating all these non-conformities may entail a significant effort and the consumption of scarce human and economic resources. A robust framework to classify and evaluate internal audit nonconformities can help in prioritising the efforts in those with real potential impact and justified mitigation. Also, such a framework would certainly facilitate the discussion and negotiation between the business units and internal audit.

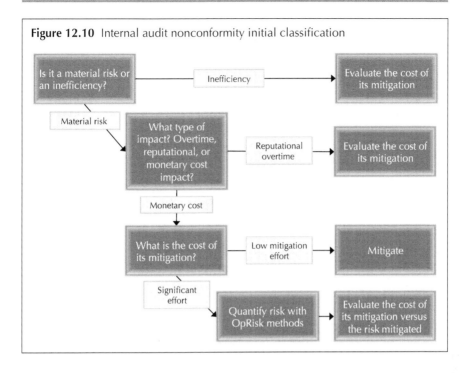

Figure 12.10 Internal audit nonconformity initial classification

The evaluation process of nonconformities can be similar to RCSA and SA, where a probability of occurrence and a potential impact are assigned to the risk for evaluating its materiality. In Figure 12.10, we present a possible simple first classification of nonconformities to identify those with the highest material impact deserving a deeper analysis. Nonconformities are first classified according to their impact and finally according to their implementation cost. When they have a material monetary cost, this is compared with their implementation cost. If the implementation cost is high, a solid process similar to SA or RCSA is then implemented to evaluate the business case for the mitigation. As a result, a negotiation/discussion with internal audit takes place, and a sound and compromised nonconformity resolution plan, schedule and priority are agreed. Finally, those non-conformities with material impact should be informed to the operational risk management function. The consistency between the risk evaluation methods will facilitate the cross information between the internal audit and operational risk management functions.

The risk evaluation of nonconformities can be done by classifying

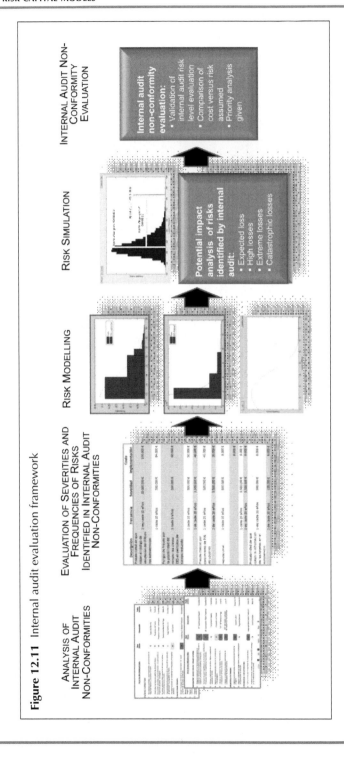

Figure 12.11 Internal audit evaluation framework

the probability of occurrence and impact into categories linked to specific monetary and frequency values respectively. Those nonconformities requiring the largest effort to conform should be evaluated under the scenario analysis elicitation methods described in Chapter 3. Then, the business case for the mitigation can be evaluated as explained above.

Figure 12.11 summarises the risk evaluations proposed for nonconformities from the internal audit. Internal audit nonconformities are first classified. Then, those most relevant are evaluated and modelled. The model is used to estimate potential losses and derive the economic impact and business case for the mitigation, comparing mitigation costs with the change of the risk profile. The evaluation of the business can be done following the methods presented in the previous section, see the examples illustrated in Figures 12.6 and 12.7.

The introduction of this analysis into the internal audit may also benefit the operational risk capital model. Using a similar approach for the risk classification, internal audit reports are more easily integrated and may be more commonly used as an input into the capital model, consolidating the risk evaluations performed by different

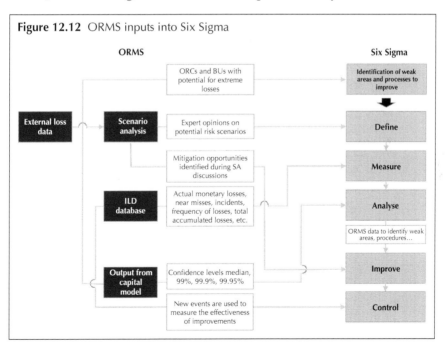

Figure 12.12 ORMS inputs into Six Sigma

functions of the organisation. In addition, risk evaluation method-ologies will be better understood and more accepted by many more departments in the institution.

PROCESS IMPROVEMENT: SIX SIGMA AND OPERATIONAL RISK[1]

The inputs, modelling and results of the operational risk capital model and, in general, ORMS provides detailed information from the operation of the different business processes and assets involved in the support of such processes. This information is of extremely high value for mitigation actions such as the identification of process in need of improvement, which could be implemented through Six Sigma methodologies.[2] The analysis of capital results and the loss data collected with the ORMS can first be used to identify weak areas for process improvements via Six Sigma. Once weak processes have been identified for improvement, the ORMS can still provide valu-able input into each of the Six Sigma phases, as Figure 12.12 shows. The Six Sigma strategy follows the phases of the so-called DMAIC cycle (define–measure–analyse–improve–control).

First, as described in Figure 12.12, the results of the operational risk capital model can help to identify any areas, business entities, ORCs and so on with potential for process improvement, due to their high capital requirements. The modelling of the full loss distribution, including the extreme possible events, in consideration of expert opinions, ED and so on, provides us with important insights not available in the standard Six Sigma analysis, generally based on internal data and average cases rather than extremely unlikely but possible scenarios.

The improvement objectives are outlined in the Define Phase. To this aim, the scenario analysis exercise provides expert opinions on potential risk scenarios that, although unlikely, could occur in the institution business units, areas and, eventually, the key variables that support them.

In the Measure Phase, the inputs into the capital model provide information from the actual functioning of the business processes such as real monetary losses, near misses, incidents, frequency of losses and total accumulated losses.

As for the Analyse Phase, the capital modelling allows for the identification of areas or even specific processes that have potential for very extreme events, thanks to the construction of their severity distributions and the use of the distributions in the estimation of unlikely severe events. The capital model results permit the understanding of potential events, combining their frequency and severity, at different confidence levels: median, 99%, 99.9%, 99.95%, etc.

All this information can be used during the Improve Phase to identify weak areas, procedures and so on, and then better redesign processes to be protected from the circumstances identified by the ORMS.

Finally, in the Control Phase, the improvements that were achieved as a result of the Improve Phase are to be sustained. The way of assuring quality is through the control of the key input variables defined in the Define Phase. A detailed control plan for these variables should be designed.

We now present an example on the interactions between the ORMS and Six Sigma applied to the process improvement of the derivative trading business in a banking institution. In a first step, the operational risk quantification team reports high, potentially strong losses in the derivative business, reflected in the high capital requirements for the activity. Although extremely large losses have not been experienced by the institution, the institution's ILD high frequency in the derivative trading department together with the use of ED and SA allows us to model the loss distribution tail more accurately, resulting in high capital requirements.

The processes of the area are reviewed starting with the Define Phase, which pulls all the collected ILD stemming from the derivative trading. This can be done, for instance, through a project chapter. The analysis of the ILD shows a very significant cost of market losses on trading errors and electronic order corrections. These errors accounted, such as ticket corrections, for a large percentage of the business unit income. In addition, the high capital requirements from the operational risk capital model left the return on equity (ROE) well below the cost of equity required for the trading activity. During the Define Phase, other inefficiencies are detected related to back-office response time, productivity issues and so forth, which affect the return on the allocated capital.

In the Measure Phase, information from scenario analysis is collected in order to derive the high percentiles (99, 99.5, 99.9 . . .) for both the loss severity and the loss joint distributions, which may produce such a large and unlikely but possible loss.

The Analyse Phase is focused on the analysis of the ILD data from trading losses and electronic corrections. The analysis is done by concentrating on the largest errors, identifying the causes, and link these causes to weaknesses of the current procedures. The extreme scenarios collected in the Measure Phase are analysed thoroughly.

During the Improve Phase, all inputs from the ORMS are used to better define new procedures and mitigation measures to reduce the frequency and the size of the errors and corrections. Also, the extreme scenarios identified during the Analysis Phase are used to define additional controls and improve procedures to prevent them.

Finally, the new data collected by the ORMS is also used during the Control Phase to verify that the procedures and mitigation measures implemented are having the desired impact. If new scenarios are identified by the ORMS, the Control Phase triggers an alert to evaluate the suitability of the current derivative trading processes.

The conclusion is that it is worthwhile applying Six Sigma within the ORMS. Six Sigma takes advantage of the mitigation opportunities identified during the operational risk analysis and the information from the ORMS data. Also, the process improvement can be complemented with the inputs of extremely unlikely scenarios from the full distribution modelling in use of SA and ED. On the other hand, operational risk management increases the quality of its inputs thanks to the interest and validation from the quality team and its distinctive perspective.

To maximise the efficiency of using Six Sigma within the ORMS, the scenario analysis questionnaires and workshops should probably be coordinated to serve for both purposes and avoid duplicated efforts. Also, the ILD collection processes should be reviewed to make sure they serve the purpose of Six Sigma. Finally, there should be a procedure to inform of the mitigation measures identified in the operational risk programme during the Six Sigma process.

OPERATIONAL LOSS PREDICTIVE ANALYTICS

The final goal of the operational risk management programme is to reduce the number of event losses and establish a more predictable operational environment through the use of different information and analytical tools. With the successful implementation of the programme, including the capital model, often facilitated by a GRC solution, the institution should have at its disposal abundant and high-quality ILD and BEICFs. All this data can be used to create predictive models of operational risk losses for the anticipation of preventive mitigation actions to reduce the frequency and severity of operational risk events. Predictive models can help to identify areas with higher risk of major losses or of incrementing loss frequency due to a deteriorating control environment, or can statistically validate the effectiveness of existing controls.

In turn, predictive analytics on operational risk loss data can help to create indicators that are more linkable to earnings at risk and financial results. This will make the ORMS better understood and accepted by the top management, eventually facilitating a stronger risk mitigation mandate.

In this section, we present some possible examples of operational loss prediction analytics:

❑ composite KRIs for higher event prediction power and aggregation of the operational risk profile;
❑ how a sophisticated Advanced Persisten Threat malware attack can compromise ATMs and money processing services exposing the institution to major losses;
❑ analytical derivation of KRI thresholds based one the real relationship between the indicator and operational events, allowing a clear link with risk appetite monitoring;
❑ a test for the evaluation of control test failures used in predicting large losses and the evaluation of its effectiveness; and
❑ predictive analytics for forward-looking capital estimations (these are presented in Chapter 6).

Note that the prediction power of these models will be highly dependent on the quality of their inputs, mainly BEICFs and ILD, which themselves depend on the technology that supports the operational risk programme, such as a GRC platform. Also, the existence of an interface into the adequate solution for the generation of the predictive analytics and the embedment of the model into the KRIs and risk appetite dashboard can make the creation and implementation of the predictive models highly efficient. And the integration of the operational risk metrics analytics directed at anticipating preventive mitigation actions will represent an additional stimulus for the collection of high-quality ILD and BEICFs, inputs of the capital model, benefiting the quality of capital estimations.

Composite KRIs

Operational risk dashboards of KRIs tend to be very rich in information made of multiple indicators and often lacking a structure allowing for the intuitive and quick understanding of the risk profile demanded by the top management. These indicators may be difficult to summarise into a single figure responding to the question, "How much operational risk is confronted?" and that can be easily linked to the institution's financial statements.

Although the disaggregated view of the operational risk profile is necessary for an effective operational risk mitigation, the use of composite indicators can help to create a consolidated view of the risk profile and to increase the loss prediction power of the ORMS metrics.

Composite KRIs can be used for aggregating the operational risk metrics. They can be used to predict changes in internal loss frequency, in total internal loss amount or in the probability of major internal loss events, providing us with insight into operational risk's root causes. Under this procedure, we can create multivariate composite KRI models where several KRIs are used as explanatory variables of the model, each providing a different piece of information concerning the dependent variable (internal loss frequency, total internal loss amount or probability of high internal loss events), increasing the prediction power of the resulting composite indicator. Explanatory variables such as RCSA and internal audit scores can be included. The frequency of the different indicators of the composite metric should be harmonised to permit the calculations. In models predicting the occurrence of major losses, internal loss frequency from previous months can act as an indicator of a relaxation of the control environment and be used as an additional explanatory variable.

The generic formulation of a composite KRI for predicting the level of internal losses may be as follows:

$$KRI_{Comp} = \alpha + \beta_1.KRI_1 + \beta_2.KRI_2 + \beta_3.KRI_3 + \dots + \beta_n.KRI_n,$$

where KRI_n are risk indicators and α and β_n are coefficients derived from regression analysis against operational loss metrics as mentioned above (operational loss frequencies, total losses and others). Thanks to the regression analysis against real losses, KRI_{Comp}

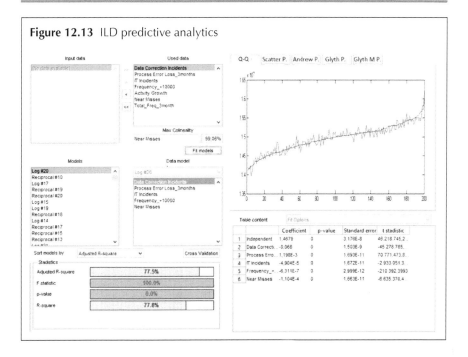

Figure 12.13 ILD predictive analytics

can be directly related to an operational loss level and be used in risk appetite monitoring.

Such a model consolidating multiple operational risk metrics into a single composite indicator can be used to summarise the risk levels of organisational entities and improve the effectiveness of the management reporting and, as it is linked to real losses and thus to the P&L, be better understood and accepted by the upper management.

Figure 12.13 describes the analytics for the creation of a composite KRI for the prediction internal loss frequencies above US$10,000, the model dependent variable. It uses explanatory variables such as internal loss frequency below US$10,000 of the three previous months, data correction incidents, process error total loss of the previous three months, IT incidents, near misses and total frequency of the previous three months. The model has a high R^2, and therefore represents a good predictor of the level of target variable, with a high significance. It can also be used to summarise the evolution of the risk profile of an organisation unit of the institution.

To increase the number of observations for the regression analysis, the sample can be segmented by organisational units or time periods.

This type of statistical analysis can be applied to stress testing.

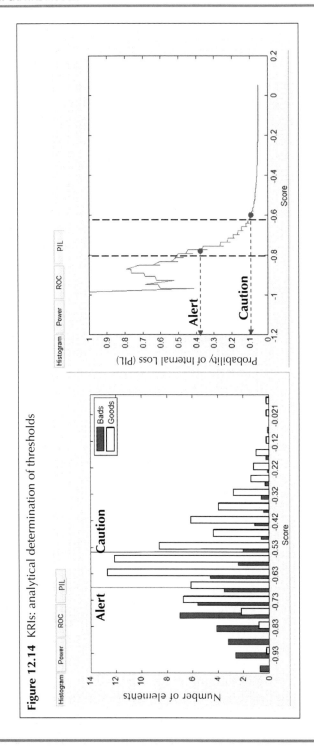

Figure 12.14 KRIs: analytical determination of thresholds

Loss frequency of average losses can be regressed versus macroeconomic, market or credit variables to determine the relationship and be used in stress scenarios that affect market, credit and operational risks. The same type of analysis can also be used to analyse other areas of management such as quality, IT incidents and others, and identify causes and create predictive analytics to anticipate management actions.

Analytical derivation of KRI thresholds

Predictive analytics can be developed to statistically derive the thresholds for KRIs. The relationship between the model score and an internal loss variable can be used to determine the appropriate thresholds for triggering alerts or limiting breaches, as it relates to the expected level of losses.

Figure 12.14 shows an example of this calculation with a composite KRI to alert from a high probability of experiencing an internal loss event larger than US$25,000. The predictive analytics permits us to determine the probability of a major internal loss event given the score resulting from the composite analytics, and determine the different KRI thresholds based on that probability. The graph on the right shows the relationship between the composite KRI score and the probability of the internal loss. From the relationship, the "caution" threshold for the KRI has been determined at –0.6, where the probability of the occurrence is approximately 0.1 and above which the probability starts growing quickly. Then, the "alert" threshold is set at –0.77, where the probability is 0.4. The histogram on the left shows the density of positive and negative elements of the sample used to develop the model and the corresponding thresholds. A similar analysis can be used to control operational risk appetite thresholds when monitoring the earnings at risk.

This type of analysis will help to give additional value to the KRI analysis, translate the thresholds level into more tangible units of loss and give additional insight into the causes of operational risk losses.

Testing the effectiveness of control tests

ILD predictive analytics can also be used to test the effectiveness of control test failures used in predicting large losses. The effectiveness

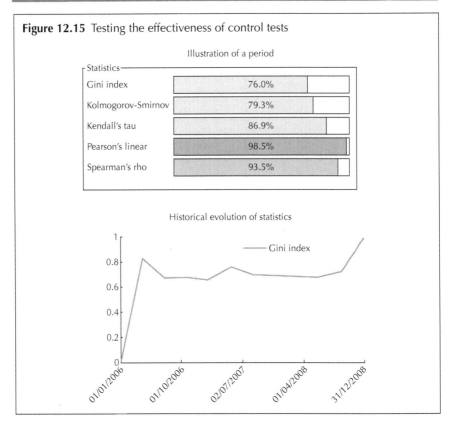

Figure 12.15 Testing the effectiveness of control tests

Illustration of a period

Statistics

Gini index	76.0%
Kolmogorov-Smirnov	79.3%
Kendall's tau	86.9%
Pearson's linear	98.5%
Spearman's rho	93.5%

Historical evolution of statistics

Gini index

of the tests can be evaluated using a standard test such as K–S or area under the curve. Comparing the control prediction with the occurrence of a large internal loss permits us to evaluate the effectiveness of the control. It can also be applied to validate the prediction power of the predictive models, KRIs and other BEICFs. Figure 12.15 shows the analysis along the time of the control tests for identifying potentially large losses. Various statistics are calculated to determine the effectiveness of the controls.

This same type of analysis can be used for the efficacy of KRI thresholds to anticipate operational risk events.

ADVERSARIAL RISK ANALYSIS: LINKING RISK MEASUREMENT WITH OPTIMAL MITIGATION

Inputs to the operational risk capital model represent precious information on the risk profile of the institution, which should be directly usable for mitigating risk exposures such as the security threats to the institution's critical infrastructure. Using capital inputs into risk mitigation actions helps to increase the trust by supervisors in the operational capital model and motivates a deeper analysis of the risk profile. It also supports the use test for the regulatory approval of the capital model. As we have mentioned before, one of the most relevant benefits of an operational risk capital model is that of obtaining a much deeper understanding of the institution's risk profile, potential threats, the surrounding environment and so forth, and the use of this information in risk mitigation.

In this section, we present an example of how to leverage SA and other risk measures in order to allocate resources for defence against security threats. For this purpose, we briefly introduce the use of adversarial risk analysis (ARA) in critical infrastructure protection (CIP), which allows for far more realistic modelling of risk and delivers an output directly implementable into risk mitigation. In fact, ARA establishes a direct link between operational risk measurement and its mitigation and can play a major role within the use test. It can also be used to define a more realistic business case for the justication of risk mitigation investments.

Appropriate responses to security threats represent one of the key challenges for states and organisations in this century, especially as far as critical infrastructure is concerned. Operational risk events such as the 9/11 terrorist attacks, the 2011 Tohoku tsunami, the Stuxnet cyber-attack and the January 2014 vortex in the US have produced very large operational losses, reminding us how vulnerable our societies and institutions actually are, and of the need to get ready and possibly respond to serious events that involve the critical infrastructure in financial institutions. As an example, the Bank of England warned that there is no doubt that "cyber-threat" has become one of the biggest problems faced by the financial system. Cyber-attacks are growing in frequency and sophistication.

Think for a while about the following operational risk events, which may endanger the critical infrastructure of your institution:

❏ how a carefully designed cyber-attack could lead to a loss of critical information in a bank or insurer;
❏ how a sophisticated Advanced Persistent Threat malware attack can compromise ATMs and money processing services exposing the institution to major losses;

❏ how a carefully placed bomb could damage the IT system of a financial institution; or

❏ how an extremely cold period could affect an entire nation, affecting the financial system as well.

Indeed, in response to potentially large-scale terrorist attacks, multi-billion-euro investments are being made to increase safety and security. This has stirred public debate about the convenience of such measures, especially within the context of limited resources within a shrinking economy.

In turn, this has motivated a great deal of interest in modelling issues in relation to security. The US National Academy of Sciences provided in 2008 an outstanding report on strategies, models and research issues in security risk analysis, focusing on the inadequacy of then available tools, either because they lacked mechanisms to deal with the potential intentionality of threats (as in standard risk-analysis approaches), or because they assumed unrealistically strong assumptions (as in standard game-theory approaches), or because they lacked operationally deliverable tools (as in standard decision-analytic approaches).

Adversarial risk analysis

ARA (Rios and Rios Insua 2012), is an analytical framework introduced to cope with risk-analysis situations in which one or more adversaries are ready to increase our risks. This is an approach that promises to revolutionise resource allocation for critical infrastructure protection (CIP), overcoming problems with earlier methodological attempts, by considering the intentionality of offenders and delivering a directly implementable output: the optimal portfolio of mitigation and security measures. As a result, not only would the risk mitigation be much more effective and focused, but the overall mitigation costs might decrease significantly.

ARA inputs are those from SA, such as threats, impacts, environment, character of the threat, existing controls and applicable policy, and represent a powerful opportunity to gain tangible value from the information collected during the SA exercise. In turn, SA and the capital estimates will benefit from the incentive of using this information in real risk mitigation, which promotes a deeper and higher-quality analysis and, thus, better inputs into the capital model.

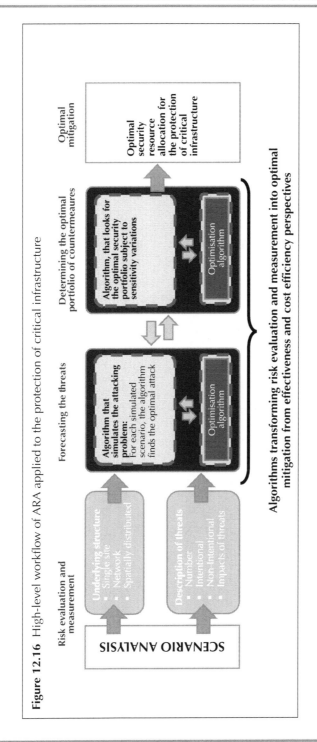

Figure 12.16 High-level workflow of ARA applied to the protection of critical infrastructure

ARA lies somewhere between both approaches mentioned above with a Bayesian game-theory flavour. In supporting one of the participants, the Defender, we view the problem as a decision-analytic one, but use principled procedures that employ the game-theory structure, and other information available, to forecast the opponents' actions. Our uncertainty of our adversaries' actions stem from our uncertainty about their preferences and beliefs when used to analyse their decision-making problems. Given our usable policy emphasis, we are able to accommodate as much information from intelligence into the analysis as we can, through a structure of nested decision models, and stop when no more information can be accommodated, ending the recursion with an uninformative distribution, which needs to pass some sensitivity analysis tests before the whole analysis is considered appropriate.

Figure 12.16 shows a high-level workflow of ARA analysis applied to the protection of a critical infrastructure (such as cybersecurity or physical security). At the workflow input lies the SA results, which feed the problem and threaten structuring. At the output of the workflow, we obtain the optimal resource allocation for the physical security and cybersecurity of the institution's critical infrastructure. "Optimal resources" means the portfolio of countermeasures that most efficiently, from a cost–benefit perspective, mitigates the security risk exposures of the institution. At the centre of the workflow, there are the processes estimating the optimal portfolio of mitigation measures, given the inputs from ORMS. These simulate the attacking problem and determine the optimal countermeasures. After multiple iterations, the algorithms converge to an optimal and cost-efficient portfolio of countermeasures. In fact, these algorithms translate the scenario analysis information into the optimal mitigation strategy and tactics.

In summary, ARA can establish a clean link between the operational risk capital model inputs and outputs and risk mitigation, representing a solid asset for the use test.

Models and extensions for operational risk mitigation

ARA methodology provides several templates applicable to the mitigation of operational risk events affecting the critical infrastructure of a financial institution including: simultaneous defend–attack models; sequential defend–attack models; sequential attack–defend models; sequential defend–attack–defend models; and sequential defend–attack models with private information.

Novel ARA methods can be combined with standard risk analysis approaches to support an organisation in allocating limited resources in the face of both intentional and standard threats. The analysis can be extended to the presence of multiple attackers and/or multiple defenders, and the need to protect multiple sites, possibly displayed around a network or distributed spatially. The analysis can be applied to the study of both physical and cyber-protection issues.

Optimised mitigation actions

Over the last few years, ARA has been expanded and applied to the latest developments in CIP resource allocation (Rios and Rios Insua 2012). Using the results of SA from security experts, the technology for modelling and algorithm implementation in ARA, models can be created to fit the institution's security needs and decide the best protection and recovery strategies for the institution's critical assets

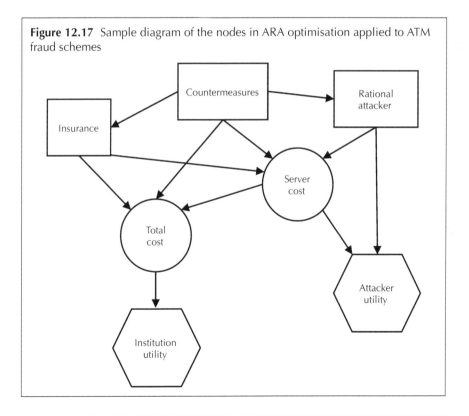

Figure 12.17 Sample diagram of the nodes in ARA optimisation applied to ATM fraud schemes

(ie, information systems), in the face of an ever-increasing complex environment with more intelligent, sophisticated or organised threats as well as stringent budgets. Examples include optimal defence strategy against denial of service (DoS) web attacks, malicious software and terrorism, and the corresponding optimal countermeasures (Rubio 2008).

Figure 12.17 shows a typical defend–attack model, in this case referring to fighting against ATM fraud schemes. White nodes refer to the institution, grey nodes to organised fraudsters, square nodes to decisions, round nodes to uncertainties, hexagonal nodes to evaluations.

In this example, ARA permits us to introduce information regarding the last successful attacks and the bounty obtained by the criminals in ATM fraud schemes. Also, the techniques and resources used in the attack can help to estimate the costs of the scheme for the criminal. This information is used to better adjust the utility function of the attackers and better estimate implicit probability of attack and its severity. Assumptions around the risk-aversion of the criminals (generally risk-neutral or risk-loving) can also be embedded into the model for simulating a more realistic attacker behaviour.

Then, the ARA algorithm simulates different attacks and corresponding responses and estimates the costs for the institution both from the countermeasures and possible successful attacks for the

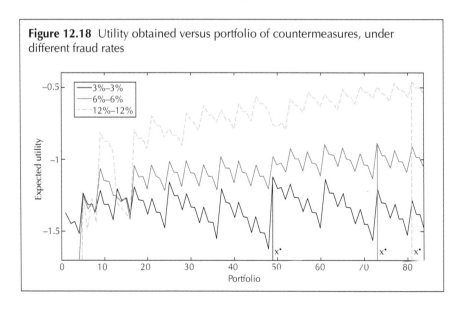

Figure 12.18 Utility obtained versus portfolio of countermeasures, under different fraud rates

estimation of the institution's utility in each response. Countermeasures may include technological solutions and also insurance, as in the figure. As a result of the simulation process, ARA delivers the optimal portfolio of countermeasures at an optimal cost.

The diagram of nodes can incorporate more elements when the same countermeasures may prevent several threats, and the optimisation can be performed for multiple risks. Threats may be intentional (terrorism, robberies, for instance) or traditional (such as fire and natural disasters).

Then, by varying the fraud rates, we may determine the optimal security portfolios under various scenarios, as it is illustrated in Figure 12.18, or identify which portfolio of measures provides the highest utility under any scenario. In the example, it is countermeasure portfolio 80 that provides the highest utility under most of the scenarios. Figure 12.18 can be used to justify the needed security expense for the institution and different threats.

In conclusion, ARA creates a clear link between risk assessments and risk mitigation, providing the optimal mitigation strategy, in consideration of their costs to the institution while also reflecting the potential decisions and behaviour of fraudsters. This results in a more effective and cost-efficient mitigation and a solid argument for the use test. Ultimately, ARA can be used to create the business case, under a risk–reward view, for the justification of mitigation investments and security expense.

In addition to security analysis, ARA can also be applied to other situations where adversaries react to our defensive strategies, including business strategy analysis. Here, competing adversaries react against our pricing or product strategies and have well-known intentions to acquire our market share or market positioning, or launch new products into similar market segments. In this context, ARA can be applied to the analysis of pricing, product strategies or brand management, for marketing decision analysis and tactics definition, although this application should be better developed in a separate document.

CONCLUSION

We have reached the end of our last chapter, where we have examined several examples for integrating the ORMS into the day-to-day management of the institution. These examples show how the business case for the mitigation action investment can be determined and how other management processes are enriched with the ORMS metrics. The proposed analysis focuses on the risk–reward relationship, rather than the single-sided, traditional risk view. The risk–reward perspective creates additional incentives for the involvement of the experts and the quality of the risk evaluations, significantly improving the effectiveness of operational risk management.

Finally, these examples permit the management of the risk profile facilitating the execution of the institution's business plan and, ultimately, the execution of the institution's risk strategy.

To conclude this book, we remind the reader of the great and unique benefits that can be obtained from the implementation of an advanced operational risk capital model. In addition to more accurate capital estimates, the greatest benefits stem from the required deep analysis of the operational risk profile and the model output integration into the risk management of the institution. The analysis of the risk profile provides us with an insightful understanding of the uncertainties the institution faces, which, in turn, permits us the implementation of far more effective risk management tools. Examples of these are the risk profile embedded into business planning and the evaluation of the effectiveness of controls and mitigation plans, in addition to the delivery of valuable information to other critical management processes in the institution. All in all, an operational risk capital model can play a critical role in the implementation of the institution's risk strategy and the effective management of its operational risk profile.

It is hard to imagine operational risk management frameworks other than the advanced capital models that can contribute more to the efficient operational risk management of an institution.

1 This section has been contributed by Javier Martinez Moguerza.
2 For a brief but detailed description of the Six Sigma methodology, see, for example, the first chapter of Cano, Moguerza and Redchuk (2012).

REFERENCES

Cano, E. L., J. M. Moguerza and A. Redchuk, 2012, *Six Sigma with R: Statistical Engineering for Process Improvement*, Vol. 36 (New York: Springer).

Rios, Jesus, and David Rios Insua, 2012, "Adversarial Risk Analysis for Counterterrorism Modeling" *Journal of Risk Analysis* Volume 32, Issue 5, pages 894–915, May.

Rubio, Juan Antonio, 2008, "Probabilistic Risk Analysis for ICT Industry", presented at joint statistical meetings, Denver.

Appendices

Appendix 1

Distributions for Modelling Operational Risk Capital

Daniel Rodriguez

Probability distributions (French and Rios Insua 2000) play a role in the operational risk modelling process that permits us to interpolate and extrapolate from the observed loss sample. Indeed, in the capital modelling, capital charge is determined through probability distributions. The number of times an operational event takes place is determined by a discrete probability distribution, such as a Poisson or a negative binomial. On the other hand, the loss amount for any of the events is determined by a continuous positive probability distribution, such as gamma, lognormal or Pareto distributions. These examples are parametric distributions, where a mathematical expression and a set of parameters completely define the probability of all attainable values. It is also possible to define distributions using empirical data, mixing two or more parametric distributions or changing the range in which the distributions are defined by means of its truncation or shifting.

Mathematically, a probability distribution is a function that describes the likelihood that a random variable can take within a given range. This relationship can be expressed by different functions, the most commonly used being:

❏ pdf (probability density function), which provides the relative likelihood for the random variable on a given value;
❏ CDF (cumulative distribution function), which describes the probability that a random variable with a given probability distribution will have a value less than or equal to it; and

❑ ICDF (inverse CDF), which is the inverse of the CDF.

The pdf is the derivative case of the CDF. The mean, standard deviation, skewness, kurtosis and other descriptive parameters of a distribution can be derived from the pdf.

The selection of an appropriate distribution for risk events (a continuous event for the severity and discrete one for the frequency), is important, not only for obtaining the right amount of capital, but for gaining an appropriate understanding of the behaviour behind different risks. This is so because, by understating the distributions, it is possible to deduce how the capital needs are caused by the repletion of events, by the existence of extreme loss events or by both with different influence. If incorrect distributions are used to model risks, it can lead to either an overestimation or an underestimation of capital.

For risks with a high frequency of occurrence, with a sufficiently broad log of historical data, an empirical distribution functions can be used for modelling the severity of the losses. This is common when the risk refers to the losses of an ORC of lower magnitude. Use of the empirical distribution functions has the advantage of accurately reproducing the historical losses. However, they have the disadvantage that they cannot be used to extrapolate results for non-observed values of historical data. Therefore they are not suitable for modelling extreme values on the tails. In fact, this concern is captured by BCSG-AMA when it says, "In particular, when the data are medium/heavy tailed (therefore very dispersed in the tail), the use of empirical curves to estimate the tail region is an unacceptable practice due to the inability to extrapolate information beyond the last observable data point."

Parametric distributions, which can be shifted, truncated and mixed, offer the possibility of modelling the likelihood and severity of extreme-value events on the tail without the need for events to have materialised in the past. In turn, parametric distributions have the disadvantage that their modelling is more complicated.

The requirement to shift or truncate a distribution can appear for several reasons, including the existence of operational risk data capture thresholds, meaning that losses below a specific amount are not reported for capital modelling. In other situations, the need for truncated distributions is due to the need of modelling the losses in differentiated severity segments, particularly when internal and external data is in use. In these cases, the use of a standard distribution is inadequate because its domain is determined between fixed values, while the fitting sample starts at the threshold and the values below the threshold are extrapolated, forcing the fit and affecting the projection of tail losses. Thus, the best solution is to use shifted or truncated distributions, which can restrict the influence of the distribution to the desired segment. A shifted distribution is simply a distribution where the distribution range has been displaced by adding or subtracting a specific amount. Furthermore, truncated distributions support a restricted range of the distribution without shifting the values. The truncation can be interpreted as if a segment of the parametric distribution above or below a specific threshold would have been cancelled.

Figure A1.1 shows the fitting of historical operational risk loss data with a threshold of 20, with a shifted and truncated distribution. The threshold is indicated by the black bar labled "Fitting thresholds" in the graph. The shifted the lognormal distribution has a shift

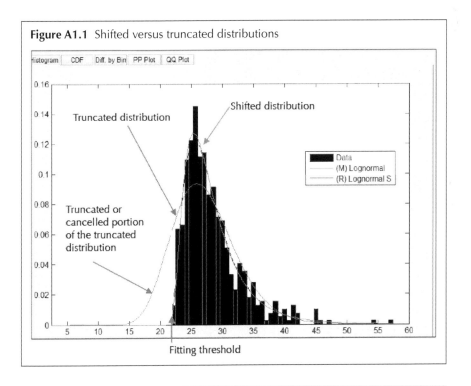

Figure A1.1 Shifted versus truncated distributions

Figure A1.2 Distribution mixture

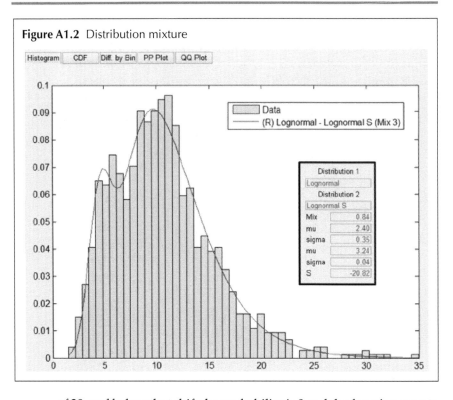

of 20, and below that shift the probability is 0 and the function goes to 0 parallel to the horizontal axis, consistent with the loss data fed into the fit. On the other hand, the truncated distribution was cut at 20 and the portion of the lognormal distribution below 20 is cancelled for calculation purposes, also in consistency with the data, although, in the illustration, it has been plotted to facilitate the understanding.

Finally, a mixture is the union of two or more parametric distributions with a certain weight. These functions are useful when it is necessary to model a risk with two (or more) different underlying causes that are difficult to separate, and the modelling sample shows clearly two behaviours.

Figure A1.2 shows a distribution mixture made of two lognormals. The mixture is able to replicate the double hump in the empirical data, which suggests events being generated by two different processes. The parameters of the mixture can be seen in the illustration and are made by the μ and σ of both lognormals, the shift parameter of one of the lognormals and the mixture weight, which is 0.84 for the first distribution and 0.16 for the second.

EMPIRICAL DISTRIBUTIONS

Empirical distribution functions are constructed directly from the dataset of historical losses. Let X be a set of n historical losses where each individual loss is dented as x_i. The construction of the empirical function requires that the distinct values of the observations then be arranged in an increasing order, denoting as y_i, where $y_1 < ... < y_m$ and $m \leq n$. The value of y_i is repeated w_i times:

$$\sum_{i=1}^{m} w_i = n \ ,$$

and

$$w_i \geq 1$$

The empirical pdf can be defined as:

$$f(y) = \begin{cases} \dfrac{w_i}{n} & \text{if } y \in \{y_1, ..., y_m\} \\ 0 & \text{otherwise} \end{cases}$$

This indicates that the empirical pdf is zero for the value of losses that have not been previously observed, and the numbers of replications divided by the number of observations if the values have been observed. This is one of the disadvantages of the empirical functions where the values that have not been previously observed have a probability density equal to zero, although this is not so in reality.

The empirical CDF can be defined as:

$$F(y) = \begin{cases} 0 & \text{for } y < y_1 \\ \dfrac{\left(\sum_{i=1}^{j} w_i\right) - 0.5}{n} & \text{for } y_j \leq y < y_{j+1}, j = 1, ... m-1 \\ 1 & \text{for } y > y_m \end{cases}$$

According to this definition for the empirical CDF, the lower value in the dataset has a cumulative probability equal to $0.5/n$, assuming that it is not repeated, and the last value $(n - 0.5)/n$, instead of zero and one respectively. This is defined in this way because, in an empirical data sample, not all the possible values are included and there is a probability that the underlying distribution has higher or lower values than those observed. It will be noticed that, as the number of samples increases, the cumulative probability of the minimum and maximum asymptotically approach zero and one, respectively.

In those functions, any value that is not on the original data sample has a probability of zero. In some cases, as in a Monte Carlo simulation, it may be necessary to have the values associated with intermediate probabilities of the table. In these cases, linear interpolation can be used to compute the intermediate cumulative probabilities.

For empirical distributions, the mean can be estimated using the expression for the sample mean of the dataset used:

$$\bar{x} = \frac{1}{n}\sum_{i=1}^{n} x_i$$

The variance of the empirical distribution can be estimated using:

$$\sigma^2 = \frac{1}{n}\sum_{i=1}^{n}(x_i - \bar{x})^2$$

In the case of the skewness and kurtosis, its values can also be obtained through its sample expressions. Skewness can be estimated using:

$$S = \frac{\frac{1}{n}\sum_{i=1}^{n}(x_i - \bar{x})^3}{\left(\frac{1}{n}\sum_{i=1}^{n}(x_i - \bar{x})^2\right)^{3/2}}$$

Kurtosis, meanwhile, can be estimated using:

$$k = \frac{\frac{1}{n}\sum_{i=1}^{n}(x_i - \bar{x})4}{\left(\frac{1}{n}\sum_{i=1}^{n}(x_i - \bar{x})^2\right)^2}$$

Figure A1.3 represents an empirical distribution example. The two columns on the left represent the quantile and percentile relationship of the empirical distribution. Values not present in the columns can be interpolated. The illustration on the right represents the histogram.

Figure A1.3 Empirical distribution representation

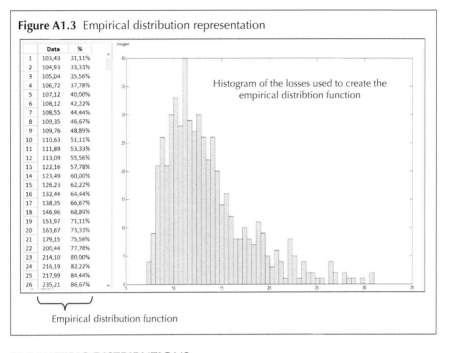

	Data	%
1	103,43	31,11%
2	104,93	33,33%
3	105,04	35,56%
4	106,72	37,78%
5	107,12	40,00%
6	108,12	42,22%
7	108,55	44,44%
8	109,35	46,67%
9	109,76	48,89%
10	110,63	51,11%
11	111,89	53,33%
12	113,09	55,56%
13	122,16	57,78%
14	123,49	60,00%
15	126,23	62,22%
16	132,44	64,44%
17	138,35	66,67%
18	146,96	68,89%
19	151,97	71,11%
20	163,67	73,33%
21	179,15	75,56%
22	200,44	77,78%
23	214,10	80,00%
24	216,19	82,22%
25	217,99	84,44%
26	235,21	86,67%

Histogram of the losses used to create the empirical distribtion function

Empirical distribution function

PARAMETRIC DISTRIBUTIONS

Parametric distributions are a set of related functions (pdf, CDF and ICDF) through which it is possible to determine the probability of occurrence of any value in a given range. Through these functions, once the parameters are set, it is possible to determine the mode, mean, median, standard deviation, skewness and kurtosis for most common parametric distributions. Parametric distributions can be divided into two categories: discrete and continuous.

The discrete distributions are those in which the data can take only discrete values.[1] In operational risk, they are typically used to represent the probability that a certain number of operational losses occur. Continuous distributions are those in which data can take any value within a specified range.

In parametric distributions, it is important to determine appropriate values for the parameters. This process can be performed through different methods. Among these the most commonly used in the bibliography are the MLE (maximum-likelihood estimation) and moments (see Chapter 4).

The normal distribution (or Gaussian distribution) is one of the most popular and widely used parametric distributions in natural and social sciences. This distribution has two parameters, μ and σ; the first is the mean (and also its median and mode), the second is its standard deviation. Its variance is therefore σ^2. The pdf is:

$$f(x) = \frac{1}{\sigma\sqrt{2\pi}} e^{-\frac{(x-\mu)^2}{2\sigma^2}}$$

While the CDF is:

$$F(x) = \frac{1}{2}\left[1 + erf\left(\frac{x-\mu}{\sqrt{2\sigma^2}}\right)\right],$$

where *erf* is the error function.

The normal distribution is a major example of parametric distribution because of its popularity, and its two parameters have a clear meaning. However, the shape of this distribution is not appropriate to represent the majority of operational risks due to its symmetry and light tail. An alternative to the normal distribution is the lognormal distribution, which is built with the logarithm of the normal. The pdf of the log-normal distribution is:

$$f(x) = \frac{1}{\sigma\sqrt{2\pi}} e^{-\frac{(\ln(x)-\mu)^2}{2\sigma^2}},$$

where ln is the natural logarithm; and the CDF is:

$$F(x) = \frac{1}{2} + \frac{1}{2} erf\left(\frac{\ln(x)-\mu}{\sqrt{2\sigma^2}}\right)$$

The mean is:

$$e^{\mu+\sigma^2/2}$$

The variance:

$$\left(e^{\sigma^2} - 1\right)e^{2\mu+\sigma^2}$$

There are dozens of families of parametric distributions used in operational risk that can be found in commercial statistical packages. A list of some distributions families can be seen in Table A1.1. When working with these distributions, care must be taken with the small differences that may exist, with the formulations of the same family in different software.

When modelling operational risk severities, the key issue is the distribution weight on the tail. Distributions are generally classified

Table A1.1 List of distributions commonly available in an operational risk package

Name	Parameters	Type	Modelling use	Tail weight	pdf
Poisson	1	Discrete	Frequency	Light	$\dfrac{\lambda^k}{x!}e^{-\lambda}$
Negative binomial	2	Discrete	Frequency	Light	$\begin{pmatrix} k+r-1 \\ k \end{pmatrix}(1-x)^r x^k,$
Exponential	1	Continuous	Severity	Light	$\lambda e^{-\lambda x}$
Gamma	2	Continuous	Severity	Light	$\dfrac{1}{\Gamma(k)\theta^k}x^{k-1}e^{-\frac{x}{\theta}}$
Lognormal	2	Continuous	Severity	Light (considered also medium weight)	$\dfrac{1}{x\sqrt{2\pi}\sigma}e^{-\frac{(\ln x-\mu)^2}{2\sigma^2}}$
Weibull	2	Continuous	Severity	Light (considered also medium weight)	$\begin{cases} \dfrac{k}{\lambda}\left(\dfrac{x}{\lambda}\right)^{k-1}e^{-(z/\lambda)^k} & x \ge 0 \\ 0 & x < 0 \end{cases}$
GEV	3	Continuous	Severity	Fat	$\dfrac{1}{\sigma}t(x)^{\xi+1}e^{-t(x)},$ where $t(x)\begin{cases} \left(1+\left(\dfrac{z-\mu}{\sigma}\right)\xi\right)^{-1/\xi} & \text{if } \xi \ne 0 \\ e^{-(z-\mu)/\sigma} & \text{if } \xi = 0 \end{cases}$
GPD	3	Continuous	Severity	Fat	$\dfrac{1}{\sigma}\left(1+\xi\dfrac{x-\mu}{\sigma}\right)^{-\frac{1}{\xi}+1}$
LogGama	2	Continuous	Severity	Fat	$\dfrac{1}{b\Gamma(a)}\left(\dfrac{\log(x)}{b}\right)^{a-1}x^{-\frac{1}{b}-1}$
Burr	2	Continuous	Severity	Fat	$ck\dfrac{x^{c-1}}{\left(1+x^c\right)^{k+1}}$
Cauchy	2	Continuous	Severity	Very fat tail, depending on the parameters	$\dfrac{1}{\pi\gamma\left[1+\left(\dfrac{x-x_0}{\gamma}\right)^2\right]}$

under light- or fat-tail distributions. A fat-tail distribution is characterised because of its strong skewness and kurtosis and, thus, potentially higher capital charges. There are various definitions of fat-tail distributions generally used. In this work we call a distribution light-tailed if it has finite moments of all orders, and heavy-tailed otherwise.[2] This means the maximal moment (the maximal moment of a distribution is the highest moment that is not infinite; in a light-tail distribution all moments have a finite value) of a fat tail distribution is a finite number. Table A1.1 presents some of the most commonly used parametric distributions for operational risk modelling.

SHIFTED DISTRIBUTIONS

Shifted distributions are parametric distributions in which the support is displaced by a value s. Their pdf is defined using the following expression:

$$f_s(x;s) = f(x-s)$$

As can be easily deduced from the expression, the mean, median and mode are shifted by an amount s, while the remainder of the central moments are unaffected.

Figure A1.4 illustrates a shifted distribution fitted to a truncation data sample. The truncation threshold is 100, which is equal to the data threshold. Below the threshold, the distribution is 0. Above the threshold the distribution is a lognormal 2, 1.29, with a shift equal to 100.

TRUNCATED DISTRIBUTIONS

When losses available for modelling lie above or below a given threshold or within a specified range defined by two thresholds, it is necessary to use truncated distributions to build a model. These distributions are constructed by setting the probability to zero outside the selected range to a parametric distribution (Billingsley 1995). Mathematically, a truncated distribution is a conditional distribution that results from restricting the domain of some other probability distribution.

Suppose an operational risk for which only losses above a given threshold have been collected, x_{th} and losses of severity below the threshold have been ignored for modelling purposes. Additionally,

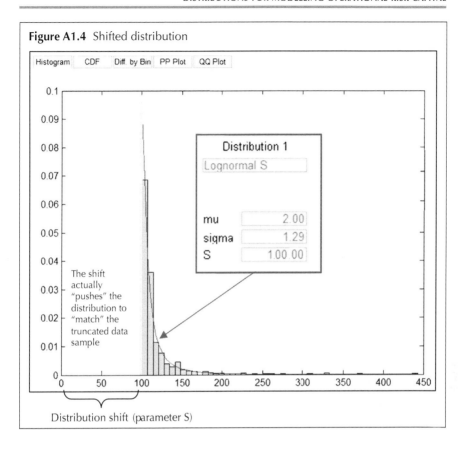

Figure A1.4 Shifted distribution

it is known that the probability of occurrence of this operational risk can be modelled by the parametric distribution whose pdf is f and CDF is F. In such cases, the pdf is:

$$f_{th}(x;x_{th}) = \begin{cases} 0 & if\ x < x_{th} \\ \dfrac{f(x)}{1 - F(x_{th})} & if\ x \geq x_{th} \end{cases}$$

In this expression, the probability of all points below the threshold is set to zero. The term appears because the integral of the pdf over the definition range must be equal to the unit and it can be calculated that the value is:

$$\int_{x_{th}}^{\infty} f(x)dx = 1 - F(x_{th})$$

$$\int_{x_{th}}^{\infty} \frac{f(x)}{1-F(x_{th})}dx = 1$$

In an analogous way, the CDF is constructed as:

$$F_{th}(x;x_{th}) = \begin{cases} 0 & if\ x < x_{th} \\ \dfrac{F(x)-F(x_{th})}{1-F(x^{th})} & if\ x \geq x_{th} \end{cases}$$

This is called a lower truncated distribution because they have a lower truncation value.

Figure A1.5 shows a truncated distribution fitted to a data sample with a threshold, X_{th}, of 100. The distribution is valued:

$$\frac{f(x)}{1-F(x_{th})}$$

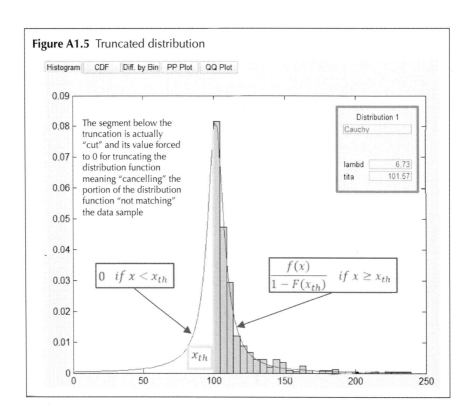

Figure A1.5 Truncated distribution

above 100, and it is valued 0 below 100. Nevertheless, the distribution has been plotted below 100 for illustrative purposes. In reality the portion of the distribution below 100 is "cut" and its value made 0.

Truncated distributions can also be defined for the situation in which loss values are recorded only below a threshold value, called upper truncated distributions. These distributions are useful when it is desired to use differentiated models for the body and tail in a consistent manner (see Figure A1.5). In case no truncated distribution is used, there will be an overlap between the body an tail loss events.

In the upper truncated distributions, the values of the losses only exist below a given threshold, x_{th}. In such cases, the pdf is:

$$f_{th}(x;x_{th}) = \begin{cases} \dfrac{f(x)}{F(x_{th})} & \text{if } x \leq x_{th} \\ 0 & \text{if } x > x_{th} \end{cases}$$

$$F_{th}(x;x_{th}) = \begin{cases} \dfrac{F(x)}{F(x_{th})} & \text{if } x \leq x_{th} \\ 1 & \text{if } x > x_{th} \end{cases}$$

Finally, it is possible to define the most general case in which there are only records of losses within a range determined by a lower, x_l, and an upper value, x_u. Now the expression used for the construction of the pdf's is:

$$f_{th}(x;x_l;x_u) = \begin{cases} 0 & \text{if } x < x_l \\ \dfrac{f(x)}{F(x_u) - F(x_l)} & \text{if } x_l \leq x \leq x_u \\ 0 & \text{if } x > x_u \end{cases}$$

$$F_{th}(x;x_l;x_u) = \begin{cases} 0 & \text{if } x < x_l \\ \dfrac{f(x) - F(x_l)}{F(x_u) - F(x_l)} & \text{if } x_l \leq x \leq x_u \\ 1 & \text{if } x > x_u \end{cases}$$

In the truncated distributions, there is no generic expression to estimate the mean, mode, variance, skewness and kurtosis from the value of the truncation point and the values in the original distribution. As can be seen in the case of the mean:

$$\overline{x_{th}} = \int_{x_{th}}^{\infty} \frac{xf(x)}{1-F(x_{th})} dx = \frac{\int_{x_{th}}^{\infty} xf(x)dx}{1-F(x_{th})},$$

and it is not trivial to express this formula in terms of the mean of the original parametric distribution. Because of this, the methods for estimating the distribution parameters must be numeric like MLE, RLS, etc.

DISTRIBUTION OF MIXTURES

In some situations, a single parametric distribution may not be sufficient to explain completely the probability of occurrence of the events of a specific risk type. This can occur because there are more than one underlying cause and it is not possible to separate into different risk types, in many cases because the risk events are materialised under the same risk classification. In the observation of historical data of these risk types, sometimes, it is possible to observe more than one mode in the histogram, indicating multiple underlying behaviours. The modelling process of these risks can be realised through mixtures.

A distribution mixture is constructed using two (or more) different parametric distributions and a distribution weight, w. For the first distribution, f is the pdf, F is the CDF and n_f is the number of parameters. In the second distribution, g is the pdf, G the CDF and n_g the number of parameters. Both distributions F and G can be of the same family but with different parameters. Using this notation, the pdf of the mixture is:

$$m(x;w) = w \times f(x) + (1-w) \times g(x)$$

and the CDF is

$$M(x;w) = w \times F(x) + (1-w) \times G(x)$$

The resulting distribution mixture is a parametric distribution with:

$$n_m = 1 + n_f + n_g$$

parameters, the weight plus the parameters of first and second distributions.

The mean of the mixture can be easily derived from the definition using:

$$\overline{x_m} = \int_{-\infty}^{\infty} x \times \left(w \times f(x) + (1-w) \times f(x) \right) dx$$
$$= w \int_{-\infty}^{\infty} x \times f(x) dx + (1-w) \int_{-\infty}^{\infty} x \times f(x) dx$$
$$= w \times \overline{x_f} + (1-w) \times \overline{x_g}$$

Thus, the average of the mixture is the weighted sum of the averages of the component distributions.

An issue is the high number of degrees of freedom on the fit, which leads to the overfitting and capital estimation instability. Also, it is possible that a single distribution dominates a great percentage of the fit and the second explains only some events at the tail, which may make the fitting even more unstable and a strong over fit in the tail.

1   In discrete distributions, the pdf is usually called probability mass function (pmf).
2   Other definitions describe a fat tail as a distribution with infinite variance, or whose maximal moment is of order 1.

REFERENCES

Billingsley, Patrick, 1995, *Probability and Measure*, 3rd edn (New York: John Wiley & Sons).

French, S., and D. Rios Insua, 2000, *Statistical Decisions Theory*, Arnolds (London: Arnolds).

Appendix 2
Credibility Theory
Daniel Rodriguez

This appendix introduces the different models of credibility theory: classical model, Bühlmann, Bühlmann–Straub and Bühlmann–Straub for small and large losses.

CLASSICAL CREDIBILITY MODELS

This section presents the classical credibility model. In classical credibility, it is assumed that the underlying data is normally distributed, which is uncommon for operational risk losses. Nevertheless, it is presented for its simplicity to facilitate the understanding of all other credibility models.

Classical credibility theory (also known as limited-fluctuation credibility) starts with two estimations obtained from different sources, denoted as estimates x and y. Each of these estimates has a specific variance denoted as σ_x^2 for x and σ_y^2 for y. Estimate x, which generally refers to the institution's ILD, is associated with a weight-named credibility factor and denoted by z, which will be between 0 and 1. The mean value of both estimates can be obtained by the expression:

$$\overline{xy} = z \times x + (1-z) \times y \qquad (A2.1)$$

This equation shows that the value of $\overline{xy}$ is between x and y. The credibility factor, z, indicates the relative importance of the estimate x. We say that estimate z has full credibility when $z = 1$. In this case, the final estimate depends only on x. When $z < 1$, it is said to have a partial estimate credibility.

Determining the amount of data needed to assign full credibility is one of the benefits obtained through classical credibility theory.

This amount of data is known as the "full credibility criterion" or the standard for full credibility.

The following subsections show how to perform the estimation of the size of a dataset, both for the frequency and severity values, to be considered full credibility and the value of the parameter z given a specific dataset available.

Full credibility

A dataset alone may fulfil the conditions for complete credibility, called standards for full credibility. The base of the analysis is the data sample with N, an average and variance . We can estimate how likely the observed value of N is representative of the true values by answering the question, "What is the probability that this value is within a percentage of the average k?" This can be expressed mathematically as:

$$\Pr\left(\mu_N - k\mu_N \le N \le \mu_N + k\mu_N\right)$$

By standardising the expression, we get:

$$\Pr\left(-\frac{k\mu_N}{\sigma_N} \le \frac{N-\mu_N}{\sigma_N} \le \frac{k\mu_N}{\sigma_N}\right)$$

Then, the required calculations need the values of N to be normally distributed. The values for the standard normal distribution facilitate the calculations. Then, we obtain:

$$\Pr\left(-\frac{k\mu_N}{\sigma_N} \le \frac{N-\mu_N}{\sigma_N} \le \frac{k\mu_N}{\sigma_N}\right) = \Phi\left(\frac{k\mu_N}{\sigma_N}\right) - \Phi\left(-\frac{k\mu_N}{\sigma_N}\right) = 2\Phi\left(\frac{k\mu_N}{\sigma_N}\right) - 1 ,$$

where Φ represents the CDF of the standard normal distribution.

In this case, it can be written as:

$$\frac{k\mu_N}{\sigma_N} = q_i - \frac{\alpha}{2}, \tag{A2.2}$$

where q_i is the percentile i of the standard normal distribution, meaning $\Phi(q_i) = i$, where there is a probability $1-\alpha$ that an observed losses occurs with a k averages. Then it can be assumed that the probability is:

$$\Pr\left(-\frac{k\mu_N}{\sigma_N} \le \frac{N-\mu_N}{\sigma_N} \le \frac{k\mu_N}{\sigma_N}\right) = 2\left(i-\frac{\alpha}{2}\right) - 1 = 2i - 1 - \alpha$$

Then, for $i = 0.01$, there is a probability:

$$\Pr\left(-\frac{k\mu_N}{\sigma_N} \le \frac{N - \mu_N}{\sigma_N} \le \frac{k\mu_N}{\sigma_N}\right) = 1 - \alpha,$$

that a frequency higher than k times μ_N is observed, provided it complies with expression (A2.2).

Now, the severity standards for full credibility is calculated based on the N events of the modelling sample, X_1, ..., X_N. In this case, it is assumed the sample size is large enough so that the values of X_i are normally distributed with a mean value of μ_X, a variance of σ_X^2/N and the sample average is events by $\overline{X}$. The condition of full credibility is associated to $\overline{X}$ when the probability of this value is around the value of $k\mu_X$ meets a margin. This can be mathematically expressed as:

$$\Pr\left(\mu_X - k\mu_X \le \overline{X} \le \mu_X + k\mu_X\right)$$

Or normalised:

$$\Pr\left(-\frac{k\mu_X}{\sigma_X/\sqrt{N}} \le \frac{\overline{X} - \mu_X}{\sigma_X/\sqrt{N}} \le \frac{k\mu_X}{\sigma_X/\sqrt{N}}\right)$$

Assuming normality:

$$\Pr\left(-\frac{k\mu_X}{\sigma_X/\sqrt{N}} \le \frac{\overline{X} - \mu_X}{\sigma_X/\sqrt{N}} \le \frac{k\mu_X}{\sigma_X/\sqrt{N}}\right) = 2\Phi\left(\frac{k\mu_X}{\sigma_X/\sqrt{N}}\right) - 1$$

Similar to the frequency calculations, in order to have a probability larger than $1 - \alpha$, the following expression should be verified:

$$\frac{k\mu_X}{\sigma_X/\sqrt{N}} = q_i - \frac{\alpha}{2}$$

It then follows that full credibility for the severity can be obtained, as long as:

$$N \ge \left(\frac{q_i - \frac{\alpha}{2}}{k}\right)^2 \left(\frac{\sigma_X}{\mu_X}\right)^2$$

These approaches have been developed under the assumption that the data can be considered as normal. This tends to be more acceptable for frequency distribution. However, it would be highly uncommon for severity distributions. When the event data is not normally distributed, the approach needs to be adapted, as we next explain.

Partial credibility

Full credibility cannot be achieved when the empirical dataset is not large enough. In these situations, it is required to assume partial credibility, and the value of z for estimate x must be less than 1 and thus z needs to be calculated. Thus, a probability needs to be calculated such that:

$$\Pr\left(z\mu_N - k\mu_N \le zN \le z\mu_N + k\mu_N\right) = 1 - \alpha$$

where α is a given value. The expression above can be standardised as:

$$\Pr\left(-\frac{k\mu_N}{z\sigma_N} \le \frac{N - \mu_N}{\sigma_N} \le \frac{k\mu_N}{z\sigma_N}\right) \ge 1 - \alpha$$

Assuming a Poisson distribution λ_N for the frequency and a normal distribution on the underlying data, we have:

$$\Pr\left(-\frac{k\mu_N}{z\sigma_N} \le \frac{N - \mu_N}{\sigma_N} \le \frac{k\mu_N}{z\sigma_N}\right) = 2\Phi\left(\frac{k\sqrt{\lambda_N}}{z\sigma_N}\right) - 1$$

Therefore, if we have that:

$$\frac{k\sqrt{\lambda_N}}{z\sigma_N} = q_i - \frac{\alpha}{2},$$

the partial credibility for frequency can be obtained through the expression:

$$z = \left(\frac{k}{q_1 - \dfrac{\alpha}{2}}\right)\sqrt{\lambda_N}$$

For the severity, the credibility factor can be obtained following analogous method and we have:

$$z = \frac{k}{q_1 - \dfrac{\alpha}{2}} \frac{\mu_X}{\sigma_X} \sqrt{N}$$

These methods have been developed under the normality assumption of the loss data. Therefore, the above methods need to be adapted, as presented in the following sections.

BÜHLMANN CREDIBILITY MODEL

The classical theory of credibility addresses the important problem of combining estimates from different sources to get a better overall estimate. However, this theory does not provide a completely suitable solution, since the method is based on the arbitrary selection of probabilities and levels of precision. Although this issue can be addressed by using standard confidence levels, the model still requires the application of restrictive assumptions about the distributions of losses such as normality.

The Bühlmann Credibility Model addresses this issue through a rigorous statistical approach that optimises the prediction by minimising square errors on the estimates. Moreover, the approach used in Bühlmann's credibility theory is sufficiently flexible to incorporate different loss distribution families. This section is a simplified presentation of Bühlmann's credibility model. More formal developments are available in Bühlmann and Gisler (2005).

In equation (A2.1), we can assume that the estimates x and y have a squared errors equal to δ_x and δ_x respectively. Therefore, the expected squared error for the total estimate will be:

$$\sigma_{\overline{xy}} = z^2 \times \delta_x + (1-z)^2 \times \delta_y$$

We can find the value of z, which minimises the total estimate error. For this purpose, we set to zero the derivative of the errors with respect to z, ie:

$$\frac{d\sigma_{\overline{xy}}}{dz} = 2 \times z \times \delta_x + 2 \times (1-z) \times \delta_y$$

Simple algebra leads to the expression:

$$z = \frac{\delta_y}{\delta_x + \delta_y} \qquad \text{(A2.3)}$$

This suggests that each of the estimate weights is proportional to the reciprocal of its square error.

Then, if there is available a data sample X_i with N elements belonging to various risk subclasses, identified as s, in different periods of time, the observed losses can be described as:

$$L_{s,t} = E[X \mid s] + \mathbb{E}_{s,t},$$

where $L_{s,t}$ are the observed losses for a risk subcategory s in period t, $E[X \mid s]$ is the expected value of losses for subcategory s, and $\mathbb{E}_{s,t}$ is the random component of subcategory s in period t. Then, if we define l as the expected losses and l_s as:

$$l_s = E[X] - E[X \mid s],$$

looking into an ORC model, the observed losses of time period t to s, can be decomposed as:

$$L_{s,t} = l + l_s + \mathbb{E}_{s,t} \tag{A2.4}$$

Without much loss of generality, we can assume that the average of both as l_s and $l_{s,t}$ is zero. The variance can be indicated by l_s:

$$\sigma_{HM}^2 = Var\left(E[l_s]\right),$$

which is usually called the variance of hypothetical means. In this definition, the hypothetical term is used because the values of the average losses cannot be observed. The random portion of each of the random component is σ_s^2, allowing us to calculate its average:

$$\mu_{pV} = E\left[\sigma_s^2\right],$$

which is usually called the expected value of the process variance.

Now, to apply the expression (A2.3), it is necessary to link x and y components to get the square errors. First, x can be identified with the losses observed at the different time periods, so that the square error of this component is:

$$\delta_x = \frac{\mu_{pV}}{N},$$

where N is the number of periods that have been observed for the estimate. Furthermore, the component y may be associated with losses of subtype s, meaning $l + ls$, so that the square error is σ_{HM}^2. Under these circumstances, by applying expression (A2.3), we obtain

$$z = \frac{\sigma_{HM}^2}{\dfrac{\mu_{pV}}{N} + \sigma_{HM}^2}$$

Multiplying the numerator and denominator by N/σ^2_{HM}, leaves the expression:

$$z = \frac{N}{\dfrac{\mu_{pV}}{\sigma^2_{HM}} + N} \text{ ,}$$

which is the original formula of Bühlmann's credibility. This expression can be simplified by defining:

$$k = \frac{\mu_{pV}}{\sigma^2_{HM}} \text{ ,}$$

which leads to:

$$z = \frac{N}{N + k}$$

BÜHLMANN–STRAUB CREDIBILITY MODEL

The previous development of the Bühlmann credibility model makes the implicit assumption that losses are evenly distributed within stable distribution characteristics. This assumption is often violated in those exposures in which the random component variance cannot be considered constant over time. In this case, Bühlmann's credibility model is corrected by the Bühlmann–Straub Model.

This model introduces a measure of exposure for each of the loss types, m_s, to address the lack of homogeneity in the distribution functions of loss types. By introducing this term, the variance of each risk subtype becomes $m_s\sigma^2_s$ and, thus, σ^2_s becomes the variance by unit of exposure. Under this circumstance, the assumption that the average deviation of the losses for each risk subtype is zero no longer holds. This is because the different subtypes of risk deviate from the average in a different amount, depending on exposure type.

One way to preserve this assumption in equation (A2.4) is to reinterpret the value of $L_{s,t}$ as the loss per unit of exposure, so that the variance of the random part becomes σ^2_s/m_s. Using this reinterpretation makes the X_i values become the average exposure losses over the N periods of time.

Based on the new assumptions, it holds that the mean squared error losses for subtype s, meaning $l + l_s$, is σ^2_{HM}. Assuming that the losses are calculated as the sum of the N time periods divided by the sum of exposures, it follows that the variance is:

$$\frac{m_s \sigma_s^2}{m_s^2} = \frac{\sigma_s^2}{m_s}$$

observed in the N time periods. Therefore, their expected average value will now be:

$$E\left[\frac{\sigma_s^2}{m_s}\right] = \frac{E[m_s]}{m_s} = \frac{\mu_{pV}}{m_s} \ ,$$

which is the squared error of the individual losses. Under these assumptions, by applying the expression (A2.3), we obtain:

$$z = \frac{\sigma_{HM}^2}{\dfrac{\mu_{pV}}{m_s} + \sigma_{HM}^2} \ ,$$

which can be simplified to:

$$z = \frac{m_s}{m_s + \dfrac{\mu_{pV}}{\sigma_{HM}^2}} = \frac{m_s}{m_s + k} \ , \tag{A2.5}$$

which is the Bühlmann–Straub Credibility Model.

BÜHLMANN–STRAUB CREDIBILITY MODEL FOR LARGE AND SMALL RISKS

The development of the Bühlmann–Straub credibility model requires the assumption that each exposure unit generates the same amount of variance in losses. This implies that large losses are expected to behave as a linear combination of lower losses. In reality, this does not hold (Hewitt 1967), and the variance from great loss events will typically be higher than that obtained by adding events with minor losses. Two factors that explain this behaviour are that risk causes changes over time and that exposure varies with the change in the economic environment, the use of new technologies, etc. An approach to address this issue is to assume that the variance can be modelled as an independent value plus another component, which increases with square of the losses. Then, the variance can be expressed as:

$$m_s \sigma_s^2 + m_s^2 \left(1+l_s\right)^2$$

In this case, the formula is complicated credibility of the form:

$$z = \frac{m_s}{m_s + \dfrac{\mu_{pV}}{\sigma_{HM}^2} + \dfrac{m_s \left(1+l_s\right)^2}{\sigma_{HM}^2}}$$

This expression reduces the value of the Bühlmann–Straub credibility when the values of losses are high since the correction introduced in the denominator becomes more important.

REFERENCES

Bühlmann, H., and A. Gisler, 2005, *A Course in Credibility Theory and its Applications* (New York: Springer Verlag).

Hewitt, C. C., 1967, "Loss Ratio Distributions: A Model". Paper presented to the Casualty Actuarial Society, PCAS LIV, p. 70.

Appendix 3

Mathematical Optimisation Methods Required for Operational Risk Modelling and Other Risk Mitigation Processes

Laureano F. Escudero

Mathematical optimisation has significant applications in risk measurement and mitigation. In particular, it is used in operational risk modelling for the determination of the severity and frequency distribution functions that best represent the operational risk profile of the institution.

Additionally, mathematical optimisation has other applications in risk management, such as the selection of portfolios of risk exposures (market and credit risk) consistent with risk-averse strategies (Escudero *et al* 2014). In fact, the choice of risk exposures can also be applied to operational risk such as in the selection of the optimal insurance programmes for the hedging of operational risk exposures (see Chapter 12).

In this appendix, we present an approach for the determination of the operational risk distribution function. Additionally, we introduce a mathematical optimisation model under uncertainty for portfolio selection, in this case the optimisation of credit exposures in order to obtain desired risk profile consistent with risk-averse strategies.

A MATHEMATICAL OPTIMISATION APPROACH FOR OPERATIONAL RISK MEASUREMENT

The process for determining the optimal distribution function that best represents the institution operational risk profile requires the use of mathematical optimisation for the implementation of MLE, LS or the other fitting methods (see Chapter 4). The variables of this optimisation process are the parameters of such distribution function and the optimisation process may include multiple conditions (represented by constraints related to nonlinear and linear functions with bounded variables) derived from ILD, ED and SA.

A very popular optimisation and easy-to-implement algorithm for the determination of distribution functions is the Nelder–Mead method (Nelder and Mead 1965). It is a derivative-free minimisation engine that provides acceptable solutions for less complex problems such as determination of the distribution function using a single data element, either ILD, ED, or SA.

Nevertheless, when fitting distributions using multiple data elements, the fitting goals might not all be perfectly consistent, representing a challenge for the convergence, in addition to adding multiple dimensions into the optimisation. Using the Nelder–Mead method in this analysis may deliver suboptimal results or even not converge into a reasonable solution, within a limited time.

An example of a severity distribution determination via optimisation incorporating multiple data elements would be as follows:

Suppose that the distribution function of severity losses is assumed to be a lognormal.

ILD is used to determine the scale of the operational risk losses, which is derived from the value of the 80th, 90th and 95th percentiles and mean, expressed through the following constraints:

$$\text{Percentile } 80 = 100, \quad F(100) = \frac{1}{2} + \frac{1}{2} erf\left(\frac{\ln(100) - \mu}{\sqrt{2\sigma^2}}\right) = 0.8$$

$$\text{Percentile } 90 = 250, \quad F(250) = \frac{1}{2} + \frac{1}{2} erf\left(\frac{\ln(250) - \mu}{\sqrt{2\sigma^2}}\right) = 0.9$$

$$\text{Percentile } 95 = 380, \quad F(380) = \frac{1}{2} + \frac{1}{2} erf\left(\frac{\ln(380) - \mu}{\sqrt{2\sigma^2}}\right) = 0.95$$

$$\text{Loss mean, } \overline{x} = e^{\mu + \sigma^2/2} = 65$$

External data is used to determine the shape of the distribution. From the analysis of external data, it is determined that the kurtosis and skewness of the risk being modelled should be equal to 120 and 13 respectively. This information adds the additional constraints:

$$\text{Skewness} = \left(e^{\sigma^2} + 2\right)\sqrt{e^{\sigma^2} - 1} = 13$$
$$\text{Kurtosis} = e^{4\sigma^2} + 2e^{3\sigma^2} + 3e^{2\sigma^2} - 6 = 120$$

Finally, expert opinions from scenario analysis are used to inform the characteristics of the distribution tail and shape. In this respect, the experts have determined that the σ parameter of the lognormal should be between 3.5 and 5. This information is introduced as bounding the σ variable, such that it can be expressed:

$$3.5 < \sigma < 5$$

Additional pieces of information can be introduced into the fitting process, such as internal data collection thresholds, which would require the use of a more complex distribution function, adding challenges to the optimisation process.

All these complex functions may make the Nelder–Mead algorithm inaccurate and costly computationally. Alternatively, there are some other more modern algorithms that can easily handle those types of constraints in an accurate way and without requiring -- much computing time, such as the derivative-free algorithms COBYLA and LINCOA, developed by Powell (1994), among others. They are more suitable for solving those difficult problems since, additionally, they seek to minimise a multivariable nonlinear function subject to nonlinear and linear constraints with unbounded and bounded variables.

A STOCHASTIC MODEL FOR RISK MANAGEMENT OF CREDIT PORTFOLIO STRUCTURING TO MAXIMISE EXPECTED RETURNS UNDER SOME SOURCES OF UNCERTAINTY

Introduction

Deterministic optimisation models have been proposed and studied extensively since the 1940s, and they have been applied to the financial sector since the 1970s. The stochastic version (where some parameters are considered uncertain and then they are random variables) were not considered for solving real-life problems until the 1980s due to the high requirement for computer facilities. So the stochastic modelling for the financial models to be dealt with in this work, rather than the traditional deterministic version, considers that some information is available on uncertain parameters, such that known or estimated probability distributions of the potential values, usually, along a time horizon are required to form a set of representative scenarios and, then, stochastic optimisation is used (Aramburu *et al* 2012; Beraldi, Violi and De Simeone 2011; Bertocchi, Moriggia and Dupacova 2006; Bradley and Crane 1972; Fong and Vasicek 1983; Geyer and Ziemba 2008; Golub *et al* 1995; Kusy and Ziemba 1986; Wallace and Ziemba 2005; Ziemba 2003; Ziemba and Mulvey 1998; Zenios *et al* 1998; Zenios and Ziemba 2006).

Notice that the majority of the financial models proposed until the 1990s are static and single-period. However, in cases where uncertainty could prevail at all periods of the time horizon under consideration, multistage dynamic models become more appropriate, even requiring specialised algorithms and more computer power. Such models are not very common at present in practical financial applications due to their complexity and the complex requirement for input data. Nevertheless, some very interesting models have been used in recent years. As an example, numerous ALM (asset-and-liability management) stochastic optimisation models have been used by pension funds, insurance companies, wealthy individuals and hedge funds.

An advantage of these scenario-based models is that the parameters are not assumed to be known but are scenario-dependent, hence they are uncertain. These models are related to capital-investment returns by the financial institutions, portfolio structuring and restructuring of personal and mortgage-based loans, funds investments and others, such that some objectives are achieved as the maximisation of the net present value (NPV) of the expected profit, the minimisation of the cash requirements of capital, the satisfaction of liabilities and the maximisation of the minimum profit over the scenarios, the conditional minimum ratio of investment in the different assets and opportunities and so forth – all of them along a given time horizon.

As we point out above, the capital management could maximise the NPV of the expected profit (as in an example considered above). Now, the expectation of profit is based on the potential realisation of the scenarios to be generated for the uncertain parameters, mainly, say, the interest rate, country risk and the relating of the issues or institutions on which the capital is invested along the time horizon. For instance, the price of an asset is directly related to the interest rate level over all of the time horizon. The interest rate is the percentage of the par value or nominal (the money you invest) that you will receive as payment when holding a asset.

However, in this appendix a stochastic model for risk management of credit portfolio structuring to maximise expected return and recover under some sources of uncertainty is presented; in stochastic terminology it is called a single-stage stochastic optimisation problem.

Let the following key definitions be used in this work:

❏ Definition 1: Default is the failure to pay back a credit (loan) on maturity, or when the terms of an agreement are fulfilled; and
❏ Definition 2: Recovery rate is the proportion of the money owed that the issuer undertakes to pay to the purchaser in case of default.

(Note: The likelihood risk of default is closely linked to the credit rating of an organisation at a given instant in time.)

The volatility of the uncertain parameters may produce a high variability of the returns over the scenarios along the time horizon. Then, the NPV expected return and recovery of the credit portfolio may have an add-value over the deterministic approach where random values of the parameters are just replaced with their expected value. Observe that the deterministic approach may have a high risk on the returns, since only the average scenario is considered, ignoring the uncertainty of the information. Notice that this scenario may not even exist at all. In any case, the maximisation of the NPV of the expected return alone does not have enough risk reduction under high variability on the realisation of the scenarios; the strategy is known as "risk-neutral". For getting a predefined risk reduction, some so-named risk-averse strategies should be considered while maximising the expected NPV of the expected return and recovery. See in Alonso-Ayuso *et al* (2014) a survey of the most appealing risk-averse strategies that in chronological order are as follows: (1) upper bounding the semi-deviation of the shortfall on reaching the expected, eg, profit over the scenarios; (2) several immunisation strategies for minimising the expected shortfall of the proposed solution with respect to the greatest profit by considering each scenario independently; (3) minimising the expected shortfall from the expected profit; (4) conditional value-at-risk (CVaR), such that the VaR profit is maximised while the weighted expected shortfall over the scenarios on reaching the VaR profit is minimised; (5) minimising the weighted probability of the occurrence of a non-wanted scenario (ie, a scenario whose profit has a shortfall on reaching a user-driven profit threshold; and (6) the so-called SD, which stands for joint first- and second-order stochastic dominance strategy, where a user-driven set of profiles should be satisfied. A profile is defined by the following 4-tupla: a profit threshold, a bound on the shortfall on reaching the threshold for any scenario, a bound on the probability of the occurrence of a scenario with a profit shortfall on the threshold, and a bound on the expected shortfall over the scenarios. See in Escudero *et al* (2014) the related SD synthesised model to consider in our work and Gollmer, Neiser and Schultz (2008) and Gollmer, Gotzes and Schultz (2011) for the original two-stage first- and second-order SDC strategies.

This appendix will now consider the main concepts on stochastic optimisation, since it is the discipline to be used in this work as well as a synthesised risk-neutral model; the risk-neutral model in detail for credit portfolio structuring; and the single-stage risk-averse strategy SD.

Stochastic optimisation methodology for multistage mixed 0–1 stochastic problems

Stochastic optimisation is one of the most robust tools for decision making. It is broadly used in real-world applications in a wide range of problems from different areas such as finance, scheduling, production planning, industrial engineering, capacity allocation, energy, air traffic and logistics.

It is well known that an optimisation problem under uncertainty (see the pioneering works of Beale 1955; Charnes and Cooper 1959; Dantzig 1955; Wets 1966) with a finite number of scenarios has a deterministic equivalent model (DEM), where the risk of providing a wrong solution is included in the model, partially at least, via a set of representative scenarios. Let us assume that we are dealing with a maximisation problem. Traditionally, special attention has been given to optimising the DEM by maximising the objective function expected value over the scenarios, subject to the satisfaction of all the problem constraints in the defined scenarios. Currently, we are able to solve huge DEMs by using different types of decomposition algorithmic approaches. However, the optimisation of the so-called risk-neutral approach has the inconvenience of providing a solution that ignores the variability of the objective value of the scenarios, and so the occurrence of scenarios with an objective value below the expected one.

Alternatively, we present in this work a risk-averse strategy for single-stage stochastic problems, as stated above. Given the dimensions of large-scale instances augmented by the new variables and constraints required by the risk measures to consider, it is unrealistic to solve the problem up to optimality by plain use of mathematical optimisation solvers. Instead, we should use decomposition algorithms of some type, see, for example, our branch-and-fix coordination algorithm presented in Escudero *et al* (2012) and Escudero *et al* (2014) as well as the stochastic dynamic programming algorithm presented in Escudero, Monge and Romero-Morales (2015) for metaheuristically-solved problems.

Let us consider the following single-stage deterministic 0–1 model:

$$Z_{EV} = \max ax$$
$$s.t. Ax = b$$
$$x_t \in \{0,1\}^{nx}, \tag{A3.1}$$

where x is the nx dimensional vector of the 0–1 variables, a is the vector of the objective function coefficients, A is the constraint matrix and b is the right-hand-side vector.

However, some of the problem coefficients (in our case) in the objective function can be uncertain, mainly in dynamic domains (ie, problems whose decisions to be made are based on data along a time horizon). There are several ways in which to express future uncertainty in the coefficients. One the most used consists of representing it by considering scenarios with known or estimated probabilities, see, for example, Birge and Louveaux (2011), among others. For this purpose, consider the following definition:

Definition 3: A scenario consists of a realisation of all the random parameters in the problem.

Let us assume that the parameters in problem (A3.1) are random ones to be presented by a set of discrete occurrences, say, a^ω for scenario $\omega \in \Omega$, where Ω is the set of scenarios under consideration, being assumed that the set represents the uncertainty in vector a. The model for maximising the expected objective value over the scenarios (ie, risk-neutral strategy) can be expressed:

$$Z_{RN} = \max \sum_{\omega \in \Omega} w^{\omega} a^{\omega} x$$

$$s.t. Ax = b$$

$$x_t \in \{0,1\}^{nx},$$

(A3.2)

where w- is a positive weight assigned to scenario $\omega \in \Omega$.

A risk-neutral model for credit portfolio structuring to maximise NPV of expected returns and recovery under some sources of uncertainty

A detailed model for credit portfolio management to maximise the NPV of the return and recovery through a time horizon, under uncertainty, satisfying credit-maximum volume for different classes and portfolio-profitable requirements, among other constraints, is presented in this section; ie, a risk-neural strategy is used. Thus, decision makers can obtain the optimal portfolio, taking into account the risk associated with the likelihood of bankruptcy or default on the part of the issuer of each credit and the weight that they themselves attribute to that risk.

Let the following notation for sets, parameters and variables that define the DEM:

Input Data
Sets
❏ $\mathcal{I}$, set of potential credits to be a member of the portfolio to structure.
❏ $\mathcal{J}$, set of credit classes based on the estimated risk, ie, the set of different credit ratings that are considered.
❏ $\mathcal{I}_j$, set of credits that belong to class $j \in \mathcal{J}$, for $\mathcal{I}_j \subset \mathcal{I}$, such that $\mathcal{I} = \cup_{j \in \mathcal{J}} \mathcal{I}_j$ and $\mathcal{I}_j \cap \mathcal{J}_{j1} = \varnothing$ for $j, j' \in \mathcal{J}: j \neq j'$.
❏ $\mathcal{T}_i$, set of periods in a time horizon at which payment returns are due from credit i, for $i \in \mathcal{I}$.

Deterministic parameters for credit $i \in \mathcal{I}$
❏ N_i, nominal amount.
❏ c_{it}, return to be generated by credit i at period t, for $t \in \mathcal{T}_i$.

❏ t_i, maturity period.

❏ $j(i) \in \mathcal{J}$, class to which it belongs to.

❏ z_i, recovery rate (as a fraction of one) in case of default (Altman, and Kishore 1996).

Other deterministic parameters

❏ M_j, Maximum volume that is allowed for credit class j, for $j \in \mathcal{J}$.

❏ M, Maximum volume that is allowed for the total credit portfolio.

❏ δ, user-driven multiplicative factor (greater than 1) of the total nominal value of the portfolio to structure; it is used for forcing the profitability of the NPV expected credit portfolio return and recovery.

Uncertain parameters for scenario $\omega \in \Omega$

❏ r_ω, risk-free interest.

❏ q_j^w, measure of risk calculated as the probability of default of a credit from class j, for $j \in \mathcal{J}$.

Variables for scenario $\omega \in \Omega$

x_i, 0–1 variable such that its value is 1 if credit i is included in the portfolio to structure and otherwise, 0, for $j \in \mathcal{J}$.

Risk-neutral deterministic equivalent model

The single-stage DEM maximises the NPV of the expected credit portfolio return and recovery over the scenarios satisfying the maximum credit volume of each class and in total, and other constraints such as the profitability lower bound on the portfolio (see below). The (risk-neutral) model can be expressed as follows:

$$X_{RN} = \max \sum_{\omega \in \Omega} \sum_{i \in \mathcal{I}} w^\omega a_i^\omega x_i$$

$$s.t. \sum_{i \in \mathcal{I}_j} N_i x_i \leq M_j \quad \forall j \in \mathcal{J}$$

$$\sum_{x \in \mathcal{I}_j} N_i x_i \leq M$$

$$\sum_{\omega \in \Omega} \sum_{i \in \mathcal{I}} w^\omega a_i^\omega x_i \geq \delta \sum_{i \in \mathcal{I}} N_i x_i$$

$$x \in \chi$$

$$x^g \in \{0,1\}^{nx} \, \forall i \in \mathcal{I}, \tag{A3.3}$$

where $\mathcal{X}$ is the set of x-values that satisfy constraints not explicitly defined and the parameter a^i can be expressed:

$$a_i \equiv \left(\sum_{t \in T_i} \frac{1}{\left(1+r^\omega\right)^t} \left(1 - q_{j(i)}^\omega\right) c_{it} \right) + \frac{1}{\left(1+r^\omega\right)^{t_i}} q_{j(i)}^\omega z_i N_i$$

Notice that model (A3.2) is the synthesised version of model (A3.3) by considering that a_i in the former gives the objective function of 0–1 variable x_i in (A3.3) and $Ax = b$ is its constraint system. The advantage of the risk-neutral model over the deterministic model (A3.1) is that in the latter the random parameters have been replaced with its expected value ignoring their variability.

SD measure for immunising NPV of expected return and recovery from the credit portfolio

The main criticism that can be made to the risk-neutral strategy represented in model (A3.3) (a very popular one on the other hand) is that it ignores the variability on the objective function value over the scenarios and, in particular, the "left" tail of the unwanted scenarios. Moreover, there are some risk-averse approaches that additionally deal with risk management (see the earlier list). We have chosen to consider the stochastic dominance (SD) strategy, to be presented in this section.

Let a user-driven risk reduction profile for the SD strategy be defined by the following 4-tupla: $(\phi_p, S_p, \beta_p, e_p)$, for $p \in \mathcal{P}$, where $\mathcal{P}$ is the set of profiles; ϕ_p is the threshold on the NPV of expected return, and recovery from the credit portfolio aimed to be satisfied by any scenario; S_p is the maximum shortfall that is allowed on reaching the threshold; β_p is the upper bound on the fraction of scenarios with shortfall; and e_p is the upper bound on the expected shortfall over the scenarios.

The modelling of the SD strategy is as follows:

$$Z_{SDC} = \max \sum_{\omega \in \Omega} w^\omega a^\omega x$$

$$s.t. Ax = b$$

$$\sum_{\omega \in \Omega} w^\omega a^\omega x + s_p^\omega \geq \phi_p \qquad \forall \omega \in \Omega, p \in \mathcal{P}$$

$$0 \leq s_p^\omega \leq S_p v_p^\omega, v_p^\omega \in \{0,1\} \qquad \forall \omega \in \Omega, p \in \mathcal{P}$$

$$\sum_{\omega \in \Omega} w^\omega s_p^\omega \leq e_p \qquad \forall p \in \mathcal{P}$$

$$\sum_{\omega \in \Omega} w^{\omega} v_p^{\omega} \leq \beta_p \qquad\qquad \forall p \in \mathcal{P}$$

$$x^g \in \{0,1\}^{nx}, \qquad\qquad\qquad\qquad (A3.4)$$

where s_p^{ω} is the variable that takes the shortfall on reaching ϕ_p for scenario ω and v_p^{ω} is a variable that takes the value 1 if there is shortfall, and otherwise 0.

Notice that model (A3.4) maximises the NPV of the expected credit portfolio return and recovery, subject to different credit volume bounds and the constraints to define the portfolio structuring. Those constraints lower bound the portfolio, the portfolio's profitability, they force the portfolio's immunisation (given the variability of the risk-free interest and the default probability of some credits) and defines the user-driven set of risk-reduction profiles.

REFERENCES

Alonso-Ayuso, A., et al, 2014, "Medium range optimisation of copper extraction planning under uncertainty in future copper prices", *European Journal of Operational Research* 233, pp. 711–26, 2014.

Altman, E. I., and V. M. Kishore, 1996, "Almost everything you wanted to know about recoveries on defaulted bonds", *Financial Analysts Journal* 52, pp. 57–64.

Aramburu, L., et al, 2012, "Stochastic models for optimising immunisation strategies in fixed-income security portfolios under some sources of uncertainty", in H. I. Gassmann and W. T. Ziemba (eds), *Applications in Finance, Energy, Planning and Logistics* (London: World Scientific Publishers), pp. 173–220.

Beale, E. M. L., 1955, "On minimising a convex function subject to linear inequalities", *Journal of the Royal Statistical Society Ser B* 17, pp. 173–84.

Beraldi, P., A. Violi and F. De Simeone, 2011, "A Decision Support System for strategic asset allocation", *Decision Support Systems* 51, pp. 549–61.

Bertocchi, M., V. Moriggia, and J. Dupacova, 2006, "Horizon and stages in applications of stochastic programming in finance", *Annals of Operations Research* 142 pp. 63–78.

Birge J. R., and F. Louveaux, 2011, *Introduction to Stochastic Programming*, 2nd edn (Berlin: Springer).

Bradley, S. P., and D. B. Crane, 1972, "A dynamic model for bond portfolio management", *Management Science* 19, pp. 139–51.

Charnes, A., and W. W. Cooper, 1959, "Chanced-constrained programming", *Management Science* 5, pp. 73–9.

Dantzig, G. B., "Linear programming under uncertainty", 1955, *Management Science* 1 pp. 197–206.

Escudero, L. F., *et al*, 2012, "An algorithmic framework for solving large scale multi-stage stochastic mixed 0–1 programs", *Computers & Operations Research* 39, pp. 1133–44.

Escudero, L. F., *et al*, 2014, "On time stochastic dominance induced by mixed integer linear recourse in multistage stochastic mixed 0–1 problems", submitted for publication.

Escudero, L. F., *et al*, 2015, "An SDP approach for multiperiod mixed 0-1 linear programming models with stochastic dominance constraints for risk management", *Computers & Operations Research* 58, pp. 32-40.

Fong, H. G., and O. Vasicek, 1983, "The tradeoff between return and risk in immunised portfolios", *Financial Analysts Journal* 39, pp. 73–8.

Geyer, A., and W. T. Ziemba, 2008, "The Innovest Austrian Pension Fund financial planning model InnoALM", *Operations Research* 56, pp. 797–810.

Gollmer, R., F. Neiser and R. Schultz, 2008, "Stochastic programs with first-order stochastic dominance constraints", *SIAM Journal on Optimisation* 19, pp. 552–71.

Gollmer, R., U. Gotzes and R. Schultz, 2011, "A note on second-order stochastic dominance constraints induced by mixed-integer recourse", *Mathematical Programming Ser A* 126, pp. 179–90.

Golub, B., *et al*, 1995, "Stochastic management models for money management", *European Journal of Operational Research* 85, pp. 282–96.

Kusy, M. I., and W. T. Ziemba, 1986, "A bank Asset and Liability Management Model", *Operations Research* 34, pp. 356–76.

Nelder, J. A., and R. Mead, 1965, "A simplex method for function minimisation", *Computer Journal* 7(38), p. 313.

Powell, M. J. D., 1994, "A direct search optimisation method that models the objective and constraint functions by linear interpolation", in S. Gomez and J-P. Hennart (eds), *Advances in Optimisation and Numerical Analysis* (Dordrecht: Kluwer Academic), pp. 51–67.

Wallace, S. W., and W. T. Ziemba (eds), 2005, *Applications of Stochastic Programming*: MPS-SIAM-Series in Optimisation.

Wets, R., 1966, "Programming under uncertainty: the equivalent convex program", *SIAM Journal on Applied Mathematics* 14, pp. 89–105.

Zenios, S. A., *et al*, 1998, "Dynamic models for fixed-income portfolio management under uncertainty", *Journal of Economic Dynamics and Control* 22, pp. 1517–41.

Zenios, S. A., and W. T. Ziemba (eds), 2006, *Handbook of Asset and Liability Modelling* (Vol. 1 on theory and methodology, Vol. 2 on applications and case studies) (North Holland: Elsevier.

Ziemba, W. T., 2003, *The stochastic programming approach to Asset Liability and Wealth Management* (Charlottesville: VA:AIMR).

Ziemba, W. T., and J. M. Mulvey (eds), 1998, *Worldwide Asset and Liability Modelling* (Cambridge: Cambridge University Press).

Appendix 4
Business Risk Quantification
Lutz Baumgarten

Typically, business risk is referred to "the risk of volumes decreasing or margins shrinking with no opportunity to offset the revenue decline with a reduction in costs …" Business risk factors include a competitive environment, the macroeconomic environment, political risks, new-product risks, strategic risks, reputational risks, regulatory risks, legal risks, tax risks and IT risks. Business risk quantification completes the universe of risks for capital requirement estimation and financial planning, and it can be implemented with the help of a scenario-based approach, as explained later in this appendix.

Historically, the development of formal risk quantification processes and corresponding capital estimations has been driven by the availability of data for quantification and of the effectiveness of the risk management actions derived from the risk quantification metrics, rather than the risk potential impact on shareholder value. Market risk quantification started to be widely adopted in the late 1980s, facilitated by RiskMetrics methods. Market risk data is the most plentiful, and risk management can be performed by buying and selling securities and derivatives in formal markets. Credit risk quantification started to be widely adopted during the mid and late 1990s by the acceptance of methodologies and products from KMV, CreditMetrics and others. Credit risk can be managed by the use of asset securitization, credit derivatives, the implementation of credit policies among others. Operational risk quantification is the latest method to be adopted, and it is still being developed, its main driver being Basel's AMA guidelines and Solvency II internal models. Operational risk data is scarce because it is very firm-specific, and operational risk management is performed via process improvement, automation, introduction of new controls, etc.

Regarding business risk, few institutions have yet implemented a quantification process and embedded its results into the day-to-day management of the institution, completing the universe of quantified risks for capital determination and financial planning. However, business risk can be the most determinant risk for shareholder value in the medium to long term, and business risk factors – such as competitive environment, pressure in margins, economic environment, political risk and strategic risk – may impact on shareholder value and its growth potential more than market, credit or operational risks. This is particularly true once a formal risk management process for market, credit or operational risks has been introduced in the institution.

The institution will benefit greatly by quantifying business risks, including the following:

❏ Necessary element for Pillar II (ICAAP) requirements of Basel II/III and Solvency II (ORSA).
❏ Completing the risk universe of enterprise risk management by modelling the changes in volumes and margins not attributable to other risks (market, credit and operational).
❏ Managing earnings volatility or "body risk"; capturing body events to maintain "business as usual"; expected dividends; planned initiatives and others.
❏ Incentivising, planning and execution quality by incorporating the business risk sources of P&L volatility and capital consumption.
❏ Improving scenario analyses and stress testing; incorporating stress components of strategic and reputational risks, which might actually be likely but not historically observed.
❏ Better identification of current changes in market and business models, which can feed directly into the management of the institution. Discussions among experts about their perceptions on market trends and business environment can be a valuable input for the business unit management as well as for the institution's board of directors. Experts' closeness to the actual business generation and execution may provide a timely and deep insight

into business risk factors that would otherwise not be collected and reported without a business risk quantification process.

A business risk model is constructed around three blocks: business risk definition, business risk drivers (risk factors to be included) and the actual model. An approach for actual business risk models is to quantify the volatility of income and expenses by modelling individual value/economic drivers of the most important income and expense components. This approach can be implemented following a scenario approach very similar to the SBA of operational risk, adhering to the steps below:

❑ Define business risk stress scenarios (including likelihood and severity), based on expert input, which can be implemented based on similar methods as those explained in Chapter 3. These methods will facilitate reflection on the non-normal character and understanding of the business risk factors.
❑ Model business risk stress scenarios, which requires handling of non-normal distributions. This can be done following similar methods to those explained in Chapters 4 and 5 and Appendix 1.
❑ Simulate total business risk distribution and allocate capital, which can be performed under the same methods of Chapter 8.

Index

(page numbers in italic type refer to figures and tables)

and modelling process,
technology supporting
17–18
and multiple data elements,
integration of 17
and operational risk
dependencies, modelling 17
and scenario analysis,
qualitative nature of 13
and sources and risk types,
variety of 15–16
and stable capital estimates,
need for 13–14, *14*
and backtesting 303–9, *306*
of annual frequency 305–8, *307*
of annual total losses 308–9
of severity of the year 304–5
Basel II defines 1
dependencies, modelling 17
and extreme events, modelling
10–11
management, role of, in ERM
343–4
modelling, splitting distribution
for 128–9
sensitivity analysis and stress
testing 303–9
and Six Sigma *375*, 376–8
stress-testing of *311*, *313*, *316*,
317, *318*, 319–23, *319*, *321*
and sensitivity analysis 309–10
see also operational risk
"Operational Risk – Supervisory
Guidelines for Advanced
Measurement Approaches"
(BCSG-AMA):
on AMAs' use and
embeddedness 330
on capital allocation 290

on extreme events 107
on frequency distributions 146
on goodness-of-fit (GoF) 150,
157
on graphical methods 162
on internally determined
correlations 253
on loss data modelling 186
on merger of data elements 219
most comprehensive
international document 8
on operational risk profile 336
on ORA 346
on ORMS 360
on purpose and use of an AMA
20, 27
on quality of fit 317
on scenario analysis (SA) 61
on thresholds 107
on verification 73, 304
operational risk appetite (ORA)
348
adherence to, monitoring 356–7
cascading *216*, *300*, *348*, 349–50,
351
and BEICFs 215–17
for monitoring strategic and
business plan 345–57
and adherence to ORA 356–7
financial resources dimension
353–4
and hard-to-quantify aspects
of or profile 355–6
strategic direction dimension
354–5
threshold levels and limit
monitoring 350–6, *352*, *354*
see also business planning and
monitoring